# Madame Vieux Carré

# MADAME
# VIEUX CARRÉ

*The French Quarter*
*in the Twentieth Century*

SCOTT S. ELLIS

UNIVERSITY PRESS OF MISSISSIPPI / JACKSON

www.upress.state.ms.us

The University Press of Mississippi is a member
of the Association of American University Presses.

First printing 2010
∞
Library of Congress Cataloging-in-Publication Data

Ellis, Scott S.
Madame Vieux Carré : the French Quarter in the
twentieth century / Scott S. Ellis.
p. cm.
Includes bibliographical references  and index.
ISBN 978-1-60473-358-7 (cloth : alk. paper)  1.  Vieux
Carré (New Orleans, La.)—History—20th century.
2.  Vieux Carré (New Orleans, La.)—Social life and
customs—20th century. 3.  Vieux Carré (New Orleans,
La.)—Politics and government—20th century. 4.  New
Orleans (La.)—History—20th century. 5.  New Orleans
(La.)—Social life and customs—20th century. 6.  New
Orleans (La.)—Politics and government—20th century.
I. Title.
F379.N56V533 2010
976.3'35—dc22                                        2009021662

British Library Cataloging-in-Publication Data available

# CONTENTS

# PREFACE *and*
# ACKNOWLEDGMENTS

For New Orleans's first century, 1718–1818, its history and that of the French Quarter were roughly congruent. The second century, 1818–1918, saw American ascendancy in the city diminishing the role of the original French settlement. The 1917 closing of Storyville, a nominal triumph of alien morals, and the loss of the French Opera House in 1919 made the Americanization of the French Quarter nearly total.

This book is a history of the French Quarter in the twentieth and early twenty-first centuries. The French Quarter does not exist in a vacuum, untouched by outside events. In its third century, the French Quarter has been buffeted by many external forces, yet retains the overall character—charm is too silly a word—that draws tourists and new residents year after year.

New Orleans, and the Quarter itself, do not strictly observe the calendar or the clock. To tell the story in a rigid chronological fashion would muddle many important views of the Quarter's history in the century just passed. The book is therefore arranged in epochs of years with interludes discussing subjects that require treatments within individual chapters.

## A NOTE ON TERMINOLOGY

The enclave of our present tale has changed names over time. *La Nouvelle-Orléans* was named in honor of the Duc d'Orléans, regent of France in 1718. At the influx of Americans after 1803, the Creole French mainly occupied the original settlement, and so *French Quarter* became common. Among the French Creoles, *Vieux Carré* (Old Square) was an affectionate name for the *Place d'Armes*, originally a parade ground and place of execution, now known as Jackson Square. Eventually, *Vieux Carré* became applied to the entire enclave. Writers in past decades, knowing Mediterranean influence had overtaken that of France, sometimes used *Latin Quarter*. At the end of the nineteenth century, *Frenchtown* became a synonym. In the twentieth century, *French Quarter, the Quarter*, and *Vieux Carré* became interchangeable, and so I have used them in this book.

Although the larger city remains New Orleans in English, two other synonyms have developed. *Crescent City* refers to the broad bend of the Mississippi between Algiers Point, opposite the Quarter, and Nine-Mile Point, upstream. It is memorialized in the inverted crescent moon surrounding the star on the badges of the New Orleans Police Department (NOPD). *Big Easy* was assigned in the same era when New York was the *Big Apple*, for its possibilities and temptations, and Pittsburgh, the *Big Smoke*, for its air pollution. The *Easy* of the name was taken to denote at once both a casual style of living and the ease with which sexual conquests could be made. Most natives despise the term. A phoneticized rendering of the lower-class pronunciation of the city's legal name is *N'awlins*. Native usage of *N'awlins* is becoming rarer by the year, although it is still popular in the tourist media.

I believe people should be free to call themselves whatever they wish. Ethnic and racial labels have shifted over time. Regarding these labels, I have used the correct form for each period of history. Quotations retain the terms— for good or ill—applied by their sources. *Creole* is a term that deserves special explanation. It originally meant a child born in the New World of French or Spanish parents. Over time, it became associated with Louisianans of French descent who were not *Acadians* expelled from Canada (today's *Cajuns*). By the 1880s, it became a prefix for any product of Louisiana. Eventually, through concubinage and intermarriage, *Creole* has also become associated with light-skinned people of mixed race. These are referred to as *Modern Creoles* in this work. The "original" *Creoles*, whose men took concubines of color in the system called *plaçage* and produced today's *Modern Creoles*, are referred to here as *French Creoles*. It is important to note that *Creole* is a cultural identification as well as an ethnic one.

The author thanks: Earl Bernhardt, Tom Bissell, Bill Borah, Gene Bourg, Clayton Boyer, Kevin Brown, Ann Case, Nathan Chapman, Mike Early, Darlene Fife, Dennis Formento, Robyn Halvorsen, Hilary Irvin, Dale Irwin, Sara Jacobelli, Dave Johnson, Florence Jumonville, Ph.D., Jim Kellogg, Esq., Greg Lambousy, Brobson Lutz, M.D., Cosimo Matassa, Glenn Meche, Jon Newlin,

James Nolan, Pat O'Rourke, Greg Osborne, Bessianne Parker, Bob Patience, Reverend Troy Perry, D.D., Sal Serio, Anthony Stanonis, Ph.D., Sally Stassi, George Tresch, Jim Van Dorin, Rodney Workman, and Joe Zahani.

These institutions have shown much patience as they gave me great assistance: Societé de St. Anne; the Historic New Orleans Collection; the Louisiana Historical Association; the Louisiana Historical Society; the Louisiana State Museum; the Vieux Carré Commission; the American-Italian Museum; the French Market Corporation; the Howard-Tilton Library at Tulane University; the Louisiana Collection at the Earl K. Long Library, University of New Orleans; the City Archives of the New Orleans Public Library, and the Library of Congress.

I also thank all those who contributed anonymously; in the Quarter, the shadows still speak to those who can hear.

Thanks go to the University Press of Mississippi, especially Craig Gill, for believing in the book, and to copy editor Carol Cox.

Amanda Glenn prepared the beautiful maps; Serena Saye was my patient editor and Tim Farmer my sturdy pillar.

Gratitude to Jay Borne, who unlocked the door, and Jim Adams, who flung it open.

In dreams, they still walk these streets with me: Joe d'Antoni, Jay Borne, Mike Cordtz, Kim Donnelly, Mike Kerley, Willie Latiolais, Joe Lindsay, Tim Nettles, José Quintanilla, William Rueff, Wally Sherwood , Larry Thompson, and Norma Williams.

# TO SET THE SCENE

La Nouvelle-Orléans was established in 1718 by Jean-Baptiste Le Moyne, sieur de Bienville, as the southern anchor of French Louisiana. The first settlement was along the northeast bank of a sharp bend of the Mississippi, on the highest ground of a mostly swampy terrain. From 1763 to 1800, New Orleans was owned by the Spanish[1] and then was retransferred to France. In 1803, Napoleon sold the Louisiana Colony to the young United States. In what has been termed the greatest land deal in history, about one-third of what would become the lower forty-eight states of America was acquired at a stroke. Of most immediate importance was the port of New Orleans—the outlet for American goods from the heartland. The British, who, ironically, had financed the Louisiana Purchase,[2] tried to wrest New Orleans from America in the War of 1812. The American victory, under General Andrew Jackson in 1815, cemented the United States' claim to the entire region.

In 1862, New Orleans was the first major city of the Confederacy to fall to northern forces. The city was under military rule until the establishment of so-called carpetbag government. At Reconstruction's end in 1877, the state and city resumed local white government.[3]

Although New Orleans remained the preeminent city of the state, and one of the top American ports, it never regained the position of economic importance it had enjoyed before the Civil War. Sugar, cotton, and other traditional agricultural products predominated the city's trade. The state government decamped to Baton Rouge in 1882.[4] However, like those countries that have both civic and religious capitals, Louisiana's Supreme Court remained in New Orleans.

Prior to the Civil War, New Orleans had a prominent group of "free people of color," Negroes who were not slaves. Some had been freed, or bought their own freedom. Some were free-born émigrés from the French Caribbean

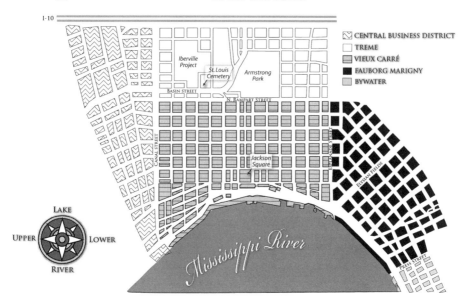

1-10

CENTRAL BUSINESS DISTRICT
TREME
VIEUX CARRÉ
FAUBORG MARIGNY
BYWATER

Iberville Project
St. Louis Cemetery
Armstrong Park
BASIN STREET
N. RAMPART STREET
CANAL STREET
Jackson Square
ELYSIAN FIELDS
PRESS STREET

LAKE
UPPER                    LOWER
RIVER

Mississippi River

The Quarter and Its Neighbors

or other French territory. After the end of Reconstruction, the lot of these people, as was true of other Negroes, descended. From the end of Reconstruction to the Louisiana Constitutional Convention of 1896, Negroes lost rights, and were effectively disenfranchised after the new constitution was passed in 1898.[5]

From the beginning, New Orleans had a reputation as a city where moral laxity was the rule. The earliest settlers, even the ruling nobility, tended to be scapegrace adventurers.[6] Paris and whatever control the crown exercised were far away, and conditions were harsh for decades. New Orleans could boast of many civic features. However, in the main, booze, brothels, and betting were its best-known attributes. Other cities had all this as well, but none had installed the pleasures of the flesh so deeply in the civic structure as New Orleans. New Orleans was where many Victorian Americans went to be naughty.

In 1900 the U.S. Census counted 287,104 New Orleanians out of a state figure of 1,381,625—roughly one out of every five Louisianans.[7]

Bienville's original settlement, grown to about a hundred blocks, became the old heart of a much larger city. The cardinal directions mean little in New Orleans. The Mississippi River and Lake Pontchartrain are the two vertical boundaries, and the directions of each are called "river" and "lake," respectively. The direction of the river's flow is called "lower," and upstream is referred to as "upper." The maps of the Quarter presented here, and the locations specified in the text, follow this convention.

By 1900, Bienville's old heart was a much-neglected slum. The story of the French Quarter's transformation from a warehouse for the poor and demimonde to its state in the early twenty-first century is our present story.

# Madame Vieux Carré

# The French Quarter - Early 1900s

CHAPTER 1

# 1900–1920

*The Quarter Faces a New Century*

### DAWN OF THE CENTURY

Let us step back to a time gone, but still, it seems, just around the next corner in this one special place. Its inhabitants believed in passing fancies, followed street mobs, and listened to long speeches. They were quick to laugh, quick to cry, and sometimes quick to anger—a people whose world was compassed by a small city, and set therein, a small village. Complete unto itself, it provided all the needs of most of its dwellers.

The blocks between Canal and Esplanade and between North Rampart and the Mississippi River were paved with rough square stones, called Belgian blocks, brought in as ship ballast. Gutters ran alongside, washing all manner of smelly debris along. In drought, the natural cleansing action was absent, and the smells of dead animals and household refuse were incredible. Crossing these streets, we would have had to avoid many horse and mule droppings. These animals still provided the motive power for most of New Orleans. We'd also have had to avoid the electrified streetcars which came to the Quarter in 1894.[1]

We would be surprised by the smoke in the air—smoke from coal and wood fires from many shops and factories, and during the brief winter, most homes. Smoke poured out of saloons and trailed along the sidewalks, called banquettes; tobacco was almost a universal habit.

3

St. Peter Street, circa 1908. Courtesy of the Williams Research Center of the Historic New Orleans Collection.

Overhead, the view of the smokey skies was laced by wires. Electric and trolley power lines ran above the streets; with the high water table, underground lines were impossible. Street lamps were usually suspended in midair by wires above the pavement. In those times, each telephone line needed its own pair of wires strung on a pole; so poles sported many cross arms.[2] The streets were alive with sound—the clip-clop of hooves and click-clack of streetcars and, from the Mississippi River, the scream of ship horns and whistles. Automobiles were a great rarity in the South, and it would be some time before the Quarter heard their engines and horns.

The streets had human voices as well. The sellers of flowers, fruits, candies, and pies all cried their wares. The milk wagon bounced along, ringing its bell.[3] Housewives called to each other from stoops and windows. In some blocks, harlots screamed greetings and profane abuse to each other. They accosted men with sweet-sounding entreaties. So much of life happened on the banquettes and streets that people spoke of living "in," not "on," a street.

The Quarter's front stoop was the Mississippi River wharf opposite Jackson Square. The river view then was obscured by the Kentucky warehouse, which persisted until 1932.[4] Here, across from a sylvan setting, longshoremen, stevedores, draymen driving mule-drawn wagons, and laborers sweated and swore over cargos of cotton, bananas, coffee, and many other tropical

The Lower Pontalba, circa 1890. Courtesy of the Louisiana State Museum.

St. Peter Street, looking towards Royal, circa 1905–1910. Courtesy of the Louisiana Division, City Archives, New Orleans Public Library.

Royal Street, 1900. Courtesy of the Library of Congress, Prints and Photographs Division, Detroit Publishing Company Collection.

The French Market, circa 1900–1910. Courtesy of the Detroit Publishing Company, Library of Congress, Prints and Photographs Division.

The French Market, fruit and vegetable aisle, 1904. Courtesy of the Williams Research Center of the Historic New Orleans Collection.

Rag dealer at the French Market, circa 1910. Collection of the author.

products. After their labors, some found comfort in the liquor and women of the nearby taverns and "sporting" houses.

Ruling Jackson Square, St. Louis Cathedral, flanked by the old seat of government, the Cabildo, and the archbishop's residence, the Presbytère, was the spiritual anchor of the French Creoles. It was here that they expected to be baptized, married, and to have their funeral masses held.[5] Flanking the square are the Pontalba apartments. Built in 1850, they had once been grand town houses above stores. As the twentieth century arrived, they had declined to tenements.[6]

Nearby was the French Market. The poor and rich alike shopped here for produce, meat, seafood (some offered live), berries brought from the woods, and game from the swamps.[7] After Sunday Mass at the Cathedral, many women did their marketing here.[8] Wagons lined up to unload in early morning, and many barefoot children helped their elders. Some of the vendors walked in[9] and sat cross-legged on a little patch of ground they claimed as their own. For what could not be found at the French Market, there were grocery stores, seemingly one on every corner.

The upriver, or "upper" boundary of the Vieux Carré, is Canal Street—the economic heart of New Orleans and its ceremonial promenade. The stores of Canal Street provided clothing, furniture, and medical and legal services. In Carnival season, Canal Street was packed with revelers viewing the floats. The downriver, or "lower" boundary, is Esplanade, which even then had some of the last fine homes of the area. North Rampart Street is the lakeside boundary. Its name derives from the old French fortifications that defined the early settlement.

## THE PEOPLE OF FRENCHTOWN

The people of the French Quarter were an interesting mix. The enclave was, in these times, called "Frenchtown" more than "the Quarter." In truth, most of the French Creoles no longer resided in Frenchtown. Even before the Civil War, the French Creoles were a minority in the Vieux Carré.[10] There were two primary reasons for the exodus. First, the enterprises they had created had outgrown the old concept of the family living above a small shop. This prosperity meant that some could now afford mansions on Esplanade Avenue, at the downriver margin of the Quarter, the most desirable Creole address of New Orleans. Secondly, as a new wave of immigrants, the Italian Sicilians, arrived in the Quarter, the Creoles disdained these "unwashed" Mediterranean peasants.[11] Although French Creoles shunned marriage outside their circumscribed group, many of the men took light-skinned women of color as concubines and produced children with them, maintaining two separate families throughout much of their lives. This system was called *plaçage*,[12] literally, "veneer." This system had declined markedly after the Civil War as the local economy slumped and the racial tensions of Reconstruction played out.[13] For those French Creoles still clinging to their Vieux Carré, it was not unusual for three generations to live under one roof. A *grandmamère* or a *tante* held a place of honor in these homes; even if *tante* was a penniless old spinster, she cared for the children and was a constant reminder of the family's former grandeur. *Grandmamère* and *tante* probably spoke nothing but French, and that language was apt to be the only tongue spoken under the roof.[14] The father may have spoken English only for business. The teenage *garçons* probably had the garret for themselves, where they could smoke, swear, and pretend to be men out of their mother's disapproving sight.

No matter what has happened to the rest of the Quarter, the French Creole universe was centered on the French Opera House, Bourbon at Toulouse. Here was the embodiment of French Creole culture and the court of what was left of their kingdom. As *Leslie's Illustrated News* observed in 1902:

> The first night of the opera season is the opening of the social season in New Orleans, and the opera itself is the most important feature of New Orleans social life. For nearly a century it has held the undisputed first place in the hearts of the people of the delightful old French-American city, and it grows each year in popularity and in pride of place. It must be understood, however, that New Orleans loves her French opera not because of the social side of the operatic season, but because she has been taught for generations to love it for the music and for art's sake . . . The music and musicians are the first consideration in this splendid old house; consequently New Orleans knows her great composers, her Mozart, Meyerbeer, Rossini, Verdi, in great detail, and knowing them so is able to listen and enjoy them understandingly. Another thing which adds to New Orleans' enjoyment of French opera, and has doubtless had much to do with the great popularity of the institution, is the fact that one-fourth of the population of the city speaks French in ordinary daily intercourse, while another two-fourths is able to understand the language perfectly.[15]

The French Opera House. Courtesy of the Williams Research Center of the Historic New Orleans Collection.

*Leslie's* notwithstanding, the social side of the French Opera was of crucial importance to the French Creoles. For this is where the debutante was presented, even if her French Creole parents had not lived in Frenchtown for years. The girl may have not grown up in the Vieux Carré; indeed, she was usually forbidden to set foot in it apart from the chaperonage of her watchful family,[16] but the Opera was the silver tray she was presented upon for the consideration of gentlemen bachelors.[17]

At the turn of the twentieth century, the Civil War was only thirty-five years distant, approximately the same span as the Vietnam War is from this writing. The Civil War, "*the* war" to that time, was very much alive in the old soldiers of the Lost Cause that paraded down Canal Street every year, and to Confederate widows, many of whom fell on hard times without any pension to sustain them. The economic slide after the war had hit some French Creoles especially hard, and some elders were living in genteel poverty by 1900.[18] Living in reduced circumstances, some had sold their grander furnishings to antique dealers on Royal Street.[19] Without pensions, lacking vocational skills, and their world fallen down 'round their ears, old French Creole widows and spinsters were fortunate if their relations would take them in. The plight of these old ladies led to the founding of La Maison Hospitalière in 1893. Beginning with a small building at 822 Barracks, La Maison Hospitalière took in twenty women, providing them with basic essentials, which they supplemented by the sale of handicrafts and staging of fund-raising fairs.[20] By century's end, approximately ninety elderly men and women would be cared for in a complex on the corner of Barracks and Dauphine.[21]

Many other ethnic groups had claimed the Quarter. Most prominent were the Italian Sicilians. There had been an Italian presence in the city since the eighteenth century, and prior to 1900 some were well-established businessmen like hotelier Antonio Monteleone.[22] In the great wave of immigration from southern Europe from 1890 to 1910, many ships arrived at New Orleans from Palermo, bearing passengers from Sicilian towns like Cefalù, Contessa, and Ustica.[23]

Beginning in 1895, planters of the Mississippi River Delta in Arkansas and Mississippi believed that European peasants would be more permanent and tractable[24] than the unhappy Negroes who were leaving the Delta in record numbers.[25] Labor agents in Italy recruited families to work the Delta cotton crop. Upon their arrival, the immigrants discovered their "free" steamship tickets were being subtracted from their future earnings, so they started their Delta lives immediately in debt.[26] Conditions of labor, sanitation, and tropical disease, for Italians as well as the Negroes, were wretched.[27] A federal investigation, requested by the Italian ambassador in 1907, revealed the Delta Italians living in the same debt peonage—wage slavery—as Delta Negroes.[28] The investigation was quashed by the intervention of President Theodore Roosevelt at the behest of his hunting buddy, planter LeRoy Percy.[29] However, a copy was sent to the Italian government, which actively discouraged any more Italians from going to the Delta.[30] In the period 1907–1913, most Italians began to leave the Delta, some absconding while in debt to their employers, a criminal offense in Mississippi.[31] Some of the Italians leaving the Delta went downstream to the nearest metropolis that had fellow countrymen. New Orleans's "French Quarter" would become, for them, a city of refuge—a role the Quarter was to play again and again for various groups throughout the century.

In New Orleans, Italian immigrants, whether fresh off the boat from the old country or fleeing the Delta, found cheap tenement lodging in Frenchtown. Here was, in the main, freedom from perpetual serfdom, freedom from usury, and an enclave to claim as their own. There was also the opportunity to practice traditional urban trades; the Italians became greengrocers, fruit sellers, cobblers, barbers, makers of pasta and gelato. Many ran fruit and vegetable stalls at the French Market.[32] In 1905, Angelo Brocato started an ice cream parlor on

Ursulines Street, which featured a separate ladies entrance. The ladies could enter and be seated while their male escorts bought the ice cream. With polychromic plaster ornamentation, the interior effect was like being surrounded by marzipan. The parlor survives to this day as Croissant D'Or.[33]

So many Sicilians were in the Quarter that the enclave acquired yet another name, Little Palermo.[34] Jazzman Danny Barker recalled that in the early years of the twentieth century, "there were thousands of Italians" all over the Quarter.[35] In 1905, the Italian consul estimated that one-third to one-half of the Quarter's population were Italian-born or second generation.[36] For many, the living conditions were appalling. Dilapidated old buildings sheltered many families, with six people to a single room not uncommon.[37] Dependant on the rainfall, a cistern supplied drinking water; unscreened, it also served as a mosquito hatchery.[38] A single privy, if it was working, had to be shared by all. The courtyards were festooned with old furniture, litter, farm animals and their droppings.[39] Many families lived in the Pontalba apartments, flanking Jackson Square. Their washing flapped over balconies like lazy flags saluting the statue of Andrew Jackson.[40] Even in the climb up from poverty in a new land, the Italians usually had large families.

The New Orleans Italians of the early 1900s faced obstacles worse than privation and disease. Anti-immigrant sentiment was running high in America at the turn of the century. In a gruesome incident in October 1890, the police chief of New Orleans, David Hennessy, was shot down by a group of assailants. Allegedly, he gasped, "Dagoes!" to a friend.[41] A group of Italians were acquitted of the murder. A mob led by the "best" citizens stormed the parish prison in what is now Armstrong Park. Eleven men were killed, by gunshots and hanging, in the worst lynching in American history.[42] The facts of Hennessy's death were obscure in that day and remain uncertain now. Regardless, the entire affair was an excuse for a tide of anti-Italian sentiment, including more murders around the country.[43] Hennessy's murder, nativist propaganda, and urban warfare among various New Orleans Italian factions made them, and their Little Palermo enclave, malodorous in the public nostril. Facing linguistic, cultural, and perceptual barriers, the New Orleans Italians had three strong institutions. One was the Catholic Church. Always a powerful presence in the city, the influx of Italians swelled its numbers and eventual influence in civic life. The second strength was the mutual aid societies. These were founded in the nineteenth century primarily to ensure decent burials for affiliated members, building large above-ground mausoleums. Eventually, they became a safety net and focus of tradition for many ethnicities. One of the best known, the Italian Hall Association, purchased 1020 Esplanade in 1912 and christened it the *Unione Italiana*. The third pillar, of course, was family. The typically large families, over succeeding generations, spread far beyond Little Palermo to the rest of the city, to suburbs like Kenner, and to satellite communities such as Slidell and Bay St. Louis, Mississippi.

The dominant political machine of New Orleans was the Democratic Choctaw Club. It catered to these new and politically isolated arrivals as a source of votes.[44] Individual rivulets of patronage, those little but essential favors in return for reliable votes, would one day combine in a mighty political stream.

Jews were well represented among furniture dealers and street vendors also. There was a small Chinatown on upper Bourbon.[45] Some Negro families lived on lower Burgundy.

Although legal segregation along ethnic and racial lines was very real, it did not enter much into the casual relationships among most families in the Quarter.[46] Jewish, Italian, Chinese, and Negro working-class children played, and their mothers conversed.[47] In religion and schooling, and later, in matters of marriage, these children would be set apart. But on the street, they mingled freely. No matter what they spoke at home, they talked to each other in the common tongue of New Orleans, a dialect of American English likened to that of Brooklyn or northern New Jersey. It borrowed words from French and hit them with a brickbat. Chartres became "sharturhs," and Burgundy, "bur-GUN-dee." The "oi" as heard in "boil" and "oil" was rendered as an "er" sound, leading to "berl" and "earl." Statements often concluded with the all-inclusive "and like dat" or "and dem." Speakers were rarely heard to go directly to any destination; they usually "went down by" a place. Veracity was assured by the tagline "for true."

The Negro parents could not be as carefree as their roaming progeny. In 1896, Homer Plessy decided he no longer cared to sit apart from whites in the city's streetcars. After the U.S. Supreme Court disallowed his challenge, the white South tightened its segregation practices.[48] The generally bad national economy of the mid- and late 1890s cost many local whites their jobs to Negroes who accepted lower wages, aggravating post-Reconstruction tensions.[49] In 1896, Negroes were 22.7 percent of registered voters in Orleans Parish; in the state at large, they were a slight majority at 50.1 percent.[50] In that same year, the Louisiana Democratic Party called a constitutional convention for the express purpose of disenfranchising Negro voters.[51] The new constitution kept all but a small number of Negroes from voting.

Racial tensions simmered in the 1900 summer heat. In July, a Negro named Robert Charles resisted a beating by white policemen and went on a shooting rampage. Before he was cut down, he killed six white men, including four policemen. In a ghastly echo of the Hennessy affair, enraged white mobs roamed the city looking for vengeance, killing at least ten Negroes and wounding dozens of others,[52] before the authorities bestirred themselves to regain control. Quickly obscured in white collective memory, Charles's deed was whispered with admiration by generations of New Orleans's Negroes.

Negro and white dockworkers had formed an integrated labor council,[53] which triumphed in two strikes in 1907 and 1908. However, advances in technology, the rise of the "open shop," and the grip of segregation weakened this alliance in subsequent years.[54] In a multitude of ways major and minor, Negroes were increasingly reminded of their place. Signs designating white and "colored" entrances, washrooms, and theater seating had to be carefully observed.[55] At 1218 Burgundy, Medard Nelson operated a private school for Negro children.[56] One of his pupils was Danny Barker, who recalled that Nelson let his pupils out one at a time to avoid a mob of children hitting the street all at once.[57] New Orleans was a refuge from peonage—slavery redux—in the despised Delta, but it was no paradise for people of dark skin.

Part of the French Creole legacy are light-skinned people of color. Two centuries of French Creole concubinage with light-skinned Negro women, referred to with dubious accuracy as "quadroons" or "octoroons," produced a caste of people unique in America. At the time called politely "café au lait" or, coarsely, "high yeller," these would also one day be called Creoles. They had their own society, which floated uneasily between that of whites and dark-skinned Negroes.[58]

Beyond the American norm of these early years, morbidity was a constant presence in the city. Yellow fever, that decimating horror of nineteenth-century New Orleans, made one final appearance in 1905.[59] Italians living in the lower Quarter were hit especially hard.[60] The link between mosquitoes and yellow fever was still new and not widely accepted.[61] The squalid conditions in the lower Quarter, like the open cisterns, poor drainage, and unscreened windows, were ideal for contagion-carrying mosquitoes. Linguistic and cultural barriers made many Italians reluctant to seek help. According to a contemporary account, deaths in Little Palermo were concentrated along Decatur and Chartres streets, between Dumaine and Barracks.[62] The public health service started a campaign to install window screens on residences and cisterns, put a film of oil on standing water, and fumigate living spaces.

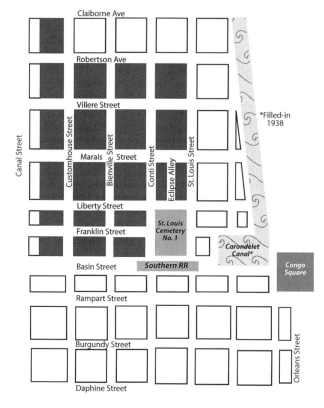

## Storyville and the Quarter c.1900

The outbreak was arrested, but not before about 452 had died.[63] Besides this final appearance of "yellow jack," tuberculosis—then called consumption—dysentery, cholera, and other ailments promoted by close quarters and poor sanitation took many lives. Syphilis, incurable before the 1910 introduction of Salvarsan, reduced many former "sporting" people to gibbering idiots shuffling towards insane asylums and early deaths.[64]

Although the 1850s murderous mayhem of Gallatin Street, near the French Market, was no more,[65] violent crime was still very common in the Vieux Carré. Drunks were easy targets for robbery and were sometimes murdered in the process. Disputes, frequently abetted by alcohol, often escalated to fights to the death between spouses, relatives, erstwhile friends, and strangers. Political rallies could turn from passionate to brawling in a twinkling. As we have seen in the Hennessy and Charles affairs, mobs could easily be incited to wholesale murder. Black was a popular shade of clothing; it took little effort to assume mourning dress. The above-ground "cities of the dead," such as St. Louis Cemetery No. 1, were often better kept than the houses of the living.

Frenchtown had a sister, called by its populace the District or the Turf, but known to outsiders as Storyville.[66] When the French Creole families were still politically strong, they joined with the Protestant American elites to try to move prostitution out of the Quarter. Alderman Sidney Story crafted an ordinance in 1897 that designated a district where that profession was tolerated but never legalized.[67] Many, but certainly not all, of the bordellos in French-town joined others already in the designated area north of Rampart Street. Storyville essentially became an autonomous village. Its government consisted of the madams, owners, and landlords of the "sporting houses" and bars. Its unofficial mayor was saloonkeeper Tom Anderson, whose political power was well respected throughout the state. Many of the madams rented furniture from prominent, legitimate businessmen, such as the Maestri family.[68]

Most civic leaders thought Storyville was a progressive, if not perfect, solution to the problem. Vice officially sanctioned, so the reasoning went, was vice controlled, and the Choctaws strongly favored keeping Storyville. However, some other progressives were scandalized that the sex trade had not been stamped out. Among these was music publisher Phillip Werlein, who, beginning in 1910 crusaded for the district's abolition.[69]

Although Storyville reduced prostitution in the Quarter, some whores and whorehouses remained therein.[70] Only a paper boundary divided the two enclaves, and sex workers freely moved between both as whim and legal circumstance dictated.[71]

After a particularly notorious gun battle between dance hall operators in 1913, many of the dance halls of Storyville were obliged to move to the Quarter.[72] These dance halls all had prostitutes, either on staff or working the floor for customers. Following the dance halls, strumpets started filtering back into the Quarter in greater numbers.[73] The lowest class of hookers rented slatted stalls called "cribs," primarily on upper Burgundy and Iberville. They called out to passing men, sometimes forcibly dragging them inside. For as little as a quarter, a man could visit briefly with a tough, unsentimental, larcenous, and often diseased woman.[74] If he had the money, he was far better off at one of the top-line houses of Storyville, such as Lulu White's, where the chandeliers gleamed and the girls were usually clean.[75]

The location of Storyville, roughly northwest of the Quarter, and the continuing presence of low-class hookers in the upper Quarter, influenced a gradual residential shift to the lower Quarter. To a cartographer, the Quarter could be bisected by Orleans Avenue, which ends at the back of the cathedral garden. But in reality, St. Ann became the dividing line, particularly on the river side of the Quarter and the busy thoroughfares of Bourbon and Royal. Above St. Ann, businesses, some still with owners living above the store, coexisted uneasily with saloons and strolling strumpets. Below St. Ann, "respectable" inhabitants lived in relative peace.

The French Quarter of the early twentieth century had a veneer of civilization. The top layers were the French Opera House and St. Louis Cathedral. By contemporary standards, this veneer floated atop a stagnant pool of general frowziness and even wretchedness. The people of the Quarter in the early 1900s probably had little notion that they were living in the middle of important history worth preserving. To most, Frenchtown was poor, old, and shabby. Livestock, particularly chickens,[76] roamed at will. It was a way station like New York's teeming Lower East Side of the same era—a place one would hope to leave as succeeding generations moved on up the American ladder.

In 1911, realizing that men down on their luck needed help, Rev. Peter Wynhoven opened a Vieux Carré mission.[77] Located in the Lower Pontalba on Jackson Square from 1911 to 1916,[78] the St. Vincent's Hotel and Free Labor Bureau provided assistance and jobs until 1936.[79]

In the Latin manner, many buildings contained shops on the ground floors and the family residence above. In some buildings, an arched passageway (porte cochere) led from a gated entry to a courtyard. On one side of the porte cochere there might be an inner staircase, winding elegantly upwards. In palmier days, the courtyard was a gracious atrium, as Harriet Joor observed in 1905:

> Yet, once within the heavy entrance door, once across the dark, damp corridor, with its wrought-iron lamp swinging in the arch at the inner end, we come upon the cool, green court, with its fountain, and its birds and blue sky. Here the noise of the street dies to a whisper, and its dust and heat are forgotten. Everywhere is a wealth of green; in pots, in boxes, in old Spanish water-jugs grow palms and great, wide-spreading ferns. Here one sees the pale green of the banana, the dark, jagged spears of Spanish bayonet, and the fleshy, spiny lobes of cacti. On brackets, on benches, on little stands, from the railing of the gallery above, from hanging-baskets swinging between its pillars, green streamers float, while the neighbor's house-wall is veiled in close-clinging vines.[80]

Once these courtyards had been the domain of Creole families of formal manners and proud honor. Now, many were cluttered common areas for several poor families living in the same house, which sagged with great weariness around the courtyard.[81] The owners had little incentive, and no official mandate, to keep the buildings in good repair. Photos of the time show peeling paint and cracked stucco everywhere. From that time until this, mosses, ferns, and even small trees grew out of chinks in the bricks and parapets. One accidental binder of style was the cheap green paint used for many shutters and doors, weathering in the subtropical climate to a family of blue-green hues.[82] Demolishing certain buildings was, given their utter decay, the only expedient. While everyone could name common building styles, like Creole cottages, shotguns, and camelbacks, there was no catechism of ornamentation. Balconies might appear or disappear on a whim. Carriageways might be covered over or adapted to suit automobiles. Wood and metal brackets were interchanged. Electric and telephone wires were tacked to the outsides or strung from house to house. Sheds and other outbuildings might spring up to crowd in even more tenants. So, many buildings in the Vieux Carré were a mishmash of styles, and only a precious few, like Madam John's Legacy on Dumaine, were battered survivors of French colonial times. After two major fires in the late eighteenth century, the architecture of Frenchtown was far more Spanish than French.[83] The public buildings, including the Presbytère and Cabildo, were also shabby.

In 1909, the Louisiana Supreme Court moved to a new Beaux Arts fortress at the intersection of Royal and Conti. Many older buildings died to give it birth.[84] Hulking, gleaming white, it was a dazzling reminder of authority in a district long known for lawlessness and laxity. In coming years, it would be a finger in the eye of those seeking a coherent vision of Quarter styles.[85] Eventually, the mantle of sheer age—architectural ancestor worship—and the Supreme Court's return to the renovated building would endear it to the guardians of Vieux Carré antiquity.

As the new century lumbered on, automobiles came to the Quarter, and as in most other cities, initially made themselves unwelcome. Mules and horses would continue to be the motive power for many of New Orleans's municipal chores into the 1930s, and the animals didn't care for the snorting machines. The narrow, streetcar-tracked cobblestone streets, perfumed with animal droppings, were challenging to early drivers. Then there was the question of where to park. Draft animals were usually stabled outside Frenchtown. But automobiles needed secure parking that was nearby to homes and businesses.

Soon, some buildings were demolished for parking lots. Others would retain some semblance of their outward looks but were gutted for garages. Hotels would have to dedicate precious floor space for indoor parking, since basements were rare in the soggy soil. Before power steering, drivers built arm muscle wrenching their cars in and out of parallel parking along the Quarter's streets. The quest for a (one hoped, legal) parking place entered the life of the Quarter, never to depart.

## The Louisiana Purchase Centennial

The 1903 centennial of the purchase was staged in New Orleans, which had been the French colonial capital and original object of Thomas Jefferson's acquisition.

The celebration centered around Jackson Square. On Saturday, December 19, the governor of Louisiana, the French ambassador, a representative of the king of Spain, and Admiral W. C. Wise, representing the president of the United States, headlined the festivities.[86] The dignitaries bellowed oratory from the balcony of the Cabildo, the old colonial capitol and then the seat of the Louisiana Supreme Court. A fleet of flag-bedecked warships paraded on the river.[87] That night, a gala ball was held at the French Opera House.[88] The next day, a Te Deum and Grand Pontifical High Mass were offered at St. Louis Cathedral. More speeches were followed by a reenactment of the purchase signing.[89]

An early formal acknowledgment of New Orleans's origins was the opening of the Colonial Museum at the old Ursuline Convent on Chartres. Professor Alcee Fortier of the Louisiana Historical Society welcomed the dignitaries to a collection of artifacts from the colonial era.[90] Transferred to the Louisiana State Museum in the Cabildo in 1906, this collection became its nucleus.[91]

## The First Stirrings of Preservation

To see the buildings of the Vieux Carré in context, and to see the Vieux Carré as an enclave of a larger history and not merely of one ethnic group, required a special vision. William Ratcliffe Irby seems to have been the first to have had both the vision and the means to do something about it. Irby, who had made a fortune in tobacco,[92] became the first of many angels to rescue the Vieux Carré at critical moments.

By 1913, the glory of French Creole society, the French Opera House, was in decline. Irby bought it, fixed it up, and donated it to Tulane University.[93] In 1920, Irby donated 417 Royal Street to Tulane; it is now Brennan's Restaurant; and Irby would rescue other important buildings.[94]

In 1915, a twenty-three-year-old writer from Baton Rouge arrived in the Quarter.[95] He took up residence at 612 Royal Street. With the exception of a few detours, Lyle Saxon would live in New Orleans until the end of his days. Saxon was one of the most influential of Madame Vieux Carré's lovers in the twentieth century. Between 1914 and 1917, he and his friend, Flo Field, wrote several articles extolling the charms of the old village.[96]

These early preservationists also faced a stealthy threat to the physical realm of the Quarter. Beginning in the 1890s, the city undertook a massive project to improve drainage. Large canals and pipes, powered by pumps, now drew water out of town and dumped it into the lake. This meant that the old back o' town swamp and the lakefront could be built upon.[97] It also meant that the muck underlying the Quarter grew drier. Many older structures in the Vieux Carré were built upon cypress grids, or "mattresses," supporting brick piers.[98] The falling water table made these mattresses sink and shift. Gradually, many Frenchtown buildings reflected the subsidence in leaning walls, cracked plaster, and uneven floors.[99] The most spectacular example was the collapse of St. Louis Cathedral's foundations in 1916, which imperilled the entire basilica.[100] This came on the heels of damage from the 1915 hurricane and a small bomb blast in 1909.[101] Prior to his death in 1917, Archbishop James Blenk appealed for funds,[102] and his appeal was answered by William Ratcliffe Irby, whose generosity allowed the restored cathedral to be reopened in a splendid ceremony as a new archbishop was installed in December 1918.[103]

## TANGO BELT, CHA-CHA-CHA

Even as there was a residential changing of the guard from French Creole to Sicilian, Frenchtown was still the place for the city to have fun. Besides the opera and carnival balls, Frenchtown remained true to its roots as a place to drink, dance, and carouse. All three thrills fit perfectly with a dance craze from Argentina. The tango's close-in syncopation between partners, its suggestive moves and stylized flairs, easily found a home in America's first Latin

capital, New Orleans. In the tango, with liquored confidence and the bonhomie of the club, couples could have their closest public pantomime of inter-
course. For that reason, the tango, and contemporary dances like the turkey
trot and bunny hug, were considered scandalous by the same high-hatters
who were appalled by jazz and ragtime. The police harassed clubs where these
dances were in vogue.[104] The tango was well established in the Quarter by the
1900s. So many clubs featured the dance that a section of the Quarter was
labeled the Tango Belt in 1915. The Tango Belt was approximately bounded
by North Rampart, Iberville, St. Louis, and Bourbon streets,[105] and featured
clubs such as the Black Orchid, 942 Conti,[106] the Haymarket at 931 Iberville,
and the Green Tree, at 401 Dauphine.[107]

Like the lowing horns and throbbing strings of a Wagner overture, the
howling hurricane of 1915 presaged tragedy to come. The old St. Louis hotel,
once a gem, had fallen to ruin several years before. The hotel's dome fell in
during the storm,[108] and the entire structure was eventually razed.[109] Wharves
at the riverfront collapsed,[110] and the French Opera House suffered serious
damage.[111] The cathedral also incurred injury.[112]

In April 1917, the United States entered World War I on the side of Brit-
ain and France. In its rescue of decadent old Europe, young America held
its head and morals high. Not since the Civil War had the nation needed
to mobilize so many men. The War Department looked at port cities and
didn't like the inevitable intersection of soldiers and sailors with whores. The
notoriety of Storyville was worldwide and viewed with sour Calvinist disap-
proval outside of south Louisiana. The secretary of the navy, Josephus Daniels, issued an edict directing closure of the district. Mayor Martin Behrman
went to Washington to plead the city's reclama to Daniels and other officials.
He was rebuffed, and on November 12, 1917,[113] Storyville, officially at least, was
no more. The madams and their charges simply moved into other parts of
town, and the Quarter, nearby and cheap, was the favored destination. Whatever gains the Quarter had made in quality of life since her sister was created
from her rib were now reversed as the tawdry relation moved back in.[114]

> Legislature voted the district down . . .
> Legislature voted the district down . . .
> Damn good way to spread the hookers over town.[115]

So went part of the parody of "Hesitation Blues," sung by jazz artists
who observed the aftermath of Storyville. For most of the remaining French

Creole families, this was the last straw, and they began to move uptown.[116] The old Storyville area lapsed into slumhood. The sex industry would continue much as before; servicemen would continue to find their pleasures; but official morality had been served.

In the summer of 1918, many Tango Belt clubs were closed for the same reasons. They were allowed to reopen later that year after the conclusion of the "Great War."[117]

## LOSS OF THE FRENCH OPERA HOUSE

Early in the morning of December 4, 1919, Lyle Saxon was awakened by clanging firebells and a general uproar. Flinging on his clothes, he ran to see the cause of the commotion. What he found stunned him and the entire city. The French Opera House was burning and beyond salvation. Joined by his friend, painter Alberta Kinsey, Saxon sat on the curb and wept.[118]

No French Creole, and not a native New Orleanian, Saxon had formed a deep bond with the Quarter and had hopes for its revival. The loss of this nexus of genteel society meant, as Saxon wrote in the *Times-Picayune* the next morning, "The heart of the old French Quarter has stopped beating."[119] At this distance in time, it is difficult to comprehend the emotional shock that reverberated across the bereft city. The Opera House was not merely the local hub of society; it was New Orleans's cultural crown jewel, displayed with pride to an admiring world that rarely associated the city with anything above the pleasures of the flesh. Despite many brave plans, the French Opera House was never rebuilt, and no other epicenter for French Creole life emerged as the Jazz Age took over American culture.

As the 1920s dawned, the Vieux Carré had suffered the double indignity of the influx of Storyville's sex workers and the loss of its cultural centerpiece. The American experiment in the prohibition of alcohol, more precious than water in New Orleans, was beginning. It was at this bleakest moment that Madame Vieux Carré found "the kindness of strangers."

## CHAPTER 2

# 1920–1930

*The Firebird of Preservation*

## "Strangers Within Our Gates"

Preservation of the old, the worn-out, and the frowsy was not an American trait just after World War I. Progress led forward on the wheels of automobiles and the wings of biplanes. The new vernacular of architecture was the skyscraper, the sprawling factory, and the tract house of muddled nineteenth-century style. The old was to cheerfully give way to the new by the good offices of the wrecking ball and bulldozer. Concrete and steel would be the new sinews of the alabaster cities.

A very few people, such as author Grace King, William Ratcliffe Irby, and Lyle Saxon, saw the need to save the old buildings defining American history. Besides buildings of monumental import, some wanted to save "ordinary" old buildings and communities. If nothing else, these places could serve as object lessons to youth on the trials of former generations.

Some early "preservationists" saw mere "quaintness." This became a cutesy term for simple, unthreatening things so far removed from modern life as to be fascinating to those of means and leisure. For better or worse, these well-intentioned folks often took bits and pieces of history out of their contexts. Aping the barons of the Gilded Age who cut up European villas and rearranged them on American estates, collectors bought everything from rusty farm implements to entire cornices to add the quaint touch to suburban residences.

Tenant housing on Dauphine Street, circa 1920–1930s. Courtesy of the Louisiana State Museum.

The French Quarter's fearsome social reputation did not deter these collectors of the early 1920s, as Elizabeth Werlein sighed in her portfolio, *The Wrought Iron Railings of the Vieux Carré, New Orleans:* "Like all prophets, unseen and unhonored in their own land, these worthy relics are being carried away by observing strangers within our gates until New Orleans is fast losing this distinctive evidence of her foreign setting and America, that unique Vieux Carré of romance and charm."[1]

What were the preservationists to preserve? Were Quarter tenements worthy of saving just because they were old? Were their litter and farm animals part of their charm? What of the public buildings from the colonial era? Property rights were then considered nearly absolute. That a city could constrain property owners from changing or demolishing their buildings was a shocking notion, not accepted for years. Why couldn't a man sell rusty iron bric-a-brac off his old building to wide-eyed rubes?

In an era when master planning, public input, and environmental impact are all in the vocabulary of public discourse, it is hard for us to imagine the nearly utter lack of controls on property use that prevailed in 1920s America. Before Storyville, a homeowner in the French Quarter might find a new whorehouse or saloon had opened next door without warning. That property owner's rights were also fairly absolute, so there was little or no recourse for those who wanted quiet enjoyment of their residences.

The Storyville experiment had temporarily relieved the Vieux Carré of some, if not all, sex industry activity. Now it was back in force. The romanticized image of prostitution leaves out the violent pimps, drug addiction, and larceny that followed the whores back to the Quarter. Despite the common

media image, the libertine aspects of the Roaring Twenties were largely confined to big cities, especially way points like New Orleans. The sex industry of
Storyville and the French Quarter had been in decline for some time,[2] but it
was not due completely to all the "nice girls" now doing "naughty things," as
the oft-repeated legend has it. America in 1920 was still, by and large, a place
of rigid social conservatism. The small gains in social progress in the first two
decades of the 1900s—female suffrage and the eight-hour workday—were
over-balanced by regressive actions like Prohibition, the Justice Department's
"Red Scare," and the rebirth of the Ku Klux Klan.

Against this backdrop, a small but influential band emerged to launch
the first phase of the Vieux Carré's revival. The shock of the loss of the French
Opera House certainly galvanized early preservationists like Saxon, Irby, and
Saxon's friend Flo Fields, who had started giving what are believed to be the
first organized tours of the Vieux Carré in the late teens.[3] To those that followed them in the next few years, the lost opera house was not their cause.
For the subsequent waves, the French Quarter was attractive simply because
it was cheap and freer of social constraints than their hometowns. Much has
been made of the artistic circle that coalesced around Saxon. Their influence
in the 1920s revival of the Vieux Carré was not due to any intrinsic celebrity,
most of which lay in the future. Writing in the local press and sending mis-
sives to prominent outsiders, their achievement was to bestir some influential and wealthy citizens to join them and achieve the first critical mass for
conservation. Saxon managed to cajole a few owners into varying degrees of
renovation.[4] An artist might buy and fix up a building, but had little influence
on the property owners on the block, most of whom were absentee landlords,
living Uptown, collecting rents from decaying tenements. They were getting
their money—why should things change?

What cannot be overstated is that this first band of preservationists left
a legacy that ultimately became the economic engine of New Orleans. Their
influence was slow and sometimes faltering, and there were reverses along the
way. But it was at the smokey, absinthe-informed parties of the 1920s Quarter
"bohemians" that the foundations for New Orleans's modern tourist industry
were laid.[5] Long after most primary industry has fled, tourism, in ways great
and small, keeps the city ever so slightly above utter destitution. Most of the
oil industry has decamped to Houston, but the hotels stay busy. The high-tech
sector may roll its eyes when thinking of Orleans Parish, but the souvenir
shops of Decatur Street still turn the goods to each new generation of tourists.
This first band scraped a few sparkling shards of "charm" from the gutter and

exposed the mother lode of unique character that is New Orleans's, and the Vieux Carré's, lifeblood.

In 1919, painter Alberta Kinsey arrived in New Orleans. Legend has it that she took a wrong turn and ended up in the Quarter.[6] Down at the heels and groaning under the transplanted Storyville sex industry, the Vieux Carré somehow charmed her. A glimmer of youthful beauty showed through the hag's cracked makeup.[7] She became acquainted with Lyle Saxon, and together they wept at the French Opera House fire. She and Saxon helped establish the Arts and Crafts Club, which would become an important center for the Quarter's artistic life and its overall revival.[8]

In 1916, a few wealthy men and women giving plays in their living rooms called themselves the Drawing Room Players. In 1919, reorganized as Le Petit Théâtre du Vieux Carré, they moved to the lower Pontalba, above the former site of Rev. Wynhoven's mission. By hard volunteer labor, they created a theater seating 184.[9]

In early February 1920, a public meeting, attended by Lyle Saxon, was held at the Monteleone Hotel. The press announced the gathering as "[t]hose sponsoring the move to organize an improvement league to preserve and advance the Vieux Carré . . ."[10] The resulting Vieux Carré Society (VCS) sent a delegation including Grace King of the Louisiana Historical Society and many prominent business leaders to meet with Mayor Martin Behrman. Encouraged by press and civic response, the VCS submitted a ten-point plan to the city commission in May 1920. Among these points are some that sound familiar to contemporary ears:

"Suspension of all questionable resorts." This, of course, was a plea for the suppression of vice.

"Protection of the chiefly residential sections of the Quarter from certain types of businesses, particularly to prohibit businesses that give off offensive odors, smoke or dust, or cause street congestion by trucks, wagons or drays" (mule or horse-drawn sideless wagons, still common at the time).

The proposed zone of protection was bounded by St. Louis, North Rampart, Chartres, and Esplanade. This was the first formal recognition that the Quarter was effectively divided into commercial, tourist, and residential zones, a partition which, for better or worse, informed many later decisions.[11]

The VCS did not merely demand that the city act. It took the lead in setting standards for renovation and upgrading of buildings, and encouraged its members to live in the Quarter if possible.[12] The VCS could cajole and act on its own, but its initiatives remained at the mercy of the city government, who was also listening to absentee landlords and owners of those "question-able resorts." Mayor Martin Behrman seemed favorable to the goals of the VCS. However, a series of newspaper articles proclaimed the corruption of this long-time mayor, and he lost his bid for reelection in 1920. The author of these articles was Lyle Saxon.[13] Not for the last time, reformers had reason to be careful what they wished for. Behrman's successor, Andrew McShane, was ineffectual, and Behrman returned to office in 1925,[14] dying less than a year into his fifth term.[15]

Meanwhile, a clarion call went out to the world, announcing New Orleans's arrival as a literary city of national rank. In a fledgling journal, Sherwood Anderson wrote an article titled "New Orleans, the *Double Dealer*, and the Modern Movement in America."[16]

The *Double Dealer* became the voice of the city's literary genius and in its brief life (1921–1926) attracted many writers to New Orleans and the Vieux Carré in particular. The magazine became a nexus for Anderson and other authors, then unknown but to become famous with time: Faulkner, Hemingway, Thornton Wilder, Robert Penn Warren, and many others.[17]

Saxon wrote several newspaper articles extolling the Vieux Carré and evangelized it as a place for the artistic to live. As one of Saxon's close friends, Robert Tallant, observed, the Quarter became "more and more of an art colony, less an underworld."[18] By 1924, Saxon told a correspondent that "the whole Quarter is filling up with artists and writers." He complained that they "yell and scream all night long like cats."[19] Nonetheless, he played host and mentor to them.[20] Many of these artists and writers lived close by Jackson Square. A popular hangout was the Green Shutter, a tearoom-bookshop operated by Martha Westfeldt—first at 633 Royal and then at 710 St. Peter.[21]

The Pontalbas had been in decline since the end of the Civil War, and evidence suggests that farm animals were stabled there by immigrant tenants. In December 1920 a group led by Alfred Danzinger bought the Upper Pontalba, and eventually it came to be owned by the city; the name City Pontalba has stuck to it ever since. William Ratcliffe Irby bought the Lower Pontalba in 1921 and willed it to the Louisiana State Museum.[22] It is known, in turn, as the State Pontalba.

In June 1921, Natalie Vivian Scott and her friend, *Double Dealer* editor Jack McClure, purchased a house at 626 Orleans (now Pirate's) Alley.[23] They operated the building as studio apartments and created an incubator for writers and artists to live in the ferment of the Vieux Carré. Among those who lived there was artist and later silversmith William Spratling, who eventually shared an apartment at 624 with William Faulkner.[24]

Close to the Scott-McClure house was the new location of Le Petit Théâtre du Vieux Carré. In 1922, Le Petit asked architect Richard Koch to restore an old building on St. Peter Street, across from the Cabildo. Koch prevailed upon them to build a new structure that conformed in style to older ones nearby. The result pleased Elizabeth Werlein, who pronounced it "[s]o harmonious with its surroundings that it is difficult to believe that it has not been stand-ing for a century."[25] Le Petit became the theatrical hub of the Vieux Carré, hosting both mainstream and experimental productions.[26] Although it could not become the social fulcrum that the old Opera House was, it established its own status as a place for the city's artistic elite. It became a nexus not only for Quarter culture, but for those, from Uptown and elsewhere, who were involved in the life of the enclave. Over the years, many famous actors have performed there, enjoying the Quarter's ambience in the bargain.[27]

Another nearby resource was the Arts and Crafts Club, at 520 Royal, whose building had been donated by William Irby.[28] The club provided work-shops, exhibition spaces, materials, and instruction in various mediums and became an incubator for many artists.[29] In the fall of 1922, Spratling became a part-time instructor there.[30] In 1927, some members of the Arts and Crafts Club organized the New Orleans Art League, which held the first outdoor art exhibitions in the Quarter.[31]

In 1924, Sherwood Anderson made a home on the second floor of the Upper Pontalba at 540B St. Peter Street.[32] The author of *Winesburg, Ohio* was already a national figure. He and his wife operated a part-salon/part-boardinghouse for many writers who came up the elegant winding steps in the echoing stairwell. Among those who passed the portals were Faulkner, who lived there prior to moving in with Spratling;[33] Carl Sandburg; and Ring Lardner.[34] Yet another was Anita Loos, author of *Gentlemen Prefer Blondes*— later made into a movie now enjoying cult status.[35] In the two years Anderson remained in the Pontalba, he was a powerful draw to the famous and hopeful apprentices alike.

The Arts and Crafts Club held freewheeling masquerade parties—not at all like the regimented, classical tableau of the exclusive old-line Carnival krewes. If one could be oneself in the Quarter, then these parties let one be some other self, giving existence to creatures from the inner psyche.[36] These parties were the direct ancestors of the pansexual fantasy krewes of the later part of the century.

In the early 1920s, a group of young female socialites started the Quartier Club, which operated a tearoom on St. Peter Street in the as-yet-ungentrified Quarter. By 1925, the club evolved into Le Petit Salon and moved from the Pontalba to 620 St. Peter, a building donated by the perennially generous William Ratcliffe Irby.[37] Author Grace King was elected the salon's first president. As she was the standard bearer for the traditions of old New Orleans, her prestige enabled her and her fellow salon members to press the city for further protection of the Quarter. On November 24, 1925, the city council approved an ordinance creating the first Vieux Carré Commission (VCC).[38] This first VCC was merely advisory and had no power to enact codes nor enforce them. It did record one small triumph: in December 1926 it prevailed on the city to deny a permit for a club on Royal Street.[39]

The VCS's most memorable achievement also occurred in 1926 with the restoration of the Old Absinthe House at 238 Bourbon.[40] Also in 1926, Natalie Scott restored the Court of Two Sisters building at 613 Royal, now home to the namesake restaurant. The Pontalba buildings began a long restoration process that year as well.[41] Overall, however, 1926 would be one of the bad years that Madame Vieux Carré's friends would sigh over for decades. The literary moths that had clustered in the Quarter began to fly away, one by one, in search of brighter lights elsewhere. Despite its pretensions, New Orleans was simply not going to displace New York as the capital of American letters. Nor could it compete with the burgeoning film industry in Hollywood. In that year, the *Double Dealer* folded, Saxon left for New York, and Anderson moved to Virginia.[42]

On November 20, 1926, William Irby called at a funeral parlor, looked at coffins, asked for a newspaper, and shot himself to death.[43] Depressed over failing health, the Quarter's real estate angel took himself from the scene.[44] The terms of his will transferred the Lower Pontalba to the Louisiana State Museum.[45]

By 1929, Natalie Scott, William Spratling, and William Faulkner were no longer full-time Quarter residents.[46] Saxon would return and continue his association with the district, owning a large house at 536 Madison,[47] although his primary salon would be conducted from a hotel on St. Charles Avenue.[48]

At the same time this literary band was helping Madame Vieux Carré from her knees to at least a sitting position, she was doing something for them, too. Aside from Grace King, Sherwood Anderson, and Lyle Saxon, none of this first cadre was well known outside New Orleans. King was the duchess of New Orleans letters, but there her celebrity ended. Anderson had

Gov. Nicholls and Royal,
1928. Courtesy of the
Williams Research Center
of the Historic New Orleans
Collection.

a national reputation before his stay in the Quarter. Saxon was just emerging
on the larger literary scene in the midtwenties. The others were, at least at
that time, unknowns. These unsung men and women were testing themselves
against New Orleans in all its somnambulance, and against the Quarter in all
its compact, frowzy, and cheap potential. And they were coming up winners.
Here, one could create a salon in humble circumstances and become a queen
bee, provided the liquor supply held out. The aspiring could find training,
mentorship, and, if lucky, references to the larger artistic life of the world. On
any besodden, convivial evening, just a story or two above the street, looking over a balcony at the dim house shapes against a sky still dark enough to
show a few stars, the feeling of success and the surety of place came easily.
From inside, laughter, clinking of ice, victrola music, and candlelight vouched
friendship; the subtropical world outside enticed with mysteries of the tanta-
lizing future. In the middle, you, purified by booze and youth to the sheerest
kell, both drawn by indoors comradery and pulled by the seductive call of the
night, its streets, and its breezes.

The Quarter and the larger city had a human scale, in architecture, society, and institutions, that was microscopic beside the canyons of New York.

The entire population of serious writers in the Vieux Carré at that time would probably have filled only a couple of the many artistic coffeehouses of Gotham. Most of the "action" was right within a span of twelve or so Vieux Carré blocks. New Orleans had no major publishing houses, no Broadway, no Tin Pan Alley, no *New York Times*, no important galleries to dangle world-class opportunities—or deal spirit-crushing rejections. Saxon, a major talent, tested himself against New York and, after four years of mixed success, returned to Louisiana.[49] He resumed his honored centerpiece in the Quarter's cultural life. No one was surprised when he was named "Mr. New Orleans"[50;] he could never have aspired to the title of "Mr. Greenwich Village," had such a mantle been available. Failure within the context of New Orleans was possible, of course. It mainly befell those who confused excess with inspiration. Having no standards of comparison other than the Quarter lifestyle, they merged into the cheerfully alcoholic mass of café society.[51]

The others in this early cadre—with one exception—remained as local and sometimes regional luminaries, content to be recognized as one of dozens at home, not ignored as one of thousands in a chilly Babylon. The exception, of course, is William Faulkner, whose embrace of Hollywood vaulted him past the big-city cataracts that had washed many talents back to their spawn streams.[52] This pattern has held true in many endeavors for many people across the century. Whether chewed up and spit out of a metropolis, or refugees from small-minded small towns, many have found their groove, niche, and measure of celebrity within the Crescent City, and with that, they are content.

## "BELLIGERENTLY WET"

New Orleans's reputation as the hardest-drinking town in America dates to the colonial era. The Gallic fondness for wine was all the more important in the frontier rigors of La Nouvelle-Orléans. The Kaintock flatboat men expected whiskey—and women—at the end of their voyages down the Mississippi, and the town was happy to oblige on both counts. Alcohol, rite of passage for the young, lubricant for the amorous, and comforter of the poor, lonely, and old, has forever been a necessity of New Orleans life. New Orleans's "moderation" is everyone else's excess. In legend and literature, everyone from Andy Jackson to Lyle Saxon calls for an absinthe frappé.[53]

We have seen how American idealism informed the decision to close Storyville. Across the nation, the temperance movement gained strength, and in January 1919, the Eighteenth Amendment was ratified, prohibiting the manufacture or sale of alcoholic beverages, with certain narrow exceptions for medicine and industry.[54] Louisiana had approved the amendment by a close margin in the summer of 1918. New Orleanians could not believe that something more essential than drinking water—and dearer to some than life itself—could be taken away.

The Bureau of Prohibition set up shop in the U.S. Customshouse, near the Quarter. Between thirty and forty agents were employed full-time, along with support personnel.[55] The city had been home to about five thousand places to buy a drink in 1919.[56] A mouse had been sent to police an elephant of liquor.

Surrounded by trackless marsh, intersected by a major river, and a hub of ocean traffic, New Orleans was a smuggler's dream. Booze was brought in on boats, ocean-going ships, and on simple rafts. With hundreds of bodies of water, vast spreads of rural acreage, and pliant local officials, rumrunners could bring in nearly any quantity of alcohol at almost any time. New Orleans was also a major port for the transhipment of liquor to other points, including Al Capone's Chicago.[57] New Orleans's well-honed skills at the business of pleasure were even applied to insurance; the Bootlegger Underwriting Company provided its members coverage against the financial stress of being busted.[58]

Distilleries of varying sizes operated throughout the Vieux Carré and the greater New Orleans area.[59] One found at 1132 Decatur Street in 1921 featured nine stills.[60] It would be busted again in 1925.[61] Yet another, uncovered in 1922 at 625–629 St. Philip, featured six stills and an elaborate system of trapdoors leading to various functional areas. Three thousand quarts of so-called "overnight whiskey"—flavored and colored raw alcohol—were seized.[62] Those buildings must have been popular with bootleggers, since, eighteen months later, another raid revealed four two-thousand-gallon mash vats and other apparatus capable of making forty-five gallons of alcohol daily.[63]

Even Quarter architecture came to the aid of the bootleggers. The eighteenth-century Spanish had introduced a building style with one low-ceilinged mezzanine floor between the retail space at street level and the living quarters above. This entresol space, rare in American domestic architecture and hard to perceive from the street, was nearly perfect for making and hiding liquor, until the Prohibition agents caught on.

The world-famous restaurants and drinking establishments of the Quarter resorted to several subterfuges to serve their patrons strong drink. In the beginning, some attempted to become "private clubs" where "members only" could be served behind closed doors.[64] The Prohibition agents' raids discouraged this, and so some places served liquor in coffee cups. Other taverns disappeared into office buildings behind strong doors to become speakeasies, or, as called in New Orleans, "blind tigers." Many of these catered to the upper classes, and there one might find the elite of civic and social life.[65]

It wasn't necessary to become a member of a blind tiger to get a drink. Booze was sold at soft-drink stands, which often doubled as cheap whorehouses,[66] by bellhops, taxi drivers, and practically everyone else.[67] Faulkner and Spratling maintained that a priest at St. Louis Cathedral was their connection when they lived in the shadow of the basilica.[68]

Celebrated Prohibition agent Izzy Einstein recorded that it took a mere thirty-five seconds to be offered liquor upon his arrival in New Orleans. Staid Washington, D.C., by contrast took over two hours to make the same offer.[69]

In 1929, Sanford Jarrell, in his *New Orleans—The Civilized and Lively City*, observed: "New Orleans is frankly and belligerently wet." He also noticed, "If a cop in uniform drops in for a drink, *he* pays for it!" (emphasis in original).[70] Jarrell's grocer would deliver wine and liquor along with the usual groceries.[71]

The Eighteenth Amendment was codified by the National Prohibition Act of 1919, which left many enforcement questions to the states. In November 1921, Louisiana passed its own implementation, the Hood Act, named after its original sponsor, state senator T. L. Hood. This act allowed the transportation of liquor for personal use, the making of home brew, and the serving of alcoholic beverages to legitimate guests in one's own home.[72] The Hood Act was a quintessential Louisiana legal sidestep that seemed to conform to the letter of the Eighteenth Amendment while allowing state residents to do pretty much as they pleased at home. Despite its watery language, the New Orleans delegation opposed the act and attempted more than once to repeal it in the hopes of making Prohibition only a federal concern in the state.[73]

With the Hood Act came the emergence of the state's home breweries and wineries.[74] Particularly for ethnic families, this method assured a stable supply of wine and beer controlled in quality and distribution by Mama and Papa, without resort to bootleggers. The materials for homemade wine were readily available and the skill easily imparted from one generation to the next. Poor families realized that wine was now a medium of exchange.[75] Several widowed or abandoned mothers, arrested for selling home brew, pled that they were only trying to keep their children from privation.[76] In general, matriarchs caught selling home brew the first time were let off with a warning; those caught the second or more times might actually serve jail time.[77] Many people also made homemade beer, and they generally avoided trouble with the law if they kept the beer to themselves and didn't traffic in it.[78]

In the face of the wishy-washy Hood Act, and the city's entwinement with booze, Prohibition enforcement by the New Orleans Police Department (NOPD) was sporadic. The federal agents operating out of the customshouse found the NOPD inconsistent at best and corrupt at worst.[79] Most of the well-publicized bootleg busts were by federal agents. One enforcement lever was the practice of padlocking establishments found in repeated violation of the law for a year. The most notorious example was the padlocking of the Old Absinthe House, Bourbon and Bienville.[80]

Louisiana already had underworld empires, political corruption, and gangland wars before 1919, but Prohibition exacerbated these woes. Liquor shipments might be hijacked, and bootleggers took the lives of others in their business and lawmen as well.[81] As in other parts of the country, bootleg liquor—whether made in illicit distilleries or brought in by rumrunners—might contain the blinding methyl ("wood") alcohol, or any number of other adulterants proven to sicken or kill.[82]

Not all New Orleans bootleggers were grizzled male gangsters of the type featured in *The Untouchables*. Some were women who sold liquor out of family restaurants, assisted husbands or boyfriends in still operations, or moved booze brought into the city.[83]


## "A NICKEL ON A NUMBER"

An old New Orleans saw maintains that the first French settlers stepped off the boat with a roulette wheel in one hand and a deck of marked cards in the other. Like liquor and free love, gambling is an integral part of the New Orleans psyche. From the tuxedoed elite wagering fancy sums at roulette in exclusive clubs to maids putting their weekly "nickel on a number" with their corner racketeer, the city gambled on every conceivable game. There was no 1920s national kibosh, like Prohibition, put on gambling. Enforcing the gambling laws was a state and local affair. Enforcement served, as with other city vices, a dual opportunity. The holders of public trust could appear righteous as they closed a few gambling halls and free-floating poker games. They could also skim a percentage of the profits in return for providing protection. The appearance of public morality was balanced with protecting the tourist trade. Bookies in New Orleans were called "handbook operators,"[84] and they were pervasive. Using "wire service" information relayed by telephone, the larger handbook operators ran parlors that offered bets on horse races, games, and boxing matches near and far.[85] Many of these establishments were archly labeled "poolrooms" although billiards were hardly the point, and most were commonly called "horse parlors." One famous 1920s Quarter example was the so-called Union Bankers' Club at the corner of Iberville and Royal.[86] The Quarter also featured a number of "chartered clubs." These had charters from the city to operate "friendly," that is to say, nonwagering card games for their members. In reality, gambling was the norm, as was liquor.[87]

Later in the 1930s, slot machines arrived in south Louisiana. In a bit of inspired legal hocus-pocus, many of these machines dispensed a small candy mint with each pull. Therefore, the player was getting something of value, and, ergo, wasn't really gambling.[88]

## THE LANDLADIES

The legendary, luxurious bordellos of Storyville were already declining when the district was shut down in 1917.[89] Although most of Storyville's sex workers went to the Quarter, some stayed in the old district. The swath of prostitution in the Quarter was very wide. From streetwalkers—some now cruising in automobiles[90]—to the crib girls, to the well-established houses, every price range and peccadillo could be satisfied. The whorehouses of the 1920s could not, however, match the pleasure palaces of old. Some of these had provided shoe shines, food, and live music in addition to the primary service.[91] The madams—or "landladies" as they liked to call themselves[92]—of the 1920s were far less interested in attending to their clients' noncarnal needs. Without the legal status of a "protected" district, they had to make their own arrangements for police and political protection.

During the 1920s, the Quarter's most enduring landlady got her start. Norma Wallace operated various bordellos, most notably at 1026 Conti, for about forty years, entertaining frat boys, conventioneers, and the city's elite.[93]

Prostitution presented a puzzle to the honest police. The city had always tolerated it. The moral issue aside—and that was rarely a factor in enforcement—prostitution then, as now, intersected with narcotics, and, during Prohibition, illegal liquor. In most cases, it was the pimps—mostly despised by landladies—who supplied the dope to make their working girls dependant on them.[94] Busting whores for their profession alone was rarely worth the effort, since all but the lowest streetwalkers could usually escape prosecution. However, a raid on a "soft-drink stand" might yield arrests for solicitation, pandering, liquor, gambling, and narcotics.[95] So, as time went on, the few cops interested in enforcement learned that even if the solicitation rap couldn't stick, there might be other charges that could.

The twenties saw the slow beginning of a new community in the Quarter, one that arrived by informed choice and not by accident of birth or pigeonhole of ethnicity. That community had kindled the spark of physical and social uplift, but it would take another decade, and then the start of yet another, to stoke the fire in the forge of preservation.

## CHAPTER 3

# 1930–1946

## *The Struggle for the* Tout Ensemble

### UNCLE, CAN YOU SPARE A DIME?

The New York stock market crash of October 1929 sent out ripples—some faster, some slower—across the country. For many reasons, the South was slow to feel the effects. The South was still largely agrarian and had suffered from depressed crop prices throughout the 1920s. Poor southerners had not been able to buy stocks on margin and so were not immediately affected by the calamity in far-off New York. Then, too, the Mississippi valley flood of 1927 had caused deep, long-lasting damage to parts of Arkansas, Mississippi, and northern Louisiana.[1]

Like much of the South, New Orleans had less to lose. This left-handed salvation would be repeated in the last years of the century, when the information technology bubble burst in far-off climes. The Great Depression, for many New Orleanians, was simply a continuation of the same stagnation and hand-to-mouth existence most had known all their lives.[2]

By 1930, New Orleans began to feel some effects. In March, a fraudulent job scheme was uncovered in the Quarter. An "employment agent'" attempted to extract five dollars from each applicant for non-existent jobs. When the scheme was uncovered, about four hundred men vented their frustration with a riot.[3]

In late 1930, the city began a limited relief effort, selling boxes of oranges to selected persons who could make a small profit selling them on the street, much as apples were being sold in New York City and other northern locales.[4] Unlike many other cities, New Orleans had no bank failures, perhaps due to the perceived safety of savings accounts over investments.[5]

The greatest problem, for the Quarter and the city at large, was the rotten shape of New Orleans's finances.[6] Franklin Roosevelt's New Deal and the river of federal money that followed were a few years away. Across Louisiana, Governor Huey Long consolidated his power. Only the intransigence of the Old Regular Democrats of New Orleans stood in his way. New Orleans rightly regarded herself as the queen city of the state, and her leaders scorned this upstart from the little town of Winnfield. The queen, however, was broke, and Long slowly but surely strangled the city's revenue from the state. The Roosevelt administration sent patronage jobs to anti-Longs, fearing—and rightfully—that federal funding would be diverted to Long's coffers.[7]

Long became a senator in 1933 and left the governorship to a stooge, Oscar K. ("OK") Allen.[8] Although Allen did what Huey told him to do, he needed a minder, and so Huey set attorney Richard Leche to watch the governor.[9] Leche went on to become governor after Allen's sudden death in 1935. Prior to the elections of 1934, Long's rubber-stamp legislature authorized a committee to investigate vice in New Orleans, hoping to embarrass the Old Regulars and their mayor, T. Semmes Walmsley, known as "Old Turkey Head" for his resemblance to that fowl. Senator Long himself acted as committee counsel and conducted the "investigation" before live radio microphones.

After a parade of anonymous witnesses came forth and gave what seemed to be coached statements, the chief of police and chief of detectives were called. Long produced evidence that indicated these men had lifestyles well above what their city salaries would suggest. They admitted no wrongdoing, but their ordeal must have made even jaded New Orleanians squirm. The investigation concluded without any indictments, but Huey had proved his point. New Orleans *was* vice-ridden—how shocking!—and the Old Regulars were responsible, which, of course, was just as true.[10]

Not content with this opéra bouffe, Long sent the Louisiana National Guard to confront the mayor's police force in a tense standoff at city hall. Quarter residents were treated to the sight of uniformed country boys ambling wide-eyed down the old banquettes.[11] Although the military situation was defused, the mayor was unmoved. With federal and state aid in limbo, the poorest New Orleanians began to go hungry and started foraging in garbage cans.[12] Walmsley wasn't starving, of course, and wouldn't budge. Long's assassination in September 1935 changed nothing. The momentum of his machine was too powerful, and after some negotiations, Walmsley finally stepped down in June 1936.[13] Long's heavy financial backer,[14] New Orleans real estate magnate[15] Robert Maestri, was appointed mayor and then, through a constitutional amendment in 1936, given a six-year term when no candidate dared run against him.[16]

A curious thing then happened. Maestri, labeled by critics as "Red Light Bob,"[17] for his family's leasing furniture to Storyville madams,[18] turned out to be an amazingly good mayor—at least in his first term.[19] The Roosevelt administration began to channel New Deal dollars into the city.[20] Maestri even used his personal fortune to make a no-interest loan to the city and gave handouts to poor people who wandered into his open-door personal audiences.[21] Maestri made frequent inspection tours of the city and promptly dealt with problems coming to his attention.[22] Awkward at speechifying,[23] he led from the handshake, from commands sprinkled with "dese," "dem," "dose," and from the heart.[24] A 1936 photo of Long cabal chieftains in Baton Rouge shows Maestri, not Governor Richard Leche nor Huey's brother Earl, seated in the middle and holding a gavel.[25]

## THE BUSINESS OF PLEASURE

The Vieux Carré blissfully continued its old ways.[26] The maladies arising from Prohibition and the screaming hypocrisy of the situation had worn out national and New Orleans's patience by 1932, and it became, along with recovery from the Depression, a major issue of the 1932 political season. Even such a stalwart reformer as Elizabeth Werlein called for repeal.[27]

After Franklin Roosevelt's election in November 1932, the Twenty-first Amendment was ratified to repeal the Eighteenth. Because the wartime Volstead act had prohibited beer, it was repealed first, and then Louisiana repealed the Hood Act. On April 13, 1933, trucks crowded the streets rushing "suds" to eager patrons of bars and restaurants. Horns of autos, trains, and ships blew at noon, and the city swigged legal beer again.[28] Legal liquor returned once more on December 5, 1933. Both occasions were celebrated much like extra Fat Tuesdays.[29]

Prohibition, even as New Orleans lightly regarded it,[30] had encouraged some to try other kicks.[31] Marijuana, once a drug out of white sight in Negro and Latin subcultures, was being sold on the city's streets even before the 1920s.[32] The same soggy boundaries that made the city a rumrunner's dream[33] allowed grass and other illegal drugs to be brought in easily.[34] In 1927, Louisiana, following hysterical newspaper stories alleging rampant pot use by children,[35] outlawed the weed.[36] The usual efforts to curb smuggling only made the growing of cannabis a hobby for devotees, and soon large numbers of plants were seized in the city and countryside.[37] The same conditions that had promoted marijuana—the illegality of alcohol, the easy access to ships and the sea— also fostered a resurgence in opiates and cocaine.[38] The Quarter was acknowledged as the heart of the illicit drug business.[39]

Without alcohol and tobacco's mantle of tradition and legal protection, marijuana and other drugs became an obsession with New Orleans's law enforcement. Reluctant to enforce the prohibition of alcohol, New Orleans police eagerly cooperated with federal narcotics agents.[40] A Quarter tavern might—and many did—feature such illegal delights as gambling, taxi dancing, drug-addicted prostitutes and rooms for servicing their "johns." With the proper payoffs, it could remain securely in business, year after year. A raid on a rooming house next door yielding a single joint was trumpeted as the bust of a "drug den," and all arrested would have their names and faces published in the papers.[41] This remained the norm for many years. When large-scale drug traffic became an important profit center for organized crime and therefore corrupt officialdom, these penny-ante busts provided cover for the city government to prove it was "doing something" about drugs.

Gambling, like alcohol and other pleasures of the flesh, is deeply intertwined with New Orleans living. A 1937 *Time* article depicted gambling as pervasive, with an unusual number of nickels being handed out in change for use in slot machines.[42] The big-time gaming was found in Jefferson Parish and other outlying areas, where land was cheap, parking plentiful, and local politicians even more pliant that those of Orleans Parish.[43]

So, as the 1930s wore on, a Vieux Carré visitor had a delightful menu from which to choose. For well-heeled "straight arrows," there was the still-fading glory of the architecture, antique hunting on Royal Street, and the pleasures of the table at places like Antoine's. Perhaps they might take in a play at Le Petit; in the 1936 season they might have chosen Lardner-Kaufman's *June Moon* or Maxwell Anderson's *Mary of Scotland*.[44] For students and would-be bohemians, there was poetry and intellectual vibrancy in the coffee shops and salons.[45] The Arts and Crafts Club was in full flower. Beyond instruction, it hosted exhibitions by world-famous artists, and its students contributed to local Works Progress Administration (WPA) projects. Arts and Crafts Club members also participated in Le Petit Théâtre and Le Petit Salon.[46] For those so inclined, liquor and gambling were readily available, and dope, particularly marijuana, could be found with little effort. Women and young men of Anthony Stanonis's felicitous description "purchasable virtue" were convenient.[47] As long as he didn't pass out on someone's stoop, or fuss about losing money at gambling, or shortchange a whore, a man could usually have a good, safe time in the Quarter and then return to whatever respectable life he lived somewhere else. Complaining about the entertainment was a bad idea. The same police that protected these pleasures also punished those who didn't play by the rules with arrests, jail, and beatings.[48] The Quarter was still largely a slum, becoming more genteel only by degrees. It could still be a dangerous place; Lyle Saxon was robbed and brutalized during an invasion of his Royal Street apartment in 1932.[49]

An interesting window into the nightclub scene of the late thirties and early forties is *The Bachelor in New Orleans*,[50] published in 1942. Robert Kinney rendered suave yet blunt advice on what, and what not, to do in the Quarter. He touts Dixie's Bar of Music, soon to move to Bourbon Street ("Dixie herself does a *mean* clarinet and vocalizes indigo")[51]; the James Bar at Royal and Toulouse, where classical records were played[52]; and Café Lafitte's, where the reader is advised that "if the bartender is passed out, go behind [the bar] and mix your own [drink]!"[53]

Kinney lays out the upper Quarter entertainment district thusly, and his words still have a ring of accuracy for the present configuration: "Here are honky-tonks and gilt-and-silver supper clubs; here are clubs with 'B-girls' by the score and clubs with strip-tease entertainers; here are floorshows with dozens of lovely dollies and floorshows with a few boney old hags grinning through their routines in horrible travesty; here is the gamut of nightlife."[54]

For young men, the Quarter offered inexpensive, if usually shabby, lodging handy to all the things a young man might need—cheap eats, hot jazz, strong drink, and sexual partners. Apartments favored by students in the Quarter might go for twenty-five to forty dollars a month. Po'boys could be had for twenty-five cents; a five- or six-course fancy lunch at Tujague's might cost fifty cents; beer—after Prohibition ended—was a nickle a glass. Hot spots for young adults included the 500 Club at 441 Bourbon; Pat O'Brien's on St. Peter; and Victor's at Chartres and Toulouse.[55]

Aside from living in college dormitories, "respectable" young southern women away from home were expected to stay in rooming houses supervised by old women interviewed by their mothers.[56] In the dual standards of the time, for a young man to move to the "Quarters" was a declaration of virile, if perhaps offbeat, independence; a young woman would be announcing her apparent moral abandonment. So it was rare for a young woman, alone, to rent an apartment in the Quarter for strictly legitimate reasons, and some landlords would not rent to a single woman, no matter how pure her resumé.

The Quarter continued to host diverse ethnicities. After the Chinese market on Tulane Avenue was torn down in 1937, some Chinese merchants moved to the 300 and 400 blocks of Bourbon.[57]

## KIND STRANGERS PRESERVE US

New Orleans has never been known as an exporter of political causes. Causes like abolition and women's suffrage that flowed from Boston and Philadelphia found little resonance in this city of old colonialism and fervent, albeit brief, Confederacy. As elsewhere, activism has come in waves in the Crescent City, but nearly all its causes are inward-looking. New Orleans has an ample navel to gaze upon.

The idealism and fervor of World War I fueled a burst of activism nationwide, but the briefness of America's participation and the unwelcome closure of Storyville spun off little enthusiasm for civic causes in New Orleans. The two primary national causes celebres of the time—prohibition and women's suffrage—were received with contempt and reluctance, respectively, in New Orleans. The activism that elevated Madame Vieux Carré's fortunes in the 1920s and 1930s stemmed from a small group largely of outsiders who rescued Madame from hometown neglect.

One positive official action was the transfer of the Upper Pontalba from the Pontalba Building Museum to the city in 1930.[58] The Lower Pontalba had been willed to the Louisiana State Museum by William Irby in 1926.[59]

Until the Long-Walmsley dispute was settled, Quarter-wide revival efforts were nearly at a standstill. Maestri's appointment as mayor was the best thing to happen to New Orleans in many decades. He had deep ties with his fellow Italian New Orleanians, many of whom still lived in the Quarter. Maestri was genuinely interested in fixing up his frowzy city, and could now tap New Deal largesse to do it. As a principal, indeed perhaps *the* principal,[60] of the Long machine, he had no fear of conflict with the state government.[61] His grateful constituents soon labeled him "Bob the Builder."[62]

When it came to the Quarter, the mayor's views seemed divided. He wanted to preserve the quality of life for his constituents there. He also wanted

WPA renovation of the Upper Pontalba, 1936. Courtesy of the Louisiana Division, City Archives, New Orleans Public Library.

to preserve the pleasure industry, with whom he had deep connections. A balance had to be struck between the wide-open joints and the residential neighborhood of this ancient *tante* he inherited from Walmsley. Where would the balance be?

In this, Maestri got help from a hurricane from the north. Elizabeth Thomas was born to money in Michigan. She was, by Edwardian sensibilities, an adventuress before her arrival in New Orleans.[63] There, in 1908, she settled down to marriage with music store magnate Phillip Werlein.[64]

Between female suffrage in the nineteen teens and women's liberation in the nineteen sixties, the clubwoman held a powerful position in American life. She was typically of noted lineage, usually married to a wealthy man, and invariably white. In an evening gown, with her own bejewelled kind, she was a patron of the arts. She could also put on an apron to serve coffee to soldiers and work for the Red Cross. Although she rarely held public office, her position in charities and advisory boards gave her great influence. These women clustered in clubs, and some held memberships in many organizations. In the South, these clubs were rooted in the benevolent societies organized after the Civil War to care for widows. These clubs could be purely social; they could be dedicated to "civic improvement," and most raised money for charity. The clubwoman had an enviable position. She was largely immune from economic vicissitudes or political pressure. Although snugly installed in social boundaries, she could, and sometimes did, champion unpopular causes and the downtrodden. Her pronouncements were occasionally schoolroom idealistic or simply daffy.[65] No matter; they always made good newspaper copy.

She was a mobilizer of women's votes and behind her was the power of her husband's fortune. Neither of these facts were lost on male politicians.

In New Orleans, clubwomen were doubly strong. Besides the roles just described, they also were matrons of Carnival krewes. The krewes contained nearly the entire weight of the city's ruling establishment, and the matrons of the krewes wielded uncontested power of acceptance and exclusion.[66]

Especially after her husband's death in 1917, Mrs. Werlein became the foremost clubwoman of the city. She headed the Louisiana Women's Suffrage Party, the Louisiana League of Women Voters, and the Orleans Club Voters. Le Petit Théâtre du Vieux Carré, the New Orleans Country Club, the board of the New Orleans Symphony, and the Spring Fiesta Association all counted her as an important member.[67] She had a deep, protective love of the Quarter and was one of the prime movers for the enclave's legal protection. In early 1936, her group lobbied the state legislature for a referendum to amend the Louisiana constitution, for "the preservation of such buildings in the Vieux Carré section of the City of New Orleans, as . . . shall be deemed to have architectural and historical value, and which buildings should be preserved for the benefit of the people of the City of New Orleans and the State of Louisiana."[68]

With the assistance of Judge John J. Wingrave and Louisiana State Museum curator J. A. Fortier, the referendum was passed and approved by the voters.[69] The amendment excluded the Canal Street blocks between Canal and Iberville, since these were already occupied by stores on the "Fifth Avenue of the South." The second Vieux Carré Commission (VCC) met for the first time on April 8, 1937.[70] Having been appointed, the new VCC didn't quite know what to do. The South's tradition of strong property owner rights and the lingering Depression mitigated against any sweeping improvement. The decay and outright destruction of Quarter properties went unchallenged. Mrs. Werlein and her allies, like historian Harnett Kane, fumed. Five months after the commission's first meeting, Kane revealed in the *States-Item* that the city architect did not bother to consult the VCC when issuing demolition or alteration permits for Vieux Carré buildings.[71] The VCC had the authority, but not the will. In 1938, Mrs. Werlein, Jacob Morrison, and others set up their own organization, the Vieux Carré Property Owners and Associates (VCPOA), to guide, cajole, and occasionally force the VCC into action.[72] Later, this group renamed itself the Vieux Carré Property Owners Residents and Associates (VCPORA) to include the many renters who had a stake in the enclave. Elizebeth Werlein served as the VCPOA's first president. Besides pressuring the VCC, Mrs. Werlein never hesitated to call Maestri, who dubbed her "the mayor of the Vieux Carré."[73] In January 1939, Mrs. Werlein met with the mayor about the VCC's inaction. She issued a vociferous communiqué afterwards, saying, among other things: "The commission has stood by idly. It meets very seldom and when it does, it does little or nothing. There are some good people on it, interested in the Quarter, but they are lost among the dead wood that make up the majority."[74] Maestri ruled that no Quarter demolition permits would be issued without the approval of the VCC. In February 1939, the VCC then tried to rubber-stamp a demolition permit for 227–233 Bourbon, for another parking lot for the almighty automobile. Jabbed by Mrs. Werlein and the VCPOA, the VCC quickly reversed itself and won the ensuing court case.[75] The lowest ebb of the 1930s VCC came in 1939 when the director of the commission was indicted for the fraudulent sale of the Bienville Hotel to Louisiana State University.[76] The members of the commission were replaced; one of the new members was Roy Alciatore, owner of Antoine's Restaurant. Alciatore had stood watchfully behind President Roosevelt, Governor Leche, and Mayor Maestri at the celebrated "Erster Dinner" of 1937.[77] Reorganized, but still carefully monitored by the VCPOA, the VCC started the 1940s with more public and self-confidence.

The trinity of the first wave of preservation—William Irby, Lyle Saxon, and Elizabeth Werlein—brought three great talents to bear. Irby had the money, Saxon was the master of publicity, and Werlein had the contacts and persistence. Irby's legacy, after his early death, was the buildings he placed under public protection. Saxon's newspaper stories and his connections with 1920s literati brought in many enthusiastic, newly minted Quarter residents. Werlein sailed the social waters of the Crescent City like an ocean liner, powerfully pressing on with her Vieux Carré agenda.[78]

Despite the money, publicity, and prestige these three brought to the fight, they remained largely outsiders to the city's political life. That world, which faded slowly in the late twentieth century, was the province of machine politics, as was common in most larger cities. By whatever name, these machines—and there were at least three in play in New Orleans in 1946[79]— had common structures. There was a boss, who might, or might not, be the mayor at the moment; there was a caucus,[80] which served as a legislature; and there were ward bosses, precinct captains, and party workers.[81] The machine boss sat atop a pyramid of interlocking favors, loyalties, and payoffs. The precinct captains ensured that the loyalists contributed to, and voted for, the machine's candidates.[82] New York City's Tammany Hall was the archetype of this arrangement.

The precinct captains had a duty to see to it, especially in the days of the ballot box, that their ward "went" for the "correct" candidates, regardless of what voters might have marked on paper ballots.[83] In return, they took care of many constituent needs.[84] Did your brother-in-law need a city job so you could eject him from your home? Did your teenage son have a scrape with the law? Was the city slow to repair your street? These and myriad other difficulties were fixed by the ward and precinct bosses.[85] Party workers, who were often also policemen, firemen, and city office workers,[86] planted campaign signs, organized rallies, and attended to a thousand other little yet essential things, all on the clock and, if need be, their own time.[87] It was common for municipal and state workers to make involuntary contributions to the machine by deductions from their paychecks.[88] Huey Long kept state contributions in the "dee-duct box," a strongbox that was carried, like an ark, wherever Huey went.[89]

In spite of occasional civil service reforms, the bosses controlled patronage, whereby the machine in power would employ its allies and discharge the leftovers from the outgoing machine.[90] City contracts were awarded in deals to reward campaign contributions, or, like kings of old marrying off their children, cement alliances between factions.

Of the preservation trinity, Elizabeth Werlein achieved the most clout with the city. By the time of Robert Maestri's elevation to the mayor's office at Gallier Hall in 1936, Irby was long dead and Saxon was absorbed by his WPA work and declining health.[91] Maestri has been rightfully painted as unsophisticated and limelight-averse.[92] However, he was far from dull and was, in some respects, more cunning than his much-feted successor, deLesseps "Chep" Morrison. Morrison spoke loudly of reform, but pulled the levers of corruption without shame; since Maestri never labeled himself as such, no one would confuse him with a reformer.

It is a pity that Maestri never wrote—or, perhaps better for all, dictated—his memoirs. This bluff, hearty man left some mysteries behind. One is how he survived as other chieftains of the Long cabal were indicted in 1939–1940.[93] Richard Leche, who had just resigned the governorship for "health reasons"; Seymour Weiss, treasurer of the cabal; and the Louisiana Commissioner of Conservation were among the indicted. Perhaps it was because Maestri was already wealthy, and, not needing graft, did not leave a trail for auditors to uncover.[94] Another mystery that bears scrutiny is his relationship with

Elizebeth Werlein. He owed her nothing. As one of Huey Long's political heirs, he was made satrap of New Orleans, and his first six years in power were simply given to him without the fuss and bother of an election.[95] If he had doubts about the constitutional amendment that established the VCC, he apparently did nothing to impede it. When city agencies attempted to circumvent the VCC, he brought them to heel. He often—but not always—granted Mrs. Werlein's wishes in Quarter matters, even if they irritated his pals in the saloon and vice trade.

It seems that Bob the Builder and Elizebeth the Scold had a synergy. He needed her for the cover of respectability and her considerable influence with women and uptown voters, at least in the election of 1942, which he won. She, lacking office or a political base, and not being especially wealthy,[96] needed his intercession with an indifferent city bureaucracy and a somnolent VCC.

Herein is yet another seeming contradiction, in a city that presents them by the dozens. Maestri was, at first glance, the kind of politician an idealist like Mrs. Werlein ought not to like. Her husband crusaded against Storyville until his death in 1917,[97] and Maestri never shook his association with that district. He had been given his office as the Old Regular Democrats were forced to kneel to the Longs.[98] In his first six years, Maestri was the machine boss par excellence. As former governor Leche and others were shuffled off to federal prison after the scandals of 1938–1939,[99] Hizzoner stood as primus inter pares of the Long cabal. Maestri was the epitome of the midcentury city boss. Efficiency, not squeaky-clean honesty, was his forte.

This efficiency worked to the favor of Mrs. Werlein and the Vieux Carré in general, at least until the war years distracted the mayor's focus. In Maestri's first term, New Orleans learned to be "corrupt and efficient at the same time,"[100] in a pattern similar to other cities with Tammany Hall–like machines. A "reform" mayor might have wanted to do all of Mrs. Werlein's bidding. But if he had been an outsider with no statehouse backing, overturning the machine structure that made the city work, he might have accomplished far less than Robert Maestri.

Most of the deeds by Mrs. Werlein and the second wave of activists were done by individual contacts, like Elizebeth's phone calls to Hizzoner, or by buttonholing politicians and businessmen at various social gatherings. Mrs. Werlein did not shun making well-chosen outbursts in the press, but her greatest effects were had away from the banquettes, as when she lined up support for the VCC's creation. This clubby sort of lobbying among fellow elites is still the usual New Orleans way. It is, of course, the polar opposite of activism in the nation at large with the sound bites, mass marches, Internet presence, and appeals to outside authority that are the staples of today's movements.

Preservation as an institution was not confined to the VCC and VCPOA. The Louisiana State Museum, which had acquired control of key buildings around Jackson Square in the 1920s, began to be a player in preservation of the larger scene. In 1930, it moved its library to the first floor of the Lower Pontalba, at the corner of St. Ann and Chartres. Beginning in 1935, the federal WPA provided 105 people to conserve many portions of the LSM holdings. This included renovations to the Cabildo, Presbytère, the Lower Pontalba,[101] and also the city-owned Upper[102] Pontalbas.

The gradual revival of the Quarter as place for "nice people" to live had emboldened the early urban pioneers to show off the Vieux Carré to the world. In 1937, Mrs. Helen Pitkin Schertz and others conceived of a Spring Fiesta. The Spring Fiesta, first held in April 1937, featured tours of homes, plantations, and gardens, in the Vieux Carré and around the area. A queen was crowned amid a court of gowned young women. The Spring Fiesta continues today as the most genteel festival hosted in New Orleans.[103]

## THE FRENCH MARKET RECONSTRUCTION

In 1932, the French Market Corporation was chartered by the city.[104] It was obvious that the ancient market needed modern refrigeration and better access for trucks.[105] The old Gallatin Street area would be sacrificed. Although families were living there, it was still associated with its nineteenth-century depravity, when it was the toughest, and deadliest, strip in a wide-open Vieux Carré.[106] In common with other Quarter streets, it also had some speakeasies. Obliterating it would remove both the old and new associations. The renovation plans were sidetracked by the Long-Walmsley fracas. After Maestri took office, funding was found and the reconstruction was completed in 1938. For various reasons, many of the old-time vendors were dissuaded from returning. It is probable that the competition from large grocery retailers and the many corner markets had driven some of them out of business.[107] Eventually, the French Market would have few sellers of food; most booths would be occupied by vendors of tourist trinkets.

## GROWING UP IN THE QUARTER

In the early 1920s a young man originally from Sicily arrived in the Quarter to work at his uncle's grocery at Chartres and Barracks. By 1924, he had opened his corner store at the lakeside, lower intersection of Dauphine and St. Philip streets. He married an Italian girl who had grown up on Barracks Street. John and Dominica "Mamie" Matassa had one child, Cosimo, who arrived in 1926. Cosimo Matassa now presides in an office that had been his parents' parlor above the grocery now run by his sons.

Cosimo went to McDonough 15 Elementary School, four blocks from home at Barracks and Dauphine, where Cabrini Park is now. His schoolmates represented all the ethnicities of the Quarter—except, of course, Negroes, who attended segregated schools. He and the many other neighborhood children—Negroes included—played in the streets within a few blocks from home. The streets were shared with vendors who had mule-drawn wagons, pushcarts, and handbaskets. Italians and Negroes sold vegetables, chanting, "Watermelon, watermelon, red to the rind." Some Jews sold balloons from arm baskets. Also sold on the street was *sfincione*, thick pizza-like slices. After school he worked in his parents' store. John Matassa operated two small bars behind his grocery store, one for blacks and one for whites in accordance with the Gay-Shattuck Law of 1908.[108] To have card tables in the black bar, he paid the beat policeman, a sergeant, ten dollars and a pack of cigarettes a week. At the tables, Louisiana favorites like pitty-pat, kotch, and bouree were played; the games were for entertainment, and the house had no take of any winnings.[109]

## THE LAKESIDE: STRIKE ONE

In 1940, Americans still believed in a common notion of progress, and slum clearance was all the rage. The New Deal, led by idealistic urban planners, mowed down acres of decaying tenement housing in major cities. Replacing them were multistory apartments, with all the essentials of "modern" life—indoor plumbing, central heating, outdoor lighting, and playgrounds. New Orleans's first taste of this effort was the Iberville project, which covered most of the area once known as Storyville. The clean, up-to-date buildings must have seemed a godsend to the eighty-seven families of white former servicemen who first moved in.[110] Like the official closing of Storyville in 1917, the slum clearance displaced many sex workers. Just as in 1917, these crossed Basin and North Rampart streets, reinfesting the lake edges of the Quarter. Prostitution had never left the Quarter, but the 1930s had seen a somewhat less open trade. Now, North Rampart, upper Iberville, and Burgundy again teemed with whores. Just as in the days immediately after Storyville, these ranged from women operating from once-elegant mansions to lone girls, some naked, calling from behind shutters in "cribs."[111] The resurgent tide of sleaze washed over the whole Quarter, threatening to undo the hard-won gains of the past decade. Maestri soon heard from Mrs. Werlein's VCPOA and other civic groups. In May 1940, they published an open letter[112] demanding enforcement of alcohol laws and more police patrols. The letter stated that February of 1939 found 71 bars; May of 1940 revealed 134 bars, 52 of which were "alleged night clubs," a more sinister connotation. The letter quoted an author who had found barmaids whose main business was prostitution. The hookers were told by a cop to close up shop for a certain convention. The sex industry eagerly awaited amorous male conventioneers, and these strumpets were keenly disappointed with the order to vanish. Their much-anticipated convention turned out to be a Eucharistic Congress.[113] The writers went on to demand that "certain sections of the Vieux Carré be completely zoned against liquor permits of any kind." The mess made national news.[114] Mrs. Werlein and her allies pressed the issue,[115] saying of the mayor, "We want him to get busy and act."[116]

A large protest meeting in August 1940 alleged that some illegal establishments were being not only operated with the connivance of, but were owned by, civic authorities. Multiple shootings, some fatal, erupted in the Quarter, wounding two visitors. The city attorney felt compelled to deny a statement attributed to police superintendent Reyer to the effect that the city attorney did not consider houses of prostitution illegal. Interestingly enough, this meeting was not simply a clutch of clubwomen and VCPOA members. The *New Orleans Item* reported that Quarter businessmen, pimps, and "possible agents of the prostitute's union or racketeer's association" attended, presumably to keep an eye on the unfolding righteous wrath.[117]

Just after this meeting, the police raided a whorehouse at 313 Dauphine and arrested five bawds and one madam. Superintendent Reyer trumpeted his department's record of arrests in the Quarter as an antidote to the outrage of the protest meeting.[118] Despite the large numbers of arrests, not many of the protesters' concerns would be satisfied. The great majority of those arrested were back on the streets quickly.

Maestri did much of what Mrs. Werlein wanted. But he could not, and would not, sanitize the Vieux Carré to satisfy her.[119]

## TOUTING THE *TOUT ENSEMBLE*

As the battle against street sleaze continued, 1941 would be a year of victory in the larger war of preservation. Two Louisiana Supreme Court decisions cemented the VCC's power over both historic and nonhistoric elements.

*City of New Orleans v. Impastato*'s outcome was that the VCC had the authority to control the external parts of a structure, even if not visible from the street,[120] "anything the exterior air touches, anything the sun shines on, anytime we can see the sky, anytime there is free exchange of air . . . ," as one member of the VCC more recently put it.[121]

In *City of New Orleans v. Pergament* (5 So. 2d 129, 131 [La. 1941]) the court ruled that the VCC could prevent the owner of a gas station from placing an oversize sign nearby. In its decision,[122] Chief Justice O'Neill sounded what has become the battle cry of Quarter preservation. He ruled that the VCC had the power to adjudicate the entire collection of elements—*tout ensemble*—that make up the Vieux Carré streetscape.

This doctrine, which resounds through subsequent Quarter controversies and decisions, covers the total visual experience of the Quarter, at least in regards to the tangibles of the street. In practice it does not extend to the interiors, where generations of landlords and now condo corporations have cut up and remade room configurations to suit themselves. Nor has it ever governed renters, who may repaint their flats in tasteful neutrals or, perhaps, paints that fluoresce under black light.

Many have argued that *tout ensemble* also extends to the character of businesses, street activities, tourism, and human behavior in the Vieux Carré. The VCPOA stemmed from this opinion as much as from disgust with the early VCC's sluggishness. To its credit, the VCC has usually, but not always, avoided overreaching its charter by attempting to intervene in these questions. Other groups, like the VCPORA, have addressed these issues in various forums over the years. Beneath the surface of this wider interpretation is a perpetual, spoken and unspoken, undercurrent of wanting the "right" people for the Quarter, the famous tolerance of the city be damned.[123] In various eras, the "right" people were not too dark, too morally loose, too poor, too openly homosexual, too nouveau riche, or too out-of-town. The "right" people, it was hoped, would also have money to buy and fix up properties. In the early years of the Quarter's revival, most of its enthusiastic new residents were renters, and renters, until recently, outnumbered owner-residents. Renters, no matter how well-intentioned or clean their habits, could not restore or maintain the outer structures. The interior life of the Quarter, whether in chandeliered mansions or cheap tiny flats, was largely unaffected by legal notions of *tout ensemble*. Behind the gates and shutters, residents could continue to commune with the calm ancientness of the high ceilings and plastered walls, and let the striving world hurry by.

In 1939, attorney Jacob Morrison and his wife, Mary, moved to the Quarter. Living at 906 Royal,[124] they fixed up their old place, and were part of the first wave of urban pioneers to homestead under the aegis of the revived VCC. In a 1977 interview, Mary observed that lack of funds among the revivalists of the twenties and thirties may have had a preservative effect. Lacking much money, these pioneers could not make major alterations. The character of their buildings was preserved, even if styles were not strictly observed. Wrecking yards around the Quarter were sources for architectural elements; among these was one at 621 St. Louis Street, at Royal, where the Omni Royal Orleans hotel now stands. The urban pioneer spirit of the time is captured in Mary's remark: "The dinner might have been cooked on a hot plate but it was served by candle light. There was a certain degree of elegance to it all."[125]

## WRITING THROUGH A QUARTER PRISM

By the late 1920s, most of the famous literary crowd that had clustered around Sherwood Anderson and Lyle Saxon was gone. Anderson himself had departed in 1926. Lacking movie studios or major publishing houses, the city could only support a few regionally significant writers. The most successful, like Faulkner, had gone to Hollywood or New York. Seen from the windows of outbound trains, the Quarter lapsed into fond memory of youthful slumming.[126] In the 1930s, Lyle Saxon remained the center of New Orleans's literary circle and operated a salon in his rooms at the St. Charles Hotel. He also renovated 536 Madison, reserving an apartment for himself. Saxon's salon gave food, liquor, and encouragement to many drifting writers. He became head of the Louisiana Federal Writers' Project in 1935.[127] Saxon almost hired a stray Missourian named Thomas Williams. However, Saxon's federal project was cut as the New Deal wound down, and Williams, now known as "Tennessee," had to survive by other means.[128]

Saxon's true protégé and literary heir was Robert Tallant, who lovingly fictionalized Saxon and his circle in his 1949 *Mr. Preen's Salon*.[129] New Orleans native Tallant collaborated with Saxon on the Federal Writers' Project city guide[130] for New Orleans. He was, with Saxon and Edward Dreyer, a co-author of *Gumbo Ya-Ya*, a classic collection of Louisiana folk tales. In midlife, Tallant moved out of his family home and roomed on Banks Street, then a midcity working-class slum. His observation of New Orleans characters at the boardinghouse led him to write *Mrs. Candy and Saturday Night*.[131] Tallant went on to write many other Louisiana-themed books—among them the 1949 *Mardi Gras . . . As It Was*, the best historical perspective on Carnival until that time, and still fresh today. Although not a "couple" in any sense, and perhaps not even close friends, Tallant and Williams doubtless knew each other through Saxon.[132]

Tennessee Williams returned to New Orleans in 1941 and, in a very productive period, produced his and New Orleans's signature play, *A Streetcar Named Desire*. Although not entirely set in the Quarter, the play and many movie versions colored outside perceptions of the Vieux Carré. Williams often returned to the Quarter and was a regular at Lafitte's (now Lafitte's Blacksmith Shop), particularly before 1952, when it was a gay-friendly bar. It was probably Williams that the 1952 *New Orleans City Guide*—revised by Tallant— was speaking of when it mentioned that a celebrity might be seen sitting by the fire at Lafitte's.[133] Williams's legacy has become a local industry. During the annual Tennessee Williams Festival, couples compete in the Stanley and Stella Shouting Contest, re-creating the movie scene made famous by Marlon Brando and Kim Hunter. Tallant and Williams did not just observe Quarter life; they lived it to saturation.[134] They mixed with horny sailors, assorted hustlers, whores, dreamy artists, society swells, and the working poor. Both came of age when gritty social realism was the paradigm of American fiction. In this groove, *Mrs. Candy* and *Streetcar* presented a new face of New Orleans to the world, one that made bourgeois city boosters squirm. The French Creoles in Tallant's works are either ghosts or soon will be.[135] The elegant, mannered affectations of Saxon's southern gentry[136] were replaced by T-shirted, sweaty men, cheerfully loose women, and shameless homosexuals. As years went by, Williams's Stanley Kowalski became the archetype of white, working-class New Orleanians, particularly from St. Bernard Parish. These are often called Yats, a contraction of their usual greeting, "Where ya at?" Along with gold-hearted madams, black jazzmen, and voodoo priestesses, the Yat would take his place in the pantheon of marketable New Orleans icons.

## WAR YEARS

After the start of World War II in Europe in 1939, America shored up her defenses. The navy base at Algiers, with its annex on Poland Avenue, down-river of the Quarter in Bywater; Belle Chase Naval Air Station; and Jackson Barracks all swelled with many soldiers, sailors, marines, and airmen. The year 1940 saw the Quarter's peak of twentieth-century population at about eleven thousand.[137]

During Prohibition, Pat O'Brien had operated a speakeasy in the 600 block of St. Peter. After liquor was re-legalized in 1933, he opened a bar across the street. In 1941, he decided to buy the eighteenth-century Casa de Flechier at 718 St. Peter. This area had many long-time residents and no bars. The notion of a tavern in this old house, close to many long-established families, stirred Elizebeth Werlein and the VCPOA to fury. Mrs. Werlein noted that the courtyards of the new Pat O's and the Court of Two Sisters would touch each other and with logical prescience said, "That means that there will be nightly bedlam; that these old families will be driven out forever; that one of the most magnificent of our residential blocks in the Quarter will be started on the down grade."[138] "Banjo Annie" was a celebrated Quarter character. She roamed the streets and bars, cadging drinks while singing ribald songs to the twang of her namesake instrument.[139] She was reputed to be Burl Ives's original mentor of the banjo.[140] Although distinctly not of Mrs. Werlein's social stratosphere, Banjo Annie supported her crusade against Pat O'Brien's, saying, "I stand with Mrs. Werlein. We have too many bars in too many places in the Quarter anyway. Let's preserve this great asset."[141]

Mrs. Werlein vowed to defend the building with a gun if necessary. In reality, her greatest weapon was her influence with Mayor Maestri. However, this time, Hizzoner would not listen to the lady he dubbed "the mayor of the Vieux Carré"; he declined to intervene. The Vieux Carré Commission, just emerging from its shaky infancy, had no purview. Pat O' Brien's installed itself at 718 St. Peter the following year and is now regarded as a Quarter institution. A long-time fixture of Pat O'Brien's was pianist and singer Mercedes Le Corgne Paulsen, fondly remembered by the thousands of servicemen who heard her performances during the war.[142]

*All Work* by Thomas Hart Benton, circa 1943. Courtesy of the Department of the Navy, the Naval Historical Center, Navy Art Collection.

*Preliminary Shakedown, New Orleans* by Thomas Hart Benton, circa 1943. Courtesy of the Department of the Navy, the Naval Historical Center, Navy Art Collection.

America's entrance into World War II in December 1941 meant a period of ostensible restraint, even for New Orleans. Although the Carnival krewes canceled their balls and parades for the duration, Carnival revelry still went on in the streets and at private parties. Aside from the lack of parades, the Quarter, on Fat Tuesdays during the war, looked much the same as in peacetime.[143]

The Niagara of servicemen energized the bars and honky-tonks as the pleasure industry of the Quarter expanded to host military visitors.[144] Their money, taken both legally and by vices ignored by the law,[145] was a profound relief to businesses staggered by the Prohibition and Depression years. For the Vieux Carré's guardians, trying to stem the tide of barrooms was now a lost cause. To the disgust of the Quarter's keepers, more bars blossomed further down Bourbon Street towards Dumaine.[146] By 1945, New Orleans had at least 16 brothels housing 145 bawds.[147] "Anything for the boys" was the catch-phrase that justified many variances of civic and social norms.

Maestri faced the voters for the first time in 1942 and, with a record of solid accomplishments, won easily.[148] In another curious turn, this activist mayor retreated from most public life. His city tours all but ceased and he allowed things to drift. The reasons are obscure. Among the speculation was that he was more interested in politics behind closed doors than taking care of voters.[149] Also, "Dr. New Deal" had become "Dr. Win the War," as the president put it.[150] The once plentiful federal urban funds now went to the war effort, and perhaps Maestri felt that his efforts were starved for lack of money.[151] In addition, Sam Jones, an anti-Longite, was governor from 1940 to 1944.[152]

While attending Tulane in the early years of the Second World War, Cosimo Matassa also serviced the jukeboxes his father owned, making his rounds to the bars and honky-tonks in the Quarter and beyond. He set up a small recording studio at 838 Rampart. Like the *Double Dealer* twenty years before, J&M Studios would have an effect far beyond the small precinct of the Vieux Carré.[153]

Like most wartime American cities, New Orleans had a sudden influx of servicepeople and defense workers, and precious little lodging for them. One enlisted man found that furnished rooms in the Quarter ranged, depending on bathing facilities, from five to ten dollars a week in early 1943.[154] Considering that a buck private made only fifty dollars a month, before any deductions,[155] this lodging was affordable only to higher-ranking enlisted personnel and officers. The handy streetcars and proximity to Jackson Barracks in the Bywater and the Navy base at Algiers made the Vieux Carré an attractive alternative to living in a barracks. However, there was an 11:30 p.m. curfew to keep servicepeople off the streets late at night.[156]

## 1946: ANNUS HORRIBILIS

After the V-J day celebrations in September 1945, New Orleans heaved a long sigh. The war years had been hard. The departure and loss of servicepeople was bad enough. Maestri's withdrawal from much of mayoral life left the city lacking what little rudder it possessed. The Quarter was open wider than before to accommodate the pleasure needs of servicemen. Carnival balls, those jeweled bearings on which the city's society turned, had been cancelled for the war. So, 1946 was anticipated with shining eyes. Carnival, officially absent for four long years, would return in full force. Those hoping to be kings, queens, dukes, and maids again began their preparations.

Robert Maestri thought he was a shoo-in for reelection. The Long machine, apart from a few cracks here and there, still controlled Louisiana. The wartime spirit of unity and the aversion of New Orleanians to change would surely keep him in office. However, the clubwomen were angry. To them, what little progress had been made in the city and Vieux Carré had been negated by Maestri's retreat and general wartime excess.[157] Using brooms as their emblem, the clubwomen demanded a reform candidate.

DeLesseps "Chep" Morrison, half-brother of Jacob Morrison, was everything Maestri was not. Young, eloquent, vigorous, a decorated war veteran, Chep campaigned hard as a reformer. After the votes were counted on January 22, Morrison had won.

March 5 was Fat Tuesday 1946, and pent-up revelry washed over the Quarter.[158] Lyle Saxon, too ill to mask and run the streets, gamely narrated the festivities for a radio microphone on the balcony of the St. Charles Hotel. He died, of cancer and hard living, on April 9, with Tallant at his bedside.[159]

Elizebeth Werlein's health had been in decline for months. Her death on April 24 at her home at 630 St. Ann ended the passionate love affair between this well-traveled Yankee and the most famous neighborhood of the South.[160]

So it was, within the space of four months, the Quarter had lost its two most ardent champions and its best official protector.

In March 1946 the city council, with the Vieux Carré Commission's acquiescence,[161] passed an ordinance[162] removing parts of the Quarter's boundaries from Vieux Carré Commission control. The areas removed by this "exempting ordinance" were Square 96, bounded by Iberville, N. Rampart, Burgundy, and Bienville; Square 97, bounded by N. Rampart, Bienville, Conti, and Burgundy; and the riverside of North Rampart, and the riverside areas between Wilkinson and Iberville. The exemption of half the riverside might be reasonable. It was a long-time commercial zone with many offices supporting the port. For years, preservationists had wanted to remove the dock sheds blocking the view from Jackson Square, and finally got their wish in 1932.[163] But the Quarter riverside was still a busy part of the port in the late 1940s.[164] Aside from squares 96 and 97, little defense can be made for removing the rest of the riverside of North Rampart. True, it had been in decline for many years, and the preservationists of the twenties and thirties had shown little interest.[165] It did not attract the urban pioneers who had made comfortable and even elegant nests in the lower Quarter. After all, most of North Rampart was a commercial strip and already down-market, so businesses were not likely to invest much beyond mortgages, rent, and utilities. North Rampart and the Basin Street areas were the lakeside buffer of the Quarter, and absorbed many of the sex workers displaced when the former Storyville was cleared for the Iberville project in 1940. Worse still, the people who lived there would have no preservation advocate, and their visibility fell into kind of a limbo.[166]

The Vieux Carré Property Owners and Associates, speaking through Jacob Morrison, were irate. Morrison slammed the Vieux Carré Commission for not developing a building code for the Quarter. Of the VCC he wrote, "It has spent its time in piecemeal approvals and rejections of minor details." He contrasted the VCC's "snooping into patios to disapprove paint color" to its inaction when a secondhand streetcar was illegally parked in a Quarter lot to serve as a hotdog stand.[167] "Snooping" into privately owned patios had no political consequences compared to fighting a business that might very well be connected to city hall, then in transition from the ten-year Maestri regime to the infant Morrison administration.

Without the VCC's oversight—such as it might have been—Rampart Street owners were allowed to do anything, or nothing, with their properties. Rampart Street began a precipitous decline that sixty years later has not been arrested. These orphan areas were left to their fate at the hands of the city council until 1964, when the lost blocks were restored to VCC control.[168]

Timidly, Madame took the hand of the young mayor. He smiled, a dazzling, powerful smile, and Madame wondered what she was in for.

## CHAPTER 4

# 1946–1961

*Official Vices and Dissenting Voices*

## A Long Anti-Long Reign Begins

Chep Morrison was unlike any mayor New Orleans had seen. Some former mayors had been readily accessible; Martin Behrman (mayor 1904–1920 and 1925–1926) often drove his own horse and buggy around the city,[1] and Maestri, at least in his first phase, popped up all over town.[2] Morrison was not simply visible; in the opening days of his mayorship, he was seen collecting garbage during a strike and stoking the incinerator.[3] Although not a native of the city, he knew how to play the factions of the Democratic machine and in his first term was nationally recognized as a new breed of southern leader. *Time* magazine, which had gleefully reported the follies of the Long cabal and snidely referred to Maestri as "squat and swarthy,"[4] featured Chep on an approving cover less than two years into his first term.[5] *Time* ran several upbeat articles about him during his mayoralty.[6] Maestri had been a reluctant public speaker; Morrison was positively telegenic as the new medium of television arrived.

He had defeated the man the Long machine had entrusted with New Orleans, and the machine wasn't happy about it. Earl Long, Huey's younger brother, had stepped forward as the machine's public leader after Huey's lieutenant, Governor Richard Leche, resigned in 1939 just prior to imprisonment for federal mail fraud.[7] Earl finished out Leche's term but was defeated in 1940 by Sam Jones, who campaigned as a reformer. Where Chep was educated, polished, and slick, "Uncle Earl" was crafty in private and publically coarse. He played to the lowest common denominator of rural Louisiana voter, which suited most of those folks just fine.[8] Earl regained the governorship in 1948 and started legislative warfare to wrest control of New Orleans from municipal officials.[9] However, there was to be no repeat of 1936. Earl's efforts backfired and made Chep a hometown hero.[10] This simmering feud would shape city and state politics until Earl's death in 1960.[11]

Chep Morrison had some significant issues, which only became apparent as he was reelected three successive times. As time went on, it was clear that Chep wanted, more than anything else, to be governor of Louisiana. Other mayors had been content to serve their terms at Gallier Hall and retire; Chep saw New Orleans as a stepping-stone to Baton Rouge and possibly Washington. This obsession colored all four of his terms in office. Chep was like the inventor who believes people will buy his product because it is so good, regardless of whether the public wants it or not. Three times, the voters decided that Chep was not what they wanted as governor; they preferred the folksy patronage of "Uncle Earl" or later, the race-baiting of John J. McKeithen.[12]

In building his political machine, the Crescent City Democratic Association, Chep, elected as a reformer, knew that he could not reshape the city's official culture in one term as mayor. His first half-term had many accomplishments, the second half being dominated by round one of his feud with Governor Earl Long, from which he emerged, at least temporarily, a heroic figure. Morrison the Reformer was also holding some cards behind his back. It was later alleged that Chep met with prostitutes, pimps, bar owners, and other demimonde figures the night before his first election and assured them that business—the vice business—as usual would prevail if he sat at Gallier Hall.[13] Chep confirmed that he had spoken to a group at the time and place specified but naturally denied that he had issued such a proclamation.[14]

At first, at least, Morrison cracked down on vice. The day after his inauguration on May 6, 1946, the police began a series of raids on gambling dens. Within a short time, most slots were either destroyed or had fled to the friendlier clime of Jefferson Parish. Many of those arrested were charged simply with "loitering," a charge so vague as to be easily dismissed, as often happened.[15] Morrison's first police superintendent, the earnest and honest Adair Watters, conducted more raids on houses of prostitution, bars, and gambling establishments between 1946 and 1948.[16] Many of the sixteen bordellos open in 1945 had closed by 1947 due to these raids.[17]

Morrison trumpeted these to the outside world as a cleanup, particularly of the Quarter. Privately, he got heat from his Bourbon Street buddies.[18] Also, many policemen resented Watters's tactics for cutting into the payoffs they enjoyed.[19] By 1949, many of the bordellos closed in this first cleanup had reopened.[20] In January 1949 Watters held a meeting with bar owners and others to ask for cooperation in cleaning up the Quarter. The *Times-Picayune* reported: "Watters said he had the word of the night club and barroom operators that they would cooperate with the police department. The audience laughed." [21] In view of the audience's connections with Chep, their mirth was understandable. Later that month, the French Quarter Residents Association received a letter from Mayor Morrison stating that he was "investigating conditions in the French Quarter" and he was "sure we will be able to stamp out some of the more conspicuous irregularities."[22] Just a month later, Watters had had enough of the farce and resigned.[23]

Just as Huey Long had in the 1930s, "Uncle Earl" used the specter of New Orleans vice against a mayor he didn't like. In late 1950, Governor Long offered to send the state police to assist New Orleans in curbing bookies, known locally as "handbook operators." Chep called his bluff, and pointed out the obvious. Enforcement in Orleans Parish would only drive the bookies' customers short distances to Jefferson and St. Bernard parishes. Illegal gambling chipped away at the legalized, and tax-generating, betting at the fairgrounds.[24]

The "cleanups" of vice under Chep's administration were mostly the same superficial kind the city had seen for two centuries. Chep had powerful contributors in the saloon and vice businesses and he was not about to harm their livelihoods.[25]

Beginning with the New Deal, American politicians were enthralled with the Big Jobs—the housing developments of the thirties, wartime heroics like the Manhattan Project, and in the fifties, civic centers, airports, and superhighways. New York City, having both money and its Caesarean parks commissioner, Robert Moses, set the standard for ruthlessly clearing away the old and constructing the new. Across the country, cities great and towns small sought to emulate these wonders as best they could, with, of course, the mayors' names attached on bronze plaques.

Chep had a taste for all this, and in his fifteen years in office, the city went on a civic building spree. Gallier Hall was relegated to ceremonial use as the city government moved into a steel and glass international style box. The city library moved into a similar building, this one with a grille to filter the

The Three Sisters, N. Rampart at Bienville, designed by Dakin and Gallier, built 1834, demolished 1952, casualties of the exempting ordinance. Courtesy of the Louisiana Division/City Archives, New Orleans Public Library.

subtropical sun. The second Mississippi bridge opened, flying high above the river to Algiers. Just as railroad passenger service was fading, Union Passenger Terminal opened, consolidating five stations into one,[26] eliminating many at-grade train crossings.[27]

Like Maestri, Chep had mixed feelings about the Vieux Carré.[28] He told *The Saturday Evening Post* magazine in 1947: "You know my prescription for New Orleans? A middle class. That's the trouble with this city. It's got no real middle class . . . Let's have real home industries with pay rolls . . . If that means we lose our rank as a first rate honky-tonk, I don't give a damn. In fact, I'd trade all the glamour of the French Quarter for a few blocks of really modern apartments housing a thriving middle class."[29]

Chep might have publicly wanted to "trade all the glamour of the French Quarter"; however, he acted with amazing—some might say disgusting—alacrity to protect the vice industry there. The Quarter's rickety houses, bohemians, and busybody socialites had little relevance to Chep's political ambitions. It was the hefty contributions of the Quarter's saloon owners and bordello operators that made the Vieux Carré memorable to the mayor.[30] This meant that Morrison, apart from a few token gestures of enforcement, had powerful incentives to keep the status quo in the Vieux Carré.

The VCC's position had been cemented by the Louisiana Supreme Court, but the VCC could not act without the cooperation of the city attorney's office. During the 1940s and 1950s, the VCC charged that the city attorney's office delayed or derailed enforcement of preservation ordinances and VCC judgements. The New Orleans Code of Ordinances was gradually amended to include the VCC's purview over architectural elements.[31] Zoning issues remain the final decision of the city council. The council has overridden the VCC's recommendations on several bitterly contested occasions, especially for demolition permits.[32] It appears that the 1950s saw the most demolitions of the postwar era.

For many years, even after the revival of the twenties, the French Quarter was a social island within New Orleans. The decay, abundance of vice, plenitude of immigrants and working poor made it a shunned member of the civic family.[33] The rest of the city assumed—correctly—that the Quarter was a place of different rules, whose events were not related to mid-twentieth-century realities or mores. The lakefront and suburbs like Metairie and Kenner were busy building the 1950s American vision of tract housing and strip development. The Quarter, with its vice lords, low-rent apartments, and persistence of ethnic identities, was closer to 1900 than 1950. Crime and scandal "down in the Quarter" were accepted with nonchalance by most of the city. Locals who liked to "mess in the Quarter" accepted the possible consequences. This indifference was not shared by the more progressive civic leaders who appreciated the Quarter's role in the tourist industry and sought to protect, and, they hoped, improve that role by suppressing, at least, the more public vices flourishing there.

A local man dying in a Quarter dive was barely newsworthy and would have been passed with a shrug and a "dat's a shame" by most New Orleanians. A prominent visitor meeting his end in a Quarter saloon was a different matter altogether. On New Year's Day, 1950, a wealthy Nashvillian, Robert Dunn, died in the Club Kilroy, 427 Bourbon,[34] from the effects of chloral hydrate—knockout drops, also called a Mickey Finn.[35] A roar of indignation came from various civic groups,[36] including the Independent Women's Organization (IWO), headed by the mayor's sister-in-law, urban pioneer Mary Morrison.[37]

All this was too much even for the otherwise blasé Mayor Morrison, and in March of that year he appointed a committee to study Quarter crime. The committee included nightclub owner Gaspar Culotta, who was a contributor and friend to Morrison.

Some of the committee's recommendations became law, but for the most part, the cleanup was superficial. The civic minders and self-appointed watchdogs were losing patience, and in February 1952 they formed the Metropolitan

Crime Commission (MCC) of New Orleans. The outraged citizens' groups had to tread carefully, however. Their disgust with "reform mayor" Morrison was matched by their fear of another Long assault on the city. If Morrison was badly damaged, or thrown out of office, the city might fall back into the clutches of the Long cabal.[38]

Beginning in 1950, the U.S. Senate's Kefauver Committee traveled to fourteen cities, holding hearings on organized crime and corruption. These hearings—some televised—caused a sensation. The tentacles of organized crime were shown to be intertwined with every level of government and to exert great influence in most large cities. In January 1951, the committee arrived in New Orleans. In his testimony, Mayor Morrison deftly blamed the Longs for the arrival of slot machines in the 1930s and deflected attention to the casinos of Jefferson Parish. New Orleans did not get a pass, however, as other persistent corruption and racketeering was uncovered. Overall, Chep was successful in portraying himself as a reformer struggling against a deeply entrenched system of crime and corruption.[39]

In late 1952 and early 1953, the Louisiana State Police conducted raids on gambling houses and bordellos in New Orleans, highlighting the city's unwillingness to confront vice and its tolerance by the police department.[40]

In the summer of 1953, the city council, despite grumbling by Mayor Morrison, funded the Special Citizens Investigating Committee (SCIC), and hired Aaron Kohn, a former FBI agent, as its chief investigator. Morrison and his minions tried their best to obstruct the investigation. The mayor personally heckled witnesses, including a prostitute who began to describe her services.[41]

Although some police officials were indicted on the basis of the SCIC findings, they were later exonerated and the immediate effects of the investigation dissipated. In March 1955, Kohn served ten days in jail for refusing to name his sources to a grand jury.[42] Undeterred, he went on to serve as managing director for the Metropolitan Crime Commission.[43]

The visible, blatant excesses of Vieux Carré vice that stirred the reformers to action were the tip of a much larger Louisiana iceberg. Behind the B-girls, hookers, gaming, and dope lay a much larger criminal octopus, one with tentacles reaching from the governor's office down to the beat policeman. New York mobster Frank Costello and Carlos Marcello, the mob boss of Louisiana, contributed heavily to favored politicians, including Earl Long. They paid off to the governor; the governor's appointees paid off to him; and the barroom, bordello, and dope operatives paid off to the local cops.[44] The reformers were not a bunch of naifs; they knew they could not, by themselves, dislodge this culture, of which the tawdry side of the Quarter was but a small part.

The entire chain of events—the knockout drops fatality, the Kefauver hearings, the SCIC, and Chep's successful rollback of any real change—crystallized the heart of the matter. New Orleans has always drawn a peculiar distinction between crime and its effects. The crime itself, if it registers at all, is usually received with nonchalance; the outrage is reserved for anything publically malodorous. Mr. Dunn was not the first victim, fatal or otherwise, of knockout drops, but the ripples from that event disturbed both saloon keepers and reformers. Prostitution was so normal as to not excite local comment; but a strumpet reciting her syllabus in a public hearing was beyond "common decency," as Chep's reaction demonstrated. Local citizens, for the most part, liked round-the-clock drinking, enjoyed gambling, felt that hookers were part of the male prerogative, and knew damn well that many officials illicitly supplemented their official incomes. However, murder of important tourists, out-of-town mobsters profiting from local slots, and whores in "respectable" settings were just too much to stomach. It's an attitude that persists to this day, even in an era that makes one almost nostalgic for the tamer vices of yesteryear. Laissez-faire, that constant drag on the wagon of New Orleans's progress, had won again.[45]

From 1900, an ice house had stood at the corner of Chartres and Gov. Nicholls. In the late 1940s, the ice company donated the property to St. Mary's Italian Church, whose sanctuary adjoins the former Ursuline Convent on the Chartres block between Gov. Nicholls and Ursulines. The congregation demolished the ice house and built a neoclassical brown-brick structure as a community center. Children, senior citizens, aspiring prize fighters, and bingo players from the Vieux Carré flocked to the center for nearly thirty years.[46]

## THE LOUISIANA PURCHASE SESQUICENTENNIAL

Although New Orleans never needs an excuse for a party, it had a corker in 1953, the 150th anniversary of Napoleon's sale of the vast Louisiana territory to Thomas Jefferson's young United States. For two weeks in October, the city had a second Carnival season of celebrations. The capstone was sunny, joyous, October 17. President Eisenhower flew into Moisant airport and was greeted by Governor McKennon and Mayor Morrison, wearing his trademark white

President Eisenhower signs a replica of the Louisiana Purchase during the Purchase Sesquicentennial, 1953. Left to right: Congressman Boggs, Mayor Morrison, French Ambassador Bonnet, President Eisenhower, Chairman Richards, and Duralde Claiborne. Courtesy of the Louisiana Division, City Archives, New Orleans Public Library.

The Rex-Comus parade in front of the Purchase Sesquicentennial reviewing stand, October 17, 1953. Courtesy of the Louisiana Division, City Archives, New Orleans Public Library.

suit. The dignitaries motored to Jackson Square where the president and the French ambassador signed a replica of the purchase document. A reviewing stand covered most of the riverside fence of the square. Above the presidential seal, Eisenhower reviewed a parade that included the first and only rolling of Rex and Comus floats on a day other than Fat Tuesday. This must have been Chep's apogee of glory, sitting beside a friendly governor and a popular president. Basking in the sunshine and presidential attention, the city, for a special day, was the favored child of the American civic family.[47]

Chep's actions towards the Quarter were modulated by his half-brother Jacob and Jacob's wife, Mary. Jacob Morrison would eventually write the definitive book *Historic Preservation Law*.[48] Having Chep's ear, Jacob and Mary became important defenders of the Quarter in the forties and the fifties.[49]

In 1955, the Jacob Morrisons and a group of their allies founded Vieux Carré Restorations, Inc. The purpose of the corporation was to buy, restore, and sell Quarter properties. The stockholders gave of their own time and labor to restore houses suffering serious neglect.[50] From 1956 to 1961, three properties were thus renovated and sold.[51] Just before the final sale, the stockholders decided to liquidate the corporation.[52] The average dividend seems to have been rather small. In a 1963 letter, Jacob Morrison acknowledged that the effort had been undercapitalized, especially in view of rising property values in the Quarter, city, and state.[53]

## "THE QUARTER'S PROBLEM"

Prior to the Storyville era, at least one bordello in New Orleans catered to men who desired other men, and the names of the prostitutes imply that these were drag queens.[54] In 1893, *The Mascot*, a reform and scandal sheet, depicted two women in an overly friendly setting. "Good God! The crimes of Sodom and Gomorrah discounted," the headline shrieked. The reference was to the lesbianism common among prostitutes of the era.[55] In 1906, the *Sunday Sun*, another scandal sheet of Storyville, reported that male homosexuals, called "jennie-men" or "its," were noticed around Canal Street and Franklin Avenue.[56]

From that time forward to the early fifties, some Quarter bars had been known as unofficial hangouts for "sodomites," later "perverts" and "deviates." The police called these bars "queer shops." Some ostensibly "straight" bars, such as Café Lafittes (now Lafitte's Blacksmith Shop) also had long-enduring gay clienteles. Gay men and women had to watch their step even in these places. They might wait until a certain bartender was on duty, or if it was a particular day of the week. Even then, they frequently entered through side doors, to reduce the chance of being observed by police, family, or co-workers.[57] Some gays who lived in the Quarter disliked loud, flamboyant gay tourists who might inspire police attention in otherwise discreet and convivial settings. Finding sexual partners who didn't become violent with sober remorse was a necessary survival skill. Avoiding entrapment by the vice squad was another.

Someone busted for vice would have his or her name and picture published in the papers. This would often lead to loss of job and place to live and to family discord.[58] Those arrested were often pressured to name other "perverts." The closet was both a refuge and a prison, even in an area so noted for personal freedom as the Quarter.

Harassment of gay clubs and gathering places was common across America in the 1950s. Boise, Idaho, Gainesville, Florida, and other communities experienced sweeping "purges" of homosexuals.[59] Homophobia was part of the operating system of 1950s American masculinity. Fear of "queers" was more terrifying, to many men, than fear of the Bomb. Even their straight sympathizers expected gays and lesbians to be "discreet" and not too loud or flamboyant. It was especially troubling to southern authorities in the heyday of Jim Crow that "perverts" had no identifying stigmata. Some moral monitors solemnly maintained that all male "homos" wore red neckties,[60] pinkie rings, or green clothing on Thursdays as in-signals. Vagrancy laws, typically used against drifters, were useless against well-established hairdressers, florists, and antique dealers. It seemed especially odd that New Orleans, labeled from its start as a city of cheerful sin, should make war on gays and lesbians. After all, straight tourists could find strippers, whores, liquor, and gambling aplenty in "respectable" Quarter establishments. Narcotics only required a little extra effort. Countless conventioneers went home with woozy heads, sated lusts, and beads round their necks.

Therein is the answer to the paradox. The "tourist trade"—drunken, carnal, and gaming—would be jeopardized if "queers" were too visible. Quarter police protection meant protection of straight sex tourism. The notion that gay and lesbian tourism could be commercially important was unthinkable to the authorities and owners of straight clubs of the 1950s and for decades to come.

The 1950s saw the unhappy intersection of McCarthyism and the resurgent civil rights movement. The threat of homosexual "invisible undesirables" mirrored the McCarthyist fear of widespread, creeping Communism. Homophobia, anti-Communism, and Jim Crow were commonly conflated by the moral imperative of white, straight, male authority. It was no stretch for southern authorities to imagine that atmospheres tolerant of "race mixing" would encourage Communism and homosexuality. Frequently, dope paranoia was tossed in for good measure. A dash of anti-Semitism was sometimes added to finish the fiendish plot against "the southern way of life."

It was equally true that the "beatnik" clubs had such atmospheres. Being "cool" meant accepting nontraditional couples, stoned poets, and feverish discussions about the state of racial matters. The denizens, the authorities maintained, needed to be yanked back to "reality" and "join the human race." So, there were ample pretexts for harassing these gatherings. Perverts, Communists, race-mixers, and dope addicts could all be arrested and publicly identified in a single raid.[61]

Since paying off various officialdom was, and is, a touchstone of successful New Orleans business life, the "beatnik" hangouts and "queer shops" that did not pay off were at a further, usually fatal, disadvantage. Police raids on any club were often a signal that the owner was late in rendering unto Caesar.

The great majority of homosexuals were not sex workers operating in establishments under the protection of the police, as was true of many straight strumpets. Most were white, so segregation laws did not work to constrain them. Many had above-the-table jobs and some were local leaders in fields like decoration, art, antiques, and design. A very few were both openly gay and had prominent civic positions. One of these was Clay Shaw. Shaw was the managing director of the International Trade Mart and also accompanied Mayor Chep Morrison to Latin America on trade missions.[62] Shaw organized the Sesquicentennial of the Louisiana Purchase celebration in 1953. Chep must have known Shaw was gay, but apparently found him too useful to shun.[63]

Apart from the moral issue—still potent in a very Catholic town—the police and city hall were vexed. They feared that the "perverts," if too visible, would scare off both family tourism and straight sex trade in the Quarter. New Orleans had an ordinance, not repealed until 1993, that stated: "No person of lewd, immoral, or dissolute character, sexual pervert . . . shall be employed in such a place of business as a . . . waiter, bartender . . . Nor shall such persons be allowed to congregate or frequent such place of business."[64] This ordinance gave the moral-minders ample purview to complain, and the police tremendous latitude of enforcement.

Jacob Morrison found the presence of "queer shops" highly objectionable and made the elimination of these places a personal crusade. Beginning in 1950, he and other concerned citizens visited the Starlet Lounge,[65] at 945 Chartres, the lake side upper corner of Chartres and St. Philip. Finding the "queer" carrying-on within not to his taste, he and others tried the threat of police and legal action to change the character of the bar. In 1953, the bar's liquor license was revoked.[66]

Jacob Morrison and his allies maintained their vigilance. Beginning in 1954, they took notice of Tony Bacino's bar, at 738 Toulouse, between Bourbon and Royal.[67] Some of the same staff from the Starlet had migrated to this new menace, and beginning in July 1958, the police began arresting the manager and two of the staff. In the week of July 22–28, the staff was arrested five times, with a final sixth arrest on August 5. Each time the charge was the same: "Person of lewd character employed as bartender."[68]

The police scandals and Chep's personal defense of the accused had worn the shine of reform off his administration.[69] As he began his fourth

term in office in 1958, he needed a distraction. By remarkable coincidence—
if that is what it was—the city council on July 22, 1958, appointed Jacob Morrison the chairman of a Committee on the Problem of Sex Deviates.[70] Here
was a great opportunity for Chep! He could again act the part of Reforming
Mayor and divert attention from corruption. This would play well with the
ladies with the brooms, his whore-mongering Bourbon Street buddies, and
upstate voters who had never permitted a Catholic, New Orleans mayor to
become governor.

As the committee pondered the "Quarter's problem," a remarkable thing
happened. The day after the final arrest at Tony Bacino's, the manager, Roy
Maggio, and two staff members stood up to the city. They filed an injunction
against the mayor and the police superintendent to prevent further harassment.
They obtained a temporary restraining order until the case could be heard.[71]
The committee's report fairly gasped at the "brazen temerity" of the suit.[72]

The plaintiffs' arguments rested on three grounds: the invasion of property rights, irreparable injury to livelihood, and the constitutionality of the
city's ordinance. The trial turned into an inquisition of the plaintiffs' well-
established police records and suspect morals. A star witness for the defendants was none other than Aaron Kohn. Certainly no friend of Chep Morrison, he nonetheless provided damning testimony about the theatrics in the
bar and his own theory linking homosexuality with violent crime.

The plaintiffs lost; an appeal was filed but ultimately abandoned in 1962.
We should not extrapolate too much from this case. It irritated the Morrisons;
after all, 1950s deviates were supposed to default to shame and slink away, ver-
min-like, after being confronted. However, it provoked little sympathy in the
city. Only in a very vague way does it relate to subsequent legal maneuvering
for civil rights. The concept of "homosexual rights" was nebulous in 1958 and
this case, by itself, sparked no contemporary movement for those rights. If
anything, the Morrisons and their allies on the committee must have felt vindicated and emboldened. If we may draw comparison with well-known civil
rights cases based on color, *Maggio et al.* was a defeat like *Plessy v. Ferguson*;
it most certainly was no victory like *Brown v. Board of Education.*

The committee's report in January 1959 was, for the time, surprisingly
pragmatic. It conceded that there was probably no "cure" for homosexuality
and that the best remedies were legal.[73] If this was a legal problem, then, so
the reasoning went, it was a police problem. Provosty Dayries, Chep's jack-
booted, tough-talking superintendent of police, wrote this amazing letter,[74]
reproduced here in full:

July 24 1958
EXHIBIT "A"

Dear Chief:

The City of New Orleans is faced with a problem which on the surface appears difficult to solve. This is the problem of homosexuals and lesbians. Apparently the French Quarter of New Orleans has an atmosphere which appeals to these people, who are an undesirable element in our community. Other types of undesirables are generally easy to handle, because, for the most part, they are vagrants who can be handled under existing legislation.

It is a different story with the homosexuals and lesbians. Most of them are gainfully employed, or have a source of income from their families, and are not engaged in crime for profit. However, the assembly of these persons for pastime, at a particular location, results in complaints from residents of the immediate vicinity. Although we know certain establishments cater almost exclusively to such persons, there is no way of proving such to be the case. We are interested in determining whether or not other cities have had such a problem, and if so, what steps have been taken to solve said Problem.

1 - Is there any special legislation for handling such undesirables? If so, copies will be appreciated.
2 - If you have no special legislation, then what action is taken, if any, to keep these persons out of your city?
3 - Do you take action against lounges or bars which cater to these persons?
4 - If action is taken against the bars is it through special Ordinance, or is it through strict enforcement of all other regulations concerning bars?

Any recommendations you might make for the solution of our problem will be appreciated.

Sincerely,
PROVOSTY A. DAYRIES
Superintendent of Police

Sent to forty-two police departments, it yielded only twenty-four responses, most of which cited quaint "crimes against nature" statutes.[75] After alleging that the "French Quarter is teeming with homosexuals who brazenly flaunt public decency in many of its barrooms and even on the street," the committee's report recommended the enactment of several new or strengthened ordinances to control barroom employment and property leasing by "deviates."[76] The committee hoped that a climate of "frigid hostility" would emerge towards homosexuals.[77] Selective police harassment and entrapment would continue de rigueur for many years, alongside with tolerance of gay and gay-friendly bars that must have had favorable, that is monetary, relations with the police.

## TWEED AND BEADS

The general reaction to Morrison's police scandals of 1954 and 1955 was a shrug. A few residents still hung on in the boozy tourist area of surrounding upper Bourbon. However, most accepted that the upper Quarter had been "that way" within living memory and no outsider was liable to force a change. Many people still remembered—and resented—the alien intervention that closed Storyville and the aftereffects on the Quarter. Vice officially protected was vice controlled, so the reasoning went, and all these investigations were just giving the Quarter and the city an undeserved "shiner."

Upper Bourbon is not the whole Quarter, and for many of the pioneers of the second wave, their 1950s Vieux Carré was comfortable indeed. The 1950s in America were not, of course, the stagnant times of innocence depicted in much subsequent media. Times were simpler because people's outlooks were simpler. The easy assumptions, the handy stereotypes, the unquestioned relationships between old and young, rich and poor, white and black, all informed the world of 1950s middle-class whites and the media that served them heaping helpings of "normality." The generation that had come of age in the Great Depression and fought World War II was now in charge. The bland suburban conformity that sophisticates derided was a comforting reaction to the poverty, family disruption, and war stress that many split-level rambler homeowners had suffered in the 1930s and 1940s.

Many of the monied mainstays of the 1950s Quarter had been the "bohemian" and "eccentric" pioneers of the late 1930s and postwar 1940s, who formed and rode the second wave of gentrification as the VCC began to assert itself. Some of these folks actually lived outside the Quarter in enclaves like Audubon Place. These people staffed the VCC, the VCPORA, and many other neighborhood groups. Defining the bandwidth of tolerance, these people guarded, and enjoyed living in, the Vieux Carré. Perhaps not overly religious, they nevertheless tended the flame of a particular lifestyle—true intellectualism, cultivation of the arts, maintaining traditions, being served by one's own waiter at the world-class restaurants—all while wearing tweed, Mamie Eisenhower hats, and white gloves. The collective memory of Saxon's tête-à-têtes inspired dozens of vital, albeit uncelebrated, salons. These folks formed what I call the Inner Quarter, both geographically and culturally.

The Vieux Carré's physical boundaries in the fifties were a very mixed lot. Canal Street was at the zenith of its commercial life, and its flagship department stores were destinations in themselves.[78] Rampart Street catered to downmarket businesses at the margin of the mostly white Quarter and the mostly Negro Tremé area. Esplanade continued to be a gallery of mansions—some cut up for apartments but most still beautiful on the outside. Decatur Street was the sweaty torso of the enclave, where sailors from many lands looked for drinks and dames as they had since 1718. These margins were the boulevards of gay life as well.[79]

Like the Tango Belt two generations before, this Inner Quarter had no precise boundaries. For our purposes, we may consider St. Peter to Barracks, and Burgundy to Royal, as the approximate marches. Many Carnival visitors have been jarred after wandering too far down Bourbon or Dauphine to find themselves suddenly in a pool of stillness, with the ruckus of the upper Quarter, where they just were, an echo far away. They are in the residential end of the village, where Fat Tuesday can be, even now, as quiet as St. Louis Cemetery Number One on a hot August afternoon.

This Inner Quarter was where the tweedy guardians of the Vieux Carré established order reigned. They were certainly not all wealthy. Of course, there were plenty of working poor; some—by New Orleans standards—middle-class; drifters; and the occasional "street girl" plying her avocation away from upper Bourbon. But it was these mainstays, still called by some preservationists, that had fought and sweated to make the VCC process work, in the face of much discouragement. They had created institutions to preserve the culture of the old village and raise a firm voice against the saloon keepers and their political cronies. They had their own allies, some shared in typical New Orleans fashion with the vice lords, as Jacob and Mary Morrison had in Mayor Chep Morrison. It surprised even worldly visitors that these mostly conservative people could second-line, beads round necks, in evening clothes, or costume as giant animals, pirates, and saloon strumpets on Fat Tuesday. All that was of a piece, however, and contradiction existed only in the insufficiently liquored minds of bemused strangers.

A prominent member of the tweed and beads set was none other than Clay Shaw, whose patrician appearance would have been well set off by a purple toga. Shaw renovated thirteen Vieux Carré properties between 1950 and 1964.[80]

So, inside fifties America was the fifties Inner Quarter, a refuge from the chromed, homogenized Zeitgeist outside. The "quaintness" and "charm" the guidebooks touted was not exported outside the city. No one was building faux French Quarters in theme parks or franchising jazz clubs based on a mythic Storyville. Conversely, out-of-towners prescribing foreign notions like urban renewal and desegregation were rebuffed as ambassadors from other planets.

## LAND OF A THOUSAND DANCES

The music of New Orleans's streets floats in through open windows. It is a city of marching bands, strutting for every occasion, great and small, sorrowful and triumphant. The blat of the tuba, the blare of the trombone, the mischievous squeal of the clarinet, and, above all, the rat-tat-tat of the drum and the call of the cornet keep pulses pulsing, hips shaking, and young musicians dreaming.

New Orleans had been a city of refuge for Negroes from the Mississippi valley for many years, and they brought with them rhythm and blues from Memphis, Clarksdale, and many other points north. By the late 1940s, the Dixieland jazz that had once been spawned in Storyville, the Quarter, and many streetcorner bands, had moved on. Jazz, once an outcast, had become the mainstream popular music, and New Orleans's Dixieland was now passé almost everywhere else.[81]

For most of the twentieth century, segregation of New Orleans musical life was part of the overall division between the races. Negroes might entertain in white clubs, but they could not be admitted as patrons. A few adventurous whites would go to Negro clubs like the Dew Drop Inn uptown on LaSalle Street, where hot jazz and drag acts were featured.[82] Whites could legally enter Negro clubs, but the Gay-Shattuck law forbade Negroes and whites to drink together, as actor Zachary Scott found out in a 1952 arrest at the Dew Drop.[83] It was not merely the police who enforced the law; cab drivers would rarely take whites to Negro clubs,[84] and white cab drivers rarely, if ever, took Negro passengers.[85] White and Negro musicians could not play together in public, and so resorted to backroom jam sessions hoping that no one would call the cops about the "noise."[86] There were also separate unions for Negro and white musicians.[87]

Not everyone was content with this musical schizophrenia. Cosimo Matassa learned to love hot music while tending the jukeboxes of his father's business. At age eighteen, he started J&M Recording Studio at 838 North Rampart, above a business half owned by his father.[88] He welcomed Negro and white musicians, and a little corner of the Quarter began to pulse with rhythm and blues, setting off ripples that would reach far indeed.

Between 1947 and 1965, on North Rampart and later Gov. Nicholls, Matassa made the first recordings of Jerry Lee Lewis, Ernie K-Doe, Fats Domino, Art Neville, Johnny Rivers, Allen Toussaint, and Mac "Dr. John" Rebennack. The list of standards he recorded is very long; just a few among them are: "Good Rocking Tonight" by Roy Brown (1947); "I Hear You Knockin'" by Smiley Lewis (1955); "Tutti Frutti" (1955), "Long Tall Sally," and "Lucille" (1956) by Little Richard; "Sea Cruise" (1959) by Frankie Ford; Ernie K-Doe's anthem, "Mother-in-Law" (1961), and "Land of 1,000 Dances" (1963) by Chris Kenner.[89]

More than anyone else, Matassa, operating far from major record companies in New York or Los Angeles, midwifed the transition from rhythm and blues to rock and roll, helping to erase the commercial and social divisions of "white" and "race" records.[90]

## THE END OF CHEP'S REIGN

Chep Morrison's long run as mayor of New Orleans coincided with many watershed events. One of these, not appreciated until long after, was the peak of New Orleans's size. The 1960 census recorded about 627,000 residents. The next census would show a drop to about 593,000, and every following census showed further declines.[91]

Jacob Morrison's closeness with the VCPORA did not shield Chep from its criticism. In 1959, VCPORA president William Long took Chep to task in an open letter: "[Y]ou did not lift a finger to help the cause of preservation which you were pleased to uphold in your campaign speech at Natchitoches" [Louisiana, during the gubernatorial campaign of 1956 ].[92]

In 1960, Chep made a public pledge of greater support for preservation, but his attention was elsewhere. He ran for governor again and was defeated by former governor Jimmie "You Are My Sunshine" Davis, who portrayed Chep as too friendly to Negro interests.[93] The school integration crisis of 1960 was the beginning of a bitter coda to Chep's administration. He was caught between federal court orders and segregation enshrined in state law, and his indecisive handling made the event what he ever sought to avoid, a public relations nightmare.[94] White housewives—called "cheerleaders"—screamed and spat at little Negro children trying to attend a formerly all-white school in the Ninth Ward, downriver from the Quarter.[95] The next day, a mob of hundreds of white teens attempted to storm the school board building. Turned back, they forced their way into city hall but could not reach the mayor, who was locked in his suite. Ordered by police to disperse, the mob stormed through downtown and the Quarter, throwing rocks and fighting with any Negroes they encountered. Across the city, whites and Negroes were apprehended while carrying riot weapons.[96] The televised images shattered white New Orleans's daydream of relative racial harmony and made the seasoned Mayor Morrison look like an overwhelmed amateur. Much of the city was nonchalant about the police scandals of the midfifties, but this was something altogether different. New Orleans was looking bad, very bad, to the rest of the world, despite its so-called reform mayor and nominally progressive business climate.

One of Mayor Morrison's much-trumpeted achievements was the 1954 city charter. In the midst of the police scandal embarrassments, this charter had been drafted with input from a wide range of business, social, and civic leadership. Perhaps in reference to the 1947 Twenty-second Amendment to the Constitution, which limited presidents to two elected terms, the charter limited New Orleans mayors, after the 1958 election, to two terms. Chep, therefore, would perforce leave office in 1962. Sixteen years, it seems, were not enough, so in 1961 Chep proposed changing the charter to permit him to succeed himself yet again. His campaign used the slogan "Change Charter—Keep Chep." His opponents turned this around with placards reading "Keep Charter—Change Chep." The public agreed with the latter, and on April 15 defeated the change.[97]

In July of 1961, Chep accepted President Kennedy's nomination as U.S. ambassador to the Organization of American States.[98] The city council chose councilman Victor Schiro as acting mayor, and he was elected to two successive terms in 1962 and 1966.

The calendar and the Quarter were not close friends until a handful of festivals were spawned from Carnival in the 1970s and 1980s, becoming notches of the year's passage. Much of what the rest of America associated with the 1950s continued to cling, barnacle-like, in New Orleans's cracks and crevices long after the tide of outside events moved on. So to say that the city's 1950s ended on the first of January 1961, or even that the "cheerleader" episode was a sorry bookend to that time, is like trying to bisect a sneeze.

However, even Clio sometimes turns a page of her tablet, and the departure of Chep Morrison in July 1961 is about as logical a place as any to demark our history.

## CHAPTER 5

# 1961–1971

## Culture and Counterculture

### THE VIEUX CARRÉ SURVEY

Monitoring the status quo of the Quarter is a daunting task. Even in such a small enclave, the dense streetscape, the gates and porte cocheres conceal much. Before the 1960s, it depended largely on the Vieux Carré Commission staff noticing changes in walkabouts, neighbors bringing complaints to the VCC, and the review of building and demolition permits. From 1961 to 1966, Tulane's School of Architecture led a collaboration to produce the Vieux Carré Survey, the first comprehensive inventory of the entire enclave.[1] A file was created for each building, with photographs, chain of title, record of VCC actions, and other information. The Vieux Carré Survey is the "baseline" by which the VCC controls the Quarter's configuration. The Vieux Carré Survey also produced a classification system, color-coding each building in order of significance. The purples are of "national architectural or historical significance," and are the buildings surrounding Jackson Square, the former Ursuline Convent, and the U.S. Mint. The browns—"objectionable or of no architectural or historical importance"—are mainly seen along the long-estranged North Rampart strip, with a few other brown-rated structures, mainly outbuildings, sprinkled throughout. The intervening classes make up the rest, with the visual majority the greens—"of local architectural or historical importance."

## ENTER THE BIG HOTELS

Prior to 1960, the largest hotel in the Quarter was the venerable, six-hundred-room Monteleone, Royal at Bienville. Its rooftop sign has been an aerial landmark for generations. The block had been one of those removed from the control of the Vieux Carré Commission by the 1946 exempting ordinance.[2] In 1960, the Royal Orleans (now Omni Royal Orleans) hotel was built on the long-vacant site of the St. Louis hotel, which had been demolished after the 1915 hurricane. This hotel was built with contributions from many old-money families, including Quarter preservationists General L. Kemper Williams and Edgar Stern, owner of WDSU-TV.[3] The Royal Orleans, with over three hundred rooms, had an echo of the St. Louis's appearance.[4]

The site of the French Opera House, 541 Bourbon at St. Louis, had stood bare since the fire in 1919, and the lot was considered a grave by some older residents.[5] In 1964, the Downtowner (now the Inn on Bourbon), with 186 rooms, was built on the site.

The downriver side of the 300 block of Bourbon had been the site of Regal Brewery, and was cleared in 1961 in anticipation of a new hotel. For various reasons, the five-hundred-room Royal Sonesta Hotel was not built until 1966, leaving a "filthy and bleak half block"[6] to greet strolling tourists.

The most heated hotel controversy was over the Bourbon Orleans, Bourbon at Orleans. It would be built upon the former Convent of the Holy Family, whose nuns educated black children. Prior to the nuns' arrival, it had been the site of the infamous Quadroon Ballroom. This was one of the places that the antebellum dance of *plaçage* played out, as young women of mixed race were presented as candidates for concubinage with well-to-do white men. It was not a site held in any esteem by the black community.[7] Yet it became the darling of white preservationists, like Martha Robinson, who fought the rezoning for two years.[8] In 1963, after the developers planned to enclose the old ballroom in a modern structure, the rezoning was approved.[9]

Quarter guardians met most of these large hotels with great ire. Demolition, even of mediocre buildings with little commercial potential, instantly polarized the discussion.[10] The construction of large, steel-frame buildings on pounded pilings caused damage to some nearby old structures.[11] The size of the new hotels—seven stories typically—was out of scale with surrounding nineteenth-century structures of three or four floors at most. Yet the new hotels were far smaller than the skyscrapers that would soon be built on Canal Street, throwing long shadows over the entire Quarter. The new buildings' designs included typical Quarter styling cues, but still attracted criticism for not seamlessly blending in, an obvious impossibility, with the old buildings.[12] New buildings, of modern materials, do not age in the same way as older buildings wearing traditional finishes. One would hope that modern Vieux Carré structures would evoke the architectural *tout ensemble*. However, thankfully, there is no single, fixed "Vieux Carré style," and so new structures will never receive universal approval.[13] Vacant lots were indefensible in the city's most valuable real estate, and the tourist traffic brought in by large hotels was welcomed by merchants. The big hotels, like the legendary Roosevelt (later the Fairmont) just off Canal on Baronne Street, became destinations in themselves, with bars, restaurants, and rooftop clubs. More lodging in the Quarter was welcomed by those looking to develop the riverfront to host conventions. The larger hotels also brought more automobile traffic, which removed curbside parking for residents.[14] The increased influx of visitors meant more pressure on the quality of residential life. In 1959, the Quarter had only 740 hotel rooms, the great majority in the Monteleone. By 1969 that number had reached 2,655.[15] In 1969, the city enacted a moratorium on new hotel construction in the Quarter, and mandated height limits on commercial buildings.[16] As we will see, the city council stretched these regulations to absurdity, and the hotels themselves simply ignored the regulations when they chose.

## "ONE-MAN RESTORATION SOCIETY"

Buying and fixing up property in the Quarter was still a novelty for individuals in the 1960s. Banks did not see the potential and were reluctant to make loans to buy or renovate property there.[17]

Slowly, with private capital and great perseverance, renovators emerged. Between 1950 and 1964, Clay Shaw, managing director of the International Trade Mart, renovated thirteen Quarter properties. His most famous project was the so-called Spanish Stables, 716 Gov. Nicholls. The old livery stable dated from 1834.[18] Many of the arched carriage stalls had been closed up, and the courtyard was neglected. Shaw fitted the arches with french doors topped with fanlights, called by some *lunettes*. Twelve apartments were created. A bronze plaque on the outer wall remembers Shaw and his renovations in the Quarter. Shaw's other restorations included his first at 537 Barracks, 908 Esplanade, 1313 Dauphine, and 505 Dauphine. The latter had the distinction of

Clay Shaw. Courtesy of the Louisiana Division, City
Archives, New Orleans Public Library.

having the first residential swimming pool in the Vieux Carré. This was one
of the few "modern" outdoor elements allowed by the VCC since its founding, and it was succeeded by many other pools. A 1964 article by preservationist and real estate agent Martha Ann Samuel proclaimed him a "one-man
restoration society."[19]

## BOURBON A GO-GO

The Quarter's main tourist artery had revved up during World War II into a
wide-open street. Barkers stood outside strip clubs and saloons, shouting at
tourists to come in, grabbing their elbows, and verbally abusing them if they
didn't enter. Inside the clubs, B-drinking and prostitution were common.[20]
Drunken tourists were sometimes robbed and brutalized in the process. The
wartime "anything for the boys" had become the peacetime "anything goes."
Despite years of citizen complaints and tut-tutting from city hall, little had
changed by the early sixties. The clubs were insulated from any real enforcement by their close ties with Mayor Chep Morrison. Nightclub owner Gasper
Gulotta was called the "little mayor of Bourbon Street" for his influence.
When he died in 1956, Mayor Morrison was a pallbearer.[21]

Mayor Victor Schiro, who had replaced Chep Morrison in mid-1961, was
elected in his own right in 1962. After the turbulence at the end of Chep's long
reign, Schiro's mustachioed grin and jovial manner seemed calming. Schiro
was certainly no reformer nor much of an activist.

In 1962, James Garrison was elected Orleans Parish district attorney. "Big Jim" Garrison, who stood six feet, six inches, was about to make a dramatic impact in the Quarter and the city at large, albeit in ways no one suspected.

In his campaign, Garrison vowed to clean up Bourbon and lower Canal Street. After the election, he certainly tried. His squads of investigators entered clubs and arrested strippers, prostitutes, bar girls, and their bosses.[22] The NOPD became temporarily energized and conducted a few joint raids with the DA's staff.[23] However, although Mayor Schiro tried cooperating with Garrison[24] and uttered supporting platitudes, he and the NOPD were not much interested in Garrison's crusade. The mayor and police cared even less after Garrison made loud, public accusations against them.[25] When asked about the display of flesh in Bourbon strip joints, Mayor Schiro cracked, "You can rest assured I'm keeping abreast of the situation."[26] Many agreed that a balance between naughty and respectable attractions had to be maintained, even as Garrison rocked the scale. In 1959, Chicagoan James C. Downs had told the chamber of commerce: "Don't turn your French Quarter over to the history buffs. They'll kill it. But so could the entrepreneurs of sex and sin. It's the balance between history and honky-tonks that makes the Vieux Carré what it is."[27]

Many observers questioned whether Garrison was acting out of purity or for publicity.[28] By October 1962, there had been no convictions resulting from the raids.[29] However, some of the Canal clubs, unable to keep going in the face of repeated raids, folded.[30] About twelve Bourbon clubs were ordered, in civil court, to operate under guaranty bonds against vice.[31] But all was not going the DA's way; the traditional connections between major Bourbon operators and the civic establishment were quickly in play. Garrison was financing his raids with the proceeds from a "fines and fees" fund. These expenditures had to be approved by a criminal district court judge. The eight criminal district court judges balked at funding Garrison's investigators acting in police roles. After a well-publicized controversy, Garrison was convicted of defaming the judges, but the charge was thrown out by the U.S. Supreme Court in 1964.[32]

Emboldened, Garrison would go on to a much larger game in 1967. This is not the place to discuss the bizarre case Garrison wove against Clay Shaw in the death of President Kennedy. However, we must appreciate the incredible shock the indictment caused.[33] Shaw was a widely respected businessman who had been a trusted ally of Mayor Morrison. One of the Quarter's most visible citizens, he was one of the leading preservationists of his day.[34]

Beyond the tortured logic of the allegations, many were offended that Garrison's assault included flippant references to Shaw's sexual orientation. Garrison described the assassination as a "homosexual thrill killing."[35] In a town where glittering gauze obscured the private lives of many prominent figures, straight and gay, this maneuver was seen as a disgusting cheap shot.

By the mid-1960s, Bourbon was somewhat tamer, but not entirely because of Big Jim. Changing tastes and mores had softened some of the harder edges. In 1943, young enlisted men fresh off the farm were mesmerized by "lovely dollies" stripping down to pasties. In the 1960s, going to a strip club was still a rite of passage for very young men, but it was no longer the street's chief draw. Society had become more relaxed about public heterosexuality, and it was no longer necessary for men to sit in strip "jernts" to admire female anatomy. Now, world-famous musicians headlined clubs patronized by men in coats and ties and women in formal dresses and white gloves. Art shops, restaurants, and clubs offering nonsexual, if slightly risqué, entertainment flourished.[36] Mercedes still held sway at Pat O'Brien's.[37] The Red Garter offered banjo-strumming "Gay 90s"—as in 1890s—entertainment at 640 Bourbon.[38] It displaced an earlier club of some notoriety, Le Rendevous.[39] Some of the entertainment seemed, like the Quarter itself, charmingly behind the times. The 809 club starred Chris Owens, billed as "Queen of the Cha Cha." It invited patrons to join their "fun-filled conga line."[40] The entertainment, apart from the remaining strip clubs, was firmly pitched to middle-aged, straight tourists, old enough to remember the cha-cha and conga lines. Rock and roll was still too far from the comfortable mainstream to have a Bourbon Street presence. Despite Garrison's attempts at cleanup, the number of Quarter "adult clubs" actually increased from 1960 to 1970.[41]

Authentic New Orleans jazz had been almost, but not quite, displaced from its hometown as jazz became mainstream music, relaxed, homogenized, and mellowed to the point of blandness. Between the overtopping tide of national taste and the color line in music, black New Orleans jazzmen, and their white admirers, were out on the margins by the late fifties and early sixties. In 1961, entrepreneur Larry Borenstein started a small, traditional jazz club at his art gallery at 726 St. Peter. In a few years, it became known as Preservation Hall. The Hall offered many aged, and some very young, musicians a chance to play for tourist donations. Liquor and food were not served, and the accommodations were spartan. Yet the Hall endured, despite sporadic competition, and revived worldwide interest in this quintessential New Orleans art.[42]

Bourbon Street had become the de facto main street of the Quarter, and as it proceeded downriver, the bars and clubs began to fade out. However, at Bourbon and Dumaine, gay life was being lived more openly. On the lower, lakeside corner stood Café Lafitte In Exile—its name remembering its roots in the bar at the other end of the block. Across the street is the Clover Grill, a wee-hours oasis for the drunk, the stoned, and the hungry. In 1961, owner Arthur Jacobs began a Fat Tuesday costume contest at the Clover, open to all. By 1970 it had evolved to a raised stage erected on Bourbon and acquired the name Bourbon Street Awards. It has become an institution each Fat Tuesday where packed throngs admire the most creative costumes seen in the Quarter. Displaced for some years to St. Ann and Burgundy, it moved closer to its roots on Dumaine Street in the early twenty-first century.[43]

## BORDERLANDS BACK IN THE FOLD

In 1946, the city council had exempted certain border areas of the Quarter from control of the Vieux Carré Commission.[44] Most notable were the riverside blocks of North Rampart Street. In nearly twenty years of lassitude, the Rampart Street buildings were severely neglected and some demolished outright.

The Vieux Carré Property Owners and Associates (VCPOA) had been founded by Elizebeth Werlein and her allies in the late thirties as a watchdog of the Vieux Carré Commission, and to address those needs falling outside the VCC's legal purview. The exempting ordinance had been a bone in the throat of VCPOA and other Quarter preservationists for nearly twenty years.

Demolitions, both in the exempted and "protected" areas for hotels and parking lots, roused concern anew in the early 1960s. Demolition, as a commercial expedience, was endangering the very "quaint and distinctive" character that drew the all-important tourist dollar.[45] The Louisiana Sugar and Rice Exchange building at N. Front and Bienville fell outside the protected area. This fine building might have been re-purposed, but in 1963, it, too, was demolished.[46]

In 1964, VCPOA filed suit to have the exempting ordinance invalidated. In addition to VCPOA, three persons who owned property just outside the exempted zones joined as plaintiffs. The City of New Orleans and the VCC were among the defendants. Prominent property owners in the exempted zone joined the defendants as intervenors.

The Louisiana Sugar Exchange, 1963. Courtesy of the Library of Congress, Prints and Photographs Division, Historic American Buildings Survey.

Besides the alarm over loss of historic structures, the individual plaintiffs had a personal complaint. The property in the exempt areas could be legally renovated without following the VCC's standards and procedures. The adjoining property in the VCC-controlled area had to abide by these sometimes costly strictures and thus was at a commercial disadvantage.

The defendants' stance in court revealed a curious reading of the amendment and the enabling ordinances of 1936. They contended that the law authorized, but did not require, the creation of the VCC and its exercise of authority. Therefore, the city could restrict the VCC's span of authority if it so desired.

In July 1964 the Louisiana Supreme Court struck down the exempting ordinance as contradicting the constitutional amendment. A key theme of the decision was that the city and the VCC's duties to the Vieux Carré were not discretionary; they were mandatory.[47] The chief defendant, the VCC, expressed "delight" at having lost. The ruling, of course, could not be retroactive.[48] The damage had been done, and could not be reversed even by supreme fiat. The renewed oversight of the VCC and accelerating pace of tourism would help North Rampart little, if at all. Over time, changing demographics and the installation of Armstrong Park would pull North Rampart into a steady downward spiral.

## THE VIEUX CARRÉ DEMONSTRATION STUDY

In 1965, the city received federal funding, augmented by money from the Bureau of Governmental Research to perform a demonstration study of the Vieux Carré. This study, which took three years and the efforts of several activities, ultimately produced nine volumes of reports.[49] Among the reports were two volumes on the effects of the proposed Riverfront Expressway. That battle was still in progress when the study was published in the autumn of 1968, and is discussed in the transportation chapter of this book.

One volume was an economic and social study, which was the most comprehensive look at these factors for the Quarter yet produced. Among other things, the study noted that property values were rising and low-income people were being forced out. The loss of these people meant less heterogeneity, or, as we would say now, less diversity.[50]

The study observed that property values had taken a sharp increase at the beginning of the 1960s. Most of the price increases were attributed to demand, during World War II, for commercial space and not because properties had been upgraded. Renovation had increased postwar, of course, and housing stock was steadily increasing in value.[51]

The Vieux Carré, and later her cousin, the Faubourg Marigny, experienced a phenomenon now known as "rent gap." That is, the rent being charged for a given unit was less than what could be obtained if the property were matched with better-heeled tenants. For landlords who had owned properties outright for generations and were investing little in maintenance, this gap was not usually important. Without a mortgage, the rent was nearly pure profit.

Outside observers saw the Quarter as undervalued and decided to exploit this rent gap. From 1962 to 1968, the Southern Land Title Corporation bought properties, almost all masonry structures, at prices far above the usual values, certainly an enticement to owners who had been resigned to hanging on to unsold old buildings. Once Southern Land bought a building, its G. Brian Corporation rental arm redivided the space to create more, and smaller, apartments. In 1964, G. Brian was involved with thirty-four buildings in the Quarter.[52] Rents increased, typically about twenty-five dollars per month. This sum was not trivial to a bartender or waiter. The increased prices for buildings and rents tended to raise asking prices and rents across the Quarter, driving out, as the Study observed, some lower-income people.[53] Not everyone was cheering. As part of the study, Tulane sociology students interviewed Quarter residents about positive and negative aspects of Vieux

Carré life. G. Brian Corporation was mentioned as a positive attribute by 4.3 percent of the respondents, but negatively by 11.3 percent.[54]

## THE IRRESISTIBLE BEAT

"Three ingredients are essential for a bohemian community to take root and flourish: creative misfits, magic and cheap rent," wrote James Nolan.[55]

The intellectual ferment of the early 1960s "Beats" had reached the young of New Orleans by way of the universities, the eternal stream of drifters, and locals who had shaken off family expectations to live in that dangerous, run-down, kooky Quarter. The "responsible elements" of society were quick to stereotype the Beats of this period, as witnessed by the character of Maynard G. Krebs, resident "beatnik" on the popular TV show *The Many Loves of Dobie Gillis*. In the media, the beatniks were cast as misfits with berets and ironed hair, who said, "Man!" as all-purpose interjection and spent their days discussing the world's problems over espresso and Gauloise cigarettes, to a background of bongos and meandering poetry.

Something much more profound was happening in the New Orleans scene. In the early 1960s, Louisiana, as was true of the rest of the South, was fighting integration by many means. The old Gay-Shattuck Law[56] was being used not merely to prevent black men from socializing with white women, but to keep any combination of the races apart. Southern authorities were on the lookout for white activists—"outside agitators" who were attempting to register black voters. In several coffeehouses around central New Orleans, blacks, whites, Creoles, gays, and straights mingled to do all those things the media said they were doing, but, most important, to break down the barriers of a multisegregated society. Although registering blacks to vote—a dangerous quest in 1964—was an important coffeehouse subtext, many elements of the Beat milieu were borrowed from black culture, particularly from jazz musicians whose footloose travels, disdain for convention, and fondness for marijuana were eagerly embraced by young whites wanting to "make the scene."[57]

The lineage of one famous coffeehouse is particularly important. In 1962, on the skidding row of North Rampart, where the Landmark Hotel is now, a few friends opened the Ryder Coffee House. In the summer of 1963 the building was sold and demolished,[58] another casualty of the 1946 exempting ordinance.

At that time the Methodist Church was sponsoring a number of coffee-houses in the South.[59] Some of the Ryder's alumni founded a new coffeehouse, the Quorum, which was located in a three-story building at 611 Esplanade, on the downriver side next to a Methodist church at the corner of Esplanade and Chartres.[60]

This meeting place of many cultures was, perhaps, not as political as the surveilling NOPD thought it was. In a time when young people "graduated" to adulthood with caste-driven notions of social order, the Quorum, and other clubs, like the Dream Palace on Frenchman Street, were level fields where very different cultures and experiences could mingle. The never-ending quest for authenticity led many fans of folk music to these clubs where they might dig a performance by renowned Mississippi blues artist Jewell "Babe" Stovall.[61] These clubs were viewed by authorities as dens of Communists, homosexu-als, dope users, and, above all, race mixers who were attempting to register black voters. Undercover agents frequented the clubs, and nonpolice harass-ment was common. On July 29, 1964, police raided the Quorum.[62] "Tuneless strumming of guitars and pointless intellectual conversation" was the pretext to arrest seventy-three patrons on the all-purpose charge of "disturbing the peace."[63] The charges were all eventually dropped, but the police continued to harass the Quorum and similar clubs as the Beat era began to give way to a movement usually called the counterculture.[64]

Lyle Saxon and his friends of the twenties, themselves the original Quar-ter "bohemians," conducted many boozy, smoky salons that were vital to neighborhood revival and intellectual invigoration. They would have been pleased to see this tradition endure in the 1960s. James Nolan remembers one such salon, operated by artist Ivan Kotterman and his lover for about twenty-five years from the midfifties:[65]

They had a monthly discussion group on Friday evenings on Bourbon Street and later on they moved to Royal. This was a place where every-body went on Friday and they usually had a topic, such as, "Does God Exist?", or "Will Integration Work?" It started out fairly rationally, but as people started drinking cheap wine out of greasy glasses, it got more and more animated and usually turned into a big fight. But this was sort of a liminal mixing, melting pot where everybody met and got to know each other; the older people from the WPA in the 1930s to high school kids like myself. It was called the Discussion Group and became known as the Disgusting Group because people got into disgusting fights.

There was a woman named Helen Gladstone who was a vaudevillian from New York, all the theater people, the arts people, the literary scene; all revolved, what I knew of it, in the 60s and early 70s, around Ivan Kotterman's Discussion Group.[66]

## WHO ARE THESE PEOPLE?

Quarter residents had been railing against "rowdy collegiates" and "hell raisers" for over a decade.[67] These "rowdies" were usually considered "good kids" in the conventional sense. Fraternity boys and sorority girls were well represented in this group. They went to the Quarter, and, of course, drank too much; they broke bottles and raised hell. Then they went back to school. In the main, they were as conservative as the parents who paid their tuition.

The hippies[68] who appeared in the mid-1960s were commonly seen as lineal descendants of the Beats, even though that relationship was about as valid as the misbegotten conjunction of "Creole" and "Cajun." Before the majority of Americans questioned the Vietnam War, the hippies' antiwar stance was seen as unpatriotic. The term "hippie" was synonymous, and rightfully so, with drugs. The slovenly clothing—including, ironically, the occasional military jacket—further offended conservatives. Above all, the long hair and beards worn by young hippie men enraged crew-cut keepers of the masculine status quo, who fought the style with school expulsions, street beatings, and trumped-up arrests. In the prevailing double standard, "hippie women" were not as threatening to the established order, since they were not dodging the draft. Many otherwise conservative men found the forbidden fruit of "hippie girls" enticing and considered them sexually exploitable.

The hippies in the Quarter were a combination of college students, runaway local youngsters, and out-of-towners who were now sampling the famously bohemian Quarter. A selection were "trying their wings" before aspiring to San Francisco or New York, the other two poles of the counterculture.[69] Some, aware of the Quarter's literary history, hoped to absorb inspiration. Others wanted a taste of Latin culture without traveling overseas. The hippies brought the drug subculture of the Quarter forward from the shadows, and aside from the colleges, the Vieux Carré became even more known as the place to get dope of various kinds.[70]

Southern authorities, still fighting desegregation, looked defiantly at the televised mayhem in Berkeley and Chicago. They believed their culture would

be "tough enough" to resist any countercultural onslaught. The South's traditions of militarism, patriarchy, and hard-shell religion would surely suffice to
keep hippiedom, and associated "kooky ideas," away from young whites. They
were very, very wrong.

A number of festivals and "happenings" around the country had convinced many young people that all such events should not only be admis-
sion-free, but also catered with food, wine, and drugs gratis.[71] The old slogan
"Mardi Gras—The Greatest Free Show On Earth!" was now being taken all
too literally by young folks who arrived, many penniless, in the Big Easy looking for this famed free show. The 1969 film *Easy Rider* portrayed New Orleans
as amenable to drinking and tripping young people. The hippies thought the
*laissez les bon temps roulez* (let the good times roll) reputation and visible
alternate lifestyles meant tolerance for their kind as well. They were also very,
very wrong.

It was not simply their garb or hairstyles that gave offense. The Quarter
hippies were far more visible than the Beats who clustered in coffeehouses,
usually off the tourist track. Large numbers of young people lolled in Jackson Square,[72] parks, and neutral grounds—any open green space—strummed
guitars, drank jug wine, smoked pot, smashed bottles, and annoyed the residents and older, so-called legitimate tourists alike, especially at Carnival.[73]

Carnival 1970 was early, with Fat Tuesday falling on February 10. The usual
crowds were swelled by larger numbers of young people than ever before, and
the city's well-oiled Mardi Gras machine was strained. An encampment of
cars and sleeping bags sprang up on the lakefront. It was raided by police,
who arrested 88 as a warning to other "loiterers" to stay home.[74] Another
sweep along the riverfront across from Jackson Square netted 103 arrests.[75]
This Carnival seemed to be not just rowdy but more violent than ever before.
The nadir came when trumpeter Al Hirt, riding a float in the Garden District,
was hit in the lip by a flying brick.[76] Although no one was arrested, the attack
was commonly blamed on "hippies" and epitomized a Carnival season that
left tradition keepers and civic leaders aghast.[77] That the hooligans might have
been the "respectable" rowdy collegiates of yore was suggested by the opinion
of observers that the worst part had been over the weekend, with Lundi Gras
and Fat Tuesday relatively quiet, since college students were mostly back in
school on those days.[78]

At least the "rowdy collegiates" of recent memory had arrived with
money and went back to school when Carnival or spring break was over. The
visible hippies were not the paying customers whose shenanigans and vices

were catered to by the tourist milieu and usually indulged by the police.[79] Unlike the "respectable" establishments with their usual array of tourist-dependant, corruption-protected vices, no one was paying the police to tolerate long-haired kids tripping on LSD or passing joints around General Jackson's statue.[80] Businesspeople and the authorities fretted that these very visible drifters might "harm the tourist trade"—a cardinal sin in the city's slim catechism of condemnations. Their arrival at Carnival provoked extra anger, since no one was allowed to tamper with the linchpin of the city's tourist industry and very soul. The normally serene Mayor Schiro was disturbed enough to say, "Unless the public takes some responsibility for controlling this hoodlumism, I am afraid that Mardi Gras will go out of existence."[81]

After the tumult of Carnival 1970, the city's authorities and pundits feared a second "hippie invasion." A group of counterculture leaders and sympathetic establishment figures formed the Mardi Gras Coalition, which discouraged young people from coming to Carnival and attempted to find lodging and emergency services if they chose to arrive.[82]

As in other places, antiwar demonstrations took place in New Orleans. Many of these centered around college campuses where ROTC was a tradition and the induction centers where draftees entered the maw of the military. Like cops in other cities, the NOPD used plainclothesmen, photographic surveillance, and agents provocateurs to harass the demonstrators.[83]

Many of the resident hippies supported themselves by selling *NOLA Express*, a so-called underground paper started in 1969. Ironically, the all-sacred paying tourists were eager buyers of the paper.[84] *NOLA Express* featured antiwar screeds and exposés of local links to the military-industrial complex.[85] It also had images authorities deemed too shocking for Bourbon Street.[86] The vendors who sold *NOLA Express* made fifteen to twenty-five cents a copy.[87] They ate at places like Buster Holmes, Burgundy at Orleans, where a filling meal of red beans and rice cost fifty cents.[88] Many hippies "crashed" at a hostel on Chartres operated by a Baptist minister, "Father" Mike Stark.[89] Stark, in a caftan and with flaming red hair and biblical beard, became the hippies' leading defender in the Quarter. Stark was a buffer between the authorities and the street kids. His Abba Foundation arranged for members of his flock to do odd jobs[90] and his hostel was a safe place for youngsters to clean up and sleep.[91]

If he was present, he would take down names of hippies being arrested—frequently for "refusal to move on"[92]—and badge numbers of the officers, essential to get the kids released quickly from jail.[93] In late 1969, Stark and volunteers from the community started the Health Emergency Aid Dispensary

(HEAD) at 1117 Decatur. Hippies needing health care encountered contempt at Charity Hospital, the city's free resource for the indigent. HEAD's volunteer physicians treated hippies suffering from ailments as mundane as sore throats and as exotic as bad acid trips.[94] It also attempted to match hippies with jobs and other supporting resources.[95]

The authorities decided to break up this support system. In the summer of 1969, they began arresting vendors of *NOLA Express* on a variety of charges. In December of that year, *NOLA Express* won an injunction forbidding the arrest of the vendors.

Frustrated by local jurisprudence, the authorities turned to the federal courts. In early January 1970, the publishers of *NOLA Express*, Robert Head and Darlene Fife, were arrested for sending obscene material through the mail. The charges were thrown out that September. The police were not about to let two courts stand in their way, and the arrests of the vendors continued. Another round in court confirmed the original injunction against the arrests.[96]

In February 1971, HEAD was raided by five agencies led by the NOPD. The authorities ransacked the clinic and living quarters. The pretext was unauthorized treatment of juveniles for VD, which, in fact, was not illegal. The director of the city health department had no objection to this practice and had actively assisted HEAD. Stark, as director of HEAD,[97] was arrested. After an outcry that included many "solid citizens" supportive of Stark's mission, the charges were dismissed.[98] Not all hippies simply drifted around the Quarter. Several, following a venerable tradition that Saxon's set would have applauded, sold arts and crafts. A month before the HEAD raid, Stark's Abba Foundation launched the Community Flea Market in the out-of-season melon sheds of the French Market. All one hundred booth spaces were filled by "freaks" selling handmade goods, middle-aged ladies selling antiques, and some dealers of "plain old-fashioned junk." Mayor Moon Landrieu showed up and praised the market.[99] This was the beginning of the "flea market" end of the French Market, which in time would come to fill the majority of the open halls once occupied by grocers, butchers, and fishmongers. The Community Flea Market created an important bridge between the "hippie" and "straight" communities. The crafts contributed to the *tout ensemble* and showed the establishment that "freaks" could work for a living. Hippies who had jobs in Quarter establishments were generally tolerated by the authorities.[100] The goodwill the market fostered may have contributed to the widespread anger over the HEAD raid a month later.

Just across from the flea market was the Jerusalem Gardens, a health food restaurant with guitars and poetry readings;[101] it was an early touchstone of the hippies, similar in some ways to the Quorum.

Besides the hippies who panhandled, members of various religious groups, notably the Hare Krishnas and the Black Muslims, also worked the streets, selling religious papers and paraphernalia. Some solicitors for real estate also prowled the banquettes. The aggressiveness shown by beggars and sellers angered Vieux Carré residents, and the city council moved to action.[102] The numbers of panhandlers and solicitors gradually dwindled, especially after the ordinances applying to them were enforced. The visible hippie population seems to have peaked around 1970, which was also the peak year for *NOLA Express* vendor arrests.[103] The reputation of New Orleans as a perpetual party, even for those without money, began to slowly fade. The NOPD had a long-standing reputation for lack of gentleness towards those who got uppity with barkeepers, "landladies," and hookers. It was then a largely white force informed by lingering segregation, homophobia, and contempt for hippies. In January of 1970, the NOPD orchestrated a well-publicized bust of the Grateful Dead at the Royal Sonesta, 300 Bourbon.[104] As the 1970s progressed, word got around that the line between freewheeling fun and police brutality and jail for young people was very thin in New Orleans. Roundups of hippie-appearing young people at Carnival continued into the seventies, with beatings of male hippies common.[105] Louisiana had a reciprocal agreement with forty-two other states—a compact—that minor misdemeanors would be awarded a summons, and then the accused could go their merry way. Residents of the seven noncompact states—which included California—were usually strip-searched and thrown in central lockup if they could not make bond. An ordinance fixing this faux pas was passed in the mid-1990s,[106] but the practice persisted for years.[107] This image—correct to a large degree—of civic hostility to young drifters surely kept many away, which was part of the city's strategy.

The decade 1960–1970 witnessed the greatest drop in the Quarter's population, a loss of about twenty-four hundred former residents to a new low of about fifty-two hundred occupants.[108] The sixties saw some marked social changes in what had been an enclave slow to alter its ways. The seventies would see some of the most profound social and physical changes the Quarter had yet experienced in the twentieth century.

## CHAPTER 6

# INTERLUDE

*"Goin' Down by My Mama's": Transportation and the Quarter*

## PERAMBULATING THE BANQUETTES

The Vieux Carré was originally laid out for pedestrians, horses, and horse-drawn wagons. A few hitching posts may still be seen, bent from many collisions with automobiles. The compact size—about a mile from one end to the other—makes the enclave eminently walkable. The Quarter is one of the last urban areas that may be walked through for sheer pleasure. In the aquarium of the long summer, air-conditioned bars and restaurants offer many waypoints to cool off and refortify. Friends are met on the banquettes, and journeys may be sidetracked.

Today it is still possible, on foot, to obtain nearly every necessity of life within the compass of the Quarter. Shopping there is still a fulfilling experience. One can buy antiques, clothing, books, hardware, pet supplies, food, and drink. Corner groceries, like Matassa's at St. Philip and Dauphine, keep faith with generations of customers. Beauty salons remain important centers of neighborhood life. The attraction of national chain stores, with their generic products and lower prices, is often overbalanced by the inconvenience of unparking the car, driving for miles, reparking—perhaps in a less favorable spot—and trudging home with armloads of merchandise. The Internet can provide whatever cannot be had within the Vieux Carré.

## Quarter Street Car Lines - 1900-1949

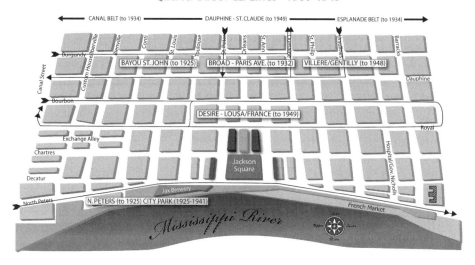

## THE STREETCARS

In the days when the Vieux Carré was also a bedroom community for work-ers at plants downriver, or in Carrollton, streetcars were essential. Relatively few folks could afford to stable horses or mules, the latter being more accli-mated to Louisiana summers. Equine-drawn omnibuses appeared early in the nineteenth century, and soon thereafter urban railroads linked the vari-ous settlements now absorbed into greater New Orleans.[1] Beginning in 1893, the system was gradually electrified.[2]

By 1922 the city boasted 225 miles of streetcar lines.[3] The Quarter alone was served by at least four lines in the twentieth century. The famous Desire line, named not for the emotion but for its destination street downriver, allowed passengers to shop on Canal Street, ride down Bourbon, loop out into Bywater, and return on Royal Street. The Desire line was just over seven miles long.[4] The City Park line offered transit along the "front stoop" of Decatur Street, and the Canal Belt line took weary shoppers from Canal down North Rampart to points downriver. Many lines connected to Canal, the retail spine of New Orleans from the 1850s through the 1970s.[5]

After the zenith of the mid-1920s, streetcar routes gradually declined. Several commercial enterprises were consolidated into New Orleans Public Service Incorporated (NOPSI) in 1922. Although this simplified the overall management of the public transit system, it created one private company with large exposure to economic vicissitudes. NOPSI simply could not afford to maintain the tracks and overhead wires of every route, so a gradual conversion to buses began.[6] The private automobile and taxi began to be more desirable than sitting or standing with a carload of jostling, sweaty strangers. As the 1930s arrived, the city's finances were in an awful condition, so municipalization of transit was out of the question.

The Desire streetcar line, for all its fame, served only from 1920 to 1948, when it was converted to buses.[7] Somehow, *A Bus Named Desire* simply does not have the same cachet. After the conversion of the Desire line, streetcar service within the Quarter ended. The Canal line held on until it too converted to buses in 1964.[8] Despite the romance of the streetcar, modern buses have a crucial advantage; they are air-conditioned—essential in the subtropical heat that dominates nine months of the New Orleans year. New Orleans retained its unair-conditioned St. Charles streetcar line, but it was considered a quaint anachronism in the Jet Age.

## Monorail a Mano

One of many wild geese eternally chased by various New Orleans mayors is a monorail, which was first conceived in the midfifties to connect the airport with downtown. The downtown portion of the route would have been placed in the neutral ground of Canal Street. True to form, Mayor Morrison invested his personal prestige in the gambit. Part of the considerable opposition came from preservationists who feared damage to the character of the Vieux Carré. A city council vote killed the idea in 1959.[9] Bill Rushton, editor of the *Vieux Carré Courier*, floated the notion of a city-wide arterial monorail in 1970. Although well thought out, it seems to have resonated only with him.[10] A very short monorail operated at the World's Fair of 1984, but it was merely an amusement ride and not a prototype of a viable urban system. Various monorail proposals were considered in the 1990s. The most comprehensive mass transit proposal, floated in 2000, was for an airport-to-downtown light rail connection; it was hooted down by skeptics who saw it, as with the earlier plan, as a tourist-only service.[11]

Yet another transit tussle loomed—one that would transform the American notion of municipal projects and their relationship to preservation, forever.

## THE EXPRESSWAY BATTLE

City parks commissioner and construction coordinator Robert Moses transformed New York City from the 1930s through the late 1960s. He bridged
waterways, built parks, pushed freeways through neighborhoods, and was
considered the pontiff of the highway lobby.[12] His power exceeded that of
most mayors he nominally served.[13]

In 1946, Moses authored an "Arterial Plan for New Orleans."[14] Mayor
Morrison's new administration had other priorities, and the proposal lay
fallow until the mid-1950s.[15] The downtown businesses realized they were
losing customers to the expanding suburbs. Auto traffic on Canal, Decatur,
and other arteries worsened. The interstate highway system would put I-10
through New Orleans, part of the ribbon of road linking Jacksonville with
Los Angeles. Downtown had no desire to be bypassed and left to wither. The
Moses plan was revived and, in 1957, a coalition of pro-freeway interests gelled
into the Central Area Committee (CAC)—a quasi-governmental cabal.[16]

I-10 was planned to cut through the center of the city.[17] It also had to
connect with the West Bank via the almost-completed Greater New Orleans
(GNO) bridge. It seemed logical that the downtown area would need a loop,[18]
connecting the I-10/GNO segment with the Pontchartrain Expressway, leading to the causeway over the lake. An elevated expressway would cut south
from I-10, fly above the neutral ground of Elysian Fields, run along the river in
front of the entire Quarter, dive under the foot of Canal in a tunnel, and connect with the Pontchartrain Expressway. This Riverfront Expressway would
be elevated about forty feet above grade, across from Decatur Street.[19] The
CAC maintained this connection would relieve arterial traffic and, simultaneously, allow shoppers easier access to the downtown shopping district. How
these two goals could be achieved at the same time was never explained.[20]
Of course, expressways also make it easier for downtown workers to nest in
suburbs, accelerating inner-city residential decay.[21]

The establishment of New Orleans, their allies in Baton Rouge and the
national highway lobby, were not used to being challenged. In New Orleans,
nearly—but not all—the city's power structure fervently wanted the expressway and the other connecting portions. The *Times-Picayune* permitted no
expressway dissent in either editorial or news coverage to be printed.[22]

In 1965, two young law students, William Borah and Richard Baumbach,
were having a drink at the Napoleon House, Chartres at St. Louis, an intelligentsia hangout for decades.[23] Both were scions of prominent local families

and were following a well-paved road of privilege and future position. Young New Orleanians, particularly of this class, were expected to defer to the judgement of elders. If, during college, they wanted to pretend to be Quarter bohemians, drink, and carouse, well, that was okay. Upon graduation they were expected to live the uptown life of interlocking conservative institutions—marriage, church, business, club, and krewe.

At the Napoleon House they heard serious concerns about the project's impact on the Vieux Carré. They went to the chamber of commerce and began researching the expressway proposal. It became obvious that alternative routes were not being considered. Also obvious was the dismissal the pro-expressway cabal poured on their concerns.[24]

Borah and Baumbach founded Help Establish Logical Planning (HELP), a nonprofit, to bring some open discussion to the process. By Carnival season of 1966, a report detailing the fixation on the Vieux Carré location, lack of traffic studies, and lack of considered alternatives was ready. It was published in the *Vieux Carré Courier* by Borah and Baumbach's ally, Bill Long, in February 1966.[25] The report needed citywide exposure; in March, HELP purchased full-page ads to reprint the report in the *Times-Picayune*[26] and the *States-Item*. In bold letters, it cried, "STOP! The Elevated Riverfront Expressway" with a rendering of how it would look from Jackson Square. When expressway proponents saw it in the early edition, they tried to intervene to stop the presses, but it was too late; the word went out.[27] It showed that every expressway plan had moved in lockstep with Moses's 1946 plan and that alternative routes, or configurations of roadways, were never considered. Other viewpoints, such as a study by Tulane in late 1965 recommending a west bank expressway, were not heeded.[28]

The report, now published in the two dailies, electrified friend and foe alike. From the vantage of forty subsequent years, Bill Borah remembers: "It went out, and I can remember the thrill of seeing that report. At that time New Orleans had never seen anything like that. That was before . . . you know, now there are all kinds of full-page various issues. At that time that just wasn't done, so it had a terrific effect. It really did. We always saw it like the flare that you send out before you invade."[29]

Baumbach and Borah were not alone. The report crystallized the concerns of many prominent preservationists; even the archbishop of New Orleans was properly horrified at the thought of an expressway so close to St. Louis Cathedral. The mantle of clubwoman defender of the Vieux Carré was now draped on the redoubtable Martha Gilmore Robinson, president of the Louisiana

Landmarks Society. Her anti-expressway sentiments were published in many out-of-town media outlets, and spawned supportive articles by others in leading news magazines and the *Washington Post*.[30] The most influential local ally was Edgar Stern, Jr. The Sterns were the owners of WDSU, Channel 4, headquartered at that time on Royal Street in the Quarter. They also operated a foundation that financed research into progressive social issues.[31]

As the details of the Riverfront Expressway came out, preservationist opposition mounted.[32] Moses-style freeways had cut off and marginalized neighborhoods across the country.[33] The destruction of the famous oaks and neighborhood disruption along New Orleans's Claiborne Avenue for I-10 in 1966 was bad enough.[34] A concrete monster and its brood of vehicles at the doorstep of the city's most sacred space was intolerable.

From the perspective of the soaring midsixties, the expressway lobby had its points. The Vieux Carré is the city's keystone, next to the Canal Street and Central Business District (CBD) areas. Trying to connect I-10 with Canal Street was a thorny problem. The Quarter had to be bypassed in some way, yet I-10 had to connect with downtown. As of early 1969, traffic in the city was growing by 6 percent per year.[35] The congestion on Canal, Decatur, Esplanade and Rampart was indeed bad. The coveted suburban shopper had to be lured back downtown, where she could shop, put her packages in her car, and whisk back to Metairie, Slidell, or Harahan. The floodwall blocked the view of the river from the Place d'Armes anyway and an elevated expressway would not change that.[36] Diverting traffic from Decatur and North Rampart would, it was thought, spare the Vieux Carré's buildings from traffic vibration, noise, and fumes.

In 1968, the Bureau of Governmental Research published the Vieux Carré Historic District Demonstration Study, which included two volumes on the effects of the proposed expressway. The summary concluded that the elevated expressway would have economic befit to the Quarter but cautioned that it "will create a visual and physical intrusion strongly alien to the traditional scale and character of the Vieux Carré. By planning the expressway as integral part of the entire Riverfront Area's redevelopment, the adverse expressway effects can be moderated, but they cannot be wholly eliminated."[37]

However, even a "high-speed" expressway would encourage through-town traffic to take that route just to rubberneck down at the Quarter. The demonstration study showed that the attendant noise and light pollution, from Café Du Monde to the Upper Pontalba, would be irritating.[38] Along with the aesthetic agony of an expressway opposite St. Louis Cathedral,[39] and the proposed destruction of lower Elysian Fields, the defenders of the Quarter pointed out the contradictions in the CAC's goals. In order to shop, drivers had to use the arterial streets at some time, and increasing Canal Street business meant increasing traffic—which was already bad. An expressway might relieve some congestion from traffic transiting the Quarter to Canal Street, but would do nothing about cars of tourists and residents cruising the Quarter looking for the oft-illusive legal parking spot.

What of alternatives? By the late 1950s, interstate passenger railroads were faltering. Moses and his allies had starved New York City's subways and commuter railroads while building conduits for automobiles.[40] The concept of urban light rail running on old freight right-of-ways was some years off. In the Quarter's case, the three through tracks at the riverfront were then still in use for freight.[41] In 1964, the Canal streetcar was taken out of service and replaced by buses. It would be forty years downstream before streetcars would return to Canal Street.[42] To pro-expressway forces, buses were for poor people, and the needs of the private automobile were paramount. Reinstating the extensive prewar web of streetcar tracks on thoroughfares was unthinkable. The high water table ruled out subways. There was the persistent rural suspicion, not unique to Louisiana, of mass transit being a disease of big cities and faintly socialistic. Legislators from rural districts could be champions of the highway lobby to the detriment of mass transit.[43] The monorail, as envisioned in 1958, would have been a shuttle for tourists between the airport and Canal Street, and would have had little impact on local commuters. Rushton's 1970 monorail proposal was similar to the arterial route plan of the then-embryonic Washington, D.C., Metro subway. However, a counterculture newspaper, which had leveled broadsides against the expressway, was not the right agitator for such a project. From examination of the evidence, it seems that mass transit was an afterthought, to all parties, in the debate and its conclusion.[44]

The preservationists found influential friends outside New Orleans.[45] Allies, and advice, were found in San Francisco, where, in 1959, preservationists had successfully halted the Embarcadero Freeway in midconstruction. In 1966, HELP hosted a forum at which the San Franciscans shared lessons learned with the Vieux Carré's defenders.[46] Many noteworthy architects and urban scholars had grown to loathe Moses and his works.[47] Most prominent of these was *New Yorker* architectural critic Lewis Mumford.[48] These critics helped the Vieux Carré defenders lobby in Washington. On December 21, 1965, Secretary of the Interior Stewart Udall declared the French Quarter to be of national historic significance, making it eligible to be a National Historic Landmark.⁴⁹ The New Orleans City Council might once have been delighted. Now, the council feared the designation would enable anti-expressway forces to perform an end run around Louisiana politics and, in a symbolic gesture, tabled acceptance.⁵⁰

The Quarter's defenders also found an unlikely, and probably unintentional, local ally. Victor Schiro had succeeded Chep Morrison as mayor in mid-1961⁵¹ when Chep departed for a presidential appointment. After the statehouse-frustrated and testy Morrison, "Vic" Schiro seemed a return to a more genial age of mayoralty. Chep, with his taste for monumentalism, would have made the expressway a matter of personal pride. Schiro wanted to appease both factions. He proposed various permutations of the expressway, such as a depressed surface roadway, or an elevated structure of only four lanes, or perhaps a riverfront tunnel.⁵² Although expressway proponents fumed, Schiro's dithering bought time for opposition to gather momentum.⁵³

The deciding voice was equally unlikely. The conservative presidency of Richard Nixon might have been expected to rubber-stamp the expressway to appease its powerful backers. However, the Nixon administration realized that uncontrolled highway development was taking a human and esthetic toll.⁵⁴ After hearing out both sides in June 1969, Assistant Secretary for Transportation for Urban Systems and Environment James D. Braman recommended to Secretary of Transportation John Volpe that the project should be cancelled. Volpe did that in a formal announcement on July 9, 1969.⁵⁵

Expressway opponents felt vindicated—the proud, self-assured windmill had fallen. Proponents reacted with incredulous anger, slow to cool. Baumbach and Borah felt a "coldness" and "isolation" from their uptown community.⁵⁶ Lou Brown had been the executive director of the CAC during the fight, and three years after the cancellation, he was still steaming in full patriarchal mode: "These kids are just demented. It's just a shame as far as their families are concerned. The irresponsibility of these kids has created such great damage to the city of New Orleans and its future . . ."⁵⁷ "These kids" were thirty-two years old when the expressway was defeated.

Eventually, I-10 was connected to North Rampart Street via the Orleans Avenue exit, which follows a dogleg route down the old Basin Street line to empty into Orleans Avenue, and permits turns onto North Rampart.

If the expressway controversy reads like an academic quarrel far in the past, bear these things in mind. Imagine boom cars shrieking obscenities to wedding parties at St. Louis Cathedral. Think of a jammed expressway full of steaming, honking cars in the summer heat. Consider holding a conversation at Café Du Monde over the constant roar of traffic. Visualize the chaos and danger of a serious fire or toxic spill in front of the square. And, finally, calculate the cost of tearing down the expressway and rerouting the road, not to mention the incalculable human and cultural displacement that might never be undone.

## STREETCARS REDUX

Elsewhere, we see how the World's Fair of 1984 affected the Vieux Carré, in both structure and street life. When the fair opened, the CSX railroad decided to abandon the freight car tracks at the riverfront. After the fair's closure on November 11, 1984, the Riverfront Transit Coalition hosted a Riverfront Awareness Conference. With the sponsorship of Congresswoman Lindy Boggs, federal money was found for a riverfront streetcar to run on the former CSX tracks. The 1988 Republican convention, held in New Orleans, gave the project an added boost as the city bureaucracy scrambled to paint the municipal face. In August 1988, just before the convention opened, the Riverfront streetcar came to life. Initially a tourist ride, with a beautiful view of Jackson Square along the way, the Riverfront line was integrated with the Canal streetcar when it returned in 2004.[58] The return of the Canal streetcar in 2004,[59] like the French Opera House two generations before, had become an idée fixe not merely among preservationists, but among a newer group of Madame Vieux Carré's lovers, whom we will call the revivalists. The revivalists are not content with simply maintaining the architectural catechism of the Quarter and preventing travesties like the expressway. Among other things, they seek to restore some of the village-like character the Quarter exhibited in its residential heyday of the twenties through the eighties.

The decline of Canal Street was, of course, not caused by the end of the streetcar, nor by the cancellation of the Riverfront Expressway. The shift of population and shopping to the suburbs was well under way in the 1950s. The ugly racial strife marking integration in 1960 triggered, as in other cities, a flight of whites to outlying towns like Metairie, Harahan, Kenner, and Slidell. Suburban whites wanted to shop the strip malls near their homes. Well-to-do white women no longer brought their daughters in rites of passage to D. H. Holmes or Maison Blanche. These and other famous anchor department stores of Canal Street faltered. The bust of the New Orleans oil industry in the 1980s drained many white-collar jobs from downtown office buildings. In the eighties and nineties nearly all the old-line businesses of Canal Street closed. In their place arrived fast food restaurants, discount clothing stores, and yet more T-shirt shops. The only exception was Canal Place, which tried to return high-end shopping to a down-market area.

The revivalists could not reverse white flight or the fortunes of the oil industry. They hope, with a vision that is still in validation, that regular air-conditioned mass transit, along the former city spine from the cemetery and City Park, to the Quarter and the Riverfront line, might trigger a renewal, as has been true in other beleaguered neighborhoods newly served by mass transit, like the U Street corridor in the District of Columbia.[60]

## COMMITTING THE SIN OF DRIVING

An enclave of narrow streets designed for pedestrian and animal traffic cannot be made car friendly. Since the first automobiles, locals and tourists alike have bemoaned the difficulty of piloting cars through the Vieux Carré. Off-street parking is prized above many other amenities, and every part-time condo resident expects a convenient, secure place to park—preferably for free as is true in the suburbs. Tourists arriving by car expect the same and are often unhappy about fees charged by parking lots and garages. Long-time residents become territorial about parking as well, feeling they should not have to compete with part-timers, tourists, and commercial vehicles.

Adding difficulty to the "sport" are tourists who tank themselves up at a watering hole and then believe it's "OK" to drive drunk in the Quarter, since drunken walking is nominally all right. Mule-drawn, plodding tourist buggies confound those who want to zip on through.

The portions of Chartres, St. Peter, and St. Ann streets framing Jackson Square became a permanent pedestrian mall in 1975.[61] This made the square safer and helped discourage cross-Quarter traffic. Portions of Bourbon and Royal become pedestrian malls in evening and weekend hours, making it possible for street performers to ply their trade in the middle of the tourist swarm.

In the 1970s, increased tourist development of the Quarter, particularly on Decatur, meant that residents had a hard time finding parking in the Quarter, let alone near their residences. The Vieux Carré instituted a residential parking program in 1983.[62] The residential stickers allow the bearer to park in the designated district without limit, save only those days of street cleaning and Carnival. Obviously, there are far fewer parking spots than permits, so the sticker is really just a lottery ticket in the parking game. Others must park for no longer than two hours from 7:00 p.m. to 7:00 a.m. Parking regulations have been fine-tuned from time to time[63] but in general have been overwhelmed by increased traffic. Although the residential stickers helped Quarter residents, other New Orleanians felt penalized by the relentless meter maids. Some city residents were ticket scofflaws; however, unpaid tickets could come back to haunt them. Out-of-towners routinely ignore parking tickets, especially if not parked in a towing zone in the upper Quarter. The number of unpaid Quarter parking tickets probably rivals the number of stars in the sky.

A saving grace is that New Orleans, and especially the Quarter, is taxicab heaven. It surprises residents of other cities to find that most New Orleans cabbies are interested in trips other than airport-hotel runs, know the city well, are relatively prompt, and actually speak English. In the Quarter, apart from Carnival and other festivals, a taxi can appear within ninety seconds of a call.

With the benefit of forty years' hindsight, we know that the Canal shopping district would have withered, Riverfront Expressway or no, from changing demographics and the invasion of national chain stores in the suburbs. The overall growth anticipated in the demonstration study simply did not happen as New Orleans's manufacturing dried up and its retail sector went steadily down-market. Whatever gains in ease of Quarter parking were had from declining population have been erased by the massive SUVs of condo residents and visitors. A Stalinist monstrosity was prevented from afflicting the Quarter; however, traffic management initiatives have been a handful of individual items like limiting tour bus size,[64] and the residential parking program. In 1974, minibuses were introduced to the Quarter, connecting with other bus lines on the perimeter. This primarily helped residents get from Canal down to Esplanade and removed full-sized buses from the interior of the Quarter. The minibuses were given a trolley-like appearance to harmonize with the *tout ensemble*.[65] However, all these efforts, good in themselves, have never been integrated into a coherent effort to minimize auto traffic in the Vieux Carré.[66]

In 1999, a brave couple founded Turtle Taxi, offering pedicab service along Canal Street and Convention Center Boulevard.[67] Pedicabs are used in many other historic districts, and it seemed they would also be a logical fit with the Quarter's narrow streets and leisurely traffic. Turtle Taxi's owners operated for a year without any license from the city, for, in fact the city had no license to give. The existing ordinances had no provisions for a service like theirs. Claiming that the issue was being researched, the city commissioned a California firm to study the problem. Turtle Taxi's owners soon got a hard lesson in the politics of New Orleans patronage. They alleged that, in return for a favorable ordinance, they would be required to give a 35 percent owner-ship share to a partner that would be picked for them.[68] The taxi companies and tour buggy operators took vocal umbrage at this tiny amount of compe-tition. Despite Turtle Taxi's clean safety record, the city-commissioned study showed the pedicabs having a "negative impact" on traffic. In August 2000, Mayor Morial dropped his support for permitting the service, and the busi-ness was effectively killed.[69] Turtle Taxi filed suit against the city claiming vio-lation of due process; they had, in fact, applied for permits that the city never formulated. While the case was in motion, the city council again floated the idea, and other parties showed some interest. Councilmen Troy Carter, who represented the Quarter as part of District C, and Councilman Scott Shea, chairman of the Ground Transportation Committee, however, were still dead set against allowing them in their most logical venue, the Quarter itself.[70] After the jury deadlocked, Turtle Taxi pondered taking the case to federal court. However, financial and emotional exhaustion took a toll, and they left town rather than fight city hall any longer. Other parties were interested in the idea, but, after a few more rounds of vacillation in the city council, the idea was shelved.[71]

Other cities have implemented perimeter parking with shuttles to carry residents and tourists alike into historic areas. It has been discussed for decades in New Orleans.[72] That approach is problematic for the Vieux Carré. To the upriver side, Canal Street businesses form a solid, if not commercially healthy, wall of structures. Towards the lake, Armstrong Park, St. Louis Cem-etery, and the Iberville housing project claim the landscape. Even as misbe-gotten and unwanted as Armstrong Park is, the notion of turning an urban park/greenspace into a car park and shuttle depot is probably a nonstarter. Downriver is the increasingly valuable housing of the Faubourg Marigny and the Frenchman Street entertainment strip. Towards the river, some parking has been created near Jax Brewery, but there is little, if any, room for expan-sion at the front stoop of the Quarter. A possible solution is to do on Canal Street what has been done in the Quarter, much to the anger of strict pres-ervationists. The old Solari's gourmet delicatessen, at Canal and Royal, with its famous dining room, was demolished in 1961 and converted to an artfully camouflaged parking garage.[73] Gutting an existing multistory building and installing a parking garage while keeping the historic façade would ease traffic pressure on the narrow streets. For tourists, especially overfed twenty-first-century Americans, strolling down Bourbon or Royal from Canal would be good exercise as well, so shuttle service might not even be needed. Other waterfront cities, like Shreveport and Baltimore, have water taxis that take tourists from venue to venue. Although the New Orleans riverfront is still a busy commercial waterway, perhaps water taxis could take some of the load off the streets and parking lots.

The demise of the Riverfront Expressway was not the end of the monumental project in New Orleans. The Superdome, whose mushroom-like form can be glimpsed far away by eager arrivals and reluctant departers on planes, remains a signature shape in New Orleans. It, too, was born of controversy, but must be judged a success by Crescent City standards. The much-needed second river bridge, named the Crescent City Connection, opened in 1988.[74]

Old-fashioned, uncritical boosterism was slain not merely by the anti-expressway preservationists. The oil bonanza of the 1970s was not invested in infrastructure; when the oil money ran out, the chance to upgrade ports, schools, and roads was lost. The black population majority—albeit an economic minority—took control of the city administration in 1978. This meant that poor neighborhoods, like Tremé, would no longer get remodeled without lengthy public input and negotiation. With the poor majority now clearly in focus, resources were diffused among many smaller projects, some sincere and some riddled with graft.

## CHAPTER 7

# 1971–1978

*Moon Rise*

## INTO THE SEVENTIES

The 1970s would be a time of tremendous change in the Vieux Carré and in New Orleans. The first half of the decade saw the beginning of a fundamental change in the character of Decatur Street, the reworking of Jackson Square, and the renovation of the French Market. The second half of the decade would see the ascendency of black political power and the beginning of the end of Louisiana's oil boom.

## THE OIL TIDES

Post-Reconstruction Louisiana had been a poor state until the discoveries, beginning in the 1920s, of major oil and natural gas fields. Those on land were joined, after 1947, by wells ranging far out into the Gulf of Mexico.[1] The income from the oil and gas industry was not only a godsend to a mainly agricultural state, but also financed political mischief deluxe. Oil could not be pumped out of the ground without payment of a federal excise tax. Oil that was pumped off the books to evade the tax was called "hot oil." In 1939, Richard Leche, who had just resigned the governorship for "health reasons," and some of his cronies were indicted for "hot oil."[2]

The rising tide of oil lifted many boats. Poor young men having few opportunities beyond high school—if they graduated at all—could now work the rigs, boats, and shipyards for wages their fathers never knew. Like the "Kaintock" flatboat men 150 years before, the oil patch boys would land from two weeks offshore with powerful thirsts and oozing testosterone. Barrooms, honky-tonks, and prostitution increased all across south Louisiana to accommodate them. The industry was—and is—a dangerous place to work, and injury and death stalked the rigs. A man getting seriously injured would usually—but not always—get a "settlement," which, after doctors' bills and the lawyer's cut, made him temporarily flush, financing mobile homes, pickup trucks, and rounds of drinks. The settlement industry became a significant part of the region's legal and medical business, with merchants eagerly awaiting the spoils.

Young Louisianans with access to college could look to the industry for jobs as engineers, chemists, and accountants. They might now have a middle-class life in their home state, not be forced to move to Houston, Atlanta, or some other strange clime where beads never rained from balconies. Until 1981, one hundred thousand Louisiana jobs depended on oil.[3]

Like other industries, oil has its cycles. The oil embargo of 1973 increased the demand for domestic production. OPEC-imposed production caps kept prices high and encouraged domestic exploration.[4] In 1973, Governor Edwin Edwards tied the severance taxes paid to the state to the price of oil, not simply to volume as had been the case. Within two years, the state's severance revenue had doubled.[5] From 1973 until about 1982, Louisiana's oil production boomed. Oil money flowed into New Orleans, where many oil companies had headquarters or large offices. Soaring new office buildings sprang up in the once-drowsy Central Business District (CBD).[6] At night, their lighted shafts looked down proudly on the old buildings of the Quarter, whose black silhouettes looked like shadows from a fairy tale. In those days a blue-collar oil industry worker could rent an apartment in the Vieux Carré for his time onshore, rarely having to leave the Quarter during his days off. White-collar workers in the CBD found the Quarter a soothing place to call home after a frantic day in a skyscraper on Poydras Street. Young renters, in a contemporary echo of Mary Morrison, described their low-rent digs as "funky." The decade 1970–1980 saw a slight uptick in the Quarter's population, perhaps because of the oil industry nearby in the CBD. The enclave registered a gain of about 360 souls to finish the decade with about 5,600 inhabitants.[7]

## FOREVER WAS NOT LONG ENOUGH

In 1970, Maurice "Moon" Landrieu became mayor, succeeding Victor Schiro. Landrieu had been one of the most liberal legislators in the Louisiana legislature and also had, as a city councilman, succeeded in passing an ordinance banning racial or religious segregation in public accommodations.[8] Unlike Schiro, who seems to have been in denial about the needs of black New Orleans,[9] Moon realized that black political power was emerging and consciously took steps to mentor men who would be in its first wave.

The economic boomlet caused by the NASA work at Michoud had tapered off dramatically by 1969 as the Saturn V moon rocket program neared its end.[10] Although the leadership of New Orleans glibly talked about new growth, it seems that they were uninterested in nonpetrochemical manufacturing. The notion of luring heavy industry with its large, living-wage base appears to have died with Chep Morrison. Many large companies were locating plants in the Old Confederacy to escape union wages and crumbling rust belt infrastructure. New Orleans's port and freedom from northern winter might have made it a candidate for such plants, but after World War II, the city rarely made the cut. Most companies considering facilities in Louisiana were scared off by governmental corruption, whose demands for bribes formed an invisible but heavy tax on business.[11] The declining Orleans Parish schools and the perceived requirement for workers to live in suburbs and commute was also off-putting. As the *Times-Picayune* opined on January 25, 1975: "It has been noted, as much in sadness as in comfort, that recession does not hit New Orleans as hard it hits some other cities because we do not have many large manufacturing plants with large skilled work forces."[12]

Aside from oil, New Orleans, as the seventies dawned, pinned its hopes on federally funded jobs, such as those sorely missed as the Saturn V program ramped down. These aerospace and defense-related businesses were brought in by congressional influence and had relatively high-wage jobs. Unfortunately, most of these jobs required skills and education rare in New Orleans, so few natives had a shot at the positions, most of which were filled by workers transferred from other states.[13] The funding for these jobs existed at the whims of congressional cloakroom politics, and every contract has an ending date. Whereas other aerospace and defense centers, like Seattle and Washington, D.C., had multiple employers to absorb any layoffs, New Orleans had very little depth in such firms. Even if transferring workers were delighted to experience New Orleans life, they had understandable anxiety about getting stuck with unsaleable property should their jobs end. Therefore, numerous workers chose to rent, and many apartments were built in New Orleans East to accommodate them. Many of these complexes, especially along Read and Bullard avenues, were built on the cheap, and looked shabby after just a few years. Slidell, which had been an obscure satellite of New Orleans before, now became a major bedroom community. It housed not only workers from Michoud and New Orleans East, but also employees of the NASA facility in Hancock County, Mississippi, just across the Pearl River from Slidell's St. Tammany Parish. Even as the Apollo program wound down, other federal agencies, such as the National Oceanic and Atmospheric Administration (NOAA) and the Naval Oceanographic Command (NAVOCEANO), moved onto the NASA reservation, which takes up about one-third of Hancock County.[14] Not a few workers "bounced" between the Avondale shipyard west of New Orleans and the Ingalls shipyard in Pascagoula, Mississippi, as jobs ebbed and flowed at each.

As the 1960s became the 1970s, many factors mitigated against large-scale progressive activism in the city. There was the well-grounded belief that the big decisions were made by older white men behind the doors of the Boston, Pickwick, and Louisiana clubs, within the dens of the old-line Carnival krewes, and by Carlos Marcello, mafia boss of Louisiana.[15]

In 1971, Tulane political scientist Charles Chai published his landmark study, "Who Rules New Orleans?" Besides confirming most of these anecdotal factors as discouraging activism, Chai also quantified the widespread feeling that politicians were of less importance than business leaders. The city's white krewe structure, based largely on birthright and ancestry, was cited as a powerful impediment to new leadership with new ideas.[16] Atlanta, Houston, Huntsville, Charlotte, all had up-and-coming leaders of business and professional life whose paths were not barred by a krewe system. Most of New Orleans's large banks were very conservative in their lending practices, and were loathe to lend money to those not within their social set—white, old New Orleans family—preferably uptown—and usually krewe-connected.[17] One renovator from the Quarter expressed it as "[the banks] which prefer to hold a silver dollar in their vaults to secure a fifty-cent loan."[18] In the days before interstate banking, this attitude rather limited capital available to entrepreneurs. Most of these banks thought the Quarter was, even then, still a slum for drifting bohemians and unworthy of any investment.[19] Although racism certainly played a part in this penurious attitude, in the main it was the desire to preserve New Orleans in some mythical state, free of outside influences, regardless if carried forward by native blacks, arriviste whites, or federal social programs.[20]

Part of this attitude stemmed from the fact that New Orleans is the last city in America where there is no shame in being poor, in contrast to the Protestant work ethic that largely controlled the country at midcentury. This lack of shame did not come from any ethnic pride; it pervaded every race and group. This does not mean that the city was egalitarian—far from it. However, living in an old house of one's own, in a community of old houses, with the bare essentials, no car or other mandatory things of modern life, was little cause for discontent. For many poor people, before neighborhood depredations of drug gangs, "getting by" New Orleans–style was pleasant. It was possible to be one of the working poor without the onus that carried up north. Many such folks worked off the books as bartenders, cooks, waiters, clerks, drivers, and domestics. Their support system was often equal parts Catholic parish and neighborhood watering hole. True, they did not have health insurance, but there was always Charity Hospital. In many southern towns, poor people—especially blacks—voted with their feet and left for big cities with ample employment. There was no such exodus from New Orleans, even in the worst of Jim Crow.[21] Most poor New Orleanians lacked the resources or skills to live independently anywhere else, and contentment was the largest part of the city's eternal soul. And, of course, no other city in America celebrates Carnival quite like New Orleans. To miss Mardi Gras causes withdrawal, anxiety, and a feeling that the new year has not quite begun. "We don't want to become Houston!" was the defiant cry of those, high and low, who thought New Orleans had nothing to learn from anywhere else.[22] Things in New Orleans, it seemed, had been that way forever. But things were about to change.


## Cabrini Park

Apart from Jackson Square and Edison (now Musical Legends) Park, the Quarter then had precious little public green space. Mirroring the decline of large families in the enclave, McDonough 15 school, at Dauphine and Barracks, was demolished in 1939 and its name transferred to a school at Royal and St. Philip. The old school yard became Cabrini Park, a leafy half-square far off the tourist path featuring playground equipment for youngsters.[23]

At night, a different clientele gathered. As true in other urban parks, gay men found Cabrini a perfect venue for nighttime sexual encounters. In January 1971, over the course of four nights, thirteen men were arrested, some through entrapment.[24] The arrests encouraged the nascent gay rights movement in New Orleans. Two weeks later, the city's first gay protest march was held at city hall, watched by police and curious spectators.[25]

Not long thereafter, Cabrini lost most of its trees and bushes,[26] and the playground equipment eventually went by the by as well. It then became a somewhat desolate greensward with a small shelter, patronized exclusively by dog owners exercising and relieving their pets.[27]

## MADAME PARTS COMPANY WITH PARADES

The ubiquitous image of Mardi Gras was of jester-laden floats passing under Quarter balconies thronged with revelers and beads a-flying. As the century progressed, the floats and crowds got larger, but the Quarter, of course, did not. Crowds would form hours in advance and stay, naturally, hours after parades had passed. In 1972, the NOPD and the Quarter-parading krewes agreed to bypass the Quarter in future Carnivals.[28] Although traditionalists sighed, the force majeure of the crowds in the confines of the Vieux Carré made this a logical move.[29] Although motorized floats would no longer drift down Quarter streets, several groups would continue walking parades, notably, the Krewe du Vieux, Pete Fountain's Half Fast Walking Club, and the Society of St. Anne.

## THE CRUCIBLE OF FIRE

For many years, Iberville Street led a twilight existence. As the first block of the Quarter, coming off Canal, it was the back street of the flagship department stores. The upriver side had been ruled out of the Vieux Carré Commission's purview by the 1936 amendment. Towards the river, it ran to warehouses and commercial buildings falling into disuse. Towards North Rampart, a string of businesses slumbered. The liveliest parts of the street, by the early seventies, were home to several bars, including Wanda's at 704. Wanda's, like many Quarter bars, and especially those near the river, had a pansexual crowd of local gays, slumming straights, and sailors fresh from the sea.[30] Iberville Street was also notable, even for the Quarter, as home to prostitution of all types.[31]

At Iberville and Chartres streets, there was an upscale gay piano bar called the Upstairs Lounge, frequented by congregants of the fledgling chapter of the Metropolitan Community Church (MCC). Being above the street, it perhaps escaped notice of many passersby, who frequented the banquette level clubs of greater notoriety.[32]

New Orleans, particularly in the Quarter, was rarely concerned with fire codes. The multitude of old wooden buildings, internally reworked and reused with little or no regulatory oversight, presented a host of fire hazards. Many buildings, wired for electricity at the turn of the century, had not been updated since. Fire escapes could not be put on existing façades, and the side and rear exits of many Quarter buildings above the street level were blocked by adjoining structures.

On Sunday, June 24, 1973, the Upstairs Lounge was lively just before 8:00 p.m. At 7:55, a passerby turned in a fire alarm, and fire trucks arrived just two minutes later, to find the entire bar engulfed in flames. When the fire was put out sixteen minutes later, an awful scene was revealed. Several patrons had been trapped by the burglar bars over the windows, and one, his head and arm roasted, lay against the bars in a last futile struggle to escape. The grisly picture shocked front-page readers of the *Times-Picayune* the next day. Twenty-eight were dead immediately; three would die in the next few days. The fire had been deliberately set in the main stairwell of the street entrance.[33]

A tale repeated to this day is that a man who had just been eighty-sixed from the bar set fire to his gasoline-soaked jacket in the stairwell. Some persons actually came forward over the years with claims of responsibility, but none were credible and the investigation went nowhere.[34] Some patrons escaped out the back, but the majority were trapped by flames roaring up from the stairwell. The man at the barred window was local MCC minister Bill Larson.[35]

The horror of the fire was just a foretaste of the stomach-churning events to come. Some of the dead, unidentified and unclaimed by families, were buried in the local potter's field.[36] The city administration, which had demonstrated its official concern in a high-rise fire taking five lives the year before, could not trouble itself to issue any words of sympathy. The chief of detectives (and later superintendent of police) Henry Morris opined, "We don't even know these [identification] papers belonged to the people we found them on. Some thieves hung out there and you know this was a queer bar."[37]

After a memorable press conference tirade by Rev. Troy Perry, head of the MCC who had flown in after the disaster, the police department issued a quiet apology for the remarks. The lack of sympathy was not limited to officialdom; one radio personality said the dead should be buried in fruit jars.[38] Finding a house of worship to hold a memorial service was a struggle. A courageous Episcopalian minister, Rev. William Richardson, offered St. George's Episcopal Church on St. Charles Avenue, which had been previously used by the MCC. Rev. Richardson's superiors were dismayed,[39] and he received hate mail and phone calls after the service.[40] A cycle of innuendo and reaction developed, with gay bars being threatened. This was a pretext for additional police harassment and consequent chilling of bar activity.[41] Upset at their loss of revenue, some bar owners confronted Perry and the other out-of-town activists, whom they blamed for loss of business. Rev. Perry later recalled the scene:

> Gay entrepreneurs suddenly wanted to have a meeting with those of us who had come into their city. They were of the opinion that we were the causes of their problems. "How dare you hold your damn news conferences!" one of them, a muscular disco owner with gold-rimmed glasses, wearing a smartly tailored linen suit, demanded. Looking at him and his mercenary associates, who had never done anything to repay the gay community for wealth they derived from it, I felt a growing warmth about my collar. "I'll tell you something," I replied, intentionally accentuating my Southern accent. "You all think the way to take care of things in New Orleans is not to talk about them? That's a grand old Southern mistake! Well, Troy Perry's from Dixie, too, and I want to tell you, the reason I'm here in New Orleans is because when it comes to city officials and business leaders like you, I find you're a greedy lot that cares about nobody but yourselves! The fact is that somebody had to do something about the oppression in this city! It's terrible! And instead of you speaking out for what is right, instead of you caring for people that need assistance now, you call us on the carpet and ask how dare we address the press! In case you haven't heard, people have died here! Gay people are hurt and official New Orleans isn't lifting a finger to help. Are you going to keep letting this be just 'another queer happening'? Are you just going to sleep and forget? No, no! The time has come, my friends, for you to reexamine your priorities. What are you able and willing to do?"[42]

A week later, Rev. Perry tried to hold another service, and found ecclesiastical doors shut tight. Eventually, the service was hosted at St. Mark's United Methodist Church at 1130 N. Rampart, with the Methodist bishop of Louisiana in attendance.[43] The concept of "perverts" as churchgoers was a novel idea, and the press was waiting just outside. Some attendees were fearful of being seen leaving. This was in an era when those arrested for crimes against nature had their names and often their faces published in the paper, with consequent loss of jobs and places to live. At Rev. Perry's exhortation, the congregants filed out of the church into the eager eye of the media.[44]

In six remarkable *Times-Picayune* articles in September 1973, Joan Treadway explored, with great objectivity, the surfacing subculture of New Orleans gay life.[45] Previous newspaper articles about gay issues, apart from identifying arrestees, had been discreetly titled and bland in copy. Now, the issues of gay identity, including psychology, religion, and official attitudes were explored with candor. One article was titled, "It's not illegal to BE gay, but certain acts are," which may have been a revelation to many readers.[46] One voice from the past was Jacob Morrison, whose homophobia had not abated, spluttering that he and others "think the influx of these people is making New Orleans the queer capital of the U.S.—they flock to their own kind here. If I was mayor and they came to me, I would have a heck of a time to keep from throwing them out bodily."[47] Like the bar owners confronting Perry, many gay people interviewed for the article were unhappy with the media attention and wished to return to lives out of the spotlight.[48]

Lest these folks be judged too harshly in a day when the love that once dared not speak its name now shouts aloud, consider these things. The crackdown and clean-up cycles of the Morrison era had created a climate of long-lasting fear. The memories of the Cabrini park roundup and Jim Garrison's persecution of Clay Shaw were very fresh. Many gay New Orleanians were refugees from small towns in the region, and still felt some responsibility to appear "respectable" to folks back home. Successful gay activism follows the same New Orleans style as other productive civic crusades. It was, and is, conducted behind closed doors by small groups of patient acolytes.[49] The gay bars existed because of a careful accommodation with the authorities, whose attitudes were slowly becoming more tolerant.[50] The Quarter and its bars were not the whole universe of New Orleans gay life. Many southern gays, even in the Quarter, lived behind lace curtains of well-practiced accommodation, discretion, and mutual confidentially. They lived, worked, and loved by these standards of privacy and did not understand why they should be questioned by outsiders, even gay activists.

The tragedy inspired the New Orleans Fire Department and the state fire marshall to actively look for fire code violations in the Vieux Carré. Unsurprisingly, they found an enormous number. That these were mainly electrical problems and that the Upstairs had been destroyed by gasoline-fueled arson was not discussed.[51] After inspecting about one-third of structures in the Vieux Carré, 946 violations were noted, including some at the Pontalbas.[52] The head of the Vieux Carré Commission reacted to the inspections and the all-too-correct public impression of the Quarter as a tinderbox. He stated that the Upstairs Lounge was not technically in the Vieux Carré, which was true from a legal standpoint, if not a cultural one. He felt that the Vieux Carré had been unfairly singled out.[53] Doubtless some corrections were made, but most Quarter buildings continued to present fire hazards intolerable anywhere else.

There was a burst of gay and lesbian organizing in the wake of the Upstairs fire. However, after a few years, most conceded that the city's gay population was more receptive to social clustering, more like the classic krewe structure, rather than a blatantly political front. The next cause célèbre was the homophobic crusade of Anita Bryant, which was conducted in a series of nationwide speaking engagements. Her approach to New Orleans set off a flurry of organizing. On June 18, 1977, about three thousand people assembled in Jackson Square, watched by many police officers. Nationally known activists Leonard Matlovich and Frank Kameny appeared. The marchers went down St. Ann to Dumaine and then on to the municipal auditorium at what would become Armstrong Park.[54]

## NON SON, NON LUMIÈRE

In the 1960s and early 1970s, European impresarios had created sound and light (*son et lumière*) shows in historic districts. Still images and movies were projected on buildings, while loudspeakers boomed music and narration. The idea was to "make the past come alive" in nighttime shows drawing tourists. In 1973, the city decided that Jackson Square was not exciting enough, and contracted to produce a *son et lumière* show. This would have been a permanent installation and not merely a one-shot deal for a particular event. The city did not bother to ask the residents of the Pontalbas what

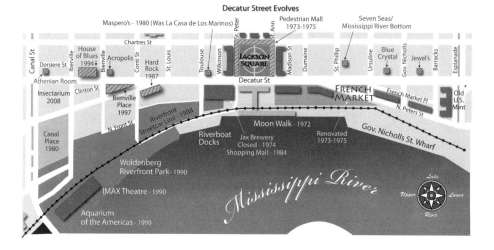

Decatur Street Evolves

they thought of this spectacle in their front yard. Nor, it seems, did the Landrieu administration bother to consult with anyone before letting a no-bid, sole-source contract.[55] VCPORA filed suit in federal court, which was dismissed for lack of jurisdiction. VCPORA and others then filed suit in state court.[56] After the civil court decided against *son et lumière*, the VCC reversed itself and approved the plan. The city proceeded to install electrical conduit supporting the installation; the square was already in renovation. Preservationists sued again, and, this time, lost. Finally, in September 1975, an appeals court reversed the earlier decision, and the city was permanently enjoined from proceeding with the idea.[57]

## DECATUR STREET

For many decades, Decatur Street had been the gateway, parlor, and bedroom of the Quarter for sailors and locals out looking for fun and sexual action. Outside the Quarter, it had a reputation as the roughest, toughest strip of the enclave.[58] One interviewee, living close by in Cabildo Alley in the seventies, remembered: "It was so fascinating, and it seemed like this big old family where everybody knew each other, and it was filthy—I mean, absolutely filthy. You would find people you know who were just passed out in the stew that would be running along the gutters and you'd make sure they were still alive. I seem to remember that there was a fair amount of use of LSD and things like that, so you'd find people sort of bouncing off the walls at that time. It was not at all Disneyland-like. It was not at all cleaned up."[59]

Decatur was also an axis of gay life. Decatur Street may be considered in three sections. The first runs from Canal to St. Peter. The second section runs from that point to the beginning of the French Market, at Ursulines, and the third is from that point to Esplanade.

This first section was neglected for decades. It held sailor bars, old ware-houses, the sputtering remnants of long-established offices, and a few small shops. The second section was the Quarter's front stoop, running in front of Jackson Square between that holy edifice and the river. This area also held the Pontalba apartments, the shops beneath them, and old fixtures like Tujague's restaurant. For decades, Jax Brewery churned out beer at St. Peter and Decatur. In 1974, it closed, vacant until the building was transformed into a shopping mall just before the World's Fair of 1984.[60] Further down, in the third portion, Central Grocery was a reminder of the Sicilian ascendency of the early 1900s. A mixture of bars and stores that sold dusty secondhand wares completed that part of the street not occupied by the former U.S. Mint. Above these stores, cheap rooming houses and apartments were found. In the 1970s, one Decatur businessman counted forty-five bars in the fifteen blocks of Decatur between Canal and Elysian Fields.[61]

Decatur seemed ripe for renovation, at least in the conventional sense. The buildings were large, if mostly run-down. They had existing commer-cial uses, and so would not conflict with residential requirements. Jackson Square, in the center, and the French Market on the downriver end, anchored the tourist experience. The slow reconnection of the Vieux Carré with its riv-erfront required Decatur Street to be worthy as a frame for the view.

The story of Decatur's transformation is an object lesson that all-encom-passing, endlessly studied, master-planned projects are not necessary to bring about diversified renewal of a declined strip. Armstrong Park had been such an exercise. It was a baby carried by five mayoral administrations and grew to be a child nobody wanted. Decatur's change was the result of several nomi-nally independent events, occurring over twenty-odd years. This was not a single, wholesale change, but rather the loss of some anchors of one culture and their replacements with anchors of another, and then yet another cul-ture. In the early and middle seventies, with the port operations still close by, the bars along Decatur catered mainly to sailors.[62] These years saw a gradual changing of the guard, in owners and customers. Decatur Street would go from a playground for sailors and locals to a tourist strip anchored by desti-nations of a scale—and ownership—beyond anything the city had yet seen. We will stroll from Canal Street to the Mint and watch the changes happen through 1978, and view the later changes in subsequent chapters.

CANAL TO ST. PETER

This portion featured bars like the Athenian Room and the Acropolis catering to Greek sailors, with ouzo and buxom young, and some very buxom and not-so-young, women of "purchasable virtue."[63] Some Greek sailors also fancied drag queens, which were picked up with full knowledge of their biological genders.[64] Daring tourists and resident bohemians might also visit La Casa de los Marinos, at 601 Decatur (at Toulouse). It featured three nested barrooms. The first was a Latino bar with Latin jukebox and conga drums chained to the wall.[65] The second was the province of a barmaid known universally as Laurel the Slut. Robyn Halvorsen remembers: "In fact, there was a big joke that one time she had two boyfriends named Darrell, so you called them Darrell #1 and Darrell #2. Darrell #2 actually got into a little trouble with the police. He shot a policeman in Clay Shaw's building in the 1000 block of St. Peters. Once he did that, he knew they were going to kill him, so he called out before they blew him away, 'Tell Laurel I love her!'"[66]

The third bar played rock music on a jukebox topped by a platform for dancing, and had German expressionist paintings on the walls.[67] James Nolan, who frequented the bar in the midsixties, recalls: "The third bar was absolute drunken insanity. I just met everyone in the Quarter right there in the third bar. At 3:00 or 4:00 in the morning women would take off their blouses and dance on the juke box and people were dancing and hooting and hollering, and it was also a place where a lot of the younger bohemian Tulane students hung out and there were lots of girls with long, straight hair who looked like they should have been playing guitars, and street musicians would go, people from the university, people from the civil rights movement, sailors, debu-tantes, drunk debutantes with a heel snapped off dancing dirty on the bar . . . and it was just a very wild place."[68]

JACKSON SQUARE REBORN

Jackson Square, as the altar before the monstrance of St. Louis Cathedral, has a history of less-than-saintly character. Authorities of the 1850s complained about passed-out drunks, and it has traditionally offered a roosting place for those with nothing but time on their hands. The square proper was fenced and is now locked at night. The automobile chugged into the square early in the twentieth century and was driven and parked in the surrounding ring of Chartres, St. Peter, St. Ann, and Decatur, convenient for residents of the

Pontalba. This also meant that Chartres remained a cross-Quarter route from Canal Street to Esplanade.

In 1971, plans were made to close the square to auto traffic and convert it into a pedestrian mall, a concept then all the rage among urban planners. From 1973 to 1975, Chartres was closed at St. Peter, resuming on the other side of the square at St. Ann. Although this certainly relieved Chartres traffic to a degree, it only increased traffic making the turn up St. Peter to Bourbon, across to St. Ann, and back down to the sharp turn into Chartres in front of the square's downriver entrance. Making the turn at Bourbon and St. Ann is never easy, and well-nigh impossible during Carnival, when that boundary between the straight and gay sections is packed with revelers.

The changes, as with the French Market renovation, were unwelcome by square denizens, particularly artists, who were displaced for several weeks.[69] The street closings were also unpopular with Pontalba residents who lost their front-door parking. Prominent preservationists like Martha Robinson decried the changes and, as with the expressway battle, attempted to enlist outside allies. These pleas gained little traction, since, unlike the expressway *fais-do-do*, automobiles were now being shut out of a protected space.[70] In the end, creating the flagstone expanse surrounding the square meant that, in addition to the long-enduring painters, vendors, fortune-tellers, musicians, and street performers now had ample room to solicit the strolling tourists. Benches offered the opportunity to sit or, if need be, to pass out. The revised square played host to the coveted tourist and the "undesirable" street person alike, a conflict which would be played out over and over as the century rolled on.

## ST. PETER TO URSULINES

Just off Decatur, at 515 St. Philip, was the Seven Seas. The Seven Seas remains fond in the memory of those who lived those times, for the eclectic mix of white, black, gay, straight, poor, rich, intellectuals, and bikers. Occasional, a celebrity would appear.[71]

## URSULINES TO ESPLANADE

Decatur from Ursulines to Esplanade was the meeting place of the young establishment and the counterculture. Boundaries, whether geographic, social, or ethnic, seemed to have not meant much here. On the riverside, at 1100, Mike Stark had his Abba Foundation flea market, which was the nucleus of the open air flea market at the downriver end of the French Market. Here artists could exhibit and sell their wares.[72] A Filipino seamen's bar was on the lakeside, at 1107. In 1974 Jim Monaghan bought the place and renamed it Molly's at the Market. Monaghan invited politicians to be guest bartenders and had jazz bands play.[73] Molly's at the Market quickly became something of a lower Quarter salon, with local intelligentsia hanging around the streetside window.[74]

Further down the block was another monument of sorts, the Abbey. For a time, the Abbey had a peculiar draw. It was the only place in the Quarter that sold the Sunday *New York Times*. Lawyers and literati would pick up the paper, drink wine, and nibble cheese—a far cry from the sailor bars of just a short time before. The legal profession was so well represented at the Abbey that the police left it alone.[75] At 1137 was the Blue Crystal, a cheerfully sleazy place whose fixture, Blow Job Shirley, performed that service for five dollars.[76]

The 1200 block, between Gov. Nicholls and Barracks, held mainly apartments in 1975. It also featured Jewel's, a sailor bar soon to mark the shift to a new era. Down the block at 1231 was the office of the *Vieux Carré Courier*, the enclave's most respected native paper. The *Vieux Carré Courier* was not an underground paper in any sense. It was the very public voice of the Quarter's concerned citizenry. Well-known journalists like Nicholas Lemann and Don Lee Keith got their start with the *Courier*. The *Courier*, under Will Long, had been prominent in the fight against the Riverfront Expressway.[77] The *Courier*'s last publisher was Philip Carter, son of Hodding Carter and grandson of Elizebeth Werlein.[78]

The enduring salty character of Decatur was reflected a block away, at Chartres and Gov. Nicholls. In 1977, the archdiocese converted the St. Mary's Recreation Center to Stella Maris, a lodging and social service center for seamen. The recreation center moved to the Carmelite Convent on North Rampart.[79]

## THE FRENCH MARKET REDUX

The French Market had last been renovated in 1938[80] and, after thirty-plus years, was again showing its age. The 1938 renovation had been focused on sanitation and improved access for trucks that had displaced the old horse- and mule-drawn wagons.

Between the 1938 renovation and the early 1970s, the market ceased to be the Quarter's main supply of meat and produce. Besides the numerous corner groceries, just outside the Quarter were chain grocery stores offering a plentiful and cheap array of foodstuffs. Parking around the market was in short supply.[81] The food wholesalers had departed. Tourists might gawk at the garlic garlands, the double-yolk eggs, the Creole tomatoes, and the fresh fish at Jimmy George's, last fishmonger in the market. They could have iced fish shipped home if they wished. But as a group, they bought few of these offerings—after all, most fresh food couldn't be taken home on an airliner, or in a hot car before air conditioning. So, the market was no longer the grocery of choice of the enclave, and few tourists were buying food there either.[82] The potential commercial value of the location, between the emerging prime tourist strip of Decatur and the floodwall, was enormous.

From 1973 to 1975, the French Market was again renovated. This time, food sellers were not catered to. The market, and an adjoining new row of matching stores, would offer goods keyed to tourist sensibilities. One hall, the old *Halle de Boucheries* (Hall of Butchers) would be allotted to food sellers.

Clay Shaw, after his notorious and frivolous prosecution by Jim Garrison, might have turned his back on New Orleans. Depleted of funds, and ever the trooper, he spent the last two years of his life managing the market renovations while fighting cancer.[83] In February 1973 he told the Kiwanis Club: "What New Orleans does best is entertain visitors and we feel this renovation could keep them here another day browsing through the 50 shops we will have." He estimated that tourists staying another day might add $500 million a year to the city's economy.[84]

Changing anything in the Quarter arouses suspicion, and renovating the colorful old (read: dilapidated) market was not universally popular. Some saw it as yet another surrender of a local institution to the tourist trade.[85] The fact that the institution, wreathed in nostalgia, had outlived its original purpose seemed not to matter.[86] Perhaps what offended was not so much the renovation per se, but the way in which it was done. The newly renovated spaces required higher rents, and Jimmy George's departed.[87] Another loss was the Morning Call Coffee Stand, which had been a caffeine and beignet ritual since 1870. Its relocation to Metairie was yet another tear in the seemingly eternal tapestry of Vieux Carré life.[88] Its slightly older competitor, Café Du Monde, survived and moved into a space next to Latrobe Park, a sunken pocket park where live music entertains the café au lait sippers and beignet munchers. For the inner life of the Vieux Carré, the most emotional loss was the closing of Battistella's restaurant. It had been a red beans and rice mainstay of art-ists, longshoremen, and market workers for several decades. The renovations demanded a doubled rent, cut the floor space in half, required 4 percent of the gross income to be spent on advertising, and mandated interior renova-tions at the owner's expense. All of this was too much for a simple hometown business, and it closed.[89]

The renovated market was dedicated on a drizzly April 1, 1975,[90] sadly without Shaw, who had died on August 14, 1974.[91] The new market featured upscale stores in a strip parallel to Decatur Street. The renovated open halls still had some food vendors, but butchers and fishmongers were not among them. Tourist trinkets produced overseas were the main course. A few native artists set up shop in the concrete expanse outside the covered area, gamely showing their stained glass, masks, and collectible old items to a curious and usually tipsy public. The renovation produced an interesting inner court-yard, named Dutch Alley, with requisite bronze plaque, after Mayor Dutch Morial,[92] where the Mardi Gras Mask-A-Thon was held each year. Two life-size bronzes, a seated girl with a basket and a derbied man in an apron, remind the public of the food sellers and grocers that had once made their living in the dusty, aromatic old halls. No bronze in the market, however, memorial-izes Clay Shaw, who gave the market his last full measure of devotion.

CHAPTER 8

# INTERLUDE

*Odd Folks*

### SHEEP MAY SAFELY CRAZE

Port cities around the world are known as havens. Havens for those at the end of the road. Havens for those whose road never started, and, taking root in a landscape of transient people and relative mores, they find refuge from the busybody world beyond.

The Vieux Carré has been a city of refuge for many such people over three centuries. The physical shelter may be just a barstool, a pool table to sleep on, or an overhanging balcony to keep the rain off. The Quarter really excelled at psychic shelter. For as long as the Quarter has existed, it has had a cast of odd characters—"eccentrics" is Rick Delaup's kind word.[1] These people had uneasy relations—sometimes little at all—with the same world inhabited by you, gentle reader, and your author. By the frowning standards of middle-class late twentieth-century America, these people were variously retarded, mentally ill, and often alcoholic. Anywhere else, they might elicit contempt or fear. Tennessee Williams remarked: "I shall always think of New Orleans—affectionately, of course—as a vagabond's paradise. In New York, eccentrics, authentic ones, are ignored. In Los Angeles, they're arrested. Only in New Orleans are they permitted to develop their eccentricities into art."[2]

In the Vieux Carré, they generated amusement and even adoration. They were not truly homeless; they were at home in the Quarter. Their home spanned many blocks and was furnished with barrooms where they

... a pool table to sleep on.
Courtesy of Glenn Meche.

entertained generations of barflies. More or less tolerated by bartenders, they used their personalities to cadge small change, drinks, and cigarettes. Some performed on the streets, earning a little money from camera-toting tourists.

Some had places to go "home" to—apartments maintained by friends, who tracked them down from time to time. Some slept wherever an undisturbed space presented itself. Many were women of middle or advanced years. The gallantry of even drunken young men to older women was their best protection against mishap, and many were adopted by the gay set as mascots— folks even stranger than themselves. Before Americans became risk-averse and protection-crazed in the early 1990s, most tourists loved these characters, and would often pay them to pose for pictures, gladly giving them smokes or a few dollars.

In my years of running the Quarter streets, I knew two best. One was the Lucky Bead Lady. A hunched hag somewhere between seventy and a hundred, she usually wore a frowsy tiara, dark clothing, and sometimes a Bell Telephone hard hat a bar-buddy of mine gave her. If observed closely—which no one did for long—her looks had a faint echo of Gloria Swanson. Various rumors swirled around her. One averred that her real name was Lola; another maintained that she had been abandoned by an aristocratic lover. She prowled the streets holding strands of beads she'd picked up from the gutter. Finding her mark, she would fix on the poor soul with coal-black, burning eyes. "You need lucky bead!" she'd pronounce in a hoarse eastern European accent. If the sap was intimidated or amused enough to take the bauble, Lucky Bead Lady would demand money, sometimes as much as ten dollars. Failure to pay brought forth screaming, vile curses. Quarter residents avoided her, going blocks out of their way.

The Lucky Bead Lady. Courtesy of Joe Zahavi.

One afternoon in the mideighties, I was sauntering down Bourbon to Mary's Hardware Store. Crossing Ursulines, I heard a familiar voice jabbering to my right. It was Lucky Bead Lady, all by herself, heading up Ursulines to Dauphine. She was having a most unpleasant conversation. "Goddamn it, I told you not say that!" she screamed. "I told you fuckers to leave me alone!" she raged to the empty block. Lovable, she was not.

In the late 1990s, no longer ambulatory, possibly from phlebitis, she was admitted to Charity Hospital. Quickly certified, she was taken to East Jackson Psychiatric Hospital, where her fate is obscured by patient privacy rules.

The character best known to me was also the most famous. Of humble origins, she achieved widespread fame. I'm proud to say that I was one of many who bought her a drink in her time in the Quarter.

Ruth Grace Moloun,[3] better known as Ruthie the Duck Lady, was, along with her brother, introduced to the streets of the Quarter by their mother in the early 1950s. In a Zen act of kindness, her mother did not institutionalize her different daughter; she planted her in an environment ideally suited to her. Ruthie began singing and dancing on the street in her teenage years. She developed a fondness for ducks, usually live but occasionally toys on a string. A fearless roller skater, she flew around the Vieux Carré, rolling swiftly into bars. She'd always ask for a drink or cigarette for "later," which meant she

Ruthie the Duck Lady, 1990. Scott Ellis.

wanted them *now*. She wore a floppy hat festooned with lapel buttons, and sometimes a wedding dress with a shabby veil.

Conversations with Ruthie were interesting. Questions were usually answered with strings of a few words, some of them non sequitur, or just laughter. Once in a while, her face would cloud over and her comments could be vitriolic. But mainly she grinned at the attention lavished on her by generations of bartenders, police officers, and gay men. Ruthie became not only a local fixture but a mini-industry, known worldwide. Note cards and refrigerator magnets were sold with images of Ruthie in a wedding dress or leading ducks down the street.

By the late 1990s, Ruthie's situation changed. She was nearing seventy and was showing some typical geriatric problems. Too, the world had changed. American society wanted people like her out of sight. The Quarter had lost much of its historic tolerance for her kind, who were seen as threats to the "family friendly" atmosphere Quarter merchants and real estate agents tried to cultivate. Her friends feared she might be victimized by the upsurge of violence ravaging New Orleans. Ruthie's legal guardian put her in a nursing home uptown. Aside from a few parties thrown in her honor, Ruthie's days on the streets that had sheltered her were over.[4] Ruthie died at age seventy-four in 2008.[5]

## THE NEW REFORMERS

The Quarter's ancient reputation as a libertine haven has drawn many plea-sure seekers, some of whom became residents. Such an enclave of happy sin also attracts those in the business of redemption. In the early years of the nineteenth century, American Protestants arrived in New Orleans. The "hard-shell" fundamentalist folk from up north were appalled at the lifestyle found downriver. They were also appalled at how "Kaintock" flatboatmen loved to wallow in the fleshy, boozy delights of New Orleans at the end of their voy-ages.[6] Everyday drunkenness, open prostitution, mixed-race concubinage, casual murder, and the dueling mania all sent these good people into apo-plexy. As the power of the French Creoles declined post–Civil War, American Protestants gained the political and social ascendency in New Orleans. Much of what they inherited from the French Creole ancien régime disgusted them, and none so much as the debauchery of the French Quarter and Basin Street areas. As we have seen, Storyville was an outcome of this process, a rational American solution to an industry based on irrational lust.

The federally forced closing of Storyville in 1917 undid this solution, and the Quarter suffered. The first Quarter preservationists were also social reformers. Apart from saving old buildings, they tried to raise the Vieux Carré above the cliché of tenement, barroom, and bordello. The half-hearted clean-ups of the 1920s and 1930s were nearly all undone, once more, by the influx of sex workers from the former Storyville area displaced for the Iberville project in 1939. Mrs. Werlein's crusades had saved much architecture, but she could not purge the Quarter of all the various vices therein.

Beginning in the early 1960s, Rev. Bob Harrington operated from a store-front at 227 Bourbon. Harrington witnessed to strippers and other denizens of the famous fairway of flesh.[7] His persistence in this unlikely religious venue earned him the title of "Chaplain of Bourbon Street" from Mayor Victor Schiro in 1962.[8]

In the current era, the Quarter attracts many self-styled evangelists who preach, sometimes in amplified harangues, to largely contemptuous crowds. To say one has preached on Bourbon Street at Mardi Gras is a major status symbol for these people when they return to their rural churches. I witnessed a delicious collision of cultures one day in the 1980s when Lucky Bead Lady approached some of these folks with her usual modus operandi.

If the piety of the religious barkers is beyond question, their connection to New Orleans realities can be tenuous. In 1985, I stood on the river side of North Rampart Street watching Proteus parade in the lakeside lanes. An old VW bus came along the open riverside roadway. A megaphoned voice screamed, "Krewe of Proteus! Abandon Greek mythology for Christ!" before speeding on towards St. Claude. The sidewalk crowd was convulsed with laughter, considering that many of the float riders were devout Catholics.

This illuminates another Crescent City verity: Carnival is a secular religion and the closest thing to an official municipal creed. It has its own apostolic hierarchy, temples, saints, and hymns. As is true in other impoverished areas having uneasy relations with Western culture, Carnival is similar to belief systems that exist beside, and are often intermingled with, Christianity, and Catholicism in particular. It provides the same comforts to poor and nonmainstream people, it is accessible without any loss of freedom or pride, and it has the weight of nearly every part of the city's establishment to promote and protect it. Stationed on the calendar by the observance of Lent, Carnival is intertwined with New Orleans Catholicism. The British sovereign is styled as Defender of the Faith; the mayors of New Orleans have the same duty towards Carnival.

Reformers have appeared in many guises. Some are far better placed and more subtle than the Bible-waving country jakes hollering on street corners. We have seen how one such crusade against gay people evolved in the 1950s. All "reformers" need some group of people to demonize. Changing mores meant that prostitution, though still available, is no longer very visible on the streets of the Vieux Carré. Aside from the usual platitudes, the drug trade is beyond anything these reformers can affect. The clean and sober movement of the 1990s slid off New Orleans like eggs off the Clover's grill. Apart from the occasional noisy outburst, demonizing gays and lesbians doesn't work anymore; officials no longer play that game. Turning down the volume of protest and counterprotest in the Quarter, the New Orleans City Council restricted the use of bullhorns in 2004.[9]

## A NEW GENERATION ON THE STREETS

The group of people collectively known as "the homeless" has been a vexing problem for America. New Orleans has not traditionally been kind to beggars. The street characters described earlier, and those like them, at least provided some entertainment for their handouts. Older Quarter residents still fondly recall "Banjo Annie" singing lewd songs about politicians.[10] Those who simply hang around and beg for alms are not treated well by police or pass-ersby. As a port, New Orleans is bound to collect its share of street people, some of whom actually have homes. The mild winter and abundance of aban-doned properties to roost in makes the city all the more attractive. As long ago as 1971, the city, and especially the Quarter, was reluctantly proclaimed as a magnet for runaway youngsters. In the years of culture vs. countercul-ture, some fled families appalled that their children had turned into "hip-pies." Some were local kids looking to escape regimented school and family life, at least for a while. Some came from abusive homes. If they were lucky, they found sympathetic adults who directed them to shelter, support, and possible reconciliation with their families. Some found adult guidance of a darker nature and were sexually victimized.[11]

Jackson Square had been a parlor and bedroom for vagrants for many years. As early as 1849, the Council of the First Municipality cited "loafers and vagabonds who are seen lying drunk under the trees."[12] No matter the national or city economy, there always seemed to be an irreducible number of street people there. As the 1990s progressed, more street people material-ized in the square.[13] Whatever "color" these folks added was overbalanced by disgusting episodes. The Cabildo suffered a serious fire in 1988, requiring the replacement of the third floor. As the structure was renovated slowly in the early 1990s, street people and their debris piled up under the arches. These were not the sleepy, Chaplinesque bums of vaudeville shticks. They publically urinated, defecated, vomited, threatened, and exposed themselves to the staff and public. In one instance, one of the vagrants grabbed a pigeon, ripped it open, and ate it on the spot.[14] The Cabildo's sister building, the Presbytère, had a fence and suffered no such indignities.

By the mid-1990s, these new denizens of the streets had a name—the gutter punks. These kids had no visible cause. Unlike the Beats of the fifties with their intellectualism, or the hippies of the sixties with their antiwar and counterculture message, the gutter punks seem to exist merely to exist. There is no credo, no rallying cry, no banner to motivate them. Some of the older ones were Deadheads adrift in the Grateful Dead's interregnum after Jerry Garcia's death in 1995. Others had been thrown out of their families or had run away from bad situations. Some were middle-class kids just slumming. Many circulate among various cities, hopping trains or catching rides. Like the hippies of two generations ago, the gutter punks are visually distinctive and therefore annoying to bourgeois sensibilities. Tattooed, pierced, with tie-dyed or pseudo-gothic clothing, the gutter punks just hung out, begged, drank, doped, and occasionally created encampments on public property before being chased away by police. With many abandoned houses and a usually mild climate, the gutter punks found lodging-"squats" easily. Businesspeople in the lower Quarter, particularly between Jackson Square and the mint, complained that the gutter punks blocked sidewalks and begged obnoxiously.[15] The wooden steps of the Moon Walk are a favorite roost, and bear carved insignia and names of gutter punks who have passed time there.[16] The gutter punks can be more aggressive, in begging and defense of "their" turf, than traditional panhandlers; some violence between themselves and others flares.[17] Out of media scrutiny, they also lost violent collisions with the working poor of New Orleans, who resent them mightily. The hippies of the sixties and seventies had a collective musk of marijuana and incense; the downwind of current street people can be a gut-wrenching miasma of old secretions, unwashed bodies, and metabolized alcohol and drugs. The gutter punks made the beret-wearing, bongo-banging Beats and the *NOLA Express*– selling, pot-smelling hippies seem, almost, well, *quaint and distinctive.*

The gutter punks joined, and then outnumbered, the usual cast of hangers-on in Jackson Square and surrounding streets. Most of the latter are older, unemployed, alcoholic men, who, in another day, were simply called "bums" or "winos." As the civic boosters and real estate agents promoted expensive properties to out-of-towners, these people became an eyesore and a liability.

In homeless people, the new reformers found their demons, and, in a new city councilwoman, found their champion. Councilwoman Jackie Clarkson's support for cleaning up the Quarter might be dismissed as just another upswing in the three-century cycle of crackdown and laissez-faire. However, this reform effort took a new twist. The artists who painted and displayed their wares in Jackson Square were pitted against street people and fortune-tellers. Clarkson had benches removed and returned with dividers installed to prohibit sleeping. After the legal fumes cleared, the fortune-tellers remained in a specific area and the painters also retained their turf. Street people of all kinds are still being officially discouraged.[18] Although an ordinance against sleeping in public was eventually enacted,[19] it was later ruled unconstitutional by a federal court.[20] Even if they were visually displeasing to some, street people did not cause trouble when they slept, and many could find shelter out of public view.

In all this, there was some measure of clear thinking. No one wanted the Vieux Carré to suffer the massive encampments of street people as seen in San Francisco, Seattle, and elsewhere. Discouraging the relatively small groups of gutter punks now, the theory went, would prevent a mass migration of their ilk.[21] Moving on and growing up, the gutter punks would, it was hoped, simply vanish into the American population like other groups before them. The gutter punks, and those who provided social services for them, pointed out that New Orleans has always had street people. Being visually different and nonconformist, they maintain, should not be reserved for those with money. After all, it was not so long ago that people simply perceived to be gay were being hassled and arrested in the Quarter. The gutter punks had some advocates who tried to provide services in a cash-strapped and hostile city.[22] However, they had no prominent champion as the hippies had had in Mike Stark, who died in 1998.[23]

In 2003, *Rolling Stone* profiled gutter punk life in New Orleans as drug ridden, desperate, and much harassed by cops.[24] This last impression was confirmed when, after the article, many gutter punks were arrested.[25] The NOPD was no more sympathetic to gutter punks than it had been thirty-five years earlier towards hippie encampments. However, after over a decade of complaints about the gutter punks,[26] and cycles of police roundups and hassling, there has been only a modest impact on their visible numbers in the area between Jackson Square and the Frenchman Triangle.

The propensity of some gutter punks to violently guard "their" space came to the fore in 2005. The building at the corner of Esplanade and Decatur had housed many clubs over the years. In the 1980s and 1990s, it had been home to the Mint, a gay and lesbian bar named after the old U.S. Mint across the street. Then it became El Matador, an eclectic nightclub that attracted many gutter punks and became the pivot of "their" neighborhood. In 2004, the building was sold by the El Matador's operator's father.[27]

The new owner was actor and prestidigitator Harry Anderson. After struggling with the typical bureaucratic obstacles, he opened Oswald's nightclub in the summer of 2005. The gutter punks, ignorant of the facts, blamed Anderson for the demise of El Matador, and he was verbally and then physically assaulted by former patrons of the club.[28] After Hurricane Katrina in August of 2005, Anderson opened the club for town hall meetings of residents and government officials. Besides the loss of customers and ruinous utility bills, in May of 2006, Anderson suffered a virtual replay of the earlier assault. In August of 2006, the Andersons had had enough, sold their property, and moved away.[29]

Why the city failed to appease the angst of business owners in the lower Quarter over the gutter punk problem is unclear. What is all too clear is that the city, and the city's media, were mostly indifferent to Anderson's travails. They were nonchalant about the departure of this nationally known and now disillusioned entrepreneur. Perhaps the spectacle of a mass roundup of young people would be unpalatable in a city with a long history of official racism and homophobia. In any case, after the Hurricane Katrina–driven evacuation of 2005, the gutter punks were one of the first groups to return, probably because they had no houses or jobs to lose to the storm, and public assistance was freely handed out, no questions asked.

Over the past century, the Quarter's guardians have wrestled with the question of tolerance. As we have noted, in various times, certain groups were actively discouraged. Yet, in nearly all cases, those very groups gained economic and social standing rivaling, and sometimes displacing, the WASPs who, in their day, had displaced the French Creoles.

The Sicilians who hung out their washing on the Pontalba balconies in 1900 rose to own a great deal of the Quarter, and spread throughout the economic and government hierarchy. Black people whose ancestors had once been discouraged from participating in the Quarter's life would become the political power brokers of the city. Jacob Morrison and Aaron Kohn would not have believed that future "queer shops" would be among the most important business anchors of the Quarter. Nor could they have stomached mayoral proclamations hailing the Southern Decadence gay bacchanal for the tourist dollars it brought. In each case, persecution has led to tolerance, to acceptance, to a melding into the mainstream of New Orleans life.

The wrestling match of "standards" versus "diversity," "local color" versus "common decency," and amusing eccentricity versus sheer depravity persists. It has become even more tortuous in the early twenty-first century as individual public behavior becomes more extreme and sanctions veer from invisible to draconian with each succeeding generation.

# INTERLUDE

*Tourism*

## TOURISM GETS ROLLING

Mass tourism and the Quarter began a long dance in the twentieth century. Even before Saxon and Flo Fields arrived in the teens, the contrast between the archaic old village and the Edwardian spirit of progress was being sold as "charm." In 1907, the Illinois Central Railroad, in its *New Orleans for the Tourist*, advised: "One must not, for instance, wander through the French Quarter and make a mental note to the effect that it is a region of narrow streets lined on either side with time-worn, old-fashion, low-storied buildings making an appearance that will not compare with the broad streets and modern buildings of some northern cities. One must, instead, carry in mind the fact that the saunter is amid surroundings rich in historical associations, and that evidences are being witnessed on every hand of a distinctive foreign epoch of civilization."[1]

The earliest marketing of Quarter tourism, then, emphasized the romance of ruins, while carefully avoiding any mention of squalor and without suggestion that the "surroundings rich in historical associations" might require preservation.

English poet John Galsworthy experienced this romance of ruins in a 1912 guided tour of the old St. Louis hotel, long fallen to dishabille. By torchlight, his guide hawked the old slave market, the once-gleaming brass now black, and the famous dome, whose fading interior images of southern heroes had

once looked down on glittering social affairs and brisk commercial maneuvers. The apotheosis of this decadence was an encounter with a gaunt horse
shuffling from room to room.[2]

The linking of tourism with preservation began with Flo Fields and her
friend Lyle Saxon, who simultaneously promoted the village as both as an
attraction and history worth saving in the late nineteen teens.[3]

For many years, Quarter tourists seemed to come in three primary vari-
eties. The first were middle-class, sometimes professional folks who came
for the famous restaurants, the jazz, and the museums. These were primarily
older, married couples but also included antiquarians, educators, and those
well established in the arts. These "straight arrow" visitors were the dream of
the Quarter's tourist industry; they bought fancy meals, and paid fancy prices
for antiques (more or less) on Royal Street. They were mostly quiet, polite,
and properly appreciative of Quarter charm, as the guidebooks presented that
intangible.

The second group was mostly young, usually on a tight budget, and drunk
much of their stay. In various times and seasons these might be conventioneers, merchant seamen, servicemen, students, drifters, and stray locals escaping their family obligations for a short, sweet time. They found endless drinking, fleshy delights—or at least the promise of them—and the freedom to be
jackasses away from the supervision of schools, parents, bosses, and spouses.[4]
These visitors were loud; sometimes passed out on stoops; spent little money
apart from liquor; and usually left with nothing more substantial than beads,
foggy memories, and colossal hangovers. The hospitality industry gritted its
teeth and humored these folks, to an extent. The hoteliers and restauranteurs
might not like them, but they brought in money. Residents avoided them if at
all possible—"that end" of Bourbon seldom sees a local after nightfall.

The third group consisted of the original French Quarter visitors—male
sex tourists. In the heyday of Storyville, men getting off trains at Basin Street
had been accosted by hawkers of *Blue Book* whorehouse guides.[5] After Storyville's and the *Blue Books*' demise in 1917, amorous men could get recommendations from helpful taxi drivers, who described their eager passengers
as "vidalias" as they delivered them to streetwalkers and bordellos.[6]

Sex tourism was an important share of the Quarter's revenue for many
years, but saw a gradual decline in the postwar forties and fifties, as more
liberal social mores meant that most men no longer had to seek out hookers
for a sexual thrill. The sex tourist found both opportunity and danger in the
Quarter. If he went to a well-entrenched brothel, wasn't too tipsy, respected

the strumpets, and departed quietly, he could have a pleasant time. Those who started trouble, or even had legitimate complaints, found that the police were on the side of landladies and their girls, not the tourists.[7]

In 1935, Lyle Saxon became the state director of the Louisiana Writers' Project of the Works Progress Administration.[8] One of the project's commissions was to write a guidebook of the city, its history, and tourist attractions. Now Saxon had a national pulpit from which to preach the reviving of the Vieux Carré. Although not as frank as *The Bachelor in New Orleans*, the 1938 WPA *New Orleans City Guide*[9] did tell its readers that some nightclubs offered "strip-teasers" and that "Negro clubs" had music "red hot." Negro tourists were not neglected; the *Guide* provided a list of accommodations for them in that segregated era. Driving tours of the city were laid out, and no facet of New Orleans life mentionable in those times was neglected. America was still in the grip of the Depression in 1938 and the first wave of post-*Guide* mass tourism turned out to be the servicepeople of World War II. The WPA issued a pamphlet with two walking tours of the Quarter for the armed forces.[10] Now there was no Storyville to shut down, and so, even with the occasional club that found itself temporarily off limits to service people, the clubs of upper Bourbon flourished. A curfew for most servicepeople kept them, to a degree, off the streets after 11:30 p.m.[11] The club owners showed commendable tolerance as they counted the profits. Aside from the usual fights, controlled by the shore patrol and military police assisted by NOPD, the club owners welcomed the business and felt patriotic. These "boys"—and many were just that—were going off to face death and destruction on a scale unknown by Americans since the Civil War. They deserved a chance to swill drinks, sing off-key to Mercedes's piano at Pat O'Brien's,[12] and make time with pretty girls—including the professionals.

## THE KIDS

College students from the surrounding region have long partied and celebrated Carnival in the Quarter, and it is an old rite of passage for out-of-town freshmen. From the early sixties, the increasing rowdyism of young people in the Vieux Carré began to irritate. In 1962, the *Vieux Carré Courier* noted that "collegiate" behavior was getting worse. In the early sixties a group of "collegiate" men killed a man perceived as gay in Pirate's Alley.[13] Al Rose, in his *Storyville, New Orleans*, was disgusted by student—"the scum of the

South"—behavior in the Quarter of the late sixties.[14] In that time, the week-end crowds of college students were still the bane of some club owners for their drunken antics.[15]

Until the late 1960s, college spring break in the eastern United States was celebrated largely on the beaches of Daytona, Fort Lauderdale, and other south Florida towns. Several movies celebrated an idyllic beach lifestyle of endless summer, surfing, dancing, and romancing. The beach-based spring break craze began to fade—temporarily—in the late sixties. Much college rec-reation then became centered on getting stoned on marijuana and listening to music. The passive devotees of these gatherings disdained the beach scene as vapid and out of step with current youth culture. Marijuana was a portable experience that could be enjoyed anywhere the authorities were absent or indifferent.

The beach towns of south Florida began to weary of spring break in the mid-1980s. The crowds were getting too large, too rowdy, and too drug-informed for the municipalities. The mayor of Fort Lauderdale told breakers they were unwelcome. Stricter alcohol laws and occupancy limits in clubs also dampened the party atmosphere.[16] As coastal real estate values climbed, the "mom and pop" hotels that had welcomed breakers were bought up and demolished for expensive condominiums and chain hotels. Upscale hotels demanded hefty deposits, minimum stays, and had little tolerance for typical breaker shenanigans. Nuclear families spent more money than breakers, and didn't fall from balconies or drug and rape coeds. As south Florida began to discourage breakers, they moved north into panhandle towns like Pensacola, Destin, and Panama City Beach.[17] At this same time, out-of-town breakers began to arrive in greater numbers in New Orleans.

Students spring-breaking in New Orleans discovered what "collegiates" had known forever: French Quarter bars rarely carded patrons, and thus teenagers could drink there with few hassles.[18] In 1984, the federal govern-ment mandated that states raise their drinking age to twenty-one, or else lose a portion of their federal highway money.[19] Louisiana, kicking and scream-ing,[20] was the last state to comply, and raised the age over a period of years.[21] Carding of would-be drinkers was officially emphasized, and, unofficially, largely ignored. Several years later, many underage visitors to the Quarter were either still not carded or found sympathetic adults who would buy them beer and liquor.[22]

The out-of-towners brought the entire spring break culture with them—minus sand and sunscreen—to the Quarter. Hotel rooms sold for four, slept six or eight; groups of students made the Bourbon bar crawl from Iberville to St. Ann, where they discovered, sometimes jarringly, the boundary between the straight and gay neighborhoods. Another rite of passage for young men was the realization that an apparently good-looking female espied on the banquette might not be a woman at all.

Because Mardi Gras day varies from February 3 through March 9, it does not always coincide with college spring breaks, which typically range from late February through April, with the majority in March. The weather of the last part of Carnival season is notoriously fickle—dry and balmy one year and frigid or rainy the next. So, the breakers do not always show up en masse for Mardi Gras.

The Quarter's business establishment greeted the breakers warily, mindful of the hippies who had just shuffled off into history. The Quarter was used to waves of revelers, and the NOPD is a model for handling large intoxicated crowds with relatively few arrests or injuries. True, breakers brought money; most students had Daddy's credit card, or at least fatter wallets, than traditional transient tourists like seamen or servicemen.However, tolerance began to wear thin as the eighties became the nineties. One factor was the emergence of high school spring breaks, which sometimes coincide with college breaks. Older teenagers had always been able to drink in the Quarter with little difficulty. Now, in the litigation-crazed 1990s, the prospect of waves of illegally drunk young minors and their lawsuit-happy parents gave business owners and tourism officials nightmares.

Traditional college culture, briefly displaced by the counterculture, saw a revival in the late 1970s, credited in part to the 1978 film *Animal House*. Many male students, particularly frat boys, seemed determined to live up—or down—to the old stereotypes of heavy drinking, brutal hazing, rape of unconscious coeds, and street fighting. Another old tradition was gay-bashing. However, frat boys who usually escaped consequences in former times now found that they were outnumbered by gays in certain parts of the Quarter, and their intended victims were fighting back. The gay community loudly publicized these incidents, and even if the police were not always interested in intervening, the public sympathy was now on the side of the gays.

The final straw was the arrival of out-of-town promoters. These producers would rent balconies, and set up video cameras to encourage and record young women flashing their breasts for crowds chanting, "Show yer tits!" and rewarding the same with strings of Carnival beads. These videos were seen on cable channels and offered on videotapes, and, later, DVDs. In 1999 *Playboy* magazine installed "bunnies" on a balcony at 327 Bourbon and sold the video as "Girls of Mardi Gras."[23] The national image of Carnival, out of control of New Orleans's own publicity machine, was now "beads for breasts." Native keepers of Carnival traditions were aghast. The prospect that upper Bourbon, and perhaps most of the Vieux Carré Carnival experience, might be abandoned to breakers, beads, and breasts was too much. Especially galling was the spread of this "bead economy" to "family friendly" parades well outside the Quarter as male float riders screamed at women to flash for beads.

Beginning in the midnineties, Bourbon Street moguls, tradition keepers, hoteliers, and tourism officials addressed this unwelcome development. Their legal options were few. Videography in a public setting was First Amendment protected. Discrimination based on age (past majority) or school affiliation was impossible. The club owners wanted to keep the hefty profits the kids brought, without the hassles. The hoteliers responded by requiring deposits and minimum stays.

After the much-publicized *Playboy* balcony incident of 1999, the city put out the word that nudity would not be tolerated at Carnival 2000. Also, the city loudly stated that it would enforce the ordinance[24]—unknown even to most natives—that forbids throwing anything from balconies.[25] In reality, and as proved in subsequent Carnival seasons, the NOPD was not about to charge into a building to apprehend a woman who had just shown her breasts from the balcony. Besides, the policemen appreciated the spectacle as much as any other straight male. Men standing on the street showing their privates for beads flung from above are a different story; they are more frequently arrested. The tourism industry wanted to simultaneously keep the profits that corporate balcony renters and breakers brought, and walk the line to keep at least a passing acquaintance with "family friendly" Carnival. As the last two frenzied weeks of Carnival 2000 rolled around, the NOPD and the city back-pedaled and denied there was a crackdown at all.[26]

This divided opinion, of traditions versus profits, resulted in pretty much the status quo. Around the country, other festivals were also experiencing the beads-for-breasts phenomenon.[27] The consensus, though by no means a universal opinion, was that "wild" behavior should be hosted in, and restricted to, the Quarter. The "family" parades should remain that way, and pressure was brought to bear on suburban krewes to forbid the battle cry of the bead economy.

After the terrorist attacks of September 11, 2001, New Orleans's tourism industry suffered, albeit to a lesser degree than some other localities. A large percentage of the city's tourists arrive from surrounding states by car and so were unaffected by fears of air travel.[28] Discouraging any tourist segment is now taboo. During short Carnival seasons, like that of 2005 or 2008, many hotels drop minimum stays if rooms go unsold even at bargain prices.

## SEX TOURISM

Historically, it has been difficult to separate sex tourism from traditional tourism in the Quarter. Until the widespread promotion of "legitimate" tourism in the 1920s, sex tourism was the vast majority of the Quarter's tourism business. Even after the preservationists of the 1920s and 1930s, Mrs. Werlein's crusades, and round after round of superficial cleanups, a baseline level of prostitution, female and male, remained,[29] and, during World War II, expanded to accommodate servicemen.

There was no published equivalent, after Storyville, of the famous *Blue Books*. Robert Kinney's *The Bachelor in New Orleans*[30] was a frank attempt to keep young straight men out of trouble as they prowled the Quarter of World War II and just after. It is interesting to note that some of the clubs Kinney discusses were, even at that time, gay tolerant, so the book may have been also used as a rather different sort of guide.

After World War II, most, but not all, streetwalkers gradually vanished from sight, but didn't change professions. The smart ones operated from the shelter of clubs that provided the police protection required to ply the trade. A few bordellos persisted. Most notable was Norma Wallace's at 1026 Conti, which stayed in business until 1962.[31]

For a teenage girl to go to D. H. Holmes for her first ball dress was an important rite of passage. Some teenage New Orleans boys, in their own rite of passage, were taken to bordellos by their fathers, or, in later times, taken down to Bourbon Street to be shown, and warned about, hookers and various scams.[32]

One of the best-known aspects of Quarter sex tourism was B-drinking. The origins of this worldwide practice must be ancient. B-drinking in the Quarter was noted many times over the years, yet it still flourished with each new crop of gullible and lonely men. Upon entering a bar, a man would be spotted by one of the house "B-girls" who would accost him and ask him to buy her a drink. The man would order drinks for both. The B-girl's drink would typically be iced tea, masquerading as bourbon, or sometimes a soda pretending to be an expensive "call drink." The man's drink would be an alcoholic beverage, of course. The B-girl would make time, chatting with the lonely visitor as he bought round after round of drinks. She might permit a little mutual affection, all carefully watched by the bartender and whatever other supervision might be around. Eventually, the man would get as drunk as he cared to, run out of money, or realize that the B-girl was not going to entertain him carnally. He would then leave or be ushered out if unhappy or falling-down drunk. In some bars the B-girls kept swizzle sticks from their drinks and turned them in at the end of their shifts, proof of their labors, much like punching a time card.[33] The B-girl would get a percentage of the take, with the house getting the rest.

B-drinking and prostitution are frequently mentioned in the same breath, yet they are mutual antagonists. B-drinking had to be hosted in a bar, which found it very profitable to keep men tempted—but unsated—as long as they bought one drink after another. Hookers, in contrast, were looking to pick up men, usually on the street, take them to a convenient and secure locale, turn the trick, and get back on the streets to resume the game. Men who were looking for hookers didn't care to hang around in bars any longer than necessary to find their quarry. So, bars that featured B-drinking didn't want hookers around to siphon off their clientele.[34]

## STRANGERS IN THE NIGHT

Prostitution is not, of course, the only aspect of sex tourism. The freewheeling atmosphere of the enclave, the boldness conferred by liquor, and the anonymity of being far from home makes getting laid very, very easy. Many Quarter visits are planned around that express purpose. One may meet plenty of "nice" people in the bars and clubs who are also interested in sexually available "nice" men and women. Long before Las Vegas used the slogan "What happens here, stays here"[35] visitors realized that the Quarter was a place set apart for the amorous as well as the architect, the hopeless romantics as well as the simply hopeless, the lonely as well as the literati. Common across all times and gender preferences is the "Carnival crush." The meeting of a stranger in an exotic locale, the uncommon freedom, the boozy corona of celebration, the mists of fantasy all separate the starry-eyed from workaday common sense. Lust is frequently mistaken for love, and a weekend in the Quarter can indeed seem like an eternity in the heart. We would have it no other way, at least until Ash Wednesday morning.

## THE MODERN PROS

As the 1960s became the 1970s, the bordellos, with very few exceptions, closed. The remaining old-time landladies had outlived their political protectors. Call girls have probably existed as long as the telephone, but new technology enabled them as never before. A manager, who might snarl at being called a madam or pimp, was now running an answering service from a comfortable office, perhaps miles from the Quarter. He or she answered calls from johns and matched them with hookers. The hookers, summoned by pagers and eventually cell phones, would arrive at hotels looking entirely presentable. Because the john had called the girl, and would have to initiate the request for sex, the strumpet's legal exposure was somewhat less than before. It was certainly less risky, and more profitable than walking the same six blocks of Bourbon in halter top, miniskirt, and fishnet hose night after night. It was also less risky for the john, who stayed in his hotel room, did not have to negotiate on the street, and was spared the possible embarrassment of mistaking a "trans" for a "real girl." The legal fig leaf was to call this an "escort service." In the early and middle eighties, the New Orleans yellow pages featured several pages of escort services, including some costly half-page ads.

Some escort services offered both call girls and call boys, whose services were also arranged in this manner. In the span between the easing of police harassment of gays in the early 1970s and the onset of AIDS in the 1980s, male prostitutes—"hustlers"—worked rather openly in the Quarter. Most, but not all, bar owners did not want them inside the clubs. A few clubs had symbiotic relationships with the hustlers. Whether these clubs, in the traditional model, paid the police to let "their" hustlers operate in peace will probably never be established; but it would not surprise anyone.

The visible street hustlers fell into two categories: the street boys and the pros. The street boys, since time immemorial, are young men, adrift and looking for quick cash. They may or may not be gay, and that is normally irrelevant. Through naïveté, they may make an approach to an undercover cop, who, if merciful, may direct them to a young persons' shelter, or if not, take them on to central lockup. An otherwise successful trick may be undone by revulsion and panic and one or both parties may be beaten up or fatally injured.

The pros were a different story. They were nearly all very handsome in the conventional sense and moved with a casual confidence. Their costumes varied, but in midsummer, that is the central six months of the year, they were often found in tight bathing trunks and white muscle shirts. Many carried, or had close by, gym bags containing their spare clothes, sex toys, and other workman's tools. In those times, many cars containing lone, usually middle-aged men would troll the Quarter, drifting in idle down St. Ann, Bourbon, Esplanade, North Rampart and looping back again. A large number of these cruising cars were from nearby communities in Jefferson and St. Tammany parishes. In the years of greater openness, the hustlers stood at popular corners like Bourbon and Dumaine or Bourbon and St. Ann, eyeballing the cruising cars and if need be, rubbing thumb and fingers together in the ancient signal. A tired office worker, carrying a gym bag, trudging back to his home in the lower Quarter from his Faubourg Marigny parking space, was accosted at 2:00 a.m. by such a trawler on Dauphine Street. The opportunity for some quick cash was demurred by the pedestrian's explanation that he was indeed just a weary resident going home after a long business trip.[36]

## SOUTHERN DECADENCE

Deep summer in New Orleans is a drowsy time. Everyone reaches an accommodation with the heat and humidity, both of which will register in the mid-nineties by noon. Chores are best done in the morning, or after nightfall, which is after 9:00 p.m. The city's famously languid pace slows even further. Those who can, flee to cooler climes, or failing that, stay close to air conditioners. Carnival looks far away, either a memory over the shoulder or just over the horizon of costuming and float building. Hotel rooms and tourist attractions get lonely. Labor Day used to demark the resumption of education, until longer school years sent kids back to classrooms in mid-August. It was a chance for one last vacation, but few families wanted to slog through the aquarium of the Deep South that time of year. With the exception of conventioneers who often bargain reduced rates in August, visitors are scarce.

The lack of things to do met with native creativity, and something special happened. In 1972 a group of costumed friends staged a gay bar crawl on the Sunday before Labor Day and called it "Southern Decadence."[37] Over

the years, the parade and attendant parties mushroomed. The grand marshall is a man in drag, frequently tall and with a lofty chapeau to empha-
size his, or rather, her, leadership of the cheerful rabble. By the mideighties,
the parade could entirely stop traffic on Decatur, Royal, and other parts of
the route. Starting at the Golden Lantern at Barracks and Royal, the throng
struts, sashays, stumbles, and marches around the Quarter in an afternoon
of bar hops, street theater, voguing, and astonished tourists. The drag might
be of the meticulous, elaborate craft New Orleans is famous for, or it might
be as simple as a thrift-store dress and beads. Drag, black leather, and bare
skin compete for attention. In the furnace heat, many men wear nothing but
trunks and sneakers, showing off tanned muscles cultivated over the summer. Although there is always an official theme, a wild range of expression
reigns. Like the Carnival Krewe du Vieux—sharing some members, in fact—
there is always at least one topical group. Their expression of the topic is well
coordinated, ever flamboyant, and usually over the edge of even present-day
taste. Before gay characters were a staple of television prime time, the shock
value of the parade was high. Most straight tourists were forewarned about
the event, and there were rarely any visible confrontations between the two
groups. Nonetheless, most tourists found the better drags and transsexuals all
too convincing and wondered aloud, with benign curiosity, if they were seeing a man or a woman, or something in between. They guffawed at the hairy
chorines and many clones of Dorothy Gale. Some of the satire, unmindful of
any political correctness, made jaws drop. A black friend of mine marched
as the Tar Baby. A group of young men dressed as school boys performed an
erotic pas de deux with an older man dressed as a priest. Some of the costumes were anatomically correct in a very large way. The cupidity of former
President Clinton inspired many rather graphic costumes. By late afternoon,
the parade melts into various packed bars as bedraggled revelers seek cool air
and cold drinks.

The authorities of the 1950s who had been terrified of visible "queers"
running off the straight tourist trade would be astounded. By the mideighties,
hotels were wondering at the sudden surge in bookings around Labor Day. In
the late nineties, it was estimated that sixty thousand would visit the Quarter
for Southern Decadence. The economic impact for 1997 was estimated at $25
million.[38] By 2004, crowd estimates were up to one hundred thousand and
the dollar figure was about $88 million.[39] The Quarter bars found Southern
Decadence to be second only to Carnival for business. The police, who once
might have tried to break up the mob of drag queens blocking traffic, were

generally mellow about the parade. In 1997 and after, the parade was made a legal public event with police escort and street sweepers. Far from discouraging the event, the city's tourism machine now promoted it far and wide, with the official blessing of a mayoral proclamation. Many gays began to prefer the event to Carnival, citing the smaller crowds, fewer drunk straight boys looking to pick fights, and the reliability of Decadence weather—always sultry, if sometimes rainy.

Unlike some gay events in San Francisco, total nudity on the street was exceedingly rare, but the line between legal clothing and exposure was constantly being tested. In Boys Town, the gay entertainment portion of the Quarter, it was extremely common for men to flash their privates on the street for the roaring, bead-tossing approval of gay bar balconies. However, it seemed that the police were less concerned about this than they were at Carnival, and arrests were rare. Perhaps the overwhelmingly gay crowd did not need to be "protected" from the spectacle. Also, the Decadence crowds of Boys Town, even in various states of undress, gave the police less cause for concern than the Carnival crowds of the upper Quarter, whose ranks are full of intoxicated high schoolers, spring breakers, and frat boys.

The durability of Southern Decadence as an institution was demonstrated on September 4, 2005, just after the onslaught of Hurricane Katrina. About forty[40] people staged a parade, pulling a boom box on a wagon, keeping the tradition unbroken.[41]

## BLACK TOURISM

In the era of de jure segregation, only a few New Orleans hotels catered to Negro tourists, and entertainment was also subject to the color line. A few adventurous whites might visit "Negro clubs" for the "red hot" music that the *City Guide* mentioned, but this cross-cultural exchange was discouraged. Black tourism in the Jim Crow South was usually limited to visiting family members. Many blacks self-selected not to tour historic sites, like plantations, associated with Confederate nostalgia. The "Old South" ambience of hoop skirts, magnolias, and "happy darkies" created for white tourists was unpalatable to blacks. Most major tourist attractions, and nearly all hotels, restaurants, theaters, washrooms, and drinking fountains were strictly divided by color. Amenities designated for "colored" use were usually inferior to those marked for "whites." So it was in New Orleans, and in particular the Quarter, where all tourist business was white-owned. Although a few Negro families lived in the Quarter throughout the segregated era, they were not welcome as tourists in their own village. For several decades, blacks found in the Quarter, and not obviously employed as menials, were harassed by police and self-appointed keepers of the status quo.[42]

The accelerating tempo of the civil rights movement in the early 1960s created an unexpected effect on Quarter tourism. National groups, based outside the South, were now sending Negro delegates to their conventions. In the South, these delegates often received second-rate accommodations and were sometimes barred from convention activities by local authorities. Organizations that took note of these Jim Crow practices in New Orleans started cancelling conventions. Seymour Weiss, former crony of Huey Long, managed the Roosevelt hotel, one of the convention anchors of New Orleans. In 1962, he was joined by Hyp Guinle, owner of Bourbon Street's Famous Door jazz club in sounding an alarm about convention cancellations: "Seymour Weiss tells me he's had five cancellations from conventions this year because he couldn't take one or two colored delegates. That's what [is] hurting the French Quarter. When conventions with 1,200 to 1,400 people cancel out, we know it on Bourbon Street. We live on conventions."[43]

After the end of legal segregation with the Civil Rights Act of 1964, de facto segregation was still deeply entrenched in the Quarter. In 1965, a group of black football players, in town for an exhibition game, had trouble getting a cab to the Quarter. They were told they had to get a "colored cab." Once in the Quarter, they were verbally abused and refused entry by several nightclub barkers, only finding welcome at Al Hirt's and Pete Fountain's clubs. The disgusted players, debating leaving town, heard some frantic pleading by local authorities. One of these was the head of the local chapter of the NAACP, civil rights attorney Ernest "Dutch" Morial. These entreaties notwithstanding, the players voted to leave.[44] Their complaints to the American Football League caused the game to be shifted to Houston.[45] The city fathers predictably blamed the victims for their troubles. Sportscaster Hap Glaudi was famous for his signature greeting, "Well, heah we ah!" He described the "Negro players" as "mutinous," an adjective leftover from slavery.[46] The city, eager to secure an NFL franchise, launched a public relations campaign to assure black athletes and tourists of a friendlier reception.[47] However, incidents like this persisted throughout the late sixties.[48]

By the 1970s, the Quarter was perceived as an entertainment venue for three largely white groups: hard-drinking college students, conventioneers, and gays. What the Quarter offered to black tourists was problematic, even after the end of de jure segregation. As homogenized, nominally multiethnic national culture crept in via the corporate clubs, black tourists should have found the clubs more welcoming. Yet there were no straight clubs in the Quarter that pursued a black tourist clientele, largely from fear of attracting natives of color, whose presence in the Quarter was still discouraged.[49] The Bayou Classic football game between Louisiana's historically black colleges, Grambling and Southern, has been a tradition since 1974. It attracted thousands of blacks to the city each year.[50] Most Quarter businessmen gritted their teeth and waited for the event to get over. They disliked the lines of cruising cars, stereos booming, snaking around the streets, the spontaneous street parties—and sometimes fights—arising from gridlock. They felt that blacks did not spend as much money as whites at events like the Sugar Bowl. Improved traffic management by the NOPD helped clear the Quarter of most automotive congestion, but the merchants were still apprehensive each Thanksgiving as the Bayou Classic and its attendant street party rolled into town.[51]

On yet another ill-starred New Year's Eve, 2005, a young black man died after being wrestled to the ground and choked by white bouncers as New Orleans police looked on. The death of Levon Jones on the banquette outside Razzoo in the 500 block of Bourbon,[52] after an altercation that is still cloudy years later, set off a wave of protest. Four bouncers were eventually indicted. Even as the criminal case wound slowly through the courts, an ordinance was passed prohibiting Vieux Carré bouncers from using sleeper choke holds.[53]

The city sent testers—"mystery shoppers" as Mayor Nagin dubbed them—of young black and white men to the bars to see if there were patterns of discrimination. To no one's surprise, it seemed that blacks faced more scrutiny about dress and were sometimes charged higher prices for drinks.[54] A briefing for bar service employees and their bosses was held after the mystery shoppers reported. A widely held opinion was voiced that blacks were perceived to be poor or nontippers. That might explain the disparity in drink prices as bartenders added their own gratuity to the bill. Some bar owners disputed the study. They claimed, among other things, that drinks might be made to differing recipes with varying cost of liquor, or that black mystery shoppers might have bought drinks just before happy hour, and their white counterparts bought their drinks after the computerized cash registers changed to happy hour prices.[55] A 1956 New Orleans ordinance requires all bars to post drink prices in two places. These "bill of fare" signs may or may not be in every bar, and like most New Orleans ordinances affecting tourism, are unevenly enforced.[56] The four bouncers in the Razzoo incident were all acquitted by October 2008,[57] leaving a lingering sense of injustice and vulnerability among black tourists.

## The Tour Guides

The early tour guides of the 1920s, like Flo Fields, must have seemed very strange to tenement dwellers. They herded gawking tourists over the uneven banquettes, pointing out features on still-eroding buildings. In her foreword to Arnold Genthe's 1926 *Impressions of Old New Orleans*, Grace King noted a Vieux Carré cicerone (tour guide) and his flock of visitors in the early twenties: "At any hour of a fair day during Winter, a little crowd of strangers may be seen following or clustering around a cicerone, who professes to relate the stories or romances as they are called of the period out of which the old quarter arose. Romances are demanded, and romances are given them by the cicerone, who has laid in a stock of them. He seems to take them out of his cedar press of memory every year and air them and dust them to make them look fresh for his auditors. Telling them does not wear them out apparently."[58] Gradually, tour buses chugged along the streets, followed by buggies drawn by mules, which withstand the subtropical heat better than horses. The buggy drivers sing out an interesting, if not always factual, spiel as the buggies roll along. Residents have to endure these oft-fanciful narrations day after day. Patience sometimes wears thin and more than one buggy driver has found himself contradicted, in a loud and salty manner, by a resident on a balcony or banquette.

In the 1990s, the "goth" movement crept out of New Orleans based on the vampire books of Anne Rice. A national adolescent fad for eighteenth-century clothes, dark makeup, and personas from the books emerged. Tapping into the goth/vampire craze, as well as the fame of the city's celebrated cemeteries, "ghost" and "haunted" tours were now in the Quarter. The veracity of the tours seemed even more suspect than the buggy-driver yarns.[59] Local actors—or sometimes derelicts—were paid to jump out of dark doorways to the shrieking delight of tourists. These tours sometimes had several dozen participants clogging the banquette, and the tour guides used megaphones to be heard. Conducted at night, when residents were trying to sleep, the tours became a flashpoint.[60] The tour operators attempted to deflect criticism by pointing out that the National Park Service and other groups give free tours, albeit not loud, nocturnal ones. That any part of the tourist experience should be "free" is anathema to the tourism industry, which resented any agency siphoning off tourists they felt to be their rightful marks. In 2003, after several rounds with the city council, restrictions were placed on tours. Among these are a limit of twenty-eight participants, separation of tour groups by fifty feet, and no megaphones.[61]

It often surprises tourists to find a National Historical Park, complete with park rangers, in the Vieux Carré. Established in 1978 as a part of the regional Jean Lafitte National Historical Park and Preserve, the French Quarter unit at 419 Decatur gives free, factual walking tours of the Vieux Carré by well-educated rangers every day save Fat Tuesday and Christmas. The headquarters also has an exhibit area and organizes folklife demonstrations including crafts and cooking.[62] Overlapping the French Quarter unit is the New Orleans Jazz National Historical Park, established in 1994.[63] Like its sister in the Vieux Carré, the Jazz NHP is a "conceptual" or "cerebral" park, as opposed to a fixed plot of land, which interprets the historic landscape associated with the development of jazz.

## THE SAVIOR BECOMES THE CAPTOR

Irby, Saxon, and Werlein saved the Quarter during the 1920s by a combination of acquisition, publicity, and networking. Preservationists, of that time through the present, often found their most powerful allies outside the parish line. Appealing to a larger audience of journalists, academics, and politicians was vital in saving Madame Vieux Carré from the wrecking ball in the 1920s and from the Riverfront Expressway in the 1960s.

Ultimately, it was the power of the tourist dollar that translated Quarter "decrepitude" into marketable "charm." The tourist dollar, nostalgia for the lost French Opera House, and shame over the decay of the city's old heart made the New Orleans establishment care about the fortunes of the Quarter and led to legal mechanisms to preserve what was left of the enclave. The coexistence of tourism, in its more naive forms, with dignified residential life was seen as necessary by the first and second wave of preservationists.

New Orleans tourism as big business gelled in the 1950s. Between the twenties and the sixties, a close-knit consortium of leading hotels, bars, restaurants, and tour companies controlled most of the tourist trade. They thrived on the lucrative convention business—white, mostly male and heterosexual—and saw no reason to further promote city tourism.[64] A 1960 study revealed that of twenty-six city convention and visitors' bureaus, New Orleans ranked last in budget, outspent by such unlikely venues as Omaha, Kansas City, and Cleveland.[65] In 1960, after several years of prodding by Mayor Morrison, the Greater New Orleans Tourist and Convention Commission was established.[66]

The traditional focus on conventioneers made the mass-market Quarter tourist experience a rather static offering. The stereotype of the conventioneer was a middle-aged man, escaping his wife and family for a brief chance to booze it up with the boys and ogle, at least, unfamiliar women. Bars, nightclubs, casinos, and hookers all made good profits serving this stereotype. New Orleans tourist venues seem to have been slow to recognize that married couples—yesteryear's "straight arrows"—might spend more money while in town than the hard-drinking, stripper-ogling conventioneer. Antiques, high-priced meals, better hotel rooms, and historic tours all might be sold if the wife was along.

Large hotels, like the Roosevelt and the Monteleone, had thrived on the margins of the Quarter. In 1959, the Quarter's first motel, the Prince Conti, opened at 830 Conti. In 1960, the Royal Orleans hotel opened at 621 St. Louis, featuring nearly four hundred rooms.[67] In succeeding years, a number of hotels located in the Quarter. They promoted themselves as party destinations in their own right with bars, restaurants, and coveted balcony space overlooking the hoopla of the upper Quarter. On their heels came the bed-and-breakfasts (B&Bs), which we will discuss in the 1994–2000 chapter.

Many well-seasoned travelers and travel agents noted occasionally indifferent service and snotty attitudes in Quarter and Canal Street hotel staffs. The Sunbelt have-a-nice-day industry standard demeanor was, understandably, a challenge for those commuting from black ghettos to service jobs in the Quarter, dealing with mostly white tourists from Middle America.

The prospect of high-rise hotels overshadowing the old structures prompted the city council to enact a moratorium on new Quarter hotels in 1969. In 1982, the moratorium was revised to permit new hotels on the declining Canal Street and in the Quarter, but only in existing buildings. The moratorium was widely believed to be merely symbolic, a flaccid, if not dead, letter. The city council granted some exceptions to allow hotels to exceed a height of seventy feet and expand into former residential buildings.[68] Even without authorization, some hotels quietly made over apartment houses into lodging.[69] Most recently, developers wanted to place a hotel in a long-vacant

1885 building at 111 Iberville, sitting in a sea of parking lots. Proponents pointed to the area's long dormancy and suggested there was nothing left to preserve.[70] Opponents feared a torrent of other hotel applications and suggested that condos might be more appropriate.[71] Condos are illegally operated as nightly rentals throughout the Quarter, so that option was no panacea. Over the objections of Councilwoman Clarkson, the city council authorized the hotel in 2005. Mayor Nagin vetoed it, and sent the concept back to the developers. In August 2006, the plan was withdrawn after opposition became too intense.[72] Post–Hurricane Katrina, the number of hotel rooms required for New Orleans's reduced tourist trade was uncertain, and adding any new rooms would be an act of faith.

As the seventies progressed, the tourist industry became diffused from a tight cluster of big hotels and well-known nightclubs on upper Bourbon to many different businesses, including the acknowledged emergence of the Quarter as a gay and lesbian tourist venue. Now the entire Quarter, including the once-sleepy lower side, was a tourist destination. Even neighborhood bodegas were now selling tourist trinkets and "authentic" New Orleans food products. As we have seen, a variety of tours emerged, to explain every aspect of Quarter history, real or imagined.

The explosion of tourism, especially in the lower Quarter, gave residents much to complain about. Bars often left doors open, even in summertime, and loud music blasted out, antagonizing residents down the block.[73] The increased competition for parking; the loud, nighttime "haunted" tours; the slow-moving and factually wobbly buggy tours; the intoxication, urination, and regurgitation; all were grating. Even well-intentioned, polite tourists may naively offend as they rest on one's stoop or gawk into inner gardens. Behavior that would never be accepted in distant hometowns is "OK" in the Quarter. The tourism industry turns upon this understanding. But the root-stock of residents' complaints is the tourist mistranslation of "few rules" into "no rules." The "few rules" that always apply, against drugs, public urination, violence, and rape are enforced with a famous unevenness. This may mean escape of consequences for some visitors, but the quality of Quarter life never escapes the consequences. The enclave's famed tolerance for juvenile antics goes down as Quarter homeowners get older and wealthier, and now have impressionable children of their own. The revivalist movement in the Quarter at the turn of the twentieth to twenty-first century hoped to upgrade the tourist experience above the stock-in-trade cliches, and eliminate irritants like obscenity-booming music and public urination that mar the tourist and resident experience alike.

A hope resounding over the decades has been to attract "a better class of tourist." As the New Orleans tourism base widened to family venues like the aquarium, the National World War II Museum, and the world-class Audubon Zoo, that hope has been partly realized. Yet the young, the loud, and the all-too-drunk still flock to the Quarter. Rather than simply discouraging these mostly youthful revelers, and hoping that more mature and wealthier crowds would fill in, a more comprehensive strategy is suggested. The young crowd is simply too much of a money machine to drive away, and there is no opportunity to remove the bars and clubs that host them, unlike the replacement of spring break hotels with expensive condos in beach towns. Better policing should help reduce the abusive behaviors that rankle residents. Better policing means more police presence throughout the Quarter, not just on tourist lanes, and policing the bouncers that operate as an unofficial police force at the clubs. The young people roaming Bourbon with big beers, big hats, and big beads today, will, it is hoped, be tomorrow's well-heeled family tourist coming back with kids in tow to spend money at the non-Quarter attractions.

"This isn't Disneyland!" snarled many residents who resented their unsought role in the entertainment. However, like it or not, residents, especially visually distinctive ones, became part of the perceived perpetual party and the *tout ensemble*. Gradually, but accelerating as the century ended, the New Orleans and Quarter presented for tourists began to shift from the authentic city and enclave to one more a part of the national culture, especially for chain clubs. These clubs had name recognition with younger visitors who had patronized other outlets of the same chains elsewhere. This national culture was topped off with New Orleans-esque touches to give the outlet a local identity. The replacement of Dixieland with nationally accepted jazz,[74] the omission of inconvenient Crescent City aspects, and the reflexive spinning of unfavorable tourist publicity reflected this shift. Some thought that Bourbon had been cleaned up too much. The old-time ambience of B-girls, screaming barkers, and tawdry shows was not "authentic" French Quarter culture, of course. It was pretty much the same as any strip of dives in any port city.

The transformation of tourism from Madame's savior to Madame's captor came about not from the tourists per se. In largest part, it was the city's horrible economic state after the early 1980s that put a huge economic burden on the back of tourism, and, therefore, on the boney shoulders of its Queen of Attractions, the Vieux Carré. Magazine Street, Frenchman Street, the revived Warehouse District, and other extra-Quarter places all now lure the tourist dollar. But it was still the Quarter that drew the crowds. Of course, even tourists who target attractions other than the Quarter inevitably wind up there. By the 1990s, many wondered if the Quarter had reached its carrying capacity for tourism. Ironically, the conversion of some buildings to condos may have prevented them from becoming even more T-shirt and tourist trinket stores. How many more tourists can the Quarter accommodate? The answer seems to be "none." During Carnival and Southern Decadence, the upper Quarter streets are crammed with almost impassable crowds. Parking is still tight and no more seems to be forthcoming. Clubs, unable to expand, must pack 'em in and pack 'em out as fast as possible during festivities, often counting patrons to ensure that occupancy limits are not exceeded.

Since the number of visitors the Quarter can accommodate at any one time is fixed, more festivals and events have been added to fill in the once-welcomed lulls in tourist waves. One recent addition is the commercial parades, hosted on tour buggies, that allow tourists to throw beads and doubloons to other tourists. Residents walk on and let the out-of-towners scramble for beads from the banquettes and gutters.

After the Katrina deluge, tourism, as the city's chief economic engine, was revived as quickly as possible, reassuring the world that the Quarter was undamaged and open for business.

## CHAPTER 10

# 1978–1994

*The Long Slide Down*

## THE PENDULUM SWINGS

Sometime around 1974, New Orleans became a majority black city.[1] *Creole New Orleans: Race and Americanization*, edited by Arnold R. Hirsch and Joseph Logsdon,[2] is a concise study of the emergence of black political power in the city. It is interesting to contrast Chai's 1971 study with the Hirsch and Logsdon volume, which cuts off at 1992. In the span of twenty-one years, the city's political leadership was dominated by elected black officialdom, with businesspeople—mainly from the tourist industry—and ministers of leading black churches also claiming important wedges of the pie chart. It is important to note that the business leadership of New Orleans at the end of the century was far different from that of Chai's day. At that time, business leaders were drawn mainly from banking, manufacturing, and primary industry. Those segments based in New Orleans have declined markedly. Now, business leadership is largely drawn from the tourism, service, and consulting firms. The latter exert powerful influence as they jockey for city hall largesse. After all, New Orleans has no shortage of problems to "study." After the election of New Orleans's first mayor of color, modern Creole Ernest "Dutch" Morial in 1978, activism in the larger city largely revolved around competition between black political organizations. This population majority is also an economic minority. Besides having persistently high unemployment, New Orleans has rates of automobile and home ownership that are very low by national standards, and anecdotal evidence suggests that perhaps one-quarter of all city residents did not have checking accounts prior to Hurricane Katrina in 2005.

The ascendency of black politicians to the top of city authority intersected with the decline in oil revenues and the overall national economic doldrums of the late seventies and early eighties. With the decline of the state's and city's fortunes, the stored-up expectations of New Orleans blacks were to go largely unfulfilled. Most of the rewards the new mayoral administrations gave out were to blacks who were already well connected and well off.[3] New Orleans began the painful process of shifting from one largely monoracial government to another.

New Orleans's mayors of color inherited a political system crafted over two centuries by white politicians into the most byzantine, corrupt, and colorful in America. If mayors of color awarded lucrative contracts on the basis of campaign contributions,[4] they were merely doing what generations of white politicians had done.[5] Corruption, as we have seen, was accepted provided the city had some degree of efficiency. That bargain began to fall apart in this era, as the municipal bureaucracy became ever more moribund. From 1946 to 1961, Mayor Chep Morrison had the advantage of a local press corps that was, by turns, sympathetic and browbeaten.[6] The first black mayors of big-city America had no such consistent amen corner in the Fifth Estate, not even in the black press.[7] In common, they all had to deal with inherited woes while trying to fulfill the expectations of poor blacks long shut out of the mainstream of American prosperity.

## THE LONG SLIDE DOWN

The boom days of oil were numbered. Oil prices fell steadily from 1981 to 1986.[8] The New Orleans Metropolitan Statistical Area's oil employment peaked in 1982 at about 21,700 and began to sink. Jobs somewhat recovered by 1987 but continued a downward trend from there on. By 2000, about half of the 1982 jobs were gone. The downward trend continued in the first years of the new century.[9] In 1988, the state ran a deficit of over a billion dollars.[10]

Oil and tourism had been the twin pillars of the area economy, and as the oil boom faded away in the mideighties, Louisiana and New Orleans fell on hard times. The tide of oil ebbed, leaving little in the way of capital improvements. Much of the money seems to have gone to tax relief, which fueled the consumer segment but built no bridges, no ports, and certainly helped no schools.[11] The primary industries of the Morrison era—shipping, metallurgy, and heavy manufacturing—were all declining. The remaining heavy industry centered on defense work, such as the sprawling Avondale shipyard west of town and smaller shipyards out Chef Menteur Highway to the east. Even those with good-paying jobs in town often chose not to live in Orleans Parish but endured the commute from Slidell, Mandeville, Kenner, and points even further away. For those who wanted suburban norms and acceptable schools, this made perfect sense.

After the wrenching struggles over integration in the early sixties, New Orleans did not experience the rioting and attendant destruction seen elsewhere in the South and certain big northern cities. However, the integration victory was Pyrrhic. White flight effectively resegregated the public schools of New Orleans.[12] The most integrated schools were the parochial schools, where upper-middle-class black and white children wore the same uniforms. White New Orleanians relapsed into a daydream of racial harmony. A few progressive whites knew that black leadership would eventually emerge. Maurice "Moon" Landrieu, mayor from 1970 to 1978, acted as mentor to the first cadre of black city officials and brought blacks into positions of responsibility.[13] Ernest "Dutch" Morial had been elected the city's first mayor of color in 1978. His qualifications as an attorney, state legislator, and judge were impressive and he had been a protégé of Landrieu.[14] Dutch Morial's first mayoralty was sold as a peaceful transition and not a revolution, as had been the case in other major cities. Dutch inherited classic big city problems, such as crumbling infrastructure, eroding tax bases, and the drug trade. Another issue was the police department, the majority of whom were Italian-American. Many policemen were openly hostile to the notion of a mayor of color.[15] Dutch's first chief of police, James Parson, imported from Birmingham, was resented for breaking up some of the long-established police graft and corruption, particularly in the Quarter.[16] These resentments blossomed into the Teamsters Union's absorption of the local police union,[17] which resulted in two strikes just before Carnival, 1979. The leading krewes backed Dutch in cancelling the parades, and Dutch and his staff craftily split the striking police into bite-sized factions, which ended the strike.[18] Although most white New Orleanians were grateful that the Teamsters would not control the NOPD, the racial dimensions surrounding the strike escaped no one, especially Dutch.

Unfortunately, for criticism, even from well-meaning would-be allies, Dutch had a thin skin. His personality created a virulent cycle of critique and reaction.[19] Dutch didn't help matters by taking rhetorical aim at powerful white institutions like the Boston Club. All of these attributes eventually alienated him from moderate whites who had been willing to give him a chance.

Dutch's reelection campaign of 1982 was bruising. His challenger was a white, thirty-one-year-old state legislator, Ron Faucheux. Although there are no strange bedfellows in New Orleans politics, it must have surprised Dutch Morial that his challenger was backed by Morial's old mentor, Moon Landrieu. Faucheux's support was biracial and included Sidney Barthelemy's Community Organization for Urban Politics (COUP).[20] Morial narrowly won the runoff by about two percentage points.[21] By the end of his administration in 1987, the atmosphere for business—in a word, white—capital investment was thoroughly poisoned, and racial dialog was severely polarized.[22]

No matter how much the city establishment resisted, Quarter culture was changing. The counterculture so savagely fought at the dawn of the 1970s was now more or less the mainstream culture of young adult America, including New Orleans. The maturity that had pushed aside some of the sleaziness was losing ground. The swarm of well-dressed patrons that once kept the jazz clubs busy was dwindling. The twenty-somethings touring Bourbon had been raised on recorded rock and roll, and that is what the clubs boomed out. Female streetwalkers had been part of the scenery for centuries. Now, masculine male prostitutes—"hustlers" and some very convincing transsexuals and transvestites—openly worked the streets, raising eyebrows of even jaded Quarter dwellers. Residents and club owners faced increasing doorway urination and passed-out partiers on their stoops. T-shirts, often with frankly lewd images and slogans, were eagerly sought trophies, and more T-shirt shops sprang up to satisfy the demand. The T-shirt shops presented these shirts, along with cheap tourist trinkets, and frequently used loud music to get young people's attention. Contrasted with the Vieux Carré's famous old restaurants, art galleries, and antique stores, the T-shirt shops were hardly "quaint and distinctive" parts of the *tout ensemble*. Parts of the old Warehouse District were being reshaped for the 1984 World's Fair, and a number of vagrants had migrated from that area into the Quarter.[23] The look of upper Bourbon, still home to a few diehard Quarter residents, reminded some of New York's then-infamous combat zone, Times Square.[24]

Clarinetist Pete Fountain had closed his club at 700 Bourbon in 1971, and it was largely vacant during this period.[25] Another landmark jazz club was Al Hirt's, at 501 Bourbon; Hirt's own residence was just around the corner on St. Louis. Hirt was disturbed by the changing culture and vanishing jazz fans.

Three T-shirt shops, five topless-bottomless strip shows, a massage parlor, and an adult film store were all located in Hirt's block of Bourbon. It was hard for a legitimate club, catering to a mature audience, to compete in this sea of sleaze.[26] In early 1983 he announced the closing of his club, citing declining business and social decay. He opined that local residents would not come to the Quarter "without an armed guard."[27] The remarks were picked up by the national press. Some of the Vieux Carré's longtime defenders agreed with him, but civic boosters were shocked. They pointed to the closing of Bourbon to create a pedestrian mall, and pinned their hopes on improvements associated with the 1984 World's Fair.[28]

The reaction from Mayor Morial was quite reminiscent of Mayor Morrison thirty years before: "'If laws are being broken', Morial said in a news conference Monday [11 July 1983], 'we're going to see that there is appropriate law enforcement to correct the conditions that he has complained of.' Morial also said a group has been formed to counteract the bad image the city received from coverage of Hirt's statements."[29]

In other words, spinning this event was more important, and had no political risk, than trying to clean up the conditions offending the famous musician. Hirt never reopened his club. However, after all, a native son, he returned to the city's good graces and trumpeted a moving "Ave Maria" for Pope John Paul II during the pontiff's 1987 visit.[30] The Quarter was not a privileged island when it came to economic vicissitudes. As had happened after the Civil War, there was again a sharp division between economic fortunes of Quarter residents. A handful of the old-money crowd—the aging remnants of the tweed and beads set of the fifties—still remained. Some new money, mainly show business folks, bought up mansions on Royal and Esplanade. Many of the Quarter dwellers were working poor or, like me and most of my friends, barely middle class. With double-digit mortgage interest[31] and a moribund city economy, real estate was in turgid stagnation and many properties sat on the market for years.

## LOOK TO THIS DAY

Nostalgia is a dangerous drug that wafts in the very air of the Vieux Carré. This cocktail of memory, imagination, and reconsidered events hangs like a nimbus over every discussion of Quarter life. For a historian, personal experience must be strained through a mesh of steel. Even so, I am not alone in regarding the period of 1975 to 1987 as the era of the greatest livability, for the greatest number, in the modern history of the Vieux Carré.[32]

Of course, I could cite many caveats. Those dependent directly on the oil industry were either moving out or grimly hanging on to jobs not yet departed to Houston. The service industry that supported the native Quarter population—the groceries, neighborhood bars, hardware stores, and fix-it men—was, in turn, having hard times. The federal tax laws, until 1986, allowed owners of decrepit properties to take write-offs as the buildings' value declined.[33] Until 2008, New Orleans's property tax structure was a crazy quilt of seven assessors who valued property based on political connection, friendship, or at best, outdated information.[34] Some Quarter properties were expressly bought for the loss write-off they allowed.[35] Obviously, owners of these write-offs had no incentive to fix up the buildings, and some renters had to make repairs with their own resources. The more genial landlords would reimburse these repairs in cash, to avoid pesky documentation. Some buildings that appeared ideal for commercial development sat idle for long years. The old Stella Maris Catholic mission, at 1201 Chartres (at Gov. Nicholls) was a brown-brick ghost from 1987 until bought and condoized in 1995.[36]

When I moved to my second apartment in April 1985, my landlord told me that about one-third of all Vieux Carré rental units were vacant, which was confirmed by subsequent statistics.[37] Some of these were former hotel rooms, converted from apartments in anticipation of the 1984 World's Fair. As the fair imploded, it was expedient to make these back into leased units. Some owner-landlords, unable to find new tenants or sell their senescent property, suffered renters to go a month or two, or more, between rent checks, in the hope that money might come in soon.

"The fifth [of the month] has come and the fifth has gone," growled a landlord to a friend as we tried to tiptoe up his stairwell on lower Bourbon. "I told ya, I'm getting paid next week," my pal intoned. "Awright," snarled the Kowalski-ish landlord. Behind closed doors, my friend smiled thinly. "He'll be back in his bottle soon, and forget he said anything, until next week, I hope."

Some absentee landlords allowed their properties to decline markedly. My first, and quickly abandoned, apartment house on lower St. Philip, was such a place. The dishwasher, disposal, and one of the window air conditioners were broken. The teenage "supers" had been chased away at knife point by squatters on the top floor and feared to return.

The Quarter frequently looked and felt empty. Apart from the tourist scene of Decatur Street and the eternal, now mostly collegiate party of upper Bourbon, residential blocks drowsed alone in the afternoons. Even on weekends the Quarter was not that crowded. Then there was crime. Several high-profile assaults and murders of tourists in the late seventies and early eighties had made the Quarter a dread to the timid.[38] As one sorts through the anecdotes, and tries to screen the racial biases, it is still apparent that crimes against property increased markedly in the eighties and nineties in the Quarter. Quarter architecture, apart from the famous "Romeo" spikes, offered plenty of opportunities for barely forced entry. Floor-to-ceiling windows, ancient, seldom-changed locks on ill-fitting doors, and dark alleyways all gave burglars ample entrée. Despite preservationist misgivings, many residents installed broken glass atop their gates and walls. Alarm systems and big dogs became popular. Automobiles were—and are—frequent targets for "smash and grabs" as well as outright theft. Drivers were advised not to leave anything, even trifles, in plain sight that might tempt drug addicts to break a window. My landlord's BMW window was broken for two dollars in change in the coin holder.

At the same time that crime was increasing, public mistrust of the police was growing. The impression was that the increasingly black NOPD was more concerned with the profits of corruption and internal politics than preventing crime or apprehending criminals. What police protection was available in the Quarter seemed devoted to the Bourbon strip and Decatur Street. To supplement the police presence, the Lower Quarter Crime Watch (LQCW) was started in the early eighties. The LQCW hires off-duty policemen to provide additional patrols. With the problems in the NOPD over the years, the LQCW's paid officer was at times the only law enforcement in the lower Quarter. Some of the membership of the LQCW overlaps that of VCPORA.[39]

Quarter residents felt that people from nearby housing projects saw the Quarter and the possessions therein as a resource to be tapped at will. Some serious, and, yes, sober discussion was devoted to turning the lower Vieux Carré into a gated community, with passes required for nonresidents. Since this was floated at the same time that the United States was pressuring South Africa to abandon apartheid and its pass system, it was politically quite impossible.

Despite these concerns, for those who had a steady paycheck, and a relatively safe and cozy place to live, life could be very sweet. Apart from some tensions at the physical edges of the enclave, gay and straight residents were getting along. Police harassment of gays and lesbians was ebbing. A few people with money were buying and fixing up properties. In this renter's market, one could be choosey. Apartments of all grades were plentiful. A friend of mine had a flat on Royal Street. On the third floor, it was reached by well-worn creaking stairs. At the landing, a rotting beam spanned the gorge above the courtyard all by itself. Why? Well, perhaps it was holding the building up. The apartment had a small kitchen with ancient spigots sticking straight out of the wall above the iron sink. A tiny rectangular opening between the kitchen and bathroom mystified. Maybe it allowed heat to be shared between the two. A double-sided fireplace, long since sealed, divided the living room from the bedroom, the walls on either side having been removed. The woodwork had many coats of thick paint. Each coat was flaking to show a memory of someone's taste in the strata below. At night, peering through the shutters, we beheld the glowing new skyscrapers of the CBD rising proudly, looking with condescension upon these old houses. Silhouetted against this glow, the old buildings rose up as shapes of black construction paper, shaped by a long-forgotten bedtime story. All this for $150 a month. Another friend of mine had an entire, large and cheerfully frowsy house, with garden, on Barracks for a mere $350 a month, a sum that did not change from 1981 to 1993.

My second apartment was a renovated attic on Gov. Nicholls. The attic ran for 110 feet under the roof of the old double shotgun, which had long since been converted to three apartments on the main floor and one in the attic above. The space was demarked by the five chimneys that rose up from the now-defunct fireplaces below, and a bathroom and kitchen clustered around the upper stairwell landing. My bedroom was at the inner end, and so was in the very heart of the quiet block. My living room had three stained-glass windows that cranked open to let in the street sounds, the fragrances, and the lure of possibilities. At the time I moved in, the building was empty, save for a gentleman in the back apartment. As time went on, two airline stewardesses moved into the middle unit and a young married couple in the front. I felt secure behind the succession of locked doors—the alley gate, the stairwell door, and my own door at the top of the stairs.

Three days after I moved in, our Neighborhood Watch had a block party, featuring wine, a three-piece band, and the inevitable Lucky Dog wagon. Mixing with my new neighbors, I realized that I was one of the poorer people on the block; but that fact arrived casually and without any snootiness or exclusion. Indeed, my wealthy neighbors across the street invited me to take pictures in the garden of their award-winning property.[40] Another insight came after Mayor Dutch Morial stopped by to address us, just at sunset. He spoke of supporting Neighborhood Watch and Lower Quarter Crime Watch, and then after polite applause, got in his limousine. As his car made the turn at Bourbon, some of my neighbors chuckled derisively at the contrast between the mayor's little pep talk and his more public pronouncements.

It was not merely one's apartment that made the experience. As part of the last cadre of the sixties and seventies counterculture, I shared that group's longing to experience something truthful and unique, something not pre-planned and prepackaged by corporate manipulation. Here was the feeling of being part of a genuinely unique society. It was the feeling that the Quarter was a huge outdoor living room, with way stations—the bars, the restaurants, and the houses of friends. In an afternoon's stroll, one might visit the cheapest flat imaginable and an elegant townhouse on Royal. Elbows could be rubbed with mainstays of the arts at one watering hole and cast-up merchant sea-men, hustlers, and small-time dope dealers at another. All were met with an extended sense of communal familiarity. "Degrees of separation" was not a phrase in public use then; we said "friend of a friend" in the same way that ancestors, no matter the antiquity, are reduced to "great-grandpa." And there were many friends of friends. What alienation might there be was felt in the tourist thoroughfares of upper Bourbon, Royal, and especially Decatur Street. The latter had become, even at that time, primarily a tourist strip, offering family-friendly fleecing of every description. Once we were acclimated, the rounds we had to make outside the Quarter were disconcerting. These excur-sions were usually to larger grocery stores or movie theaters within the city or shopping in places like Metairie. For Quarter and Marigny denizens who thought nothing of twelve-block journeys on foot, Metairie and the other suburbs looked far away, even with an automobile. They were foreign enough to require different behavior, to remind ourselves that we were no longer in the Quarter and induce a feeling of relief when we were back within the bounds of the sacred precinct.

## THE FOUNDING OF "BOYS TOWN"

In January 1980, there were at least nineteen gay and lesbian bars in the Quar-ter.[41] Some were long-time hangouts and some were relatively new, occupying bars once straight. The openness of gay life in the Quarter would have astonished both "perverts" and their persecutors of a mere twenty years before.

Lafitte's Blacksmith Shop, at the lakeside upper corner of Bourbon and St. Philip, was the legendary "front" of the pirate Jean Lafitte and his brother. The little building, forever looking to be on the verge of collapse, had been a gay-friendly watering hole for decades. In 1953, its ownership changed and gays were no longer welcomed. The displaced staff then went up the block to 900 Bourbon, and founded Café Lafitte In Exile, which would become the pivot point of the gay neighborhood. Between that shift and the early 1980s, there were many independent bars that welcomed gays and lesbians. These places did not identify themselves as exclusively gay taverns, and people of many groups and cultures partied together.[42] The Seven Seas, at 515 St. Philip, and Johnny Matassa's, behind the family grocery at Dauphine and St. Philip, were two such bars.[43]

In 1981, Café Lafitte's In Exile came into the possession of Tom Wood. Over the early and mid-1980s, Wood Enterprises opened or bought other gay bars and gay-supportive businesses.[44] One of the first was the Great American Refuge at the upper lakeside corner of Ursulines and Royal. The Refuge was unlike any gay bar the Quarter had yet seen. The typical Quarter gay spot of the era was simply an existing bar, renamed, and decorated with a mix of beverage industry paraphernalia, a few suggestive posters, and the ubiquitous Carnival leftovers. The Refuge was modeled after a classic men's club with leather easy chairs, sofas, and coordinated design. Whoever considered themselves "A list"—a contemporary fantasy among social climbers—gravitated there. Others, perhaps not looking to pose and network, now realized that gay bars didn't have to be tawdry and leave one feeling soiled. The Refuge was the Crescent City's first gay "lifestyle" establishment.

In succession, the mixed show bar Play It Again Sam at St. Ann and Burgundy became Rawhides, a country and western–themed spot; the Louisiana Purchase at St. Ann and Dauphine, a pansexual, notoriously rough dive, went to charm school and emerged as Good Friends. Good Friends, after the closing of the Refuge in 1984, became the upscale bar of the family. The Clover Grill, across Bourbon from Lafitte's, and Mary's Hardware, just a few doors down, were also acquired. Other bars of this neighborhood and period included the Bourbon Pub and, just across Bourbon at St. Ann, the dance bar Oz, formerly Pete Fountain's club. St. Ann at Bourbon became the demarking line between the straight and gay parts of Bourbon Street, with curious and sometimes wistful straights peering across the divide. Bars also did a thriving business on North Rampart, even then an edgy Casablanca on the margin between the Quarter and Tremé. Quarter bars saw few social distinctions, and in the bars of North Rampart, the leather and drag communities enjoyed a synergy.[45] Towards the river, the Golden Lantern was a neighborhood institution.

Gay bars were reflected in the changes along Decatur Street. The Seven Seas became Andy Boudreaux's Mississippi River Bottom. Jewel's Tavern was bought by David Jolly and Jack White in 1982.[46] Having warmed up at other, tamer bars elsewhere in the Quarter, habitués would normally venture down to Jewel's at around midnight. The downstairs was a dark, cave-like space reflecting its former life as a sailors' bar. An old painting on the wall was of a steamship sporting the name of *S.S. Jewels*. Flags of many nations hung down from the rafters. In an era when breaks between songs were the rule in clubs, the disc jockeys played some of the first mixes heard in town. A powerful sound system vibrated the beat into every orifice. Stairs led up to a quieter second floor, where conversation was possible and a tiny balcony overlooking the street beckoned.

No longer scurrying from bar to bar, sneaking in side doors, gays and lesbians could now casually drink, dine, dance, and do business in their own neighborhood. Called "Boys Town" by gays and straights alike, the neighborhood is bounded by St. Ann, Bourbon, North Rampart, and St. Philip. The Vieux Carré was seeing the creation of a gay enclave, similar to the Castro in San Francisco or Christopher Street in New York. However, comparisons between these three districts should be taken with care. The Quarter has had a significant gay and lesbian population for many decades, and it did not displace any existing group. Boys Town evolved within a district that was already in architectural conservation. New Orleans, being a backwater of American trends and much smaller than San Francisco or New York, was one of the last to experience this "gayification" of an area in the twentieth century.

Gays and lesbians were now addressing the political process as well. In 1981, the district police captain actually asked gays not to stand on the streets of the Quarter, saying that gays should "keep moving" so that the police could concentrate their efforts on law enforcement. Gay activists worked to overcome these edicts by meeting with the superintendent of police, Henry Morris, who had, as evidenced after the Upstairs fire in 1973, demonstrated a less than tolerant mind-set.[47]

In April 1984, a gay rights ordinance was brought before the city council. Although it was defeated, that it was presented at all was a watershed event.[48]

Police entrapment and harassment were, however, slowly ebbing, as police-men from the Morrison and Schiro eras retired or just quit. However, it was not as though a wave of tolerance suddenly struck the NOPD. Harrassing gays swishing down a sidewalk, or having sex in the backroom of a club, was simply not profitable to a new generation of cops, so they were, in the main, not interested.

In 1986, gay pride parades resumed, traveling from Armstrong Park up St. Philip, and down to Washington Square in the Marigny. As a marcher, I recall how empty the Quarter seemed. It felt like every gay and lesbian in town was in the parade, and the sidewalks seemed vacant of either supporters or detractors until we turned down Elysian Fields to Washington Square.

## THE 1984 WORLD'S FAIR

The Warehouse District and its wharves just upriver of the Quarter had not bustled for many years. Containerization and other port improvements had passed it by. Fewer sailors were seen on Decatur as their ships docked elsewhere. Many of the buildings were unused, and the area was mostly pitch dark at night. Its only function, by the seventies, was as a nocturnal playground for daring gay men who went looking for sexual encounters beyond the bars and bathhouses. The metal buildings, standing open, and the space under the wharves offered opportunities to bold cruisers. They offered dangers, too, mainly from derelicts who might mug gays for money to buy another bottle.[49]

Developer Lester Kabacoff owned or leased large portions of this area, which was upriver from the Hilton hotel he built at the foot of Canal Street, once the ceremonial landing for official visitors alighting from the river. Kaba-coff, and a cadre of others, wanted to develop a convention facility enabling New Orleans to host the largest trade shows. The Kabacoff property would be a prime site for such a facility. It was decided that the convention center would need to be born of a surrogate mother. The statewide controversy over fund-ing the Superdome was still fresh, and perhaps another public bond issue was unthinkable. In any event, a World's Fair was chosen to carry the embryonic convention center. The federal government, with great reluctance, agreed to green-light the fair. The approval was contingent upon the fair's backers rais-ing more capital, which materialized after some frantic begging of corporate sponsors. Even after these commitments, the fair was undercapitalized and dependant on optimistic attendance projections to simply break even. As the opening day for the fair approached, further calls for funding implied a seemingly bottomless money pit. Amazed that these resources were channeled into an extravaganza for tourists while the city was in such dire straits, local critics were bitter. Then there were the persistent doubts on what even a successful fair would bring, long-term, to the city. The fair's shaky finances and last-minute rush to completion were already well publicized before opening day, and that may have kept people from visiting an event that might be insignificant or closed by the time they arrived.[50]

As the fair was getting off to a rocky start, the preparation for it was visiting indignities on the Vieux Carré. Anticipating throngs of fair guests, hotels continued to flout the 1969 moratorium on new inns in the Quarter. Most of this was invisible from the street. A hotel would buy or lease a building. To avoid alerting the Vieux Carré Commission, the façade was kept intact and no outward signs displayed. The interior of the building now became hotel rooms, unapproved by any government body. Worse was the conversion of long-time apartment buildings into hotel rooms. Hopeful of fair-driven profits, some landlords kicked out apartment tenants and rented their former homes by the night.[51] Small regulatory staffs and the cheek-by-jowl buildings all made enforcement difficult. Each illegal day's stay had to be prosecuted as a separate case—an impossible workload for city attorneys. The director of the city's safety and permits department conceded in 1983 that the city had never won a suit against a suspected violator.[52]

Because the fair was within walking distance of the Quarter, many decrepit sidewalks in the primary tourist area were dug up and bricked over, with, of course, Mayor Morial's name on bronze plaques. Quarter merchants were salivating at the increased traffic the fair would bring, but were also unhappy with the disruptions attending its construction. Dutch Morial, responding in one of his more beneficent moods, proposed that a festival for locals be held in the Quarter. The first French Quarter Festival was held in April 1983 and featured booths from Quarter restaurants and music stages, and was promoted to the hometown crowd. It has been a rite of Aprils ever since and is generally regarded as the most local and family-friendly event held in the Vieux Carré.[53]

The preparation for the fair caused the last—one would hope—surge of official homophobia in the Quarter. Previous major events had usually triggered a crackdown on "undesirables," as streetwalkers were urged to take it indoors and visible gays and lesbians were hassled. Once again, NOPD and

Gates of the 1984 World's Fair.
Scott Ellis.

the city administration thought it could push gays into the background, so as not to endanger the frantically "family-friendly" atmosphere.

In the Quarter itself, cops had been hassling gatherings of three or more apparent gays and lesbians, asking for multiple IDs. Women outside Brady's, a lesbian spot at North Rampart at St. Peter, had been arrested. Raising the visibility of the harassment, about a hundred gays gathered outside Jewel's on Decatur Street and allowed themselves to be arrested—"blocking the sidewalk" being a convenient charge. The resulting publicity aroused city hall to arrange a meeting between the superintendent of police, Henry Morris, and three community activists. In an offhand and disrespectful manner, he said the city was trying to "clean up" the Quarter ahead of the fair. Superintendent Morris asked the delegates to tell other gays and lesbians to contain themselves to no more than two or three per block![54] This queer quota system didn't fly with the community, and eventually the police backed off.

The Louisiana World Exposition, as the fair was titled, opened on May 12, 1984, without President Reagan, who declined to grace the ceremonies.[55] The fair's boosters, led by Governor Edwin Edwards, put on a brave face as the gates opened. New Orleans was promoted as a funky, vital, and cosmopolitan city. The official theme, "Fresh Water as a Source of Life," may have been scientifically debatable, but jibed with the city's ancient claim to be queen of the Mississippi.

The fair occupied 150 acres of land along the riverfront.[56] It featured pavilions from, among others, Korea, Japan, the European Commonwealth, the Vatican, the United States, and, of course, Louisiana. The fair experience was actually rather pleasant for adults who could stroll, drink, dine, and attend concerts. The gates were guarded by enormous and voluptuously barebreasted mermaid figures which drew snorts from the prudish. Passing these plaster sirens, visitors found a variety of engagements. The Vatican pavilion was especially popular despite an additional entry fee. The Louisiana pavilion was perhaps the most original and memorable. Visitors got into small boats linked by a chain, à la a carny tunnel of love. Into a long dark passage lit at first only by swirling colored lights, the boats glided past well-crafted displays of the state's past and present. Outdoors, a short monorail echoed the Seattle fair of 1962. A long multicolored Wonder Wall of diverse architectural façades became the fair's signature image.

After the initial fanfare, the fair's money woes increased. The daily attendance was about half of what was required to break even.[57] The adult admission of fifteen dollars seemed high in a poor city, especially when the properly connected could get free passes—which is how I got in. Ultimately, attendance was never close to the boosters' hopes. Eleven million visitors was the lowest estimate presented at the outset.[58] About 7,300,000 showed up.[59] Globally, the World's Fair concept was growing tired. Even the most recent, and financially sound, World's Fair, in Knoxville two years before, had sparked little enthusiasm.[60]

Local contractors loudly complained of slow or no payments.[61] The fair's official mascot was a cheerful, top-hatted pelican, "Seymour De Fair." The stiffed contractors offered their own symbol, "Seymour De Rat."

The fair, along with the Moon Walk installed in the 1970s, helped New Orleanians reconnect with the raison d'etre for the city's very existence—the Mississippi River. The dock area had been closed off to the public for years, and the tall floodwall installed across from Jackson Square in 1953 further obscured the view. Now, the fair reopened a portion of the waterfront to the populace.

The most visible and longest-enduring artifact of the fair was the gondola—actually a cable car system—across the river to Algiers. Towers on each side of the river supported cables carrying small pods back and forth. The ride, despite its height far above the water, and occasional jams, became extremely popular with commuters from the West Bank who could sip café au lait and look down at the sprawling vista as they floated to the East Bank. It also featured in *French Quarter Undercover*, a 1986 movie about a bioterrorism plot to sabotage the fair.

As the fair went on through the summer and fall of 1984, the criticism got louder and the gate receipts got smaller. The fair tried to encourage regional visitors, with limited success; many had already seen the fair once and did not care to repeat. On November 6, 1984, it became the first World's Fair to declare bankruptcy while operating.[62] When the fair closed on November 11, 1984,[63] it left many stiffed contractors and $120 million in debt.[64] The gondola towers stood for several years, lonely sentinels of an abandoned dream.

The national media gleefully reported the fair as boosterism run amuck.[65] The CBS news program *60 Minutes* ran an extremely unflattering segment six weeks after the fair closed.[66] In common with other New Orleans get-rich-quick schemes, the fair made money and commercial opportunities primarily for a small group of already wealthy people. Their fortunes, unlike those of the small contractors they stiffed, were not on the line. For those evicted from apartments, arrested for blocking the sidewalk, bankrupt from nonpayment, or never able to afford the entry fee, the fair left bitter dregs indeed.

However, the fair did leave some positive residue for the city at large. One of its buildings, as planned, was the start of the Ernest Morial Convention Center and the adjoining Riverwalk shopping mall. The Warehouse District attracted interest from developers who eventually remodeled some old buildings into condos and shops.[67] Another centerpiece of the revived area, opened in 2000, was the D-Day Museum, now called the National World War II Museum.[68]

## DARKNESS RISING AT NOON

After the well-organized repression of the Morrison era, New Orleans gay life began to blossom more publicly in the 1970s. The Quarter's old reputation as a place of sexual license was now endorsed for gays and lesbians as well as straights, and sexual freedom was carnally celebrated in the bars, on the balconies, and, at certain times, on the streets.

By 1983, gays had reached a parity—perhaps even an ascendency—with other groups in the Quarter. The easing, if not complete end of police harassment, the openness and commercial solidity of Boys Town, and the number of gay-owned businesses all spoke of a vibrant community. In the Castro and Greenwich Village, it had long been possible to live a completely gay life. Now that was possible, in the open air, in the Quarter. Openly gay doctors, lawyers, restaurants, florists, clothiers, and other service providers were now available and plentiful. Gay and lesbian life had created an enclave within an enclave.

*However . . .*

In a little village where mild intoxication is a typical mood, and heavy drinking is accepted, the lens of the real, the acceptable, and the safe becomes blurred. There have always been so many with peculiar fixations, fantastic schemes, and delusional systems. People whose conversations and actions would set off alarm bells anywhere else are dismissed with a wave, a laugh, and another swig of liquor. For over two centuries, girls were warned away from the Quarter with rumors—which had their basis in dreadful fact—of "white slavery."[69] It was certainly true enough that most whores were addicted to something, and, thus enslaved, kept the yoke of prostitution to support the habit. People could disappear from the Quarter easily, the river conveniently carrying bodies out to sea.

Despite the goth/vampire industry, all the dead do is sleep in the many graveyards around New Orleans. The colonial men who fought idiotic duels, falling sometimes at the hands of friends, do not rise from their crypts in the St. Louis cemeteries. If any shades have the right to lurk in the Vieux Carré, they are Lyle Saxon and Tennessee Williams, doubtless displeased at being buried in Baton Rouge and St. Louis. The boozy, carefree atmosphere has, from time to time, given real goblins good hunting grounds. They are not romanticized by Hollywood, and teenagers aren't dressing like them. Indeed, no one alive knows what they look like. More's the horror.

One—or more—of these monsters killed three gay men, and wounded another in 1984. The victims were found in their own apartments, their skulls beaten in. The tidings of the "Hammer Murderer" swept the bars.[70] This is not to say there were no safety mechanisms. Conditioned by years of repression, gay men of that era were more cautious. Police entrapment had not completely ended, and "fag bashing" was still an occasional Quarter problem. Bartenders, although loathe to be matchmakers, would usually warn customers away from men known to be "bad news." Most of these were well-known hustlers whose tastes ran to occasional larceny and battery but not murder. The Hammer Murderer had no such public onus. No bartender had a mental file on him; the victims all seemed to have let him in willingly, which indicated an aura of trustworthiness. Although the spree came to an end quickly, the fiend was never caught.

Despite the celebratory atmosphere, New Orleans was a calm backwater of gay life. It did not set trends, as did New York; it did not produce national leadership, as did San Francisco; it was simply a place to party and get laid. Efforts to politically organize the gay community had seen so many fits and starts that most would-be organizers had simply given up by the mideighties.[71] Mirroring the straight krewes, the gay krewes emerged as the de facto organization of the community.[72] Gay life in New Orleans was just as self-referential as other aspects of the town.

In 1980, a murmur began to circulate in New Orleans. Gay men in San Francisco and New York were becoming ill and dying suddenly. Perceived at first as an environmental byproduct of big-city gay life, the illness was called gay related immune disorder, or GRID. By 1983, the illness was traced to a virus, and labeled acquired immune deficiency syndrome (AIDS).[73] The news of AIDS was received at first with skepticism and sangfroid in New Orleans. Boys Town was not an epicenter of national gay activity like the Castro or Greenwich Village. Many New Orleans gays and lesbians did not have the means to travel to gay hot spots and so stayed, spider-like, in the Crescent City, awaiting visitors to come to them. As decades of official and social oppression began to lift, the idea that repression in the form of a virus should come at this time seemed incredible. The disturbing news from the east and west coasts was undeniable; its import for the Crescent City was uncertain. Uneasily, some believed that their backwater could not be affected by the illness. The first cases of AIDS in New Orleans, as presented by pneumocystis pneumonia, appear to have surfaced about 1982.[74]

In the early stages of the pandemic, pieces of fact and rumor circulated in the bars of the Quarter. A prominent DJ had collapsed at a club and was dead within a few days. Another man—the first patient I knew personally—was ill by the summer of 1985, but was known to be an IV drug user. Men visiting from San Francisco and New York were advised to claim residency elsewhere, Oakland and Albany being glib choices.

The onslaught of AIDS came to town slowly. By 1985 it had been scything gay men in larger cities for half a decade, but was still just getting started in New Orleans. New Orleans benefitted not only from the advance warning from bigger gay centers but also from a unique medical attitude. The city had long experience with the pandemic of yellow fever and, more recently, the influenza of 1918. As a major port, the city's doctors had seen many unfamiliar ailments brought in by visitors. New Orleans doctors were not, as a group, as skittish about treating patients with strange diseases as physicians elsewhere.[75] San Francisco and other cities had struggled with closing gay bath-houses, widely perceived as being nexuses of the contagion.[76] New Orleans's city administration never moved to close the bathhouses, at least not on the pretext of disease prevention. The bathhouses cooperated with public health officials in disseminating AIDS prevention information to a large at-risk population.[77]

As the dimensions of the epidemic became apparent, the federal government made block grants available to cities. In Louisiana, however, this money was filtered through the state health department, and was merely a trickle by the time it reached New Orleans. In the beginning, the amounts requested by the state were ludicrously small—in one year at the height of the epidemic, a mere thirty-five thousand dollars. It seems that the state did not want to trouble itself with administering these grants on a large scale.[78]

By comparison to other cities, AIDS may have taken a leisurely stroll into New Orleans. However, the Quarter was the center of gay life, and so zip code 70116, the Vieux Carré and a few blocks of Tremé, bore most of the reported cases.[79] After yellow fever ended in 1905, other groups in the city did not have widespread casualties. There was always someone to help bury the dead, console the living, and bring a covered dish. When the ranks of gay krewes began to fall to the pandemic, there were few who were not ill themselves or not caring for a sick partner or friend. Before AIDS, there had been fifteen gay krewes, although not all were active simultaneously. By 2005, only six were active.[80] Other groups and ethnicities had deeply entrenched support nets of churches and benevolent associations, making even poverty somewhat tolerable. Beyond the gay krewes, most gay men did not have anything like a support system capable of dealing with the pandemic. Before effective treatments, AIDS was not simply a sentence of a lingering and sometimes horrific death. Before the end, it was a death sentence for careers and independent living, as the seriously ill lost employment and then rent money. Prior to viatical settlements, there were few options. Men who had lived prosperously, openly, and proudly gay in the Quarter might now have to return—often minus their lovers—to their stunned parents in rural communities, to die at "home." Their passing was usually locally window-dressed as "pneumonia" or "heart failure." Those unable or unwilling to do this might die in a bed at Charity Hospital or on a friend's couch. A somber pall settled on once cruisey bars, laundromats, and gyms around town.

The local gay papers carried many obituaries, sometimes of men seemingly hale and hearty just weeks before. In 1987, I walked into a patio sale on lower Bourbon. In such a cosmopolitan area, these sales were fun and yielded interesting finds. This day was quite different. An older woman was handling the haggling and selling. A gaunt young man, handsomeness and vigor quickly draining away, sat on a folding chair at the back of the patio, quietly thanking all who stopped by. Through mutual friends, I realized he was selling off his possessions in a last effort to raise some cash before he died.

There are no reliable figures of how many Quarter gays died before AIDS was a treatable disease. The existing statistics drop dark hints. The 1990 census reported that 38.4 percent of all Vieux Carré housing units were vacant—up from 21.9 percent in 1980. The inner census tract, Tract 42, between Conti and St. Philip, where most of the apartment houses were, had a 1990 vacancy rate of 44.8 percent. That area also lost over 33 percent of its population between 1980 and 1990.[81] Part of this was attributable to the decline of the city's economy, but part of it is also due to AIDS. AIDS accelerated the trend, started by the 1970s–1980s emigration to the Marigny, that transformed the Quarter from a gay residential district to a gay entertainment district. Gays would continue to live in the Vieux Carré, but their presence would never again approach what it had been, for a short, sweet season.

## THE MIDEIGHTIES

Guardians of the Vieux Carré have frequently acknowledged that poverty has been a preservative.[82] Lack of free capital has meant that some properties have been kept at an earlier, and, one would hope, more authentic state. It also has meant that needed repairs have been postponed, sometimes for years. In the midst of the real-estate slump of the 1980s, when interest rates were high and restorative capital scarce in New Orleans, the Vieux Carré Commission issued design guidelines.[83] These guidelines protect the "quaint and distinctive character" of the enclave. They also prevent such affronts as modern metal windows, burglar bars, and concertina wire—all very popular in other parts of town. In a concession to security, the guidelines permit the topping of walls with broken glass set in mortar. The kind of loud Easter-egg paint schemes seen on gingerbreaded Victorians in the Marigny and other historic districts were not permitted. Aberrations could happen, since taste, even in a regulated district as the Quarter is, cannot be fine-tuned. About this same time, a particular building on lower Dauphine was allowed to be painted a deep glistening brown, which earned it unfavorable comparison with the *merde de chien* of the banquette.

Decatur Street had been slowly changing. The shift to containerized cargo and the removal of many port operations from the immediate Quarter riverfront reduced the ranks of seamen out looking for good times on

Decatur. Their old haunts were changing, too; straight professionals and gay men were beginning to claim parts of the street. Decatur properties also reflected a marked change in 1985 over what they had been ten years before. Interestingly, bars actually decreased by 41 percent. Vacancies fell by 25 percent and retail increased by 52 percent. When the shops of the renovated Jax Brewery are included, the number of Decatur retail outlets rose a dizzying 67 percent.[84]

The Jax Brewery complex, renovated at a cost of $6 million, created a magnetic field that drew other venues, large and small, to Decatur. Most of Decatur's revival in this era happened from the brewery on down to the French Market. At the very end of Decatur, on the lakeside corner, the Mint bar opened in 1986. One of the few bars catering to a mixed crowd of gay men and lesbians, it was the setting for many community shows and ceremonies until the mid-1990s.[85]

In 1986, Dutch Morial departed city hall, dying three years later. Like Chep Morrison, Dutch Morial was expected to cast a lively shadow over city politics long after he left office, but did not live to do so. Dutch's successor was his oft-times nemesis, Sidney Barthelemy. Like Morial, a modern Creole, Barthelemy, or "Sid," as the inevitable nickname went, had been a state senator and had been groomed by the Landrieu administration for eventual leadership.[86] In his first term, Barthelemy confronted a severe fiscal crisis. The city suffered a decline in revenue from $304 million in 1985 to $271 million in 1989.[87] Through drastic, painful cost-cutting, the city managed to keep afloat.[88] Coming on the heels of the World's Fair fiasco, the city and state looked like poor stewards of the public purse.

Barthelemy, like Victor Schiro succeeding Chep Morrison, was a cool gentle breeze after Dutch's eight-year sirocco. Barthelemy's friendly style, financial control in the face of considerable opposition, and outreach to potential business made him the media-endorsed favorite to win reelection over a white challenger in 1990.

In 1992, Barthelemy appointed a Vieux Carré Task Force.[89] The task force, which met intermittently throughout the early and mid-1990s, did succeed in obtaining a ban on large tour buses from the Quarter and defining a bus-free zone in the lower Quarter.[90] The mayor made fateful choices in the leadership of the NOPD. During his second administration, the NOPD, under investigation by the federal government, was confirmed as being one of the most brutal and corrupt in America.[91] The incoming waves of black recruits were, the perception went, helping themselves to the fruits of white-established corruption on a scale unseen even in Morrison's day. The documented complicity of some police in drug trafficking staggered even blasé, lifelong residents. If the 1950s cop on the beat had helped himself to a free po'boy, winked at streetwalkers, or collected a fee for ignoring backroom gambling, the involvement of officers in moving large quantities of drugs was a new level of scandal.

## QUALITY OF LIFE UNDER SIEGE

Everyone's salad days are someone else's famine. As one group has supplanted another in the Vieux Carré, the supplanted look back with nostalgia, some of which does not bear close scrutiny.

Lyle Saxon and his friends had rescued Madame in her darkest moments, and created a freewheeling artistic culture usually labeled as "bohemian." Yet, as early as 1927, Saxon's friend Roark Bradford wrote Saxon, then in New York, complaining, "Too many country boys and girls are coming in to be Bohemians."[92] Not surprisingly, this atmosphere had drawn the silly as well as the serious, the party people as well as the philosophers.

Perhaps the second wave of urban pioneers—our tweed and beads friends—felt that the emergence of an open, commercially thriving gay enclave was a sad development. Not everyone appreciated the crowds and booming music that had now worked their way down Bourbon to Dumaine. They could not argue, however, with the anchor of prosperity that Boys Town established, nor with a large population of preservation- and history-conscious gay men. If some objected to the brief gay ascendancy in the Quarter, what happened next quickly relegated that controversy to the rearview mirror of history.

Some had been willing to accept the balm of commercial poverty for its preservative effects, discounting the inexorable physical deterioration allowed by lack of capital. Accepting physical shabbiness of buildings was one thing. The first and second wave of preservationists had raised the Quarter from slumhood to a veneer of gentility over two generations These hard-won gains could not be cast aside just because the economy was poor. Concern about quality of life in the Quarter began to displace sheer physical preservation as a cause. The expansion of tourism, particularly after big-money clubs came to town in the late eighties and early nineties, pressured residential life. The Quarter had changed, over about thirty years, from a largely residential community with a few tourist strips to an all-pervasive tourist destination, with a

residual residential aspect. In 1993 the director of the Vieux Carré Commission noted that city-wide, tourist traffic had tripled between 1972 and 1992.[93]
Business that supported Quarter residents declined markedly between 1950
and 1990.[94] The old distinctions between the tourist strips and residential
areas began to blur. Even though upper Bourbon was still the locus of the
party scene, tourists, usually drunk on their arrival and always drunker on
their departure, were wandering through the lower Quarter from parking in
the Marigny and on Elysian Fields. The intoxicated visitors left a trail of trash,
vomit, urine, and sometimes passed-out friends along the way. If the stagger-
ing partygoers were noisy on foot, booming car stereos and loud motorcycles
were worse. Tour buses and heavy trucks crawled down the narrow streets,
drivers sometimes lost and frantically searching for an on-ramp back to the
interstate. The neighborhood shops that had offered unique goods were being
displaced by souvenir stores, collectively called T-shirt shops for their main
wares. These tourist-driven venues could outbid other, resident-oriented
retailers for Quarter rental space, which, of course, was and is a fixed com-
modity, particularly in the areas with heaviest tourist traffic.[95]

Reining in the T-shirt shops was a major initiative of Councilman Mike
Early, who represented District C from 1976 to 1990. Mr. Early remembers the
efforts and the reaction:

> Every business in the Quarter, whether a restaurant, T-shirt shop, sou-
> venir shop, retail, whatever—you would have to apply every year for a
> renewal of your occupancy permit. Well, in order to get that renewal,
> you would have to show us that you were in compliance with the law. If
> you are Mr. T-Shirt Shop Owner and you come in and slip in a T-shirt
> shop under the guise of a dress shop, when you come up for renewal
> at the end of that year, we're going to catch you. We're going to look at
> your permit and we're going to say, "When you applied and opened, you
> put 'dress shop.' Look at what it is now. There's not a dress in here. It's
> nothing but a T-shirt shop." So we're going to catch you in that violation
> of the law. And the same with restaurant owners. They just thought that
> I was Hitler for introducing that, but we went to public hearing with it
> twice and it did not have a lot of support. If it [the proposed ordinance]
> had been enforced and made part of the comprehensive zoning ordi-
> nance of this city in the mid '80s, the French Quarter would be a very
> different place today—a much better place today. It would not be over-
> run with the T-shirt shops. The number of souvenir shops would not be

nearly as many as they are right now. There would be more quality retail across the board in the Quarter than there is today.[96]

As finally adopted, in 2001, the zoning ordinance requires a distance of six hundred feet from one T-shirt shop to the next, and restricts the display of T-shirts and other tourist trinkets to not more than 35 percent of the display area.[97] As is true with other ordinances, the devil was in the lack of enforcement. A prime factor in Louisiana lawmaking is the desire not to offend anyone, especially monied interests, or cause any hardship in the execution of a law. So, many regulations come with loopholes and grandfather clauses. Although land use is regulated under the general police power of the state, a very large loophole exists. A land use—not including signage—which does not conform to regulations is legalized if, after some period of time, the authorities do not take action. This "nonconforming" use may be continued by successive owners, provided there is no gap in use greater than six months.[98]

In the mid-1990s, Jean Boebel, then president of VCPORA, got the legislature to extend the time required for new nonconforming uses from two to five years in historic districts. In 2000, the window was increased to ten years.[99]

The loophole of "existing nonconforming uses" and "conditional use" permits allowed these requirements to be disregarded if the errant shop could evade any legal action for the prescribed time. Where the city has not acted on a nonconforming use, activist groups may sue, and they often do. If the city enforcement process is measured in eternities, civil litigation is not swift either. An action filed in 1998 by VCPORA against an illegal hotel expansion is still in process as of this writing (2009).[100] During the litigation, the nonconforming use goes on and each passing year further cements the defendant's claim to potential economic injury and loss of customer goodwill.

In 1994, the city implemented a revised parking plan that increased the number of parking meters and expanded freight zones. Now even residents with bona fide parking stickers had thirty-one fewer parking spaces.[101]

If Quarter life in the late seventies to mideighties had been enjoyable for people of average means, that era was now ending. Many residents felt their concerns were being sublimated to the cause of tourism, and residential quality of life was being sacrificed to the needs of tourists. In some ways, this was an echo of the pre- and post-Storyville eras, when whorehouses and saloons roared full-blast next to helpless homeowners. In May of 1994, the *Times-Picayune* quoted Mary Morrison, now the senior member of the original tweed and beads set: "It's a much harder place to live now. We have the feeling that the city fathers and the business community are not interested in the residential character of the French Quarter. We're just losing ground everywhere. Oh yeah, the residential character must be maintained—they all say that. But we can't get much support for maintaining it, I can tell you that. What they say and what they do are two different things."[102]

These pressures on Quarter life did not abate, and the city rarely roused itself to enforce existing statutes. The commercial aspect of the Vieux Carré was changing, and so was the residential. Within a few years, money would rain down the Quarter, and the character of residential life would change dramatically.

## MOVING OUT

The Quarter has long had a reputation as a village of transients, as well as a place of very long-time residents. In the early part of the twentieth century, upward mobility was the chief reason for immigrants to leave. There has always been a shifting population, with as many reasons for arriving, and leaving, as each soul. Between 1980 and 1990, the Vieux Carré said farewell to about sixteen hundred people, ending the decade with about four thousand residents.[103] The Quarter was not the only neighborhood losing people. By 1990, one of every six housing units in New Orleans was vacant, the highest vacancy rate of any major American city. Urban pioneers in neighborhoods like Bywater saw hard-won gentrification erode as owners and renters fled. Abandoned properties attracted squatters, who often dealt drugs out of the houses, and the resulting shabbiness snowballed into more derelict, people-less properties.[104]

One must be very strong to live in New Orleans and even stronger to live in the Vieux Carré. For many working-class people, the initial blush of easy answers and widespread camaraderie gives way to dullness from booze and/or drugs, a grind of never-changing struggle for the daily dollar, and the down-at-the heels flats available to those with little money. Even those of greater means get discouraged as they try to keep their properties up in the face of the unforgiving climate, vandalism, and slothful bureaucracy. Everyone, regardless of station, must develop a strong stomach for governmental lassitude, corruption, noisome trash, human folly played out in public, and the abject poverty just outside the old ramparts.

For bar workers, stable employment could be elusive. Bar servers must survive the influence of the dispensed goods—legal and not—mercurial owners, drunken patrons, officialdom looking for handouts, and clueless tourists. Even after corporations and their human resource departments took over most taverns, bar service remains intrinsically a hard life. It has traditionally been the province of the young, who still see a wide road ahead, and the past-middle-aged, who realize that this is their narrow path for the remainder of life. Even for those who have economic stability, life as a resident[105] can wear as well as comfort. The Vieux Carré reassurance of little change can become a nagging sense of limbo in a place exactly between heaven and hell and having many signal traits of both.

If the decision to move to the Quarter was—before soaring property values—quick, trivial, and often made with the toss of a drink, the decision to move out is rarely so casual. The Quarter exerts a hold on people, long after they move away.

Leaving is often the result of growing up. Two young amours may pool resources and find a house downriver, or even embrace suburban domesticity. The attractions of Quarter life for singles may suddenly become a liability for keeping a relationship.[106] The Quarter, despite its international cachet, has not been perceived as a "hip, happening" place for several years. Artists seeking studio space find much better pickings in the Marigny, Bywater, or on Magazine Street.

Even in the doldrums of the mideighties, house prices in the Quarter were usually out of reach of working-class or lower-echelon white collar workers. Mortgage interest rates were high in the early and middle eighties, ranging from 15.8 percent in 1981 downward to 9.29 percent in 1986.[107] If a Quarter house was affordable to people of average means, that meant it needed expensive renovations. Quarter apartments tended to be smallish after decades of subdivision. My apartment with its one thousand usable square feet was considered large by Vieux Carré standards. My building, with four rental units in the most desirable part of the Quarter, sold for $225,000 in the summer of 1985. At the same time, that sum would have bought about three decent-sized houses downriver in the Faubourg Marigny, particularly in that portion beyond Elysian Fields.[108] True, these also needed fixing up, ranging from mere repainting to deep renovation. But they represented the American housing dream, transmogrified from Ward and June to Danny and Mike, or Sheila and Suzy. There was much better parking, no mule-drawn buggies to slow traffic, and no gawking, puking tourists. The Marigny, which begins on the other side of Esplanade and runs to the railroad tracks at Press Street,[109] had been part of the old plantation of famed gambler Bernard Marigny (1785–1868). He sectioned and sold off pieces of land to create a new suburb of what was then central New Orleans—the Vieux Carré itself.[110] As the seventies became the eighties, the Marigny was a very mixed community. A great number of Italian and some German families had once lived there. Now the children were grown up and had moved away, leaving Mama looking out a screen door at Burgundy Street, wondering where the years had gone. The large Marigny Catholic churches, like St. Peter and St. Paul at Burgundy and Marigny, and Holy Trinity, Ferdinand at Dauphine, saw fewer parishioners each year, masses being said to a shrinking number of old women, the litany echoing through the vast sanctuaries. Some working-class blacks lived in the Marigny, some owning these homes for generations. Service industry workers, who never even had a rental shot at Quarter living, were there, too, catching the Desire bus to jobs in the Quarter and CBD. A trickle of gay residents arrived in the early 1960s.[111] In the early 1970s, a professor of architecture, Eugene Cizek, performed a survey of historic Marigny properties and attempted to match these properties with potential buyers, usually gay men. Cizek went on to found the Faubourg Marigny Improvement Association (FMIA), which remains the premiere Marigny organization. Unlike the Quarter, with its many sometimes fractious and overlapping organizations, the FMIA became the dominant community voice in the Marigny. The Marigny was listed on the National Register of Historic Places in 1975, and obtained Historic District designation from the city in 1978.[112] As such, the Historic District exercises a degree of control over outward appearance, similar to, but lesser in scope and precedent, that of the VCC.

Apart from Cizek's intercessions, a series of real estate maneuvers—some legal and some not—also brought a number of gay first-time homeowners to the Marigny in the late seventies to mideighties. These real estate events would not have been possible without the reservoir of gay men who were living in the Quarter and wanted home ownership, or at least better rentals than the Quarter could offer.[113] The readily available Marigny properties and "creative" financing therefore may have "pulled" gays from the Quarter as much as decrepit building stock and rising prices "pushed" them out.[114]

In the mideighties the Marigny presented an interesting picture. Strolling down any Marigny block of Dauphine, or Royal, or Burgundy in the afternoon, one might see several houses boarded up.[115] Others, although occupied, were in various states of decay. Then, one would encounter, like a vision, a spruced-up house with a blazing paint scheme, crisp gingerbread, and wind-chimes a-tinkling in the sultry air. It required no *City Guide* to discern that this was gentrification and, most likely, owned by gays. Unlike the Quarter, the new white residents lived close by existing neighbors of various ethnicities. Relations varied from welcoming—the old neighborhood was being fixed up by nice residents at last—to resentment—gentrification was making prices go up for people of lesser means. In these early days, the Marigny was still considered somewhat marginal, verging on dangerous.[116] As is often true in the Quarter, police protection was something consigned to nostalgia, and the gentrifiers learned that alarm systems and big dogs were just as essential as faux marble paint effects.

The Marigny slowly became a new community, gays and straights achieving a type of cohesion across lines of class not seen in most other parts of town. Because it was far off the beaten tourist track, it was left alone by purveyors of big-project get-rich-quick schemes like the fair and the temporary casino. Much of the building stock, especially beyond Elysian Fields, did not lend itself to condoization. The remaining decrepitude was sufficient to frighten off most naive yuppies from parts unknown. The opportunity to have a house and a bit of yard attracted a different type of resident from the apartment-dwellers and condo-roosters of the late-century Quarter. Marigny house buyers tended to be more settled and had already had their times in the clubs of the Quarter and university areas. The Marigny bars, for the most part, were small and decidedly unflamboyant, even in Carnival season. They tended to have the same clientele, year after year, serving as living room, confessional, and sometimes dining room for their devotees. A few times a year, bars host memorial services. In a frappé of liquor, jambalaya, and tears, the departed are remembered and their barstools rewarmed. Most residents, new and old, agreed that the Marigny is what the Quarter once was—multiethnic, affordable, and with a population dedicated to fixing up and maintaining the neighborhood.

## YET ANOTHER BATTLE OF NEW ORLEANS

Nature, sometimes thwarted, sometimes aided by man, forever tries to reclaim New Orleans. In the 1990s, the city faced a new invader, one that even Andrew Jackson could not defeat.

Formosan termites had arrived on ships returning to the port of New Orleans and the navy base at Algiers from the Pacific in World War II.[117] The

use of chlordane compounds had kept them out of public view; they bur-
rowed into living trees, railroad ties, and other places away from humanity.
Unlike the familiar subterranean termite, the Formosans also made nests far
above ground in buildings and trees. Chlordane compounds were banned in
1988, although existing stocks were used for a few more years.[118]

In 1992, Hurricane Andrew brushed by the city. The winds toppled venerable and seemingly healthy oaks. One-sixth of these trees were shockingly
hollow, their hearts vanished.[119] Investigation revealed that the Formosans,
no longer repelled from civilization by chlordane, were eating the city alive.
Schoolroom chalkboards crashed down, eaten up to the slate.[120] Mantelpieces,
looking perfect from the outside, were mere shells of paint and crumbled to
the touch.[121] Anything wooden was being consumed. Unlike more familiar
termites, the Formosans make "carton" nests of a cementious excretion.[122] In
many cases, these nests are as strong, or stronger, than the wooden elements
they replaced and were left in place after the colonies were killed.[123] Formosans swarm, in brief flights, around April. The swarms make eerie halos
around lights and get in the hair of passersby. The discarded wings leave a
silvery sheen on sidewalks. In scenes Alfred Hitchcock would have loved,
some swarms took place indoors. Thousands of the fluttering insects clouded
living spaces, to the horror of the occupants.[124]

The Quarter presents the ideal conditions for the Formosans to establish huge, hidden colonies. Buildings usually share common walls; wood is
plentiful; moisture collects easily in the soft old orange bricks. A multitude of
cracks and crevices abound. Stucco protects the old bricks but traps moisture
and hides termite activities.[125] Buildings, cheek by jowl, have many different
owners, some far removed from town, making coordinated action difficult.
The VCC's regulations prohibit wholesale replacement of wooden elements
with metal or cement clones.[126] In the Quarter, many buildings had Formosan
damage, including famous landmarks like St. Louis Cathedral, the Cabildo,
the Presbytère, the Pontalbas, and the Beauregard-Keyes house.[127]

The federal government rode to the rescue, as it had at the Battle of Chal-
mette in 1815 and the 1969 coup de grace of the Riverfront Expressway. In
1998, the U.S. Department of Agriculture, in cooperation with other agencies,
universities, and the private sector, launched Operation Full Stop.

Beginning in sixteen Quarter blocks, the program set up monitoring stations on lampposts and set into sidewalk wells. Full Stop dispensed funding
for those wishing to treat the infestations with newly developed baits and
pesticides.[128] The program was gradually expanded to more of the Vieux

Carré and surrounding areas like Armstrong Park. The initial results were encouraging, but two factors dampened any premature rejoicing. First, not all property owners in the targeted zones cooperated, leading to persistent infestations. Second, like olden tides of human conquests, new Formosans often moved into nests vacated by exterminated comrades.[129]

By 2005, only 6 percent of inspected structures in the Vieux Carré were infested, a remarkable success. Full Stop's administrators urged the public to remain vigilant, since the Formosans were managed inconsistently in the rest of the city.[130] The year 2006, Hurricane Katrina not withstanding, saw a 50 percent reduction in infestation of the forty-four targeted Quarter blocks and the riverfront area.[131]

## Shooing the Insectarium

Every generation of Vieux Carré guardians has new concerns, and sometimes dragons to slay. In the 1900s, the overflow from Storyville and the loss of the French Opera House were calls to action. In the 1920s, it was piecemeal decay and demolition. The 1930s saw the establishment of the Vieux Carré Commission. The 1940s saw the removal of certain areas from VCC protection. The 1960s had the uberbattle of the Riverfront Expressway. The 1970s witnessed the beginning of gentrification of the Decatur Street corridor and surrounding areas. The 1980s drowsed in lassitude and economic slumber.

Many cities have redeveloped their riverfronts. The Inner Harbor at Baltimore is a model of how a down-at-the-heels wharf area can be transformed into a thriving tourist magnet. Other cities, like San Diego and San Francisco, have also reworked parts of their waterfront as shipping and heavy industry gave way to tourism.

As the port of New Orleans was gradually remodeled into a modern container operation, the old wharves above and below the Quarter's Moon Walk fell into disuse. The Moon Walk, and its commercially successful neighbors in the new French Market, drew crowds eager to connect to the river— and spend money while doing it. The Audubon Institute had turned its zoo from mediocrity to one of the premier zoos of America. In 1990 it opened an aquarium on the site of the former Bienville Street wharf, not far from the old World's Fair site.[132] The aquarium and its IMAX theater immediately became a major tourist draw. It seemed logical that disused wharves downriver from the Moon Walk could be reshaped into another pack-'em-in attraction.

Much local mirth resounded in 1991 when Audubon announced its plan for a zoo and museum devoted to insects. New Orleans teems with insect life, and its cockroaches are celebrated for their size and aggressiveness.[133] The proposed Insectarium for the wharves between Esplanade and Elysian Fields was immediately the victim of its own hype. Audubon predicted six hundred thousand visitors yearly. This aroused Quarter defenders to point out the tremendous impact this mass of tourists would have on the lower Quarter. Boosters replied that the existing wharves were unsightly and ripe for redevelopment. The riverfront, they argued, would be redeveloped anyway, and the Insectarium, with parking in a structure on Elysian Fields, would offer the lowest impact to the Quarter. The wharves, the Vieux Carré defenders rejoined, were indeed unsightly but mercifully out of sight behind the floodwall. The impact of the aquarium—considered a rousing success—was compared with the expected footprint of the insectarium. However, the aquarium was located just outside of the upper Quarter, which was nearly all commercial. The insectarium, by contrast, edged the mostly residential lower Quarter, where some of the enclave's defenders lived. By 1994, the Insectarium had obtained all necessary approvals, save one. The U.S. Army Corps of Engineers controls the bulwarks of levees and floodwalls at the river and must pass on each alteration thereto. The corps has not been noted for aesthetic faculties; its fortes have been massive, unstylish projects like spillways and levees. Yet in May 1994, the corps declined to issue its permit, calling the insectarium's design incompatible with the surrounding neighborhood and seconding concerns over traffic impacts.[134] The dock board also finally demurred. Audubon cast about for a new location. The U.S. Custom House, occupying the 400 block of Canal at N. Peters, had room, and in 1995 Audubon began to remodel vacant space therein. The Custom House, being a National Historic Landmark, imposed many restrictions on the job, and funding ebbed and flowed.[135] The insectarium finally opened in 2008.

CHAPTER 11

# INTERLUDE

*The Lakeside, Strike Three*

The area of North Rampart Street abutting the Quarter had fallen on hard times after the construction of the Iberville housing project in 1940. Removed from the oversight of the VCC in 1946, it had fallen into a political and social limbo. Across North Rampart lay the Faubourg Tremé, a long-established black middle-class neighborhood. Opposite the Quarter side of Orleans Avenue lay Congo Square. Before the Civil War, this had been a place for slaves to socialize and dance the bamboula, an echo of which may be heard in the works of New Orleans composer Louis Moreau Gottschalk (1829–1869). After the Civil War, the square was renamed for a hometown hero, the Confederate general Pierre Beauregard. On the Basin Street side, the municipal auditorium was built in 1930 and was the scene of many Carnival balls.[1]

The Tremé area, cheek by jowl with the Iberville project and St. Louis Cemetery No.1, went into a decline in the 1940s and 1950s. One of Mayor Chep Morrison's pet projects was a Union Passenger Terminal, which would consolidate rail passenger traffic from five stations into one.[2] The old Southern Railway Station at Basin Street, where generations of men were accosted by the sex industry, would be demolished.[3] In 1954, the city planning commission identified the area around the municipal auditorium as needing rehabilitation.

In 1961, a culture center was envisioned for this location. In 1965, the city held public hearings for those Tremé residents who would be forced to move to accommodate the grandiose project.[4] In the late sixties, demolition

184

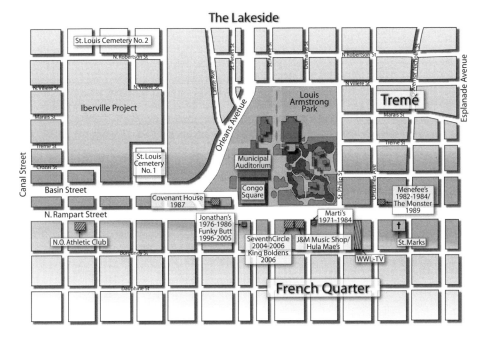

began, displacing about 180 families.[5] Many of these were scattered into housing projects. The remaining Tremé residents were markedly unhappy about
the disruption and their exclusion from jobs associated with the project. In
1972, after a series of protests,[6] work was halted after the construction of the
first major building, dubbed the Opera House in a nod to the long-vanished
French Creole citadel. Seeking to rescue the unfinished work, Mayor Moon
Landrieu visited the famous Tivoli Gardens in Copenhagen in the fall of 1972.
Similar in size, perhaps the complex could become a Tivoli-esque center of
entertainment to relieve some tourist load from the Quarter and revitalize
the Rampart Street corridor.[7] Finding the kind of engagements to make the
park a Tivoli was difficult. Like Jackson Square and other public spaces, Louis
Armstrong Park—as it was now called—would be fenced. Tremé residents
saw the fence as a hateful barrier to keep them out, but it remained.[8] The
money and political commitment, waxing and waning over twenty years,
meant that a simplified Armstrong Park was finally dedicated by Landrieu's
successor, Dutch Morial, on April 15, 1980.[9] One touch of Tivoli did arrive; a
sparkling sign of electric lights, proclaiming the park's name, over the St. Ann
Street gate. At night, the pretty sign invited tourists to find a complex that was
locked up tight.[10]

The park was there, but what to do with it? It became, like the Supreme Court building in the 1900s, an unwelcome and unloved reminder of cultural imperialism, New Orleans style. In 1986, Moon Landrieu conceded: "In looking at the long-term plan, it became apparent that it was a terrible waste of land and destruction to the neighborhood. What had been planned 25 years before was not practical."[11]

Mayor Sidney Barthelemy also felt the need to visit the Copenhagen Tivoli himself in 1986, but for Armstrong Park, any inspiration so gleaned came to naught.[12]

In January 1987, a white tourist from Ohio, Patricia Lobaugh, wandered into the park and shortly thereafter was shot dead by a black man who lived nearby.[13] Armstrong Park became a watchword of dread in the Quarter, and tourists were pointedly warned to stay out of the park by concierges, bartenders, and travel planners. There was not much to do in the park, even if safety could be assured; the murder had driven away any potential amusements. As a tourist destination, Armstrong Park died with Patricia Lobaugh.

The fourteen riverside blocks of North Rampart Street began a brief upswing in the early and mid-1970s. Performances at the municipal auditorium and Mahalia Jackson Theater for the Performing Arts—the "new opera house"—drew thousands of well-dressed patrons to upscale restaurants like Marti's, which opened in 1971 at N. Rampart and Dumaine.[14] In 1976, three partners poured a million dollars into 714 N. Rampart and created Jonathan's, an art-deco restaurant that drew a four-star culinary rating and raves for extravagant decor, including a two-story glass installation.[15] Other developers bought North Rampart properties and began to rehabilitate them.[16]

Local gay bar owner Jerry Menefee invested $2 million into renovation of a two-story building on the lakeside of North Rampart at Ursulines. The restaurant, nightclub, gym, and pool complex opened in 1982. The mauve building stood out like a beacon on the otherwise frowsy strip. New Orleans had never seen a modern "destination" club like this.[17]

In the late seventies and early eighties, the Theater for the Performing Arts began to lose performances to the Saenger Performing Arts Center, N. Rampart at Canal, and later to the University of New Orleans Lakefront Arena. With smaller after-theater crowds, Marti's, Jonathan's, and other businesses suffered. Marti's gave up in 1984;[18] Jonathan's hung on until 1986 and then declared bankruptcy. So bad was the market that the Small Business Administration auction sale went through two rounds of bidding before the former deco palace, mostly stripped of its interior finery, was sold for a mere

$165,000 in December 1987.[19] Jerry Menefee died young in 1984. The Menefee complex was idle until 1989 when it became the short-lived Monster.[20] The Monster closed that same year, and the place slumbered until 1994, when it became the French Quarter Courtyard Hotel.[21]

In the late 1980s, a few long-established retail stores remained on North Rampart, and some restaurants, like Mama Rosa's, seemed eternal. The New Orleans Athletic Club, WWL-TV, and a couple of churches, notably St. Mark's of the Vieux Carré, stood fast. Cheap walk-up apartments could still be found in the buildings along the strip. Gradually, most retail businesses closed, and their storefronts were screened and abandoned. Vagrants dozed in doorways. In 1985, the businesses of North Rampart brought in only about 0.7 percent of all retail sales attributable to the Quarter.[22] North Rampart saw a succession of bars, mostly gay, in the eighties. Rents were cheaper there than the main area of Boys Town. These bars were not the lifestyle clubs Wood Enterprises was introducing in the central Quarter. The Rampart Street clubs were very much traditional gay bars. Dark, redecorated, but rarely renovated, their distinction derived from their clientele—drag at TTs, leather at The Finale II, and hustlers and their patrons at several other spots.

New Orleans has been a magnet for runaways since its founding. North Rampart Street, with its connection to the off-ramp of the Orleans Avenue exit from I-10, is a primary entry point for footloose youngsters. In 1987, Covenant House established a shelter and service center at the site of the old Lamana-Panno-Fallo funeral home at 611–625 N. Rampart (at Toulouse).[23]

The Quarter portion of North Rampart is the upper, or western, arm of the St. Claude corridor, and as such, is on the bus line shuttling passengers from the CBD and Quarter out to the poorer, and predominantly black, Ninth Ward. The proximity of the Iberville project and Tremé, and the bus passengers leaving jobs in the Quarter to go down the line to St. Claude, all made the strip an uneasy meeting place of black working-class and mainly white gay street cultures.

In 1994, the National Park Service created the New Orleans Jazz National Historical Park, a "cerebral" entity, which floats above the boundaries of the Quarter and Tremé. The jazz park seeks to "interpret the origins, history and progression of jazz."[24] In 1999, Mayor Marc Morial granted the jazz park a ninety-nine-year lease on certain buildings within Armstrong Park.[25] The National Park Service became embroiled in a long-simmering, multiheaded dispute between Tremé residents, radio station WWOZ, who had its studio in one of the leased buildings, neighborhood activists, and the many city agencies that have a hand in management of the complex. The dispute centered on the desire of WWOZ to expand its operations, building over some greenspace.[26] The jazz park would—and should—like to take the lead for shaping the future of Armstrong Park to make it the respectable centerpiece of the jazz park operation.

Mississippi had legalized local option gaming in 1990,[27] and a dozen barge-based casinos sprang up along the once-sleepy shoreline of Gulfport and Biloxi. Louisiana's politicians wrangled over the spoils of legal gaming before they even arrived, and so by 1995 the Mississippi casinos were well entrenched. In May 1995, Harrah's set up a temporary casino in the municipal auditorium, awaiting construction permits for the "permanent" casino at the foot of Canal Street. The temporary casino went broke and closed in November of that year.[28] After three years, Harrah's would open its casino at Canal and South Peters streets.

Cosimo Matassa's first, legendary studio at 838 N. Rampart became Hula Mae's Tropic Wash in the late 1990s. In 1999, the city designated it a historic landmark. Matassa, Antoine "Fats" Domino, and other pioneers of New Orleans R&B attended a ceremony with a commemorative plaque. Like many Quarter buildings, 838 remembers its former identity with a tiled threshold, this one stating "J&M Music Shop."[29]

North Rampart's late twentieth century seedy reputation drove down house prices in the adjoining blocks, particularly in the lower Quarter. Some far-sighted buyers found relative bargains on these blocks. Far off the tourist tracks, these blocks tended to be quiet, apart from the usual siren songs of North Rampart.[30]

As the twentieth century turned to the twenty-first, Armstrong Park continued its slumber. Weeds grew through the steps of the Mahalia Jackson Center for the Performing Arts, algae coated the lagoon, and the park's open space saw only occasional use.

In the opening years of the twenty-first century, a new controversy developed. The restoration of the Canal streetcar inspired a hope that the old Desire line could be revived, providing nonautomotive conveyance down the St. Claude corridor. The groundswell of interest fueled real estate speculation—now realized as rather premature—on St. Claude. One scheme called for tracks to be laid in the neutral ground of North Rampart. Quarter advocacy groups were appalled, feeling that the streetcar would only add more traffic to the corridor without any benefit. After all, the reasoning went, there were no destinations for much-coveted nuclear family tourists on North Rampart, and no sightseeing as on the iconic St. Charles route. The Desire streetcar project was derailed in 2003 when the U.S. Department of Transportation gave the project a "not recommended" rating due to poor cost effectiveness. Additionally, the Regional Transportation Authority and the Norfolk Southern Railroad came to an impasse. The proposed streetcar would cross the Norfolk Southern tracks at Press Street. Community input ran against an above-grade crossing for the streetcar and a below-grade crossing would certainly flood in heavy rainstorms.[31] After Katrina, the RTA was absorbed with restoring the St. Charles Avenue and Canal Street lines, so the Desire line proposal has been shelved.

Many hopes for reviving North Rampart have come and gone. The old Jonathan's location was the Funky Butt music club from 1996 to just before Katrina in 2005, when it closed due to infrastructure problems and lack of patrons.[32] An attempted revival as a live music venue was shot down in October of 2005, even as the city was begging tourists to return. Councilwoman Jackie Clarkson, while professing to love live jazz, opposed any new nightclubs on North Rampart, preferring residential development.[33]

Even before Katrina, some wanted to demolish the Iberville project and install condos. The closing of some of the city's other housing projects may mean that their residents might move to Iberville. The mere suggestion of altering any of the projects elicits a loud immune response from self-styled activists, some of whom do not live in the projects themselves.[34] Armstrong Park remains a nullity. A silent, stuffed moose head overlooking the North Rampart parlor, it neither offends with noise and crowds nor does it host much life. WWOZ's offices were damaged in Katrina, and the station moved to North Peters Street, a world away in the Quarter's universe.

Gentrified neighborhoods may change in ways their first rescuers could not imagine. In San Francisco's Castro, and New Orleans's Marigny as well, gay ghettos give way with some angst to straight couples who may have children instead of cats, and moderate politics instead of agendas.[35] Sheer economics are driving changes to hard-won gay enclaves, and the market is just as deaf to spurious cries of "homophobia" as it is to pleas for diversity and affordability. Accepted norms for largely gay neighborhoods, established in the 1970s and 1980s, may not be acceptable for nongay residents in the twenty-first century.

Some suburban home buyers purchase two lots, one for a house and one for distance from the neighbors. It is often true that some early gentrifiers also approve of vacant structures and empty lots flanking their property.

Urban pioneers, having invested considerable time, money, and sweat some-times fall into a peculiar sort of NIMBYism, in this case, *"Nothing* In My Back Yard." Emptiness is insulation. No neighbors are no neighbors making noise or trouble. The current Quarter gentry could never live in the Quarter of eighty years past, with dozens of multiracial children frolicking in the streets and banquettes, mothers bellowing out windows, and vendors and strumpets crying their wares all the livelong day.

For those who want to roll the dice on North Rampart, the odds remain long. The city's catch-as-catch-can zoning enforcement tripped up a promis-ing live music venue in 2006. The Seventh Circle, a gay bar featuring male dancers, vacated 840 North Rampart after two years in operation. Its replace-ment, King Bolden's, featured live jazz music as well as that provided by DJs. The new owners assumed, incorrectly, that their club would be grandfathered in for live entertainment. However, young men gyrating nearly naked on counter tops and live jazz music were two very different "entertainments" for the city and the neighbors. A politically active neighbor, who had approved of the prior club with its loud music, alerted the city.[36] The owners had also failed to transfer the liquor license from the old bar and so did not have a legal permit to sell drinks, the coup de grace for any Quarter nightclub.[37] The club, despite support from many in the music business, was, in fact, outside the law. The Quarter has only two zones for live entertainment, on Bourbon and part of upper Decatur.[38] The fact that other clubs were offering live music outside those zones was no defense. Without political support that might have overridden zoning, as is often true, the club had no choice but to close. During the controversy, the president of the French Quarter Citizens for the Preservation of Residential Quality stated that art galleries, not jazz clubs, were wanted on North Rampart.[39]

Art galleries are all very fine, but North Rampart Street, due to the Iber-ville project, the void of Armstrong Park, and the mixture of black, gay, and gutter punk culture, has demonstrated no talent as a tourist strip. The dearth of Quarter and CBD stores selling essentials to residents suggests a new use for North Rampart, one that is not pitched to tourists. As recently as the 1980s, the street held a grocery store, a furniture store, an auto dealership, and other businesses supporting residents. Perhaps North Rampart, with its undervalued properties, could again host stores like these. Not glamourous, nor depending on fickle tourism, these sorts of firms could employ and sup-port residents.

On a night in mid-2007, I stood outside one of the street's clubs with a native old friend who was working the door. We saw no activists, no lawyers, no code enforcers, and no investors in the humid evening—just the street-wise pedestrian commuters trudging to and from jobs, and the regular bar patrons. Cop cars and ambulances came by in a rush of blue and red lights—urban fireflies often seen here. We talked about all the things we had seen in our years on this street, and concluded that things hadn't changed that much. Maybe that is best, I thought. Everything else imposed from above has ended in fiasco, and maybe North Rampart can be left to fend for itself for another generation.

## CHAPTER 12

# INTERLUDE

*Time and Life in the Quarter*

## TIME IS DIFFERENT HERE

Time is different in New Orleans and especially so in the Quarter. Yes, there are calendars and clocks, but in the main, they are simply onlookers, not pacesetters of life as elsewhere. Time here ebbs, flows, loops back on itself, passes slower than molasses and faster than a schnapps shooter. The rising of the sun signals the end of a night in the bars. The phases of the moon track the temperature of passion. The varying date of Mardi Gras was devised as a religious mechanism long before New Orleans existed. It is very New Orleans that its primary holiday changes from year to year. Time to go to the bar, time to go home. Time to prepare to party, and time to wind down. Time to think about food, and time to eat. Time to love, and time to dream. The Quarter, after the usual adjustments, felt like an old, frowzy but warm coat that one put on, and when away from home, missed when it was off.

The experience of living in the Quarter has indeed changed, albeit slowly, over the century past. Some of the changes have stemmed from security concerns, tracking the darkening, suspicious mood of the city and nation in general. Some of the changes flow from property values that skyrocketed after the 1990s. The French Quarter measures progress as fresh coats of (approved) paint on old buildings. Fixtures that persist for generations and then go away are mourned as lost relatives. Over the past two decades, New Orleans has lost several local institutions—K&B Drugs, Schwegmann groceries, MacKenzie's bakeries, and others. Although none of these chains operated in the Quarter, the Quarter dwellers and all New Orleanians missed them dearly.

The 1938 *New Orleans City Guide* wrote, "The Vieux Carré is definitely the place where people go to live their own lives."[1] It might have added, "and live close to the lives of others." Above and beyond the cachet of living in a famous enclave, Quarter residents share physical proximity, the challenge of living in old buildings, the same constricted streets, the same lack of parking, the same sidewalk avoidance of human vomit and dog feces. Before television and air conditioning, family life was played out for all to hear. For twenty-first-century Americans, feeling entitled to a bubble of "personal space," the Vieux Carré seems very close quarters indeed. To live so close to others requires a degree of tolerance that the Quarter has always had beyond the American suburban norm.

Americans have very short social memories. Few now remember the rigid religious, ethnic, social, and class lines that defined city neighborhoods just three generations ago. Living "with one's own kind" was not merely a choice; it was a matter of safety. Men venturing into a strange neighborhood, even of their ethnicity, risked attack from local youths—"good boys"—who saw themselves as guardians. Few would sell or rent to those not of their race, religion, or ethnic group. In segregated times, laws prohibited most blacks from free choice of domicile.

In the Quarter, these lines blurred, but did not completely fade. Before nondiscrimination laws, blacks who did not own property there had little entrée; and some landlords would not rent to Jews or obvious homosexuals. However, most people who wanted to live there could, shedding most, if not all, of the onerous labels the rest of society found so convenient. The couple upstairs would be "living in sin" anywhere else, but not here. The young men sitting on the stoop next door were more than roommates, but here, no one cared. The tweedy older man seen lurching home from the bar might be a famous author, but you called him by his first name and, when he was in his cups, helped him unlock his gate. You heard the arguments of the people downstairs, and knew they heard your trysts through the ceiling.

The Quarter has a kind of shabby stateliness that exists nowhere else in America. Not a synthetic portion of the past like the reconstructed Colonial Williamsburg, nor a theme park, this very old district embraces very new residents with a hug of antique looks, feels, and smells that push away the sterile, the prepackaged, and the sanitized. Like an ancient city of refuge, the Vieux Carré has been a place to run to, but not to hide. The Quarter evokes feelings like those imparted by the open ocean or great mountains—a presence of age and history so great as to induce a comforting sense of personal insignificance. It is a place to be free and exhilarated by extraordinary human acceptance as an ordinary thing, a place of intricate grandeur on a human scale, often collectively called the *tout ensemble* by its legal guardians.

For poor or barely middle-class people, the Vieux Carré offered a kind of lifestyle unavailable in other urban areas or the suburbs. The apartments might be dilapidated with sputtering appliances, but until recently, it was possible for street performers, bar staff, waiters, artists, and sheer dreamers to live on very little.

To live in the Quarter or its close cousin, the Faubourg Marigny, one acquires the scent of the tea olive, the cocktail extended from the stoop, French bread carried rifle fashion, and river fogs making mysterious feelings visible. One reacquires the skill of parallel parking, preferably with a friend to watch.

To visit, let alone live in the Quarter, means developing a finely tuned screen for the unpleasant. The smell of garbage on hot days, teenagers puking their first hurricanes, zealots haranguing the ample supply of sinners are all passed by in nonchalance. Negotiating the heaving sidewalks is a challenge for the sober, much less the inebriated. The befuddled tourists and those too far displaced from even New Orleans's reality are steered around.

Making it all worthwhile is sitting on a balcony, drink in hand, looking out at a noble skyline and down at poor mortals below. Hurrying gets us there no faster; worrying, no smarter. Notes from the riverboat calliope float across Jackson Square, punctuated by the click-clack of tapdancers and the wailing of street musicians. Immune from most bourgeois striving outside, the Quarter kept its own standards.

## CLEANLINESS IS NEXT TO . . .

Sometimes in polite whispers, sometimes in drunken bellows, people ask this question: "Why is the Quarter so dirty?" It's a stigma that, until recently, seemed to be permanent. It is crusaded against, scrubbed, and played down. Yet it is slow to go away. No discussion of the Quarter can omit it, so we will put on our old shoes, rubber gloves, and dive in.

The Quarter, and the other parts of the old natural levee, are the highest points in the city. Four to six feet above sea level is not very high, but this modest elevation should give the Quarter better drainage than many parts of town.

The Quarter, since the early 1900s, no longer has sewage, tossed from chamberpots on high, washing down the gutters. Dead animals no longer decompose in the streets. The last of the Vieux Carré's oyster packing houses closed in the mid-1980s, removing that unique perfume from hot summer afternoons.[2] Yet, by the sanitized standards of current American life, the streets smell, sometimes badly, and curbside trash must be swerved around in the traipse from bar to bar.

The commercial and residential trash is easy to understand. The cheek-by-jowl buildings allow little space for Dumpsters, so trash must sit at the curb until pickup. In the 1970s, the city installed in-sidewalk cylinders to hold trash cans. This wonderful idea kept trash out of sight and off the sidewalks until pickup. Alas, good intentions came undone. The little cylinders could not hold much trash; their lids and containers got bashed in or stolen, and pedestrians fell in the holes. Most—but not all—were filled with cement, leaving yet another tourist curiosity.[3] Although trash is picked up six days a week, city trash cans are not serviced at night when they ingest the most. The garbage trucks cannot lumber down the Bourbon pedestrian mall crowded with tipsy tourists.

The street trash, loathsome as it is, also yields to a quick analysis. The main party zone of the Quarter, Bourbon from Bienville to St. Philip, is a mere ten blocks, including the St. Ann branch of Boys Town. During Carnival, upwards of two hundred thousand people may be crammed into that area at any given time. Nearly all have a drink in hand, and some are trying to drink, eat, smoke, walk, and gawk all at once. Of course, people also leave excretions of all kinds on the streets, stoops, and gates of residents. Even with many trash cans, increasing in number over the years, a lot of trash just doesn't make it into the receptacles. People who, when sober in a hometown mall would never drop a gum wrapper, drop all manner of debris when drunk in the Quarter. For many years, city boosters took a perverse pride in how much trash was collected on Ash Wednesday. A big haul meant a commercially healthy Carnival.[4] Finally, more polite statistics supplanted these trashy tons.[5]

The sidewalks of the enclave, "banquettes" to residents, present visitors with a crazy quilt of cracks, dips, humps, cliffs, and paving styles. It's difficult to appreciate the architecture if one must always watch one's step. Although the geographical firmament of the Vieux Carré is stable by New Orleans standards, it varies enough to crack concrete within a few years and mandates careful tending of any paving. From time to time, the city has repaved certain areas, such as Jackson Square in 1974 and the bricked sidewalks laid down before the 1984 World's Fair. The majority of the Quarter's banquettes have not been repaved in decades. Their cracks and fissures collect trash and stagnate liquids.

Before Hurricane Katrina, the city's drainage system was considered a marvel. After large-scale reconstruction from about 1900 to 1940, most of the city's open drainage ditches and canals were covered and serviced by pumps.[6] New Orleanians fondly remarked that their city had more miles of canals than Venice.[7]

The additional drainage caused widespread subsidence of existing structures. It also opened up new land in the old back o' town swamp for those who thought man could overrule nature forever.[8] Heavy rains might cause some street flooding elsewhere, but the high ground of the old natural levee—"the sliver by the river"—stayed mostly dry. That rainy-day comfort depends on catch basins, called storm drains anywhere else. They are normally ignored, and often confused with sanitary drains. The Quarter's catch basins swallow rainwater, wash water, pollutants, go-cups, food, and at least one cell phone—the author's. Eventually, if all goes well, everything winds up in the lake, another frequently forgotten fact. To work, they must be cleaned out at intervals—a nasty business for the strong of stomach. Even before Katrina, merchants were complaining that the Vieux Carré catch basins were not being promptly cleaned after Fat Tuesday. Backed-up filthy water was dashed all over pedestrians by passing vehicles.[9] The catch basins were eventually cleaned. The Bourbon Street Alliance, a group of over eighty Quarter firms, welded metal mesh screens over the catch basins along Bourbon from the 900 block to Canal and one block either side. The mesh screens kept solid waste from clogging the drains and allowed street sweepers to scoop up solid debris.[10] By 2007 wear and tear from truck traffic had abraded the mesh screens and they needed replacement.[11]

Animal droppings had been a common sight on Quarter streets for centuries, baking in the sun. At the end of the twentieth century, the last remaining draft animals were mules drawing tourist buggies. The compost-like mule droppings were a frequently cited nuisance. Councilwoman Clarkson fitted the mules with canvas diapers.[12] That helped, but as any parent knows, diapers sometimes leak. Dogs also walk the banquettes, and even though "picking up" is now ingrained into owners, *merde de chien* remains an ambulatory hazard.

When I lived in the Quarter in the mideighties, my friends and I called the stretch of Ursulines between Bourbon and Dauphine "Rue Doggie Deux" for its plentiful canine souvenirs.

Regulations and public training are all essential, but the city's famed heat and humidity work to create and waft pungent smells during most of the year. A native friend gave me a valuable tip for dealing with seafood shells. He froze them until garbage day and then put them out for collection.

Hosing down sidewalks is a daily ritual for business owners, and some residents do it also. A few hardy souls splash a little ammonia on the banquette to cut the eternal grubby film.

In 2006, the city let a new sanitation contract, with SDT Waste & Debris Services, LLC. In a few months, residents and visitors noticed a new cleanliness in the Quarter, even after Carnival. This remarkable transformation won plaudits even from long-time residents.[13] During the French Quarter Festival of April 2007, I noticed the SDT personnel cleaning up while the festival was in progress. This, in contrast to years past, when city sanitation tended to wait until festivities ended before moving in to clean up. SDT even washes the streets with a lemon-scented solution.[14] One can hope that this level of attention will endure and the Quarter will get a new reputation, one for cleanliness.

## A DAY IN THE QUARTER

To Americans who often think of 1776 as Year Zero, the Quarter, antedating the nation by fifty-eight years, seems ancient indeed. Residents draw comfort from this age, and the (until recently) slow trammel of change. The real palpable difference of time in the Quarter is best felt by walking around it in early hours and coming back out—after a suitable nap in the deep swoon of summer afternoon—at night.

Starting down Bourbon from Canal, we encounter the nightclubs restocking from trucks parked in the street, cases of spirits, food, and cigarettes being handled by beefy drivers who live many miles away. The barroom doors are wide open as workers give the joints a swabbing. The *parfumeurs* of old Paris could not imagine the mixed smell of beer, urine, and chlorine bleach that is the signature of the early morning air. The music is still there, but subdued as the last of the bleary-eyed waitstaff of the graveyard shift count the time till they can totter home.

Further down, and along the side streets, other trucks are servicing the restaurants, which will not be open until 11 a.m. We detour around the latest crop of tattooed busboys, smoking at the curb. They were probably working offshore not long ago, and may return yet again. We encounter a few smartly dressed people toting briefcases, probably on their way to that bastion of authority on Royal Street where the state Supreme Court sits.

Breakfast is best spent at the Clover Grill, deep in Boys Town, where the staff serves up entertainment and good, heavy food. We see a cross section of the mid-Quarter; waitstaff changing shifts, tourists surprised by the dawn ("Oh, that moon is bright!"), hustlers and dancers now off duty, and older residents nostalgic for their roots of not so long ago.

Moving further on to the little shops and corner stores, we find them stocked by the most wide-awake people we've yet seen, with the keen interest that only proprietorship can give—greeting customers with "babe" regardless of age or gender, signing receipts for the delivery drivers, and having chats with fellow residents. Sidewalks are being hosed down and what little outside cleaning is ever done is swiftly accomplished before the furnace of typical midday.

In the lower Quarter people are trudging off to work, usually in the Central Business District (CBD) or elsewhere, giving the blank stare that only the jaded resident can give. Looping back up Barracks, we stop by the Golden Lantern for an eye-opener, lest we face Decatur Street with no fortification at all. Along with a Bloody Mary or a mimosa, we hear some interesting "dish," to be stored away for consideration. Fortified, we walk up Decatur, already humming with traffic, though the banquettes are calm just now. The heavy shopping blocks between the market and Jackson Square are strangely quiet, as the tourists are mostly abed and the shops just beginning to open. At the square, the first few tourist buggies stand by, the mules with their eternal, doleful stare behind blinders, pawing a little in anticipation of the day's trots. Walking up St. Peter in the Square, a few artists, fortune-tellers, and musicians are setting up. Some folk—called by whatever name now—are dozing upright on the benches, denied the privilege of lying down by welded iron censure. We see the first of the day's tour groups being sheparded along by a park ranger, giving the latest cadre of tourists the real lowdown.

Down Royal now, the prime rib of Quarter shopping, stores of treasure and still, reassuringly, a few of trash, are opening with hopes for the traveler's dollar. Past McDonogh 15 school at St. Philip, the laughter and yells of youngsters remind us that families are still here and a few lucky kids get to go to school within a living, breathing village of long history.

Noon passes with chores, errands, and quotidian duties. In the summer afternoons, residential blocks are quiet, shimmering with reflected heat. A late cold lunch refreshes, and now it is time to nap. In younger days, we called this a disco nap; middle age has truncated that to simply a necessary lie-down.

Shut the door, draw the veil, strip down to diaphanous garb or nothing at all, turn on the air conditioner and perhaps fan. Lie down with misty yellow fingers of light caressing the room through the drapes. The calliope's notes faintly waft through, soap bubbles of sound, memory and imagination carrying our fading wakefulness away. An occasional thump from a passing truck or boom car draws us near, but not to, the surface of waking. It is now nighttime, and in summer if we get up by eight o'clock we may see a fleeting deep turquoise sky from the palette of Maxfield Parrish.

On the other hand, getting up at eight may be too early, if our mission is a night in the bars ending in an assignation. Perhaps we have aged beyond that as our usual late-night errand. We may want to meet old friends for dinner and then retire to a neighborhood bar to have a few drinks before bedtime. The neighborhood bars are still here, at least for now, and recognition upon arrival is instantaneous. Even for nonsmokers, the cologne of cigarette smoke and spilled liquor with a top note of disinfectant is comforting. Avoiding cigarette smoke is well-nigh impossible; New Orleanians, and particularly Quarter denizens, continue to smoke far above the falling national norm. Here is the extended family, here is where the gains are celebrated and losses grieved. Here is where the new beaux are shown off and hopefully not scandalized. Here is where they remember your costume of last Carnival, and perhaps the one before that.

When it is time to go home, we walk, in that self-conscious walk of the tipsy over uneven ground, trying to be vigilant, and quickly let ourselves in, bolting the portals behind us. The bed we got up from just a while ago still waits, and our shadows are tall on the high walls. Tucked in, we dimly hear the lullaby of Quarter sounds, coming from just beyond the horizon of the air conditioner. The smells of decades of cooking and washing and of old wood, with a faint note of natural gas, surround us, and at some point, we journey to the Quarter of dreams that is always just across the threshold of waking life.

## CHAPTER 13

# 1994–2000

*A Dance Before the Rain*

## LEMONS TO CHERRIES: THE CASINO

Mississippi, New Orleans's morally dour, sometimes sour, and ever-conservative eastern neighbor, had authorized casino gambling, on a local-option basis, in 1990.[1] Other communities, such as Deadwood, South Dakota, had authorized gambling, hoping to emulate the riches of Atlantic City and Las Vegas. Natives of the Mississippi Gulf Coast, which forms part of New Orleans's solar system, thought perhaps a few casinos would arrive. To the astonishment of all, twelve casinos were in operation by 2004.[2]

The casinos offered cheap all-you-can-eat buffets, killing some longtime local eateries. The casinos built hotels and theaters for shows, albeit not the typical Vegas fare. The girlie aspect was toned down for Bible Belt audiences, and the touring acts usually featured country music and "golden oldie" revivals. The towns of the coast had long lived hand to mouth, on meager payrolls and revenues from downmarket tourism, military spending, and the seafood industry. Now Biloxi could replace its fleet of police cruisers and build an ultramodern high school. Young men who might have once toiled long hours in the sun in shipyards or on shrimp boats could now work in an air-conditioned cash cage, with benefits.

Louisiana's flamboyant governor, Edwin Edwards, looked hungrily at his sister state's new banquet. Louisiana and Mississippi usually vied for forty-ninth and fiftieth place on national tallies such as education, public spending, and personal income. Louisiana was reeling from a loss of oil revenues, and gambling was thought to be a quick fix. In 1992, the state authorized casinos. Barge-based casinos were licensed in Shreveport and elsewhere. New Orleans, with its centuries of illegal gambling and party industry, would be the location of choice for a legal, land-based casino. This time an industry courted the state—only one permit would be awarded in New Orleans—and the city's abysmal schools and crumbling infrastructure would not deter a casino operator, as they might conventional industry. Harrah's got the state approval, but in a shotgun wedding born of state and city politics, Harrah's would join in a consortium with Caesar's Palace, in a firm called Harrah's Jazz,[3] which committed to build a new casino. In the interim, it set up shop in early 1995 in the municipal auditorium in that perennial stepchild, Armstrong Park.[4] The temporary casino was misbegotten from the start. Located on the least desirable edge of the Quarter, it was not within visitor-safe walking distance of any of the "family" attractions that had been so carefully nurtured on the riverfront.

The nearest businesses to the casino were edgy gay bars, not at all what boosters wanted tourists to see. The old stench from the 1987 murder in the park was reventilated. The park backed up to Tremé, a downturned area still seething with resentment over its rape in the creation of the park in the 1970s. Tremé activists forced some changes to prevent the isolation of Congo Square by casino traffic patterns.[5] Locally, the temporary casino competed with casinos in Jefferson Parish, which drew gamblers with more income from the suburbs.[6] The Mississippi Gulf Coast casinos on the beach, a mere ninety road miles away, trumpeted a "down home" atmosphere, with alternate lifestyles, minorities, and slums kept mostly out of sight. Within six months, the casino in Armstrong Park filed for bankruptcy, and twenty-five hundred workers lost their jobs to another empty promise.[7]

Had the casino cabal bothered to ask residents, it might have learned something from their collective memory. Illegal gambling had indeed been pervasive for a long time. From the late 1930s until 1946, when they were driven across the parish line by Mayor Chep Morrison, slot machines had been widespread in New Orleans.[8] By definition, illegal gaming was exempt from pesky regulations. Various people, including Chep Morrison, had proposed legalization and taxation.[9] Besides resistance from the guardians of public morality, folks had good reasons for gambling to stay sub rosa. People liked the convenience of placing bets with their bartender, barber, or other neighborhood "handbook operator." This privacy was appealing to those solid citizens who wouldn't be caught dead in a "gambling house." Confidentiality was also attractive to those who got a little side money out of view of their spouses. The immunity of winnings from taxes also pleased. Generations of politicians and policemen supplemented their incomes with bribes to protect "horse parlors," "sports results parlors," handbook operators, and backroom gaming.

Construction on the permanent casino on Canal Street stopped for three years. In 1998, the new casino finally opened, under two conditions. It could not offer a restaurant nor a hotel, lest it compete with French Quarter eateries and overbuilt local lodging. By this time, of course, the Gulf Coast casinos were numerous and well entrenched. Biloxi, Gulfport, and Bay St. Louis, once poor stepchildren to New Orleans, had developed a thriving gaming industry while Louisiana politicians fought over future spoils and patronage.[10] In 2001, Harrah's owners again sought bankruptcy protection. The fiat against a casino hotel and restaurant was lifted,[11] and before Hurricane Katrina in 2005, Harrah's was doing well.[12]

Besides casinos, the state also legalized the first lottery in nearly a century, as well as video poker. The video poker machines blossomed in bars statewide. They lured bored lounge lizards with colorful displays and recorded enticements. What started as objects of curiosity quickly became money machines for the bars and the franchisees. This combination of home-bar socializing, drinking, and gambling was irresistible to people who couldn't be bothered with going to casinos. Like the little old ladies playing casino slots by the hour, bar patrons began to play video poker obsessively. Besides the occasional wins, the machines made losing a private affair for folks too shy to gamble in public. The bars get their contractual cut, and, of course, some winnings are recycled into rounds of drinks.

## THE MIDNINETIES

Dutch Morial's son, Marc, was elected mayor in 1994 at age thirty-six. Unlike his famously cranky father, Marc exhibited the happy-go-lucky persona of the up-and-coming young single man he was. His father's legacy had given him the mayoralty and he was now enjoying it. He was seen fighting "training" fires with the fire department. Instantly, he became the city's most eligible bachelor. But this crown prince had inherited a kingdom near collapse. By the early nineties, most New Orleanians, even those who were usually protective of the city's grubby image, thought things were at rock bottom. The city's leadership began to shift perspective. Slowly, influential whites began to wake up from the hypnosis of stagnation as preservation. Black politicians, now that the combative Dutch was gone, began to move past the politics of resentment and revenge. However, as we have seen, outsiders met stiff resistance when presenting out-of-town, and therefore suspect, ideas in New Orleans. About the only real conduit for new ideas to decision makers were the many studies commissioned by the city administrations in the 1980s and 1990s. These studies were all performed by politically connected consultants, some of whom stood to reap benefits should their ideas be adopted. Therefore, all these studies were tainted from the start by a need for political expediency and private profitability. The studies by politically connected consultants got the publicity, and were forgotten with the next mayoral administration, who had its own consultants to feed. The studies by academics in this period were far more important. The living laboratory of the Quarter and the larger city begged investigation by eager young students of urban sciences. The University of New Orleans College of Urban and Public Affairs (CUPA), Tulane University, and other institutions all published numerous studies of the evolving Vieux Carré.

Every sovereign rules with the backing of his army, and Marc knew that "his" police force was in deep trouble. The rising tide of crime and the cancer of corruption within the ranks had created a nightmare. In former times, poor blacks had rightfully complained of white police brutality. Now, their chief grievance was police—including black police—indifference to open black gang warfare, whose whizzing bullets were cutting down young innocents and "gangstas" alike.

In Louisiana until 1994, minor traffic violators from all but seven states could simply receive a ticket, to be paid by mail. The other forty-two states had an interstate compact guaranteeing reciprocal enforcement of each other's traffic laws. Residents of the other seven noncompact states could be strip-searched and thrown in jail if they could not make bond. A couple of high-profile indignities finally prodded the city to change the law to permit drivers from noncompact states to surrender their licenses until payment of tickets.[13] However, the law notwithstanding, the abuses continued, and a class-action suit against the Orleans Parish Criminal Sheriff was only settled in December 2006.[14] The NOPD's image was further tarnished as some cops lashed out at tourists. In most cases, the tourists were victimized either in the course of minor traffic violations or were doing nothing illegal at all.

A state representative complained of brutality on New Year's Eve 1993, and other incidents made ugly national news.[15] Soon after his first inauguration, Marc searched for a new police chief. He chose Richard Pennington, who had been assistant police chief of Washington, D.C. His welcome to New Orleans included the murder of a woman on orders from a police officer. Just after he took command, the FBI told him of an investigation into corruption that eventually indicted nine officers.[16] Over the next eight years, Pennington rescued NOPD and solved most, if not all, of its more flagrant problems. Between 1997 and 1999, New Orleans had the steepest drop in annual murders of the thirty-four largest cities in America.[17] From 1995 to 2002, the number of murders dropped by 30 percent. In that same period, New Orleans's crime index dropped by 37 percent.[18]

The NOPD's relationship with the Quarter residents continued to be uneasy, at best. At meetings and on the street, residents sounded claims that policing was reserved for tourist areas and tourism priorities, leaving residents to their own devices.

Residents of St. Peter Street were frustrated with police indifference, especially to crowds of young people circulating around the neighborhood at night, doing drugs and vandalizing property. In early 1995, they hired off-duty levee board police to patrol their neighborhood. The levee board cops curbed much of the rowdiness and vandalism that had plagued the area.[19] The NOPD reacted with astonishment and anger. It maintained that the neighborhood should have hired off-duty NOPD officers first and that the levee board cops were out of their jurisdiction. After a furious exchange of letters between NOPD Chief Pennington and levee board president Robert Harvey, the levee cops withdrew.[20]

## THE CONDO CONUNDRUM

In the 1990s, particularly the later half of the decade, it seemed to be raining money in America. The explosive growth of the information technology (IT) industry had made millionaires and billionaires on a scale unknown before. After the dissolution of the Iron Curtain and temporary shock of the first Gulf War in 1991, the national economy settled into a period of great expansion. There seemed to be lots of money available for investment of all kinds, and real-estate speculation, along with Silicon Valley IT investments, was red hot. New Orleans did not participate in this economy, at least not in the

earning part. Like the boom of the 1920s, the 1990s IT money was generated elsewhere. All this money had to be spent somewhere, and real estate,
particularly in prime tourist areas, was snapped up. Outside investors began
looking at not only the Vieux Carré, but other New Orleans neighborhoods,
as undervalued opportunities, ripe for the picking. The Historic Preservation
Tax Credit Program of 1986 gave incentives for restoring historic properties.[21]
New Orleans summer, like Russian winter, had long been a potent defense
against interlopers. Now, air conditioning, except for a sweaty jaunt from
car to condo, made that a moot point. Buildings that had not seen serious
renovation for decades could be fixed up—voila!—with now-ample funding. Many Quarter buildings had been owned for generations by the same
families. They had transformed them from the family store-and-home of
lean years to apartments or whole-house rentals of later, middle-class years.
Now, the current generation was being offered fabulous sums for the building where great-mammaw grew up. And some were selling out.[22] The new
owners, in most cases, were not the kind of owner-resident urban pioneers
like the Jacob Morrisons in the thirties or the Marigny gay gentrifiers of the
eighties. They were often corporations whose express purpose was real estate
investment. Condoization of apartment buildings usually forced out existing
renters. Often, these folks had paid the same rent for many years and had no
resources to sign a mortgage. The new owners put units on the market for
speculation and seasonal occupancy. Between 1980 and 1995, one hundred
Quarter rental units had been converted to condos. In the second half of the
decade, condoization accelerated. Between 1996 and 1999, eighty-one new
condos appeared.[23] The condos did not merely force out long-time renters.
Because the condos are usually occupied for short times throughout the year,
their dwellers do not support the Quarter retail infrastructure day in and day
out like the long-time renters did. Condo people, and especially guests they
let use the units,[24] often bring their own food and liquor from out of town.
The renters had their clothes dry-cleaned by Wing Lee on Chartres, bought
liquor at the A&P on Royal, got po-boys from Quarter Master on Bourbon,
made groceries at Matassa's on Dauphine, bought hardware at Mary's on
Bourbon, and went to plays at Le Petit on St. Peter. The condo people, if they
even knew these establishments existed, were rarely in town long enough
to patronize them. So, the retail infrastructure suffered as well.[25] The renters found a voice beyond their means and station in groups, like VCPORA,
that knit the fabric of residential life. "Weekenders" in condos had no time
or incentive to staff the community groups. Unlike renters, who shared the

vicissitudes of Quarter life and toil, the condo people had little in common beyond their condo association, which was usually a remote entity dispensing legalistic direction. Of course, some condos are full-time residences, usually for those who have the means to buy a unit but not the means to buy an entire house nor inclination to live elsewhere. The full-time condo residents of the Vieux Carré have at once the best and worst of apartments and ownership. They have associations to take care of the building and common areas, usually a resident manager, and professionals to obtain services and run the rapids of the city bureaucracy. They also have to put up with people loaned or—illegally—rented neighboring units for holidays, Carnival in particular. These visitors bring noise, trash, and disregard for parking conventions. It may be argued that owners, even part-timers, have more economic stake in the economy of the Vieux Carré than renters. By their association dues, they contribute to the maintenance of buildings that, in former times, had been allowed to decay. Some condo residents are actually renters, the owners either seeking a return on their investment or renting out the place because it isn't selling. These rents, of course, are far above rents of old.

The Quarter had seen slow, patchwork gentrification—by its own standards—from the twenties through the eighties. Now, it was the subject of "supergentrification"[26]—a dramatic up-luxing and up-pricing of properties that had already been gentrified to formerly middle-class standards. The Formica and linoleum that had seemed so modern in midcentury now gave way to granite and terrazzo flooring. Quarter building stock is largely fixed, and condo sizes cannot appreciably grow, so amenities increase and prices soar. One sample for comparison: my building on Gov. Nicholls had sold for $225,000 in the summer of 1985. In 2002, my old attic apartment—now deemed a "second floor condo"—was for sale for the same amount. Even modest cottages now were priced above $600,000.

In some cases, condoization was reversed as buildings were reconverted into single-family homes. In mid-1994, the *Times-Picayune* reported that approximately twenty-five Quarter properties had been reconverted to single-family residences in the early part of the decade.[27] My old building on Gov. Nicholls had been a single-family home when built in the 1880s. It had been cut up into apartments, internally remodeled in 1978, and, in the 1990s, became condos. Then it was briefly a single-family home, and, in the early part of the twenty-first century, became condos again.

The condos were not the only pressures on rental residential space in the Quarter. Hotels, despite a 1969 moratorium[28] on new hostelries in the Vieux

Carré, continued illegal expansions. Some hotels leased rooms in buildings for overflow guests. In 1999, VCPORA sued Decatur Hotel Corporation and Bruno Properties. The suit averred that rooms at 513–523 Decatur had been leased as hotel rooms in violation of the law. The defendants' response was not surprising. The city, they countered, had been aware of the arrangement more than two years before. That made it a "legal nonconforming use."[29] The suit is still in process, more than ten years on.[30] The moratorium, like other regulations, was plaint enough for politics. In 1982, the moratorium was revised to permit new hotels in existing buildings.[31] In 2004, the city planning commission granted a single exception for a new hotel in former warehouse space, which had been vacant for years. That exception was fought to a standstill, and the developers withdrew their application before a city council vote in 2006.[32]

Bed-and-breakfasts (B&Bs) had become a fashion of the seventies. An existing house would be converted into a small hotel, and the owners, usually residing on the property, would provide breakfast and tourism advice. The B&Bs were sold as a friendly alternative to impersonal and often indifferent chain hotels, particularly in prime tourist areas. The better B&Bs cultivated clienteles that returned, season after season, with permanent reservations. New Orleans saw a proliferation of B&Bs in the eighties and nineties. The then-inexpensive housing of the Marigny offered the B&B entrepreneurs a way to pay mortgages and have some fun in the process. Ramshackle houses got fixed up and maintained as B&Bs. The tourists soaked up the local charm and ground truth from the owners. Some B&Bs catered to distinct groups— gays, lesbians, the disabled, and even divers. The city attempted to regulate B&Bs by limiting their numbers in the Quarter and requiring the owners to live on the premises.

Evasion of New Orleans taxes and fees spans all eras and classes. There is a widespread feeling that money paid to the city's coffers will just be wasted or stolen. The law is nothing if not flexible in New Orleans, and soon many illegal B&Bs popped up in the better parts of town.[33] Some illicit operators complained that the fees were burdensome and the city bureaucracy too difficult to deal with. In 1999, a *Times-Picayune* survey of ninety-six B&Bs found only thirty-three licensed by the city. Some real estate agents pitched the B&B—legal or not—as a way for purchasers to finance the soaring costs of Vieux Carré properties.[34] One woman, driven out of her Quarter apartment to clear the path for a B&B, videotaped tourists coming and going, and the tape was shown on television and to the city council. After a few pious observations that the existing laws were adequate, the council went on to other business. Neighbors then became the enforcers of the laws, videotaping tourists, recording license plates, and filing lawsuits. Nonetheless, B&Bs, legal and not, persisted, whittling down the affordable housing stock in the Quarter, Marigny, and elsewhere.[35]

## THE CORPORATE CLUBS AND LOCAL COLOR

Upper Bourbon had been almost, but not quite, abandoned to nightclubs and bars for many years. These were, in the main, run by locals well connected to city hall, and some sheltered working girls under their eaves. Many of the music clubs were operated by the featured performers, like Pete Fountain and Al Hirt. Before the 1970s, some of these clubs had been upscale destinations where adult patrons dressed up to see nationally known entertainers.[36] Most of the famous jazz clubs faded away in the 1980s. Beginning in the early 1990s, the remaining long-time native owners were approached by real estate agents with buyers who would pay fabulous sums. In some cases, the owners would not sell, but raised rents to what the market would bear, meaning corporate clubs with deep pockets. In many cases, the newly sold or rented buildings had been neglected by their long-time owners and needed major renovations. Chain clubs owned by out-of-town corporations took root. Rents on Bourbon started a phenomenal rise—50% between 1997 and 2002.[37]

The chains featured entertainment and ambience carefully calibrated to targeted demographics, with the all-important this-is-New Orleans touches. The remaining hookers were chased off; most had already started working out of "escort services" anyway. The old-time clubs of upper Bourbon had featured Kinsey's "lovely dollies" or "boney hags" gyrating to mostly live music, interspersed with singers, jazz bands, and other live entertainment. The rising male generation still wanted strippers, but had no patience for the lengthy peek-a-boo tableaux of giant oyster shells, balloons, and fans of yesteryear.[38] Now in strip clubs, girls swung around poles to very loud recorded music, and spaces were carved out for dance floors. Even the "exotic dancers" now had to compete for the boys' attention with girls showing their bosoms from balconies. Jazz lived on at Preservation Hall and a few other places in the Quarter, but was hard to find in the blare of disco music.

Even bars, that cornerstone business, started to devolve into daiquiri shops. With the minimal investment and low overhead of a few daiquiri machines, and maybe some basic seating, the daiquiri shops turned the prod-uct—flavored alcohol—quickly to strollers who wanted an icy drink while wandering down the steaming street.[39]

The arrival of chain clubs was not confined to upper Bourbon. In 1992, the city rezoned the first two blocks of Decatur Street as the Vieux Carré Entertainment District.[40] This corner of the Quarter had been the sugar and rice district up to midcentury, with brokerage offices on one side of Decatur and warehouses on the other.[41] It now held mostly vacant office buildings. Beginning in the late eighties, national nightclub chains opened operations along upper Decatur. The short-lived Fashion Café flashed at 619 Decatur in 1996; Hard Rock opened at 440 N. Peters, near Jax Brewery in 1987; House of Blues at 225 Decatur in 1994; and Planet Hollywood opened in 1995 at 620 Decatur.[42] On lower Decatur, Jimmy Buffet's Margaritaville Café opened, replacing the Bombay furniture outlet in a stretch, close to the French Mar-ket, better known for dusty secondhand stores.

The chain clubs, connected to the global pop culture, had immediate name recognition with young tourists who had probably visited the same chain outlets in other cities.[43] The ball-capped patrons were looking for a familiar, dependable experience, and probably never heard of native clubs like Tipitina's or the Rock 'N' Bowl. Chain clubs often showed a tabloidish fetish for the cast-off detritus of "celebs," most of whom had no association with New Orleans.[44] New Orleans natives are not impressed with imported celeb-rities; genuflection is reserved for hometown heroes such as Fats Domino, Mac "Dr. John" Rebennack, the Neville family, Cosimo Matassa, and Harry Connick, Jr.

In all this corporate culture-mongering, the concepts of "New Orleans," and most particularly, the "French Quarter" were homogenized into a mar-ketable gumbo. Not so spicy—or truthful—as to scare off big-spending nuclear families, but not too bland, with fine-tuned naughtiness giving young adults overt permission to drink, dance, and party. The finer points of the city's culture were rounded off in the blare of marketing hype. The wildly absurd and offensive conflation of "Cajun" and "Creole" became a hyphen-ated label used to market food, music, and costumes. The Voodoo belief sys-tem was presented by nonadherents as an amusing fantasy, akin to wishing on a lottery ticket. The image of a black saxophonist, blowing away beneath a Bourbon Street sign, was made to represent all local African Americans. The Quarter's "local color," once the splattered, battered palette of many indi-vidual opinions, was now whatever the tourist and development authorities thought it should be. No infrared heat of simmering poor black resentment. No salty blue-gray of sailors out looking for booze, broads, ouzo, and floozies. No ultraviolet of "eccentric" people acting out their alternate worlds. A dash of lavender was now "OK," thanks to changing mores and revenue generated by the gay clubs. For the most part, local color would now be rendered in pastels, shaded neither to offend nor arouse curiosity about the dangerous, glorious, confounding, messy inner life of the city.

## DEFENDING MADAME

Gift and T-shirt shops continued to proliferate, selling "souvenirs" mainly cranked out in China. The combination of new, nonnative real estate capital and corporate culture-control has led to what some call a "colonization" of the Vieux Carré.[45] That is, the district is now more in thrall, financially and culturally, to outside owners, investors, and corporations than to any traditional local ownership and influence. Before the real-estate slump of the 1980s, the Quarter was controlled in a fairly balanced native triangle of nightclub owners allied with political pals; resident owners; and self-appointed defenders—including our old friends, the blue-blooded club-women. "Outsiders," even those with money, were not really welcomed into the ranks of the nightclub barons, nor into the social elite, some of whom lived in the Garden District but partook in the guardianship of the Quarter. The irony, of course, is that many of Madame Vieux Carré's most vociferous defenders have been "outsiders" by the standards of their day. New residents (if they were the "right people") were welcomed, but, unless well connected by marriage or blood, found it very difficult to break into the upper tiers of social or political life.[46]

The points of this old triangle slowly rubbed off. The old nightclub moguls died or sold out to new owners and corporations.[47] Most of the clubwomen's distaff descendants, if inclined to advocacy, were absorbed into groups whose issues are larger than the Quarter. The original tweed and beads set died off or got too old to put up with Quarter life and moved away. Now, the power diagram is anchored by the corporate tourist and entertainment wing, the absentee owner/landlords, and, to a lesser degree, activist groups and owner-residents. They tug at one corner of the commercialization balloon to keep it from floating the Vieux Carré entirely away. The cumulative pressures on the Quarter earned it a place on the list of most endangered places from the

National Trust for Historic Preservation in 1995.[48] If this was a wake-up call to the city, it seemed to have dozed through the alarm.

The VCC could do little by itself to reverse this trend. It had no power over zoning and could only regulate the exterior portions of the buildings.[49] Color schemes and appropriate hardware were within its purview; decisions—like zoning—affecting big money were not. Those were the province of the city council. Traditionally, a council member's wishes for his or her own district were usually endorsed by the full council. That comity allowed each district some autonomy, but where the Quarter was concerned it sometimes broke down. The Quarter has national visibility, statutory controls, advocacy groups, and the tourism revenue all influencing the council process. This often made for very long decision-making cycles.

The city's reluctance to enforce regulations is mirrored in the tiny staffs detailed to such purpose. In 1999, your author and a friend developed food poisoning after eating at a long-established Quarter restaurant. The city's health department was sympathetic but stated they had only four inspectors to police over three thousand establishments licensed to serve food, and could not investigate a case of only two unfortunates.

The Quarter may look like a static neighborhood to the occasional visitor. It is quietly dynamic, however, and the old buildings have had many incarnations as homes, shops, bars, and apartments. Mere adherence to architectural guidelines is not enough to ensure neighborly tranquility. As the twentieth century tottered to its end, Quarter businesses came under increasing scrutiny. VCPORA had long been in the forefront of vigilance over quality of life, as perceived by each generation. VCPORA and other activist groups flowed into the gaps between simple adherence to the VCC's rules and the city's non-enforcement of existing regulations. This lack of enforcement, and the political machinations attending city council actions, have steered activist groups into three tacts.

The first tact is to oppose any grant of exception from ordinances and regulations. The feeling is that any exception creates a precedent, which leads to yet another exception, and ultimately, to repeal of the regulation in question. These exceptions may occur over many years and changes of staff at the VCC and other agencies. So, a poorly justified exception, once granted, may only be remembered as a successful bypass of regulations, and defeating the next risky request will be harder. However, this approach has also garnered preservationists the reputation for reflexively opposing any variances, even those that strike a measured balance between conservation and commerce.

The second tact is to scrutinize each increment of the regulatory process to ensure that authorities follow their own rules to the letter. That is the approach VCPORA took to the Corps of Engineers' approval for the aquarium.[50]

The third tact asserts standing to sue as an "aggrieved" party when there is a *tout ensemble* issue that is not a clear violation of existing law or when, as usual, existing regulations are not being enforced.

This third tact points up a tension between the traditional preservationists and the newer revivalists, both of whom profess many of the same values. Preservation of the Vieux Carré is sometimes perceived as a static status quo, without a consideration of the flow of commerce benefitting the larger city, or the rights of property owners to have an enterprise at least nominally in keeping with the received historic character. Some business owners opine that modern preservationists would rather have an empty building in the Quarter than see it used in a slightly "nonconforming" way, even if still "quaint and distinctive."

The revivalists seek, among other things, a return to the kind of close-knit, mature, extended family Quarter that began to fade in the 1980s. Keystones of that former mood were clubs like the Bourbon House, 700 on its namesake street. From 1936 until its sale in 1964, the Bourbon House numbered many celebrated figures in its clientele and served as post office and base of operations for many unsung Quarter denizens.[51] Another was the Napoleon House, where the anti-expressway spark was kindled. Corner groceries that stocked special foods and liquors for certain customers and the little shops where cocktails took precedence over commerce were also mainstays of that life. The loud, juvenile straight clubs of upper Bourbon, and the gyrating, testosterone-fueled bars of Boys Town all have their place. But the residential nexuses are critical to revival of the Vieux Carré as a coherent neighborhood. Perhaps some of those former haunts would not have withstood modern scrutiny of their stylistic piety or conduct of business.

The Quarter activists must look, and act, beyond the legal bounds of the Quarter. It is generally acknowledged that nearly all the city's visitors go to the Quarter at one time or another.[52] So, attractions outside the Quarter, and particularly those within walking distance, generate more Quarter tourist traffic. This mixed blessing brings, in the main, more upscale family groups, as well as free-spending single adults. If almost all visitors go to the Quarter, then how can they be lured away by other attractions? The Warehouse District, Frenchman Street, the riverfront, the aquarium, all have been successful tourist draws in their own right. Yet, those visitors will probably wind up in the Vieux Carré at some point. Obviously, the city's tourist load cannot be restricted in favor of the Quarter. Managing that tourist load, and the impacts it creates, is an ongoing challenge for the Vieux Carré's guardians.

## MURDERS AT THE MARKET

The divide between the recent city hall of color and the mostly white Quarter was thrown into sharp, painful relief in December 1996. One Sunday morning, three employees—two white and one black—were killed, execution style, in the course of a robbery of the Louisiana Pizza Kitchen, Gov. Nicholls at the French Market. Their murderers, three black men, were quickly apprehended after identification by the lone survivor of the assault. Up until then, the Quarter had seen little of the drug gang–fueled violence ravaging the city's housing projects and poorer neighborhoods. The increase in Quarter crime had primarily been crimes against property, with the occasional shooting or stabbing related to dope dealing or prostitution. The eruption of these multiple murders triggered a shock wave of rage in the Quarter, and the city's media shrieked in an awful pitch.[53] A few days after the murders, a delegation of Quarter residents marched to city hall to express their anger and demands for better policing. There they collided with a largely black "peace rally" organized by Mayor Marc Morial to disrupt the Quarter march.[54] The "peace rally" featured the obligatory brass band to drown out the Quarter emissaries. The focus of the "peace rally" was that this kind of crime was prevalent in the poorer parts of town, and largely ignored by whites. Perhaps, the reasoning went, if the white and touristy parts of town were now seeing this plague, the city would bestir itself to address the roots of crime across all of New Orleans. The Quarter marchers sympathized with the needs beyond the ramparts, but felt that three successive black administrations had created an implied license for uncontrolled black-on-black and now, black-on-white crime throughout the city. Mayor Morial declined to attend the rally, citing fears for his safety. As one marcher replied, "Well, we are here because we are afraid for *our* safety. That's the whole point."[55] In the end, the city council passed a police budget increase of $4 million requested by Chief Pennington, although the extra funding's relationship to improved policing was nebulous.

In 1950, the murder of one tourist in the Quarter aroused the city to defend the tourist trade; the murders of three residents in 1996 were met

with official indifference. In 1950, the city administration provided cover
for the saloons and vice lords who were big contributors. In 1950 and 1996,
residents, and those who gave a damn about the city's image, had to fend for
themselves.

At the beginning of the twenty-first century, the city is no longer providing the kind of legal cover for the "adult entertainment" business it did
fifty years before. On the other hand, spin-doctoring of unfortunate events is
cheap, presents no legal exposure, and, of course, changes nothing.

## PLANNING FOR NOTHING

In the mid-twentieth century, master planning had been touted as a tonic for
urban decay, strip development, and lack of esthetic coherence. Many areas,
redeveloped in this way, seemed at first to be success stories. Often, disap-
pointment set in. Some redeveloped urban areas failed to reattract anchor
stores, already fled to suburban malls. The gleaming new downtown enclaves
had to fight durable memories of former crime and sleaze. Even those
who cheered the cleaned-up zones often found them sterile, with the same
national chains and tourist experiences as anywhere else in homogenized
Middle America. Fisherman's Wharf in San Francisco is a case in point. New
Orleans's only American rival in urban distinctiveness, San Francisco has a
multitude of unique elements for the tourist visit. Yet at the Wharf, operant-
conditioned visitors line up at the Hard Rock Café to buy yet another T-shirt.
In the master-planned areas, tourists are expected—virtually required—to
shop and dine at chain outlets. Visitors are often steered away from local culture, which might be unscripted, unbourgeois and, heaven forbid, not "family
friendly." Local entrepreneurs frequently find minimum store sizes and rents
in the new malls prohibitive. In the Quarter, a Royal Street store thrived for
decades selling lead soldiers. This very special niche would never have fit into
the shopping mall Jax Brewery became.

Residential life was upset by master planning as well. Longtime down-
market apartment houses and residential hotels—flophouses—vanished,
replaced by condos targeted to the upwardly mobile. The displacement of
residents who could not afford to adapt was deemed a private matter between
tenant and landlord. Rarely did plans include housing affordable for people
pushed aside by "revitalization." The tragedy of Armstrong Park was the
New Orleans installment of this folly. Planning dilettantes simper over parks

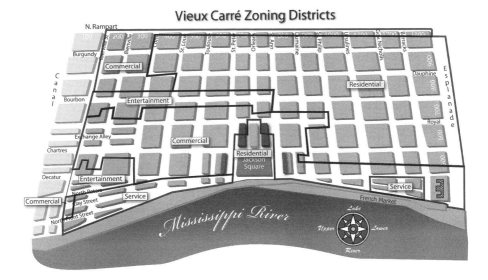

Vieux Carré Zoning Districts

and "greenspace," holding them in higher esteem than buildings of any type. Perhaps some postindustrial lots, termed "brown fields," can never be reutilized for homes, and may best serve as community gardens, but each new park in the urban core reduces the land available for housing. Many newly created urban parks attracted elements the consultants did not plan for; gay men looking for outdoor sex, dog owners relieving their pets, drug distributors, and the "homeless." Cabrini Park was a lush urban expanse until cruising gay men were evicted after a series of raids in 1971. Much vegetation was removed,[56] and today Cabrini, aside from occasional festivals, serves as the "dog doo" park of the Quarter.[57] The former Edison—now Musical Legends—Park at 311 Bourbon is another park passion gone wrong. At the epicenter of the upper Quarter party tumult, the sunken little space became a catch basin for trash and derelicts, and was chained off for years.[58] It is ironic that the modern Quarter's most balanced redevelopment—Decatur Street—was not the result of any master plan but rather several disjointed events over three decades.[59]

Most New Orleans residents, especially those who had lived in other major cities, were wary of master planning. Not all of this wariness can be ascribed to the usual N'awlins insularity, nor even to racial paranoia. Small investors fear that master planning will squeeze them out of the opportunity to have a little something of their own, done in their own way. High-end, well-heeled developers—not without reason—trust their own esthetic judgment

more than any master plan that has been homogenized by a lengthy and ago-
nized political process. In some instances, highway planning becomes the de
facto master plan, as witness the destruction of the Claiborne Avenue corridor for I-10 and the near-tragedy of the proposed Riverfront Expressway.

Beginning in 1997, the city planning commission attempted to formulate
a master plan for New Orleans.[60] Immediately, a conflict developed between
those who wanted the planning to encourage development and those who
wanted the status quo. Particularly in the Vieux Carré, those few residents
who were part of the process did not want additional "planning"; they wanted
existing zoning ordinances, particularly concerning B&Bs and hotel expansion, enforced.[61] The Quarter residents were understandably skeptical of the
planning process, particularly after the mayor's rejection of VCPORA-nom-
inated persons to serve on the master plan panel.[62] A member of VCPORA
commented: "We don't believe this will resolve everything; we are just going
along. It's good to know what's going on."[63]

As with other post-1978 controversies, there was a racial dynamic. It
appeared that black interests favored planning to encourage job growth;
white interests seemed aligned with preservation as a static environment.[64]

In the end, the master plan was never finished prior to Hurricanes Katrina
and Rita in 2005.[65] It would have changed nothing for the Quarter. Nor did
it bode much for the city at large. The City Planning Commission and the
Board of Zoning Adjustments are seen as mere speed bumps in the entire
process, since the city council still has ultimate authority. Where big money
was on the table, it often authorized spot zoning. All the planning could not
reverse the flight of companies and jobs. Nor does planning guarantee investment. The lack of enforcement persisted. In any event, the planning process
left the VCC's purview neither diminished nor expanded.

A critical aspect of planning is public involvement. In past times, a small
cadre of interests would present a project to the city administration. After
political tweaking and assignment of spoils, the project would go through,
with the wishes of ordinary citizens never solicited. All this passed as "progress." By the 1980s, planning could only be done with citizen involvement. In
town hall meetings and focus groups, the plans would be presented and citizen
input heard. The idea was to democratize the process, and, as an important
byproduct, head off opposition by claiming "buy-in" from a broad base from
the affected community. But all these outreach and focus meetings might be
an elaborate charade, as well. The development executives rarely attended
the meetings. Not wishing to become lightning rods, they sent facile staffers

who were not empowered to make commitments. The "finished, community-vetted" plans might have surprises as well. Larger buildings or features never discussed in the public meetings might suddenly appear on the plans. These had been quietly "cleared' with politicians and, therefore, approval was nearly assured. If the politicians could not deliver, developers were starting to take a harder line. Since the 1970s, New Orleans has been ever poorer and lacks the leverage of still-growing cities of similar size. The developers, not surprisingly, thought the city should be grateful for any investment and accept, with only cosmetic changes, whatever it was offered. Otherwise, the marbles would be collected and the player would move on.

The shrinking industrial base forced the city to depend more and more on tourism, of which the Quarter is the epicenter. Yet it frustrated the pro-growth faction that the Quarter seemed to have plateaued in that regard. There was a glut of hotel rooms across the city, many not far from the Quarter with rates less than Quarter lodging.[66] Quarter parking seemed fixed and many would-be Quarter visitors were put off by lack of a place to park their SUV, with any assurance it would be intact upon their return. Shuttling tourists en masse from extra-Quarter attractions, like the zoo or the National World War II Museum, to and from the Quarter was not well considered. The zoo could be reached by a long streetcar ride, connecting, for a brief time before Hurricane Katrina, with the Canal and Riverfront lines. Water taxis could be one part of the solution, but it seems nobody thought of that. Even though hotel expansion continued—legally or not—the jobs so created were mainly low-wage and only a tiny fraction of what was needed in the city at large.

Despite its limited purview, the VCC's authority derives from the state constitution, and it is not a creature of the city's whims. The state is unlikely to ever cede the VCC's powers, and esthetic judgement, to the city.

## DECATUR: BIENVILLE PARK

The curves of the river are reflected in the acutely angled streets between Decatur and the water's edge. On the upper side, North Peters Street cuts into Decatur just at Conti. At this triangle, a gas station sat for many years. In 1988, the city and the VCC approved the creation of a park on the site. After a four-year court struggle, the part owners of the plot won more compensation.[67] In 1996, a twenty-six-foot-high bronze statue of Bienville, his priest, and an

Indian was moved from Union Passenger Terminal to the park, believed to be close to Bienville's 1718 landing.[68]

## THE FENCING MATCH

In the colonial era, male New Orleanians, particularly of the upper class, had a brittle sense of honor. A misunderstanding, an unintentional slight, or even the intoxicated desire for action was enough to provoke duels. A number of French Creole fencing masters made a handsome living instructing privileged young men in the manly and sometimes fatal art of fencing. In many cases, the first draw of blood was enough to satisfy the debt of honor; in other cases, the duel did not end until one or both parties lay bleeding to death under the old oaks of what is now City Park. Swords were gradually displaced by pistols, and dueling was more or less suppressed after the Civil War.[69]

Government agencies, being human instrumentalities, have human pride as well. The Louisiana State Museum (LSM), a state agency, originated in 1906. By 1908 the Cabildo and Presbytère were transferred to its protection and control.[70] Later, the Lower Pontalba, the old U.S. Mint, and other historic buildings would also fall under its jurisdiction.[71] The Vieux Carré Commission, as we have seen, was created by the state, enshrined in the state constitution by the voters, and is an agency of the city.

The Cabildo was undergoing renovation in 1988 when a fire erupted on the third floor. While repairs were made over the next few years, street people took shelter under the Cabildo's arches. Openly urinating, defecating, and vomiting, they threatened and exposed themselves to the staff and public.[72] One of the vagrants grabbed a pigeon and ate it alive.[73] The Cabildo's near-twin sister on the other side of St. Louis Cathedral, the Presbytère, had a fence dating from 1840 and suffered no such indignities.[74]

In 1995, the LSM found funding for a Cabildo fence. With the cooperation of the VCC, the LSM took great pains to ensure that the Cabildo fence would be an exact replica in configuration, materials, and workmanship to the one protecting the Presbytère.[75] In early 1997, as the fence was nearing completion, the VCC suddenly refused to issue the permits it thought necessary for the work to proceed. It also filed suit for a stop-work order against the contractor. The mystified LSM pointed out that no permit was sought or required for repairs and renovations performed on the Presbytère, U.S. Mint, Lower Pontalba, or Cabildo proper.[76] The VCC had also permitted the city to erect a historically inaccurate fence around Jackson Square proper to prevent trespass at night.[77] The LSM received an attorney general's opinion that the LSM was not subject to the VCC's control.[78] The directors of the VCC and the LSM mutually averred that they would bring in law enforcement, on the part of the VCC, to stop the work and, in the case of the LSM, defend the state's interests.[79] Two months after the suit, the VCC voted to deny any permit for the fence. The LSM told the trial court that the LSM was not subject to the VCC; the court agreed. The Preservation Resource Center, the Louisiana Landmarks Society, and VCPORA filed amicus curiae briefs supporting the VCC's position.[80] The Fourth Louisiana Circuit reversed the first ruling; the LSM appealed to the Supreme Court.

The stage was now set for a clash of bureaucracies and egos in the state's highest arena, in a matter that cannot be thought of as a friendly test case in any way. At this same time, the Louisiana Supreme Court was renovating its own piece of the Quarter. The court had moved out of the once-despised white elephant at 400 Royal in 1958, and the building had been known as the Fish and Wildlife building since that time. In 1996, Chief Justice Pascal Calogero convinced the legislature to renovate the building to permit the court to return.[81] In a 1998 decision, the Louisiana Supreme Court reversed the Fourth Circuit and found for the LSM. The need for the fence and its authenticity were not at issue, the court observed. The court, using the ancient language of censure, found the VCC's actions "unreasonable, arbitrary and capricious, resulting in an impermissible interference with and abridgement of the police power of the State."[82]

A close reading of the decision indicates that the justices did not determine whether a state agency must be subject to the VCC.[83] Rather, it was the VCC's picayunish inaction that brought the argument to the bar at all. In my opinion, had the VCC followed through on its cooperation and issued the permit, it would have created a precedent that it could have used to the VCC's advantage in any future tiff with a state agency.

## THE NEW NATIVE JOURNALISM

Literary lights shone brightly, and briefly, in the 1920s Vieux Carré. Then, with few exceptions, they left for more favorable climes. Some, like Faulkner, became internationally famous after leaving town. In the main, figures of national cultural import treated the city as a curiosity, to be visited, slummed in, but best not lingered in too long. On just the basis of *Streetcar*, many believed that New Orleans was the epicenter of the southern Gothic culture as popularized by Tennessee Williams. That this was false was not proved until John Kennedy Toole's *A Confederacy of Dunces* gave voice to another vein of authentic New Orleans life, albeit published a couple of decades in retrospect. Among American municipalities, New Orleans was the crazy old great-aunt kept in the back room, fabulous in her showy dishabille and clucked at for her scapegrace antics.

Beginning in the 1980s, some already well-established writers moved to New Orleans and embraced it as a long-lost home. Romanian-born poet, essayist, and National Public Radio personality Andrei Codrescu became a regular at Molly's at the Market on Decatur. His *New Orleans, Mon Amour* covers twenty years of bittersweet city life, and he has been an important post-Katrina voice to the outside world.

Chris Rose, originally from Maryland, arrived in New Orleans in 1984 and writes a column that is part irony, part humor, and part outrage for the *Times-Picayune*.[84] In a city that wears its contradictions and ironies in a diadem, Rose has no shortage of material.

English-born James Gill came to New Orleans in 1979.[85] His opinion columns for the *Times-Picayune* deftly skewer the foibles of local and state politicians. His *Lords of Misrule* has become a standard text on the origins of the krewe system and the controversy surrounding the Carnival "nondiscrimination" ordinance of 1992.[86]

Well before the vampire books of Anne Rice, there had been a school of literature that savored the very high meat of the city's physical and social decay. Photographer Clarence John Laughlin's *Haunter of Ruins* is a collection of images taken from 1935 to 1950. The images of life among urban shambles, along with essays by city historians, seem just as timely and somehow more urgent now. *Geopsychic Wonders of New Orleans* by D. Eric Bookhardt and essayist Jon Newlin illuminates the very thin veil between the living world of New Orleans and the perceived spiritual realm felt to be so close at hand. The images are of mystic, symbolic architecture, eclectic shrines, and spaces where the spirit of the earth (the "geopsychic") has reclaimed the efforts of man. More recently, *New Orleans: Elegance and Decadence* by Randolph Delehanty and Richard Sexton brought the best of both eponymous phases to the coffee-table trade.

Commentators in the early twentieth century had reviled the shabbiness of "Little Palermo" and some had argued for its demolition. The run-down people and the run-down environs they inhabited were the fodder for *Street-car* and a host of similar, if lesser, works.

Sympathy for these characters was mixed with a certain disdain for their "primitiveness" and "provincialism"—in other words, for being typically New Orleanian. It was also darkly hinted that some of these folks were certifiable—an amusing notion to those of us who shared the streets with Lucky Bead Lady and Ruthie, and were, ourselves, not so tightly wound.

However, these new natives were not usually urging reform of a lifestyle decidedly more Third World and nineteenth century than the Middle American norm. Nor were they cooing over it as "quaint." More grandiose, to them, were the ruins of old grandeur than their original state. More wonderful than Nobel laureates were the street characters and the ordinary folk who sat on their stoops and watched everything with well-worn eyes. Filmmaker and archivist Rick Delaup chronicled the life of "Ruthie The Duck Girl."[87] His Web site illuminates the lives of other past "eccentrics" and those still working the clubs and bars. Cartoonist Bunny Matthews has a long-running strip devoted to *uber*-Yats Vic & Nat'ly. No longer did aspiring writers, photographers, and poets have to wait for the fickle and molasses-like publishing process. The Web now saw many sites celebrating unique aspects of New Orleans culture.

Each year since 1986, the literary heritage of Tennessee Williams has been celebrated during the Tennessee Williams/New Orleans Literary Festival. A popular sidelight is the Stella and Stanley Shouting Contest in Jackson Square, reinterpreting the scene made famous by Marlon Brando and Kim Hunter in the movie production of *Streetcar.*

In 2003, the Saints and Sinners Literary Festival was established. Although not exclusively focused on New Orleans, its purpose is for gay and lesbian writers to meet and obtain public exposure. The festival has given a venue for writers treading the same metaphorical and tangible banquettes as Saxon, Tallant, and Williams.[88]

Earlier, I alluded to the persistence of 1950s culture in the city throughout the 1980s. Even as the "kookiness" of the Quarter faded, it persisted in places like the Marigny and Bywater. In this new journalism, whether by print or by Web, wisdom was to be found not in tweedy institutions but backrooms and barrooms. Alcohol-granted verities are treasured more than degrees. Even casual researchers made the discovery, as I eventually did, that many drinkers imbibe to feel and think, not to get numb and forget. It is sometimes the stark "alcoholic certainties," lurking just under the quasi-sober municipal surface, that frighten drinkers into giving up the bottle, as much as the "accidents" and bad judgments made under the influence. Our health and sobriety-obsessed early twenty-first-century nation could never understand this. Maybe with a thousand nights in barrooms and understanding the alcohol way of knowledge, it would.

## GOING ROUND IN THE SQUARE

The three interior streets surrounding Jackson Square were converted to a pedestrian mall in the mid-1970s. The expanded area is now legally referred to as the Jackson Square Pedestrian Park, although Jackson Square is still the common name.

The square has always been the focal point of the Vieux Carré, and as such hosts many simultaneous and not always compatible activities. Painters, street performers, religious workers, musicians, alms seekers, churchgoers, drunks, and bums all claimed it as their own. The Pontalbas were built to include shops on the ground floor, which long ago shifted to the tourist trade. The commercial interests were restricted to the St. Peter, St. Ann, Chartres, and Decatur streets portions framing the square. Jackson Square proper is the realm of strolling tourists, and is locked up at night, lest unseemly activities take place. Jackson Square is not only the province of tourism, it is also the front yard of those who live in the Pontalbas.

The doors of St. Louis Cathedral open onto the square, leading into an instantaneous, unbuffered meeting ground of the sacred and profane. The square has been the setting for civic ceremonies, such as the Louisiana Purchase observances of 1903, 1953, and 2003. It hosts the New Year's Eve crowds who wait for a "gumbo kettle" to drop at the top of Jax Brewery. Images of the square have graced the covers of countless books and pamphlets about the Quarter and the larger city. The façade of the cathedral is the signature image of New Orleans.

The debate over the square's identity is the distilled essence of the larger debate of what the Quarter should be. In the rest of the Quarter, subneighborhoods have evolved—upper Bourbon, Boys Town, the increasingly wealthy lower Quarter, and so on. Within each of these minienclaves, consensus, not always settled, has evolved that defines their identities. The square, so it seems, belongs to everyone and therefore to no one. The abusive antics of derelicts that triggered the Cabildo fence case are out of bounds by any standards.

The question of who may hustle tourists is one of the two central issues of the square. The other, which I will discuss in a moment, is noise. Street

Jackson Square and vicinity, 1984. Courtesy of the Louisiana Division/City Archives, New Orleans Public Library.

performers have plied their trade in the Quarter forever, and were considered part of the local color. The best-known street performers are the painters, who from the 1920s onward hung their works on the fences of the square in Pirate's Alley and also Royal Street behind the cathedral garden. Many of these twenties painters chose south Louisiana and Vieux Carré themes,[89] then new to American art and the foundation of the "bayou school." Traditionally, most worked at the upper side of the square, along St. Peter. At one point the city imposed a limit of two hundred painters in the square. After the closing of St. Peter, Chartres, and St. Ann streets to frame the square in a pedestrian mall in the mid-1970s, painters saw more competition for the tourist dollar. Balloon artists, fortune-tellers, tarot card readers, musicians, dancers, mimes, and sheer beggars all grabbed for their perceived fair share of the cash stream. Painters especially took umbrage at workers in the "psychic arts" who, they felt, were giving nothing of value for their services.[90] Painters also faced competition from a larger number of galleries on Royal and elsewhere. Many of these galleries sold prints that could be rolled up and taken home easily, as opposed to framed canvases that had to be shipped or packed with clothes. The painters claimed precedence of longevity and artistic merit over other performers. Shouting matches between the various square denizens, over turf and poaching of potential customers, were not uncommon. Tourists dragged their kids away as profanity flew. The other square buskers also claimed legitimacy. Working for the tourist coin, they maintained, was not the exclusive province of the famous restaurants, hotels, and institutional attractions. Someone who had been born and raised in the city felt every right to go to the square and cast a net for his portion, however small, of what the tourist trade might yield. Old cons, like the bet about knowing where someone "got dem shoes," or asking for donations for nonexistent charities, persisted. Sometimes university students would try these tricks—as experiments in psychology, you understand—and later chortle over drinks bought with the proceeds.

Noise was the other flash point. The congregants of St. Louis Cathedral did not care to have divine services disturbed by brass bands, guitarists strumming through amplifiers, or the boom boxes of dancers right outside their doors. The spiritual heart and icon of New Orleans, the cathedral had powerful advocates in the temporal realms. In 1998, the city, working with performers, passed an ordinance that restricts noise in a buffer zone around the cathedral, provided that the basilica post signs indicating that services were being held.[91] The following year, Louisiana passed an even more restrictive noise law, one not specific to the cathedral. Immediately, the state law ran afoul of New Orleans realities. Carnival parades, second lines and jazz funerals, with their brass bands and singing, swaying members, routinely pass by churches and hospitals. A lawsuit, filed by a diverse group of performers, reached federal court in 1999.[92] In striking down the state law, federal judge Sarah Vance observed: "The regulation at issue applies to public streets and parks in New Orleans, the very heart of a city favored by citizens and tourists alike for a culture grounded in live music and outdoor celebration. Hospitals and churches exist all over the city in areas saturated in the sounds of urban life. Various Mardi Gras and other holiday parades take place on public streets, pass within 10 feet of many hospitals and churches, and produce sounds well in excess of the human voice in normal conversation."[93]

Policing the turf struggles and controlling noise was done with the same unevenness as enforcement of other regulations. The administration of Mayor Marc Morial had a hard time finding the will to crack down in the Quarter, let alone in the square itself. Mayor Morial observed, with some accuracy, "A lot of what the complaining is about really has to do with the comeback of the entire city. The Quarter is not a suburban neighborhood."[94]

His administration did find the will to cleanse and secure the square, evicting everyone, just before, and after, his wedding in St. Louis Cathedral on September 11, 1999.[95]

## THE BUS FUSS

The streets of the Vieux Carré were designed, as we have noted, for pedestrians and animal-drawn wagons. Automobiles have not been a good fit. The lumbering buses of the mid-twentieth century had a hard time negotiating the narrow streets and tight intersections of the Quarter. They also shook the old buildings, belched diesel smoke, idled throbbing engines for hours, and made a general nuisance of themselves.[96] Sometimes they rolled over and crushed sidewalks and collided with balcony columns.[97] A few bus drivers got their vehicles wedged at intersections, requiring rescue by bystanders to direct them out of the trap. Quarter residents complained for years about the large buses, to no avail.

In early 1993, Mayor Barthelemy's Vieux Carré Task Force issued its report. Among many familiar themes was a call to ban large buses from the Quarter.[98] Tourists arriving from out of town would have to debark and then take smaller buses to Quarter hotels. Those hotels, predictably, fought the idea tooth and nail. The Regional Transit Authority (RTA) would also have to operate smaller buses in the district. Three years of wrangling later, a modified bus ban was adopted. Buses longer than thirty-one feet were banned from the interior streets of the Quarter, and long idling was forbidden. As with many other ordinances protecting the Vieux Carré, this one was rarely enforced. By 2000, enraged residents were stopping illegal buses on their own authority and detaining them for police,[99] some of whom were apparently unaware of the law.[100]

## CHAPTER 14

# 2000 AND ON

*Into the New Century*

## INTO THE NEW CENTURY

The Vieux Carré and its full-time residents live on an island shrinking in intangible but palpable ways. As condos displace apartments, the number of year-round residents has dropped to historic lows. At this writing, the number of permanent residents seems somewhere in the low thousands.

The Vieux Carré's status as the crown jewel of the city's tourist trade keeps that aspect on the mind of the city government. It also pushes residential concerns into the background. The small permanent population, a minority in its own district,[1] has little electoral clout.

## COME TO THE REVIVAL

By the end of the twentieth century, physical preservation was so ingrained in the Zeitgeist of the Quarter that it was almost taken for granted. The Quarter, widely—and falsely—believed to be the wealthiest enclave of the city, had the VCC and citizens' groups watching over it. Some Quarter residents, particularly businesspeople, thought that preservation had crossed the line into reflexive stagnation, the collective historic authorities rejecting any changes out of hand, not considering economic vitality. Vieux Carré groups had opposed such extra-Quarter projects as the aquarium, Canal Place, and the insectarium. The reasoning was that all tourists visit the Quarter during their stay, and attractions close by meant more tourist traffic. Proponents believed that groups like VCPORA had left their well-acknowledged sphere of influence, and were now opposing gambits that might benefit the larger city. Some called this "preservation by prevention."

In the last two decades of the twentieth century, New Orleans began to lose institutions that defined the city's unique character. Shrinking inner-city population, competition from national chains, mergers and mismanagement put many local merchants in dire straits. The Schwegmann groceries, K&B drugstores, MacKenzie's bakeries, the D. H. Holmes department store, and other stars in a seemingly eternal retail firmament twinkled out. New Orleanians were left with either shuttered stores or national chains that did not cater to local sensibilities.

The Catholic Church had long been a major New Orleans power, buttressed after 1900 by waves of Italians. The church schools educated generations of girls in plaid skirts and boys in rumpled white shirts, Catholic and Protestant alike. Churches and church schools were neighborhood anchors. With few exceptions, the Catholic establishment had a long-standing modus vivendi with the lords temporal and carnal. To buy a beer from a nun, at a bingo game, in a church school, in the middle of the Quarter, was no contradiction at all. It was part of the New Orleans Order of Things.

The out-migration of Catholics, and the falling away of some of the remaining flock, began to empty the churches. The buildings, some over 150 years old and needing major repair, saw fewer parishioners each year. The archdiocese had to close and consolidate many churches, leaving the old basilicas empty and silent, like sealed tombs on lonely streets.[2]

The loss of these touchstones, the slide of life quality, and the drumbeat of unfavorable publicity had aroused passionate defense of the city in the late eighties and nineties, as things went from bad to worse in nearly all parts of town. In the late eighties, bumper stickers proclaiming "New Orleans, Proud to Call It Home" appeared. They were quickly joined by a similar sticker, with a cockroach rampant—"New Orleans, Proud to Crawl Home." The city's defenders rushed to contradict media that cast the city in a bad, which usually meant a truthful, light, and "New Orleans bashing" became one of the few civic cardinal sins.

As the twentieth century staggered to its end, a new kind of Crescent City civic patriot appeared. Not just focused on the Quarter, these looked to reviving the city and its traditional folkways, eroding from economics, out-migration, and the tide of national culture. These "revivalists" are harder to define than the "preservationists." Indeed, many proudly claim both labels and see no conflict between the agendas of each. For our purposes, we may draw the distinction thus. A preservationist is one who desires to keep the current order of physical things and their existing human interactions intact. Preservationists tend to reject changes in the use of a building, even if the physical elements are maintained.

A revivalist is not content with merely preserving a status quo, but seeks to revive the overall canopy of life that once covered the city, and still clings, over some neighborhoods, in tattered clouds. That some of this is the product of rose-colored nostalgia is not disputed, by observers nor adherents. An important component of revivalism is rolling back changes seen as tragic, intrusive, and un-N'awlins. Revivalist vision includes the recoherence of neighborhoods, the return of locally focused merchants, and those democratic arteries, streetcars, re-knitting the inner city.

Quarter revivalism focuses on upgrading the slipping quality of residential life. Those arrivistes paying gated community prices often expected gated community norms of quietude, cleanliness, and behavior. Long-time residents had more modest, but still usually unfulfilled, expectations. As tourism spread into the lower Quarter and its cross-Esplanade cousin, the Marigny Triangle, the noxious byproducts of tourism—noise, vandalism, and revelers roosting on homeowners' stoops—grew worse in once-quiet residential areas. Residents were angered that police presence seemed to be reserved for tourist areas.

Mitigating the collision of tourist and residential cultures was not the only aspect of Quarter revivalism. The desire to return the Quarter to a community of long-term residents, bound by an interior life of little shops, neighborhood bars, salons, and services for the natives is very strong. It is, however, much harder to re-create these vanishing pillars of the old life than it is to simply prevent new affronts from the tourism sphere. When I lived in the Quarter, an Englishwoman had a small business at 519 Dumaine called The Useful Shop. An eclectic array of household goods, gadgets, sewing notions, and advice were dispensed, mainly to locals. Increasing real estate values and the decline of full-time residents means opening a shop like this now would be a tremendous gamble with lots of money riding on the bet.

Revivalists care about the visitors' experience and impressions of the Vieux Carré as well. A couple should be able to hear Dixieland in the Quarter, unalloyed with disco; stroll down twilight streets without hearing booming obscenities passing as free speech; and sniff air scented by tea olives, not punk piss. The physical elements seemed assured by their now-extravagant financial values. It is the social that must be mended. Revivalism went briefly into high gear just after the turn of the twenty-first century.

Jacquelyn Brechtel Clarkson was the District C councilwoman from 1990 to 1994 and again from 2002 to 2006. Between those terms, she was a state representative from her home base of Algiers. Clarkson, a New Orleans native, was a real estate agent and Democratic Party mainstay. In her first term, she was frequently in the minority of the city council, along with the other white councilwoman, Peggy Wilson. She and Wilson opposed the so-called antidiscrimination ordinance, which prohibited krewes that discriminated in their membership from using public facilities or resources.[3] Her second term saw a boldness in her actions that made her the toast of most—if not all—Quarter residents and left opponents gasping.

Jackson Square underwent a restoration in 2001 and 2002. The Jackson Square Pedestrian Park would get its first facelift since 1976. In May of 2002, a festival for tourism operatives was held in the park. Before the festival opened, the square's metal benches were removed on Clarkson's orders. Those street people of the square who used the benches as couches and beds were outraged. Clarkson rejoined that the benches needed repair, were an obstacle for the festival, and blocked fire lanes needed for renovations of the cathedral. She added that the benches would be returned with dividers, to prevent people from lying down.[4]

At the same time, Clarkson moved against the tarot readers, tap dancers, and other street performers who had, it seemed, displaced painters. The upper side of Jackson Square had been a traditional painters' space, with plein air painting and selling of works. This area was a long-time tourist draw, and most media articles on the Quarter featured a picture of this "artists' colony." Encouraged by Clarkson, eighth district police captain Louis Dabdoub III began to stringently enforce laws against vagrancy, public urination, solicitation, and other "quality of life" crimes throughout the Quarter. Between June and mid-July 2002, the eighth district made almost four times the number of arrests as in the same period the year before.[5] The con artists, some still working the old "betcha I know where you got dem shoes" racket, began to disappear. For a brief spell, the square seemed purged of the "undesirables" that had proliferated as the nineties wore on. The nonpainter performers fought back, and eventually were granted space in front of the cathedral. The painters kept their historic turf between the upper Pontalba and the park.

The *Times-Picayune* cheered Clarkson's and Dabdoub's crackdown. An editorial of July 18, 2002 intoned: "Let's admit upfront that there's nothing quaint or romantic about the smell of urine, stale beer and vomit, especially not in the stifling summer heat . . . What visitors think of the French Quarter often determines what they think of New Orleans. That's not exactly fair—there are other parts of the city just as interesting—but it's the reality nonetheless."[6]

In October, a pro-Clarkson rally was held in the square. To shouts of adulation, Clarkson inveighed: "Those of you who want to use and abuse our French Quarter are no longer welcome here. We don't have to give it [the Quarter] away to those who don't care about [it] as much as you or me."

This pep rally was followed by a small counterdemonstration, including some homeless men who felt they had been run out of their bedroom.[7] Besides her efforts in the square, Clarkson also put diapers on the tour buggy mules, and had the streets and catch basins cleaned more often.[8] While Clarkson was cheered for getting long-overdue action, her opponents groused. They felt that she was trying "sanitize" the Quarter and make it too much like Colonial Williamsburg—a sterile, scripted reproduction. They took umbrage that street people, who felt ownership in the enclave too, were being pushed aside in favor of wealthy residents and middle-American tourists.[9] Street performers, including adult dancers, mimes, and musicians, felt that they were a legitimate part of the *tout ensemble* and were being swept up in an indiscriminate dragnet.[10]

In a 2003 interview, Clarkson laid out her vision: "I just want the Quarter to be like it was in the 1940s. It was bohemian, but it didn't smell and it didn't have garbage on the streets and there weren't people accosting you and there weren't underage children tap-dancing or people sleeping on benches. The vomit and the urine and the stench from the garbage that hasn't been picked up—that's not bohemian. Bohemian is the mixture of cultures, a place that inspires writing, painting, music, creativity. We still have that. And fortunately, that's something nobody can clean up. Even me."[11]

The shades of Elizebeth Werlein and Mary Morrison may have smiled, but not all the quick were as approving as the famous dead. By the twenty-first century, Americans demanded more public involvement in civic life; the top-down direction that Mayors Maestri and Morrison casually gave were no more. Contemporary culture expects public hearings, currying of every self-proclaimed activist group and consensus building. In New Orleans, and elsewhere, this process often consumed much time with diluted, or no, action. Clarkson simply ordered the benches removed, and they were. Other council members had the same autonomy within their districts, and even mayors feared to tamper with those prerogatives. However, the Quarter is center stage, front row of New Orleans, and Clarkson's edicts got citywide plaudits—and brickbats.

Children—and adults—have danced for money in the Quarter for generations. When break dancing was a fad, youngsters would spin and shimmy on waxed cardboard for eager camcording tourists. Children would sometimes put bottle caps in their shoe soles and tap-dance for tourist coins. Now, Dabdoub and Clarkson cast a cold eye on children tapping. In a city with high truancy rates, these kids needed to be in school. Times had changed, and if the Quarter was no longer safe for Ruthie the Duck Lady, it was hardly safe for young children with no visible adults. In May 2004, a mother of three was arrested for letting her children beg for money as they tapped unsupervised on Bourbon. She was convicted of contributing to delinquency, and as part of the plea deal, the family was banned from the Quarter for a year.[12]

This cleanup was not simply a roundup and purge. Captain Dabdoub launched the Homeless Assistance Collaborative. This effort provides transportation to shelters for the chronically homeless. It was recognized as a humane and effective alternative to jailing indigent street people.[13]

Illegal rentals were another problem Clarkson addressed. In 2004, she sponsored, and the city council passed, an ordinance requiring licensing of Vieux Carré properties offered for stays of sixty days or less.[14]

The Quarter revivalists had found their champion at last. However, in mid-2004, Clarkson overreached herself. At her urging, Captain Dabdoub sent police around the Quarter, checking up on business permits and looking for code violations. A bar was shut down for code infractions, something rarely seen since Jacob Morrison's 1950s crusade. Rousting the usual suspects from Jackson Square was one thing. Stepping on the toes of the tourist industry was another. Dabdoub and one of his officers were reassigned without Clarkson being consulted. Plainly, her code enforcement effort was not vetted with Mayor Nagin. "They [Nagin and police chief Compass] don't allow me in that little circle," Clarkson acknowledged.[15] Captain Dabdoub—and the Quarter—paid the price. After this rebuff, Clarkson was perceived as disengaging from the Quarter and Marigny, to concentrate on Algiers. This withdrawal was felt particularly in the Marigny. Many in that neighborhood became openly hostile to her. In 2006, she ran for council member at large, but lost the runoff. James Carter, a young African American attorney, won the

District C seat.[16] Clarkson returned to the council in 2007, filling an at-large seat and tipping the council to its first white majority in decades.[17]

Much of the revivalist hope is a rerun of the same contention, argued without much success since the 1940s, that New Orleans needs to rebuild its middle class. That in turn depends on increased white-collar jobs, improved education, and a perception that crime is held to an acceptable level.

In a small way, the Quarter has been experiencing revival as a family neighborhood. Houses, some formerly apartmentized, have been bought and restored to single-family use.[18] This latest raft of kind strangers are wealthy and well educated, the kind of residents Saxon and Werlein could only dream of. But revivalism did not, and perhaps cannot, restore that crucial ingredient in James Nolan's formula for a bohemian community, cheap rent. So, the revivalism of the Quarter, at least, seemed to work to the advantage of those who already had economic security. Another era of Quarter bohemians must wait upon lower housing costs.

The Faubourg Marigny is perhaps the longest-running and best-known example of neighborhood revival. Beyond gentrification, the Marigny has, in patches, restored a degree of the old lifestyle. Bars, restaurants, coffee shops, and neighborhood associations knit together a community largely of full-time residents, few of them wealthy.

In the opening years of the twenty-first century, New Orleans collectively was about 65 percent black, and a substantial number of those were poor. The city administrations, mirroring the city, have been majority black since 1978 and, prior to Hurricane Katrina, these demographics seemed unlikely to change. No matter how well-informed their vision, it is politically impossible for these administrations to give much attention to about a few thousand, mostly white, mostly upper-middle-class people living in a small enclave. The dismantling of housing projects and their attendant open-air drug markets was a weightier matter than whether street people can sleep on Jackson Square benches. The family-unfriendly "indecency" of drunks flashing each other from Quarter balconies shrank besides the genuine obscenity of the corruption-eroded public schools. The legitimate tragedy of a tourist meeting his doom on Bourbon Street—usually on New Year's Eve—rather paled beside the appalling toll of black-on-black murders in neighborhoods like Gert Town and Holy Cross.

It has been suggested that if the Vieux Carré Commission had final authority over Quarter zoning, then the expansion of hotels, the illegal B&Bs, and the condo cancer would stop. Perhaps giving the VCC that power would be a good start. But nearly all "progressive" legislation in Louisiana comes with layers of grandfather clauses that allow existing practices to endure. It is also true that the more costly a property, the more political its zoning becomes. Opening a bodega in Bywater rarely arouses any interest from the city council. Big money on the line in the Quarter, especially for the tourist industry, sends solons scrambling for position and advantage. Even if the VCC were given exclusive zoning authority, and grandfather clauses were not imposed, rolling back the expanded portions of hotels would have significant political cost. Property owners' rights aside, consider the spectacle of putting hundreds of hotel maids, doormen, and other employees on the street, to satisfy an elite committee's notion of *tout ensemble*.

Shutting down the illegal B&Bs would require that something else occupy them. Again, disregarding owners' rights, would an empowered VCC mandate the reconversion into apartments for working-class people? It is far more likely that the property would be sold and transformed into yet another condoized building for wealthy out-of-towners.

Condos may prove impossible for any government agency to roll back, unless Louisiana finds perhaps the foolish courage to revoke the charters of the associations. Then some agency would have to deal with hundreds of angry, well-to-do condo owners, who could tie the process up for years with a class-action lawsuit. A moratorium on future condos might be the only feasible solution.

The current zoning process is via the City Planning Commission, the Board of Zoning adjustments, and then the city council. The VCC has a say, but the ultimate authority rests with the city council. It has long frustrated that the zoning ordinance is treated as a flimsy reed, to be massaged and if necessary bent at a council meeting. The other layers are seen as mere speed bumps to be rolled over as painlessly as possible, before the "big show" at city hall.[19]

If the VCC was given Quarter zoning authority, without recourse to other parts of the bureaucracy, then one elected and two appointed layers of government would be removed and replaced by one appointed board. Applicants might feel, not without reason, that the larger interests of the city might be overlooked with a Vieux Carré–only focus. The aquarium, the insectarium, Canal Place, and other large extra-Quarter developments had all been challenged because they would increase Quarter tourist traffic. The same battles would still have to be fought in the city council by the Quarter's defenders.

Perhaps the best we can hope for is that the VCC will be given zoning authority, with the usual grandfather bar on retroactivity. Naturally, it is unlikely that the city council will passively submit to being cut out of the action for the city's most costly real estate. The VCC, if so inclined, would have to line up support from upstate legislators who are looking to tweak the city government's nose during one of the perennial New Orleans versus upstate Louisiana feuds.

Even if it was politically possible for the Quarter to receive its share of attention from city government, the city's financial needs even before Katrina were enormous. The declining tax base cannot support the crumbling infrastructure. The post-Katrina largesse is being diffused, like a well-used tea bag, through oceans of commissions and subcontracting until only a few pale droplets of essence remain for the average citizen. Oil and gas prices may improve, but there is little chance that the city would ever see a second petro-boom. The industry's corporate offices and white-collar workers have largely decamped to Houston and are unlikely to return. Out-of-town state legislators, mostly white and conservative, see mostly black and relatively liberal New Orleans as no longer pulling its weight in the state's economy and becoming a bottomless pit of needs.

The city's inability to address the Quarter's larger needs, and the VCC's lack of purview over zoning and internal issues, leaves only one reality, the one the Vieux Carré is already in. The simple, sad fact is that, apart from stylistic issues, the fate of the Quarter is largely in the hands of developers, real estate agents, and condominium corporations, some native and some not. The saving grace is that the sheer value of the housing stock—at least for the present—is a tremendous incentive to maintain it in accordance with the VCC's directives. The increasing wealth of the typical Quarter homeowner may be a positive thing. These owner-residents have more money and education and are more inclined to fight wholesale changes in the traditional ways of preservation. The monied preservationists of the 1920s made it possible for later "bohemians" to thrive during decades of cheap rent. Ironically, this current phase of high property values may make it possible for future bohemians to live cheaply in the same buildings after a massive economic downturn.

As the twenty-first century emerged, the entry-level fee for a single-family home in the Vieux Carré was an average of about seven hundred thousand dollars, with off-street parking adding possibly two hundred thousand more.[20]

Despite—and in some ways because of—the value of the buildings, there is no denying that the Quarter's sense of unique community has been slipping away for over twenty years. Condo dwellers who may see each other on weekends or holidays cannot do much bonding. The service industry workers who used to lived in cheap apartments had at least the camaraderie of youth, poverty, and daily life in the bars and restaurants in common.

The terrorist attacks on New York and Washington, D.C., on September 11, 2001, caused a severe downturn in most American tourism. The fear of another airliner hijacking, the heightened, and at first, quirky, security imposed at airports all kept most tourists home for many months afterwards. Although New Orleans suffered, too—some conventions were canceled—its tourism was not as badly damaged as other destinations. Many tourists drive to New Orleans from surrounding states and so were unfazed by fears of air terrorism. The effects on New Orleans seemed to stem more from a glut of overbuilt hotels that now had to compete for smaller conventions and the business of more price-conscious travelers.[21]

From time to time, celebrations have buoyed, at least temporarily, the tourist tides of New Orleans. The Louisiana Purchase Sesquicentennial of 1953 was fondly remembered for its pageantry and presidential attention. As the bicentennial of the purchase approached in 2003, boosters hoped for another celebration of favorable publicity and lucrative returns. The entire state, and other states born from the purchase, joined in a year-long calender of events that yielded a welcome "bounce" of tourism.[22] In 1953, President Eisenhower and the French ambassador headlined the hullabaloo. In 2003, the bicentennial organizers gleefully awaited the attendance of President George W. Bush, King Juan Carlos of Spain, and French president Jacques Chirac. However, Chirac's opposition to the American intervention in Iraq spoiled the event's international bonhomie. Louisiana governor Mike Foster aggravated matters by publicly calling Chirac "a snake."[23] Only a head of state may issue an invitation to another head of state, and the White House was pointedly silent. The observance of December 20, 2003, featured soldiers in Napoleonic uniforms, booming cannons, and speeches. However, President Bush could not find time to attend, and, therefore, no other heads of state appeared.[24]

Although this book is nominally about the fortunes of Madame Vieux Carré in the twentieth century, her life has had a continuum of triumphs and tribulations from the eighteenth through the twenty-first centuries. To draw a line at 2001 would ignore the impact on tourism of the terrorist attacks of September of that year. More important, it would exclude the most momentous event in New Orleans's history since the end of yellow fever—Hurricane Katrina, which struck New Orleans and the Mississippi Gulf Coast on August 29, 2005.

## KATRINA: CATHARSIS AND RECOVERY

The people of the New Orleans area had weathered many storms, meteorological and otherwise, in the twentieth century, and convincing a significant fraction to evacuate in advance of a hurricane has always been difficult. The tendency to cling to long-time family property, the apprehension of getting stuck on the open road, considerations of pets, and the well-justified fear of looting all weigh against official mandates to leave.

I lived in the Quarter in 1985 when Hurricane Elena did a crazy dance along the Gulf Coast, threatening Louisiana more than once. Local weathermen fed from each other's excitement to the brink of hysteria, telling residents of various areas—without any legal authority—to "get out now." My neighbors nailed down their shutters, added to stocks of food, water, and liquor and carried on with life as usual. Leaving a second-story apartment, on the highest residential ground in town, and taking to a bumper-to-bumper road with two cats in a pickup truck seemed foolish. Even in the near-miss of Hurricane Georges in 1998, as most businesses boarded up, few people left the Vieux Carré.[25]

A closed-up Vieux Carré is a strange place. For those accustomed to the vigor, the rhythms, the crowds, and noise in all its guises, the boarded-up, shuttered streetscape feels not unlike an empty Hollywood back lot. The corner groceries and bars are normally the last merchants to close, and some bars simply never close in any circumstances.

The first storm wave of Katrina was felt in New Orleans on Sunday, August 28. Mayor Nagin announced a mandatory evacuation at 11 a.m.[26] It is probable that a few hundred people stayed in the Quarter despite the mandatory evacuation. The close-knit social ties, honed by many soggy evenings at bars and pot luck dinners on patios, now bound people into determined bands of survivors. From the Quarter's vantage, by the early afternoon of Monday, August 29, the worst seemed over. The Quarter, and other neighborhoods along the old natural levee, escaped significant damage from flooding that destroyed vast tracts of the city. Quarter buildings had some wind and water intrusion damage, but in the main these effects were manageable. One building on Dumaine collapsed. Outwardly, the Quarter looked no worse than on any Ash Wednesday, with less litter, aside from the refrigerators at the curb, holding their cargos of well-rotted food. The dreadful, if necessary, X marks that rescuers later applied to buildings all over the city as they searched for

the dead, were mercifully painted on the banquettes in the Quarter, sparing the costly, regulated color schemes.

There was mopping and cleaning up to do, but, in general, no worse, as people emerged from behind the shutters.[27] A few groceries, like Matassa's, opened for customers they knew. When the water supply failed, on Wednesday, August 31, swimming pools furnished water to flush toilets.[28] Quarter resident and former city director of public health Dr. Brobson Lutz practiced "sidewalk medicine" at Johnny White's bar on Bourbon.[29] The bar became a community center for the holdouts.[30] At night, with the power off, the stars shown brightly over the old village as they had not in over a century. Despite the loss of all other utilities, some holdouts still had landline telephone service.[31] The loss of water pressure and the use of candles resurrected an ancient fear—widespread fire, like those that had devastated the original village in the eighteenth century. Some fires did occur but were put out by helicopter-dropped buckets of water.[32]

Although the Quarter had been largely spared, conditions in the rest of the city were deteriorating to depths of desperation and savagery not seen in America since the Civil War. Quarter residents did not roam far from home, except perhaps to the river to get water. They feared not only street violence but National Guardsmen who might shanghai them to the Superdome or Convention Center, both of which had become hellish pits of misery as refugees awaited transport.[33]

Sunday of the Labor Day weekend has been Southern Decadence since the late 1970s, and the remaining Quarter dwellers were not about to let a disaster break the continuity. On September 4, about forty[34] people, towing a boom box on a wagon and carrying a sign that said "Life Goes On?," maintained the tradition.[35]

Even those dwellings that had not suffered damage were found moldy, as the closed-up, damp, and unair-conditioned residences cooked in the sun, day after day.

Most of the returnees lived along the old natural levee and had some resources to start repairs. But many of the displaced were poor and middle-class blacks from the Lower Ninth Ward and other hard-hit areas. These people did not merely lack resources to rebuild. Many were also being exposed, for the first time, to life outside the city. Most found open arms, good-to-excellent schools, and progressive political atmospheres in their places of refuge.[36] For many, to return to the cycles of poverty, false hopes, violence, and drugs that the storm had only temporarily erased was unthinkable.[37] Pundits began to speculate that the future population of the city would be at best half of the prestorm 480,000, and there might once again be a white majority.

Before Katrina, New Orleans was a city that demanded to control its own image and be judged only by its own standards. Unless backed with large sums, outside opinions were distinctly unwelcome. Even wealthy messengers of change could be received coldly.[38] Comparisons with cities of similar size and ethnic makeup were rejected out of hand at every turn. The New Orleans Way was touted defiantly to a nation whose general culture seemed to be homogenizing in a European manner. For residents and expatriates, New Orleans life, despite its frustrations, was comforting, familiar, and very slow to change. In the early 1990s, for those fleeing the yuppie competition and overbearing political correctness of Washington, D.C., it was a visceral and spiritual relief to buy drinks from bars set up in the baggage claim of the New Orleans airport. The Yat accent of the United cabbie that took us into town seemed like a lullaby, and the Zapp's potato chips and Hubig's Pies eaten without guilt in the wee, tipsy hours were pure manna. If, with each visit, we noticed a little more decay, a little more failing, we simply had another drink and reminded ourselves that here the illusions *were* the realities. Unfortunately, so did everyone else.

After the initial worldwide outpouring of sympathy and generosity in the wake of Katrina, New Orleans was judged—and harshly—by outside standards. Every old, comforting, and sometimes maddeningly wrong notion that had governed the city was now held up to national scrutiny and often ridicule.

Whatever progress had been made in racial harmony was washed away to a saddening echo of the worst days of Dutch Morial. The rhetoric and images embarrassed New Orleanians of all races who felt that this ugliness was a thing of the past, and in any case, should not be given an out-of-town airing. The repolarization of racial attitudes was, in part, a consequence of white disengagement during the years of majority black rule. With few exceptions, white administrations had been engaged with blacks in a patriarchal pattern. When majority black rule began in 1978, whites felt pushed out of the governing process and so devoted their energies to pursuits that rarely influenced the city's overall direction. The furor over the so-called Carnival nondiscrimination ordinance of 1993 brought matters to a head. The ordinance really had nothing to do with the krewes per se. It was a legalistic, and ultimately unsuccessful, attack on white clubs as centers of wealth and business activity. The anomie that most whites felt after the affair meant that the city continued to drift from one Carnival and festival to the next, with little effective planning beyond the latest scheme for more tourist trade.

The storm ripped asunder layers of masks that concealed both pretty and ugly realities. That south Louisiana was, in part, victimized by poor federal stewardship was well agreed. Besides the loss of life and the physical losses, New Orleanians lost something else. Even for those that had no tangible losses, the agony of evacuation and uncertainty in exile was deeply wounding. The foundation of certainties that underlay every aspect of Crescent City life was now deeply cracked, no longer feeling stable under our feet. The emergence from the candlelight of common illusion to the glare outside was stunning. In some ways, the post-Katrina state was what the city might have been in twenty years anyway. Extrapolating from well-known trends, the reduced population, out-of-control crime, blight, and economic torpor were predictable. The storm was a time machine, throwing the town forward to a future-present for which no one was prepared.

Concerned academics began to clamor for protection of historic structures that might still be salvaged. The city, state, and federal governments began a squabble over the amount and control of funds. The Mississippi Gulf Coast had, in some areas, suffered even worse damage than greater New Orleans, but its solons swiftly lined up aid from a friendly Republican administration.

In the aftermath of the storm, before the mandatory evacuation, widespread looting took place, some apparently with police connivance. Some of the apparent looting was, in fact, distressed residents taking food and water. Some bars in the Quarter were looted for their liquor and video poker machines' money, but the majority of businesses robbed were pharmacies, gun stores, liquor stores, pawnshops, and expensive boutiques elsewhere. Canal Place, home to the most upscale inner-city shopping, was looted and set afire. The televised images of looters—almost all black—helping themselves to the goods highlighted the resentment that seethed in the ghettos.

Much of the Quarter's preservation was due to the high concentration of law enforcement and emergency personnel, who, receiving their assignments at Harrah's casino, parked their vehicles and bivouacked along the riverfront. A special recognition is due the responders from New York City, in reciprocity for Louisiana's assistance after the attacks of September 11, 2001.

The First District police station, located above North Rampart, between the Iberville project and Armstrong Park, housed a hundred officers in those

Looted Quarter bar. Courtesy of John Daley.

Military patrol in the Quarter. Courtesy of John Daley.

chaotic poststorm days. These officers were the first, and perhaps only, line of defense for the Quarter's naked lakeside border. The commander of the First District, Capt. James Scott, recalled: "We were the line in the sand, the buffer zone for the French Quarter. Just the fact that we were here probably saved thousands of dollars of property from looting. If the French Quarter had been burned down, that would have been the end of New Orleans as we know it. I don't think the city could have rallied."[39]

The neighborhoods surrounding the Quarter were reexamined in the wake of the storm. North Rampart Street had suffered the triple indignity of a long removal from the VCC's purview, the misbegotten Armstrong Park, and the decline of the Iberville project. In particular, Iberville had sat, like a tumor, on the Vieux Carré's lakeside marches for six decades. Neither the political will to remove it nor the resources to provide for displaced occupants could be found. At a time when other city housing projects were being bulldozed and their dwellers scattered across town, Iberville seemed to be the original immovable object on the chessboard of downtown real estate. Any mention of its removal triggered an immune response of self-proclaimed activists who claimed that developers were eager to evict the poor to house the rich. Now, Iberville had taken some storm damage and its inhabitants were scattered across America. The notion of demolishing Iberville once and for all now had new legitimacy. Some gourmets of architecture proposed saving the sturdy old buildings and rebuilding them into condos to support the rebirth of the Canal Street corridor.

Post-Katrina planning had many fits and starts. The initial plan called for shrinking the footprint of the city, allowing the lowest, most damaged areas to return to wetlands as buffers for future storms. This concept, endorsed by many outside urbanists, was quickly, and falsely, attacked as an attempted eviction of mostly black residents who had been forced to settle in these least desirable areas in times of segregation. The plan became a political liability in an election year and was disowned by both incumbent Mayor Nagin and the challenger, Lt. Gov. Mitch Landrieu.[40] The second plan, optimistically called the Unified New Orleans Plan (UNOP), consisted of a series of neighborhood visions, contingent on continued federal money flow. In reality, every citywide rebuilding plan amounted to a charade, a ticket to be punched for federal funding and then disregarded. Those home and business owners who could rebuild did so, even if they were the only residents of an otherwise devastated block. Developers continued to push their projects through the political wickets.

Those who wanted to rebuild were hamstrung by slow insurance settlements, inconsistent utility restoration, and a chronically mismanaged state grant program. Worse, even for those who had no damage, were predatory insurance rate increases and inexplicable cancellations.

The Quarter had escaped some of the immediate effects, but the pain kept unfolding. In September 2006, Maison Hospitaliere's board of directors, citing scarce staff and few residents, decided to close the 113-year-old nursing home and sell the property.[41]

## ONWARD AND . . .

As the first decade of the twenty-first century stumbled on, the French Quarter was the focus of real-estate speculation beyond anything yet seen. After Katrina, the value of property on the natural levee, called by some the Sliver by the River, increased dramatically.

Residents displaced from other parts of town looked to the Sliver for homes and apartments on higher ground. Some owners elected to sell and get out. Real estate agents approached Quarter owners and promised them amazing—even by Quarter standards—sales prices. The Marigny, relegated for twenty years to the role of bohemian/gay ghetto, suddenly saw a flurry of speculation. Some owners fixed up their houses and then hoped to reap high prices. Rents in both neighborhoods rose dramatically. Control, such as it was, over illegal apartments and condos went out the window. In January 2007, a Jackson Square painter spoke of renting an eight-by-fifteen-foot room for a thousand dollars a month.[42]

The initial blush of big-dollar dreams began to dissipate in mid- and late 2006. The worsening problems of crime, lack of planning, utility, and insurance crises held back most would-be buyers and investors. There was an oversupply of homes on the market as sellers refused to scale back the 20 to 30 percent premiums charged—and sometimes paid—less than a year before.[43]

Despite these reversals, it seems clear that the admission price of living in the Quarter and the Marigny would remain significantly higher than in years past. The gentrification of the seventies and eighties had given way to supergentrification in the 1990s, and now, ultragentrification. The first round of gentrification had, in a general sense, raised some of these Victorian properties to contemporary middle-class suburban norms. The supergentrification of the 1990s added designer touches. Ultragentrification, besides speculative pricing, brings properties, and behavioral expectations, up to the norms of gated, million-dollar home sites elsewhere in the country.

America is the land where people from all over the earth come to reinvent themselves. Americans, with our famous mobility, move around to reinvent ourselves as well. The American capacity for reinvention seemed, at least until recently, limitless. New Orleans and the Vieux Carré had hosted many people who were assuming new identities, or maybe hiding from old ones. New Orleans has had the ability—and willingness—to absorb outcasts, scapegraces, starry-eyed wanderers, the demimonde, and those just tired of life elsewhere. All these people nourished the inner life of the town, even if they were not always model citizens by exterior mores. Post-Katrina, the old tolerances and opportunities for these people were harder to find in New Orleans.

New Orleans's long-term survival, quite apart from the post-Katrina recovery, remains in doubt. The science of climatology has only bad news for the American Gulf Coast. The increasing tempo and ferocity of tropical storms is the most immediate threat. The subsidence of south Louisiana is a slower, but real, danger. It is, however, the creeping but inexorable rise of sea levels that may destroy most of the Gulf Coast.[44] A rise of only three feet would leave the city largely isolated. A few more feet will turn the Sliver by the River into the Isle of Orleans "for true." If the sea keeps rising, and the city keeps sinking, only the most heroic of national efforts could save even the old natural levee. A very high, very strong wall, with footings deeper than any before, might save the highest ground, at least for a while. As we have seen post-Katrina, American political will is a fickle thing. If this fate befalls New Orleans, it befalls most of the Gulf Coast as well.

Whatever the course of nature and man, all who have a stake in the Vieux Carré fight on for the unique, fine, quaint, and distinctive. To maintain these qualities in the face of a national culture celebrating disposable common denominators is no easy task. To preserve, for the intelligentsia, the inebriated, the lovers, the literate, the carnal, and the confused, some balance of enlightenment and contentment requires hope and hard work. The Quarter must remain a place where people can stake claims of property, curiosity, and passion. Discovery, inspiration, and appreciation should await all seekers coming to these old houses, looking out these old vistas, and finding something new in themselves.

# NOTES

## To Set the Scene

1. John Smith Kendall, *History of New Orleans*, transcribed by Bill Thayer (Chicago: Lewis Publishing, 1922), 40, http://penelope.uchicago.edu/Thayer/E/Gazetteer/Places/America/United_States/Louisiana/New_Orleans/_Texts/KENHNO/home.html.

2. John Steele Gordon, "We Banked on Them," *American Heritage Magazine* 46, no. 4 (July/August 1995).

3. Kendall, *History of New Orleans*, 405.

4. Ibid., 438.

5. George M. Reynolds, *Machine Politics in New Orleans 1897–1926*, 2nd ed. (New York: AMS Press, 1968), 36.

6. Ibid., 11.

7. U.S. Census Bureau, "U.S. Census of 1900." http://www.census.gov/population/cencounts/la190090.txt.

## Chapter 1

1. Luis C. Hennick and E. Harper Charlton, *The Streetcars of New Orleans* (Gretna: Firebird Press, 2000), 24.

2. Bernard Lemann, *The Vieux Carré: A General Statement* (New Orleans: Tulane University School of Architecture, 1966), 24.

3. John Smith Kendall, "The French Quarter Sixty Years Ago," *The Louisiana Historical Quarterly* 34, no. 2 (April 1951): 98–99.

4. Leonard V. Huber, *Jackson Square Through the Years* (New Orleans: Friends of the Cabildo, 1982), 92.

5. Kendall, "The French Quarter Sixty Years Ago," 95.

6. Leonard V. Huber and Samuel Wilson, Jr., *Baroness Pontalba's Buildings and the Remarkable Woman Who Built Them*, 2nd ed. (New Orleans: New Orleans Chapter of the Louisiana Landmarks Society and the Friends of the Cabildo, 1966), 54–55.

7. Kendall, "The French Quarter Sixty Years Ago," 97–98.

8. Ibid., 97.

9. S. Frederick Starr, ed., *Inventing New Orleans: Writings of Lafcadio Hearn* (Jackson: University Press of Mississippi, 2001), 22–30.

10. Joseph G. Tregle, Jr., "Creoles and Americans," in *Creole New Orleans: Race and Americanization*, ed. Arnold Hirsch and Joseph Logsdon (Baton Rouge: Louisiana State University Press, 1992), 165-166.

11. James Nolan, interview by Scott S. Ellis, New Orleans, October 13, 2007.

12. Joan M. Martin, "*Plaçage* and the Louisiana *Gens de Couler Libre*," in *Creole: The History and Legacy of Louisiana's Free People of Color*, ed. Sybil Kein (Baton Rouge: Louisiana State University Press, 2000), 57–58.

13. Tregle, "Creoles and Americans," 182–184.

14. Madelene Babin, interview by Christine Durbas, New Orleans, Friends of the Cabildo, Oral History Project, May 10, 1982.

15. *Leslie's Weekly*, December 11, 1902.

16. Robert Tallant, *The Romantic New Orleanians* (New York: E. P. Dutton, 1950), 307.

17. Kendall, "The French Quarter Sixty Years Ago," 95.

18. Ibid., 94.

19. James Hungerford, *The Personality of American Cities* (New York: McBride, Nast Company, 1913), 244; Lyle Saxon, *A Walk Through the Vieux Carré*, 4th ed. (New Orleans: Dinkler Hotels, 1940), 9.

20. Lillian Fortier Zeringer, *Accent on Dedication: The Story of La Maison Hospitaliere* (New Orleans: La Societe des Dames Hospitalieres, 1985), 6–7.

21. La Maison Hospitaliere Web site, http://www.maisonhospitaliere.org/ (accessed June 14, 2005).

22. Joseph Maselli and Dominic Candelero, *Italians in New Orleans* (Charleston: Arcadia Publishing, 2004), 17.

23. Ibid., 13.

24. Rudolph H. Boehm, "Mary Grace Quackenbos and the Federal Campaign Against Peonage: The Case of Sunnyside Plantation," *Arkansas Historical Quarterly* 50, no. 1 (Spring 1991): 41.

25. Bertram Wyatt-Brown, "LeRoy Percy and Sunnyside: Planter Mentality and Italian Peonage in the Mississippi Delta," *Arkansas Historical Quarterly* 50, no. 1 (Spring 1991): 71.

26. Boehm, "Mary Grace Quackenbos," 44.

27. Ernesto R. Milani, "Peonage at Sunnyside and the Reaction of the Italian Government," *Arkansas Historical Quarterly* 50, no. 1 (Spring 1991): 32.

28. Boehm, "Mary Grace Quackenbos," 44; Wyatt-Brown, "LeRoy Percy," 63.

29. Boehm, "Mary Grace Quackenbos," 57.

30. Wyatt-Brown, "LeRoy Percy," 81.

31. Boehm, "Mary Grace Quackenbos," 42, 51.

32. Maselli and Candelero, *Italians in New Orleans*, 25.

33. Ibid., 33.

34. Eleanor McMain, "Behind the Yellow Fever in Little Palermo," *Charities* 5 (November 4, 1905): 152–159, transcribed by Bill Thayer and published online at http://penelope. uchicago.edu/Thayer/E/Gazetteer/Places/America/United_States/Louisiana/New_Orleans/_ Texts/Yellow_Fever_in_Little_Palermo*.html (accessed May 3, 2006).

35. Danny Barker, interview by John Healy, New Orleans Public Library, Jambalaya Project, October 24, 1979.

36. Louise Edwards, "Yellow Fever and the Sicilian Community in New Orleans," Minneapolis, University of Minnesota, May 30, 1989.

37. McMain, "Behind the Yellow Fever," 157.

38. Lemann, *The Vieux Carré*, 24.

39. McMain, "Behind the Yellow Fever," 152.

40. Harriet Joor, "New Orleans, The City of Iron Lace," *Craftsman*, New York, November 1905, unpaginated, transcribed by Bill Thayer and published online at http://penelope.

uchicago.edu/Thayer/E/Gazetteer/Places/America/United_States/Louisiana/New_Orleans/_
Texts/Iron_Lace*.html (accessed May 3, 2006).

41. Richard Gambino, *Vendetta* (Toronto: Guernica, 1998), 4.

42. Ibid., 81–85.

43. Ibid., 111. Those wishing a definitive discussion of the Hennessy affair should read
*Vendetta*, which was adapted for an HBO movie in 1999.

44. George M. Reynolds, *Machine Politics in New Orleans 1897–1926*, 2nd ed. (New York:
AMS Press, 1968), 13.

45. Cosimo Matassa, interview by Scott S. Ellis, New Orleans, April 24, 2004.

46. Daniel Rosenberg, *New Orleans Dockworkers* (Albany: State University of New York,
1988), 18.

47. Matassa interview; Barker interview.

48. Rosenberg, *New Orleans Dockworkers*, 17–18.

49. William Ivy Hair, *Carnival of Fury* (Baton Rouge: Louisiana State University
Press,1976), 137.

50. Reynolds, *Machine Politics*, 37. Calculations are by Scott S. Ellis and are rounded to
the nearest one-tenth of a percent. However, *Louisiana et al v. United States*, 380 US 145
(1965), claims that in 1896 44 percent of registered Louisiana voters were Negroes.

51. Ibid., 36. The outcome was reflected in the Louisiana Constitution of 1898, Article 197.

52. Ida B.Wells-Barnett, *Mob Rule in New Orleans: Robert Charles and His Fight to the
Death, the Story of His Life, Burning Human Beings Alive, Other Lynching Statistics* (Chicago:
Unknown publisher, 1900). Republished by Project Gutenberg at http://www.gutenberg.org/
dirs/1/4/9/7/14976/14976-h/14976-h.htm (accessed April 20, 2005).

53. Rosenberg, *New Orleans Dockworkers*, 56.

54. Ibid., 174–184. In 1931, a city ordinance proposed by the head of the white
dockworkers' union only allowed registered voters to work on the waterfront, effectively
forcing already disenfranchised Negroes off the docks.

55. Barker interview.

56. Bruce Eggler, "Historic Doll House for Sale," *Times-Picayune*, August 14, 2005.

57. Barker interview.

58. Martin, "*Plaçage* and the Louisiana *Gens de Couler Libre*," 69.

59. New Orleans Public Library, Louisiana Division, "Yellow Fever Deaths In New
Orleans," http://nutrias.org/~nopl/facts/feverdeaths.htm (accessed November 16, 2004).

60. Martin Behrman, *Martin Behrman of New Orleans*, ed. John R. Kemp (Baton Rouge:
Louisiana State University Press, 1977), 139, note 29.

61. Benjamin H. Trask, *Fearful Ravages: Yellow Fever in New Orleans 1796–1905*
(Lafayette: Center for Louisiana Studies, University of Louisiana at Lafayette, 2005), 105.

62. McMain, "Behind the Yellow Fever."

63. Trask, *Fearful Ravages*, 108–110, 121.

64. Al Rose, *Storyville, New Orleans* (Tuscaloosa: University of Alabama Press, 1974),
70; "Nobel Lectures, Physiology or Medicine, 1901–1921" (Amsterdam: Elsevier Publishing
Company, 1967), http://nobelprize.org/medicine/laureates/1908/ehrlich-bio.html (accessed
October 27, 2004).

65. Herbert Asbury, *The French Quarter: An Informal History of the New Orleans
Underworld* (New York: Garden City Publishing, 1938), 328–330.

66. Rose, *Storyville*, 39. In official accounts it was called the "restricted district." Sidney
Story was appalled that his name became attached to it.

67. Ibid., 192–193. Council Series Ordinance 13, 032.

68. Rose, *Storyville*, 39; Russell Levy, "Of Bards and Bawds: New Orleans Sporting Life Before and During the Storyville Era, 1897–1917" (M.A thesis, Tulane University, 1967), 66.

69. Reynolds, *Machine Politics*, 158–159.

70. Levy, "Of Bards and Bawds," appendix I, "Houses Outside the Storyville District," 165–169.

71. Ibid., 100–101.

72. Ibid., 81–84.

73. Christine Wiltz, *The Last Madam: A Life in the New Orleans Underworld* (Cambridge, MA: Da Capo Press, 2000), 16.

74. Ibid., 19.

75. Rose, *Storyville*, 80–81.

76. Chance Harvey, *The Life and Selected Letters of Lyle Saxon* (Gretna: Pelican Publishing, 2003), 61; Tallant, *The Romantic New Orleanians*, 307.

77. Marie Louise Hoffmann, "The St. Vincent's Hotel" (M.A. thesis, Tulane University, 1933), 4.

78. Ibid., 20.

79. Ibid., 22.

80. Joor, "New Orleans, the City of Iron Lace."

81. Ibid.

82. Starr, ed., *Inventing New Orleans*, 7.

83. Charles Gayarré, *History of Louisiana* (New York: William J. Widleton, 1867), vol. 3, 204 (1788 fire); vol. 3, 336 (1794 fire), transcribed by Bill Thayer and published online at http://penelope.uchicago.edu/Thayer/E/Gazetteer/Places/America/UnitedStates/ Louisiana/ Texts/GAYHLA/4/4*.html (accessed October 13, 2006).

84. Bruce Eggler, "High Court," *Times-Picayune*, May 9, 2004.

85. Lemann, *Vieux Carré*, 23.

86. "Opening of the Louisiana Transfer Celebration," *Times-Democrat*, December 19, 1903, 1.

87. "Tributes by Representatives of the People of Three Nations," *Times-Democrat*, December 20, 1903, 2.

88. Louisiana Historical Society, "Programme of the Celebration in Honor of the Hundredth Anniversary of the Transfer of Louisiana from France to the United States," December 18–20, 1903. The Historic New Orleans Collection, 57-10-L.5.

89. "Fitting Finale to the Louisiana Celebration," *Times-Democrat*, December 21, 1903, 1.

90. "The Colonial Museum Is Formally Opened," *Times-Democrat*, December 21, 1903, 16.

91. Sally Reeves, Louisiana Historical Society, to Scott S. Ellis, March 12, 2008, "Re: 1903 Colonial Museum History Inquiry."

92. "W. R. Irby Calls at Undertakers and Shoots Self," *Times-Picayune*, November 21, 1926.

93. Ibid.

94. Tallant, *The Romantic New Orleanians*, 319.

95. Harvey, *The Life and Selected Letters of Lyle Saxon*, 44.

96. Ibid., 63.

97. Martin Behrman, "A History of Three Great Public Utilities, Sewerage, Water and Drainage and Their Influence Upon the Health and Progress of a Big City." Presented at convention of the League of American Municipalities, Milwaukee, WI, September 29, 1914, New Orleans, Brandao Print, n.d., ca. 1914, transcribed by Bill Thayer and published online at http://penelope.uchicago.edu/Thayer/E/Gazetteer/Places/America/United_States/ Louisiana/New_Orleans/_Texts/Behrman*.html. (accessed February 1, 2007).

98. Malcolm Heard, *French Quarter Manual: An Architectural Guide to New Orleans' Vieux Carré* (New Orleans: Tulane School of Architecture, 1997), 145. The French term for this foundation is *poteaux sur sole*. Pile drivers erecting modern buildings also damaged the cypress mattresses. "Mrs. Robinson Blasts Motel," *Times-Picayune*, January 17, 1963.

99. Walter Lowery, *912 Orleans Street: The Story of a Rescue* (New Orleans: Hauser Printing, 1965), 41.

100. John Smith Kendall, *History of New Orleans* (Chicago: Lewis Publishing, 1922), 707, transcribed by Bill Thayer and published online at http://penelope.uchicago.edu/Thayer/E/ Gazetteer/Places/America/Un ited_ States/Louisiana/New_Orleans/_Texts/KENHNO/ home.html.

101. "Cathedral Dynamited," *Times-Picayune*, April 26, 1909.

102. James Blenk, *An Appeal to the Citizens of New Orleans and Louisiana to Restore St. Louis Cathedral* (New Orleans: St. Louis Cathedral, 1917), 12.

103. Leonard V. Huber and Samuel Wilson, Jr., *The Basilica on Jackson Square* (New Orleans: St. Louis Cathedral, 1972), 42–43.

104. Levy, "Of Bards and Bawds," 159–160.

105. Wiltz, *The Last Madam*, 17.

106. National Park Service. "New Orleans Jazz Neighborhood History Map." New Orleans Jazz National Historical Park Web site, http://www.nps.gov/archive/jazz/Maps_ neighborhoods.htm (retrieved July 7, 2007).

107. Levy, "Of Bards and Bawds," 101.

108. Anthony Stanonis, "An Old House in the Quarter: Vice in the Vieux Carré of the 1930s," 2 of downloaded edition (New Orleans: Loyola University Student Historical Journals, 1997), vol. 28, http://www.loyno.edu/~history/journal/1996-7/Stanonis.html (accessed October 18, 2003).

109. Lemann, *Vieux Carré*, 23.

110. New Orleans Public Library, Louisiana Photograph Collection, David Barrow Fischer Steamboat Collection. Image published in part nine of "Crescent City Memory," 1997 exhibit. Published online at http://nutrias.org/~nopl/exhibits/ccmem.htm (accessed December 16, 2008).

111. Wayne Everard and Irene Wainwright, "The Evil Wind: Hurricanes in South Louisiana." New Orleans Public Library, 1995. Published online at http://www.nutrias .org/~nopl/exhibits/hurricane1.htm (accessed December 15, 2008).

112. Kendall, *History of New Orleans*, 707.

113. Rose, *Storyville*, 168.

114. Ibid., 170.

115. Ibid., 166. In the public domain.

116. Babin interview.

117. "Noted Gin Mills May Turn Tamely to Coffee Houses," *Times-Picayune*, January 17, 1919, 1, col. 5.

118. Tallant, *The Romantic New Orleanians*, 311.

119. Lyle Saxon, "French Opera House to Rise Again From Ruins," *Times-Picayune*, December 5, 1919, 1.

## Chapter 2

1. Mrs. Phillip (Elizabeth) Werlein, *The Wrought Iron Railings of the Vieux Carré, New Orleans* (publisher unknown, n.d., ca. 1917–1921).

2. Al Rose, *Storyville, New Orleans* (Tuscaloosa: University of Alabama Press, 1974), 70–71.

3. Chance Harvey, *The Life and Selected Letters of Lyle Saxon* (Gretna, LA: Pelican Publishing, 2003), 62–63.

4. Ibid., 69.

5. Ibid., 61, 108.

6. Ibid., 67.

7. John W. Scott, "William Spratling and the New Orleans Renaissance," *Journal of the Louisiana Historical Association* 45, no.3 (Summer 2004): 288; Robert Tallant, *The Romantic New Orleanians* (New York: E. P. Dutton, 1950), 311.

8. Harvey, *The Life and Selected Letters of Lyle Saxon*, 67–68.

9. Le Petit Théâtre du Vieux Carré, *Le Petit Théâtre du Vieux Carré* (New Orleans: Le Petit Théâtre du Vieux Carré, 1940).

10. "Vieux Carré Folk Meet Thursday to Advance Plans for Improvement," *New Orleans Item*, February 5, 1920, 10.

11. "Father Antoine Favors Cleanup," *New Orleans States*, May 4, 1920.

12. John Wyeth Scott II, "Natalie Vivian Scott: The Origins, People and Times of the French Quarter Renaissance (1920–1930), Volume I" (Ph.D. diss., Louisiana State University,1999), 56–59.

13. James W. Thomas, *Lyle Saxon: A Critical Biography* (Birmingham, AL: Summa Publishing Inc, 1991), 23.

14. Jeannette S. Raffray, "Origins of the Vieux Carré Commission 1920–1941: A Reappraisal" (M.A. thesis, University of New Orleans,1993), 3.

15. Martin Behrman, *Martin Behrman of New Orleans*, ed. John R. Kemp (Baton Rouge: Louisiana State University Press, 1977), 341.

16. Scott, "William Spratling and the New Orleans Renaissance," 296.

17. Thomas Bonner, Jr., "The *Double Dealer* and the Little-Magazine Tradition in New Orleans," in *Literary New Orleans in the Modern World*, ed. Richard S. Kennedy (Baton Rouge: Louisiana State University, 1998), 31.

18. Lyle Saxon, *Fabulous New Orleans*, 2nd ed. (New Orleans: Robert Crager & Company, 1950). The statement is from Robert Tallant's introduction to the second edition, xiv. From *Fabulous New Orleans* by Lyle Saxon © 1989 Pelican Publishing. Used by permission of the publisher, Pelican Publishing Company, Inc.

19. Harvey, *The Life and Selected Letters of Lyle Saxon*, 82.

20. Thomas, *Lyle Saxon*, 40.

21. The Historic New Orleans Collection, "The Long Weekend: The Arts and the Vieux Carré Between the World Wars 1918–1941." Part 1, The 1920s: From Armistice to the Crash. Exhibit of January 16–May 1, 1993, Exhibit 53.

22. Leonard V. Huber and Samuel Wilson, Jr., *Baroness Pontalba's Buildings and the Remarkable Woman Who Built Them*, 2nd ed. (New Orleans: New Orleans Chapter of the Louisiana Landmarks Society and the Friends of the Cabildo, 1966), 57.

23. Scott, "Natalie Vivian Scott," 82.

24. Scott, "William Spratling and the New Orleans Renaissance," 299.

25. Hillary S. Irvin, "Vieux Carré Commission History," Vieux Carré Commission, 1986.

26. Le Petit Théâtre du Vieux Carré, *Le Petit Théâtre du Vieux Carré*.

27. Recollection of the author, who saw Patricia Neal there in the fall of 2003.

28. Scott, "William Spratling and the New Orleans Renaissance," 295; Tallant, *The Romantic New Orleanians*, 317; Harnett T. Kane, *Queen New Orleans: City by the River* (New York: William Morrow & Company, 1949), 258.

29. Judith H. Bonner, *The New Orleans Arts & Crafts Club: An Artistic Legacy*, The New Orleans Museum of Art and The Historic New Orleans Collection, New Orleans, 2007.

30. Scott, "William Spratling and the New Orleans Renaissance," 294.

31. The Historic New Orleans Collection, "The Long Weekend," Exhibit 46.

32. Scott, "William Spratling and the New Orleans Renaissance," 295; Susan Larson, *The Booklover's Guide to New Orleans* (Baton Rouge: Louisiana State University Press, 1999), 47.

33. Ibid., 70.

34. Ibid., 48.

35. Scott, "William Spratling and the New Orleans Renaissance," 301.

36. Ibid., 300–301.

37. Tallant, *The Romantic New Orleanians*, 229–230.

38. "French Quarter Guardians Named," *Times-Picayune*, November 25, 1925, sect 1, 2.

39. Raffray, "Origins of the Vieux Carré Commission," 13.

40. Irvin, "Vieux Carré Commission History."

41. Lyle Saxon, "Baroness Pontalba Portrait Goes Home," *Times-Picayune*, October 10, 1926.

42. Scott, "William Spratling and the New Orleans Renaissance," 313.

43. "W. R. Irby Calls at Undertakers and Shoots Self," *Times-Picayune*, November 21, 1926.

44. Harvey, *The Life and Selected Letters of Lyle Saxon*, 143.

45. Huber and Wilson, *Baroness Pontalba's Buildings*, 58.

46. Scott, "William Spratling and the New Orleans Renaissance," 313, 322.

47. Harvey, *The Life and Selected Letters of Lyle Saxon*, 191.

48. Ibid., 194.

49. Ibid., 157.

50. Thomas, *Lyle Saxon*, 177.

51. Tallant, *The Romantic New Orleanians*, 325.

52. John B. Padgett, "William Faulkner," Oxford, MS: The Mississippi Writers Page, http://www.olemiss.edu/mwp/dir/faulkner_william/index.html. (accessed January 30, 2007).

53. A long-running, but baseless, legend maintains that Andrew Jackson and Jean Laffite planned the 1815 defense of New Orleans over absinthe frappés. In factual life, Lyle Saxon was fond of the drink. Harvey, *The Life and Selected Letters of Lyle Saxon*, 187.

54. Joy Jackson, "Prohibition in New Orleans: The Unlikeliest Crusade," *Louisiana History, Journal of the Louisiana Historical Association* 19 (1978): 264.

55. Ibid., 266.

56. Ibid., 262.

57. Louis Vyhnanek, *Unorganized Crime: New Orleans in the 1920s* (Layfayette: The Center for Louisiana Studies, 1998), 58.

58. Tanya Marie Sanchez, "The Feminine Side of Bootlegging: Women, Drink and Prohibition in New Orleans" (M.A. thesis, University of New Orleans,1998), 16.

59. Vyhnanek, *Unorganized Crime*, 66.

60. "Dry Agents Find Orleans Largest Whiskey Factory," *Times-Picayune*, October 14, 1921, 1.

61. "Perfumery Rivals Coconut as Shield in Liquor Circles," *Times-Picayune*, January 9, 1925, 1, col. 2.

62. "'Imported Rum' Factory Found by Dry Raiders," *Times-Picayune*, January 6, 1922.

63. "Dry Agents Seize Alcohol Still," *Times-Picayune*, June 22, 1923.

64. Jackson, "Prohibition in New Orleans," 267–268.

65. Sanford Jarrell, *New Orleans—The Civilized and Lively City* (Girard, Kansas: Haldeman-Julius Publications, 1929), Little Blue Book No. 1410, 21; Vyhnanek, *Unorganized Crime*, 68.

66. Vyhnanek, *Unorganized Crime*, 130.

67. Ibid., 68.

68. Scott, "William Spratling and the New Orleans Renaissance," 315, note 40.

69. "A Matter of Record," *Time*, December 31, 1923, http://time-proxy.yaga.com/time/archive/preview/0,10987,717262,00.html (accessed July 6, 2005).

70. Jarrell, *New Orleans*, 19.

71. Ibid., 22.

72. Vyhnanek, *Unorganized Crime*, 52.

73. Ibid., 52.

74. Jackson, "Prohibition in New Orleans," 269.

75. Vyhnanek, *Unorganized Crime*, 65.

76. Sanchez, "The Feminine Side of Bootlegging," 6–7.

77. Ibid., 5.

78. Vyhnanek, *Unorganized Crime*, 66.

79. Ibid., 84–85.

80. Ibid., 78; Sanchez, "The Feminine Side of Bootlegging," 17–18.

81. Jackson, "Prohibition in New Orleans," 273, 281; Vyhannek, *Unorganized Crime*, 55 .

82. Jackson, "Prohibition in New Orleans," 282.

83. Sanchez, "The Feminine Side of Bootlegging," 28–34; Vyhannek, *Unorganized Crime*, 81.

84. Ibid., 90.

85. Edward F. Haas, "New Orleans on the Half-Shell," *Journal of the Louisiana Historical Association* 13, no. 3 (1972): 298.

86. Vyahnnek, *Unorganized Crime*, 96.

87. Ibid., 97.

88. Leonard Katz, *Uncle Frank: The Biography of Frank Costello* (New York: Pocket Books, 1975),100–101.

89. Rose, *Storyville*, 70–71.

90. Christine Wiltz, *The Last Madam: A Life in the New Orleans Underworld* (Cambridge, MA: Da Capo Press, 2000), 26.

91. Herbert Asbury, *The French Quarter: An Informal History of the New Orleans Underworld* (New York: Garden City Publishing, 1938), 361–362.

92. Wiltz, *The Last Madam*, 17.

93. Ibid., 66.

94. Cosimo Matassa, interview by Scott S. Ellis, New Orleans, April 24, 2004.

95. Louis Vyhnanek, "'Muggles,' 'Inchy,' and 'Mud': Illegal Drugs in New Orleans During the 1920s," *Louisiana History, Journal of the Louisiana Historical Association* 22, no.3 (Summer 1981): 263.

## Chapter 3

1. Pete Daniel, *Deep'n As It Come: The 1927 Mississippi River Flood* (Fayetteville: University of Arkansas Press, 1996), 186–195.

2. Martine Geronimi, "The French Market New Orleans Style: Preservation of the Past Patrimonal Alibi and Glorification of Commerce." Ottawa: Society for the Study of Architecture in Canada (SSAC), 2001 autumn issue, 4 of downloaded edition, http://membres.lycos.fr/mappamundi/market.html (accessed November 15, 2001).

3. "Offer of Work Causes Rioting Among Jobless," *Times-Picayune*, March 11, 1930.

4. Roman Heleniak, "Local Reaction to the Great Depression in New Orleans," *Louisiana History, The Journal of the Louisiana Historical Association* 10, no. 4 (1969): 296.

5. Ibid., 304.

6. Edward F. Haas, "New Orleans on the Half-Shell," *Louisiana History, The Journal of the Louisiana Historical Association* 13, no. 3 (1972): 284.

7. T. Harry Williams, *Huey Long* (New York: Alfred A. Knopf, 1969), 638–639.

8. Ibid., 539–540.

9. Ibid., 567.

10. Ibid., 727–730.

11. Gary Boulard, *Huey Long Invades New Orleans: The Siege of a City, 1934–36* (Gretna, LA: Pelican Publishing Company,1998), 150.

12. Ibid., 142.

13. Ibid., 203.

14. Williams, *Huey Long*, 253.

15. "Maestri Rides Again," *Time*, January 19, 1942, at http://time-proxy.yaga.com/time/archive/preview/0,10987,766290,00.html. (accessed July 6, 2005).

16. Haas, "New Orleans on the Half-Shell," 288.

17. "State Machine Ticket Hand Picked Product," *The Voice of the People*, January 1936, http://louisdl.louislibraries.org/HPL/image/661461925112003_202.sid. (accessed April 12, 2004).

18. Williams, *Huey Long*, 253.

19. Haas, "New Orleans on the Half-Shell," 297.

20. Boulard, *Huey Long Invades New Orleans*, 203.

21. Haas, "New Orleans on the Half-Shell," 292, 296–297.

22. Ibid., 296.

23. Edward F. Haas, *DeLesseps S. Morrison and the Image of Reform: New Orleans Politics, 1946–1961* (Baton Rouge: Louisiana State University Press 1974), 13.

24. Haas, "New Orleans on the Half-Shell," 283.

25. Joseph Maselli and Dominic Candelero, *Italians in New Orleans* (Charleston: Arcadia Publishing, 2004), 84.

26. Haas, *DeLesseps S. Morrison*, 19.

27. "Mrs. Werlein to Lead State Wet Force," *New Orleans Morning Tribune*, May 3, 1932, 1.

28. "City Breweries Sell Out; Joyous Throngs Toast New and Old," *Times-Picayune*, April 14, 1933.

29. Joy Jackson, "Prohibition in New Orleans: The Unlikeliest Crusade," *Journal of the Louisiana Historical Association* 19 (1978): 284.

30. Sanford Jarrell, *New Orleans—The Civilized and Lively City* (Girard, Kansas: Haldeman-Julius Publications, 1929), Little Blue Book, No. 1410, 19.

31. Anthony Stanonis, "An Old House in the Quarter: Vice in the Vieux Carré of the 1930s," Loyola University Student Historical Journals, 1997, vol. 28, 5 of downloaded version, http://www.loyno.edu/~history/journal/1996-7/Stanonis.html (accessed October 18, 2003).

32. Al Rose, *Storyville, New Orleans* (Tuscaloosa: University of Alabama Press, 1974), 94.

33. Jackson, "Prohibition in New Orleans," 277.

34. Louis Vyhnanek, "'Muggles,' 'Inchy,' and 'Mud': Illegal Drugs in New Orleans During the 1920s," *Louisiana History, The Journal of the Louisiana Historical Association* 22, no. 3 (Summer 1981): 257–258.

35. Ibid., 267–268.

36. Edward M.Rececher and the editors of *Consumer Reports*, *The Consumers Union Report on Licit and Illicit Drugs* (Yonkers: Consumers Union, 1972), 2, www.drugtext.org/library/reports/cu/cu55.html (accessed November 12, 2003).

37. Ibid.

38. Stanonis, "An Old House in the Quarter," 5.

39. Vyhnanek, "'Muggles,'" 262.

40. Ibid., 270.

41. "Dope Raid Ends in Nine Arrests," *Times-Picayune*, June 9, 1949, sect. 1, 6.

42. "For Tarpon," *Time*, May 10, 1937, published online at www.time.com/time/magazine/article/0,9171,757744,00.html (accessed September 15, 2007).

43. U.S. Congress, Senate Special Committee to Investigate Organized Crime in Interstate Commerce 1951, *Third Interim Report*, 82nd Cong., 1st sess., S. Rep. 307, 85, 88–89.

44. Le Petit Théâtre du Vieux Carré, *Le Petit Théâtre du Vieux Carré* (New Orleans: Le Petit Théâtre du Vieux Carré, 1940), 30.

45. Jarrell, *New Orleans—The Civilized and Lively City*, 26.

46. Judith H. Bonner, *The New Orleans Arts & Crafts Club: An Artistic Legacy* (New Orleans: The New Orleans Museum of Art and the Historic New Orleans Collection, 2007), 12.

47. Stanonis, "An Old House in the Quarter," 5; Allean Hale, "Two on a Streetcar," *The Tennessee Williams Literary Journal* 1, no. 1 (1989): 33.

48. Stanonis, "An Old House in the Quarter," 6.

49. Chance Harvey, *The Life and Selected Letters of Lyle Saxon* (Gretna: Pelican Publishing, 2003), 165–166.

50. Kinney, Robert. *The Bachelor in New Orleans* (New Orleans: Bob Riley Studios, 1942).

51. Ibid., 21.

52. Ibid., 25.

53. Ibid., 28. Kinney is speaking of the bar now called Lafitte's Blacksmith Shop at 941 Bourbon.

54. Ibid., 98.

55. Peter Graffagnino, "New Orleans in the Thirties," *Muscogee County (Georgia) Medical Bulletin* 20, no. 1 (1979).

56. Recollection of the author's mother, who lived in Louisiana from 1927 to 1950.

57. Bruce Eggler, "The Final Link, Last Vestige of Chinatown May Fall; Old Site Slated to Be Garage for New Hotel," *Times-Picayune*, October 15, 2004; Matassa interview, April 24, 2004.

58. New Orleans Ordinance 11,949 Commission Council Series, 1930. "Vieux Carré Pontalba Buildings. Accepting from the Pontalba Building Museum Association, Inc., that certain portion of ground and the improvements there on known as the Upper Pontalba Building, and fixing the terms and conditions controlling said donation."

59. Leonard V. Huber and Samuel Wilson, Jr., *Baroness Pontalba's Buildings and the Remarkable Woman Who Built Them*, 2nd ed. (New Orleans: New Orleans Chapter of the Louisiana Landmarks Society and the Friends of the Cabildo, 1966), 57.

60. Allan P. Sindler, *Huey Long's Louisiana: State Politics, 1920–1952* (Baltimore: The Johns Hopkins Press, 1956), 2nd printing, 1971, 141, note 65.

61. Haas, "New Orleans on the Half-Shell," 289.

62. Ibid., 300.

63. Robert Tallant, *The Romantic New Orleanians* (New York: E. P. Dutton, 1950), 320.

64. "Last Rites Today for Mrs. Werlein," *Times-Picayune*, April 25, 1946, 2, col. 2.

65. William Manchester, *Goodbye, Darkness* (New York: Dell Publishing, 1982). Manchester (318) cites a New York clubwoman who suggested that marines returning from combat in World War II—"trained killers"—be sent to reorientation camps in the Panama Canal zone and made to wear identification patches.

66. Robert Tallant, *Mardi Gras . . . As It Was* (Gretna: Pelican Publishing Company, 2000), 178–179; Tallant, *The Romantic New Orleanians*, 234–235.

67. "Last Rites Today for Mrs. Werlein," *Times-Picayune*, April 25, 1946, 2; Tallant, *The Romantic New Orleanians*, 320.

68. Hillary S. Irvin, "Vieux Carré Commission History" (New Orleans: Vieux Carré Commission, 1986).

69. Marsha Bourgeois, "The Preservation of the Vieux Carré and Its Grassroots Beginnings," Loyola University Student Historical Journals,1988, vol. 20, 3, http://www .loyno.edu/history/journal/1988-9/bourgeois.htm (accessed August 4, 2003); Jeannette S. Raffray, "Origins of the Vieux Carré Commission 1920–1941: A Reappraisal" (M.A. thesis, University of New Orleans,1993), 21.

70. Irvin, "Vieux Carré Commission History." The legal basis for the Vieux Carré Commission is found in: Louisiana Constitution of 1921, Article XIV, subsection 22A; reaffirmed in Louisiana Constitution of 1974, Article VI, subsection 17, New Orleans Charter, Chapter 7, section 5-701, and Municipal Ordinance 14,538 of March 3, 1937, New Orleans Code of Ordinances, Section 166-31 (current as of 2006).

71. Walter W. Gallas, "Neighborhood Preservation and Politics in New Orleans: Vieux Carré Property Owners, Residents and Associates, Inc. and City Government, 1938–1983" (M.A. thesis, University of New Orleans, 1996), 23.

72. Ibid., 24–25.

73. Ibid., 21–22.

74. "Vieux Carré Group Raps Commission," *New Orleans Item*, January 12, 1939, 1, col. 1.

75. Gallas, "Neighborhood Preservation," 25.

76. Irwin, "Vieux Carré Commission History."

77. As the official party dined on oysters Rockefeller, Mayor Maestri, apparently bashful about speaking in his New Orleans dialect to the urbane chief executive, finally blurted out, "How ya like dem ersters?" Haas, *DeLesseps S. Morrison*, 13.

78. Anthony Stanonis, "'A Woman of Boundless Energy': Elizebeth Werlein and Her Times," *Louisiana History, The Journal of the Louisiana Historical Association* 46, no.1, 5–26 (Winter 2005): 22–25.

79. The Crescent City Democratic Association; the Old Regular Democrats, whose formal name was the Choctaw Club; and the Longites.

80. Martin Behrman, *Martin Behrman of New Orleans*, ed. John R. Kemp (Baton Rouge: Louisiana State University Press, 1977), xiii.

81. Lorin Peterson, *The Day of the Mugwumps* (New York: Random House, 1961), 212–213; George M. Reynolds, *Machine Politics in New Orleans 1897–1926*, 2nd ed. (New York: AMS Press, 1968), 109–110.

82. Haas, "New Orleans on the Half-Shell," 299; Behrman, *Martin Behrman*, xiv.

83. Cosimo Matassa, interview by Scott S. Ellis, New Orleans, April 24, 2004.

84. Reynolds, *Machine Politics*, 112–113.

85. Matassa interview, April 24, 2004.

86. Peterson, *The Day of the Mugwumps*, 213.

87. Reynolds, *Machine Politics*, 110; Haas, "New Orleans on the Half-Shell," 299.

88. Sindler, *Huey Long's Louisiana*, 133.

89. Williams, *Huey Long*, 821–822.

90. Haas, "New Orleans on the Half-Shell," 299.

91. James W. Thomas, *Lyle Saxon: A Critical Biography* (Birmingham, AL: Summa Publishing Inc, 1991), 160.

92. Haas, "New Orleans on the Half-Shell," 284.

93. Sindler, *Huey Long's Louisiana*, 138–139.

94. "Maestri Rides Again," *Time*, January 19, 1942, http://time-proxy.yaga.com/time/archive/preview/0,10987,766290,00.html (accessed July 6, 2005).

95. Haas, "New Orleans on the Half-Shell," 288.

96. Stanonis, "A Woman of Boundless Energy," 24.

97. Behrman, *Martin Behrman*, 303; Reynolds, *Machine Politics*, 158–159.

98. Haas, "New Orleans on the Half-Shell," 287.

99. Sindler, *Huey Long's Louisiana*, 138–139; "One Down," *Time*, September 25, 1939, http://time-proxy.yaga.com/time/archive/preview/0,10987,761953,00.html. (accessed July 6, 2005).

100. I am indebted to John Griffin for this phrase.

101. Joseph L.Herndon and Mary L. Oehrlein, "Historic Structures Report: 1850 House Museum, Lower Pontalba Building, Jackson Square, New Orleans, Louisiana," Washington, D.C., Building Conservation Technology, August 1, 1977.

102. New Orleans Public Library, WPA Photograph Collection, Series 11.54 through 11.56, Upper Pontalba, 1935–1937, http://www.nutrias.org/~nopl/photos/wpa/wpaphotos.htm (accessed July 14, 2007).

103. Ted Liuzza, "Spring Fiesta Opens with Crowning of Queen Sunday," *New Orleans Item*, March 6, 1942.

104. Geronimi, "The French Market New Orleans Style," 3 of downloaded edition.

105. Emile V. Stier and James B. Keeling, *Glorified French Market* (New Orleans: The French Market Corporation, 1938).

106. Herbert Asbury, *The French Quarter: An Informal History of the New Orleans Underworld* (New York: Garden City Publishing, 1938), 328.

107. J. E. Burgoyne, "Winds of Change Shift French Market Smells," *Times-Picayune*, December 17, 1972, sec. 3, 8.

108. Karen Trahan Leathem, "Luring Young Girls to Their Ruin: Liquor, Women and the 1908 Gay-Shattuck Law." Presented at the Louisiana Historical Association Annual Meeting, Lafayette, LA, March 14, 1997.

109. Matassa interview, April 24, 2004.

110. New Orleans Public Library, WPA Photograph Collection, Series 36.109, "Recreation; Recreation Project for Whites. Regular recreational activities are conducted by WPA recreation leaders at the Iberville Housing Project. Shown here is a track meet in which boy residents of the project participated. Exterior," June 15, 1942, http://nutrias.org/~nopl/photos/wpa/wpa36.htm (accessed August 2, 2007); City of New Orleans, "Iberville Project Neighborhood Profile," December 1978, 304.

111. Courtney Ryley Cooper, *Designs in Scarlett* (Boston: Little, Brown and Company, 1939), 131.

112. "Open Letter Asks Law in Vieux Carré," *New Orleans States-Item*, May 15, 1940, 1, 10.

113. Cooper, *Designs in Scarlett*, 131–135.

114. "Vieux Carré," *Newsweek*, August 12, 1940, 16.

115. "Vieux Carré Charges to Be Studied," *New Orleans Item*, May 16, 1940.

116. "Push Drive for Cleanup in Quarter," *New Orleans Item-Tribune*, May 19, 1940.

117. "Push Drive to Mop Up Quarter," *New Orleans Item*, August 13, 1940.

118. "5464 French Quarter Arrests Shown in Report by Reyer," *New Orleans Item*, August 13, 1940.

119. Haas, "New Orleans on the Half-Shell," 309.

120. Irvin,"Vieux Carré Commission History."

121. Tom Bissell, interview by Scott S. Ellis, New Orleans, March 19, 2005.

122. Gallas, "Neighborhood Preservation," 26.

123. John Foley, "New Orleans' French Quarter: Framing Diverse Visions of Urban Living," University of New Orleans, College of Urban & Public Affairs. Presented at Association of Collegiate Schools of Planning (ACSP) Annual Conference, November 5–8, 1998, Pasadena, CA,13. http://louisdl.louislibraries.org/CUPA/image/57936182072004_Corel_Office_Document.pdf (accessed August 17, 2005).

124. Mary Meeks Morrison and Jacob Morrison Papers, MSS 553, Historic New Orleans Collection.

125. Mrs. Jacob (Mary Meeks) Morrison, interview by John Geyser, New Orleans, Friends of the Cabildo Oral History Project, 1977. Used by permission of Friends of the Cabildo.

126. John W. Scott, "William Spratling and the New Orleans Renaissance," *Louisiana History, The Journal of the Louisiana Historical Association* 45, no. 3 (Summer 2004): 313.

127. Harvey, *The Life and Selected Letters of Lyle Saxon*, 177–178.

128. Hale, "Two on a Streetcar," 34.

129. Robert Tallant, *Mr. Preen's Salon* (Garden City: Doubleday, 1949).

130. Federal Writers' Project, Works Progress Administration, *New Orleans City Guide*, 1st ed. (Cambridge MA: Riverside Press, 1938).

131. Hale, "Two on a Streetcar," 37–38.

132. Ibid., 36.

133. Federal Writers' Project, Works Progress Administration, *New Orleans City Guide*, 2nd ed., ed. Robert Tallant (New York: Houghton Mifflin, 1952), xxxviii.

134. Hale, "Two on a Streetcar," 36.

135. Ibid., 41.

136. Harvey, *The Life and Selected Letters of Lyle Saxon*, 89.

137. Maureen Olle, *French Quarter Population, "Re: Request for Specific Census Data,"* e-mail to Scott S. Ellis, Louisiana State University Library, August 7, 2003.

138. Harnett T. Kane, "Guns, Barflys, Petticoats Feature Vieux Carré Bar War," *New Orleans Item*, May 22, 1941.

139. Delaup, Rick. "Gallery of Eccentrics," http://www.eccentricneworleans.com/gallery_of_eccentrics.htm (accessed November 2, 2006).

140. Clarence Doucet, "Bourbon House Declared Dead," *Times-Picayune*, October 1, 1964.

141. Kane, "Guns, Barflys, Petticoats."

142. Fannie B. Campbell Welsh, *Mercedes: A New Orleans Hurricane!* (Houston: The Anson Jones Press, 1948), 114–116.

143. Cosimo Matassa, interview by Scott S. Ellis, New Orleans, March 19, 2005.

144. Bureau of Governmental Research, *Vieux Carré Historic District Demonstration Study; Economic and Social Study* (Washington: Marcou, O'Leary and Associates, 1968), 102.

145. Michael L. Kurtz and Morgan D. Peoples, *Earl K. Long: The Saga of Uncle Earl and Louisiana Politics* (Baton Rouge: Louisiana State University Press, 1990), 118.

146. Mary Morrison interview.

147. Charles Winick and Paul M. Kinsie, *The Lively Commerce: Prostitution in the United States* (Chicago: Quadrangle Books, 1971), 242.

148. "Maestri Rides Again," *Time*, January 19, 1942, at http://time-proxy.yaga.com/time/archive/preview/0,10987,766290,00.html (accessed July 6, 2005).

149. Haas, "New Orleans on the Half-Shell," 303.

150. Samuel I. Rosenman, ed., *The Public Papers and Addresses of Franklin D. Roosevelt*, 1943 volume, "The Tide Turns" (New York: Harper Brothers, 1950), 569–575.

151. Haas, "New Orleans on the Half-Shell," 304.

152. "Maestri Rides Again," *Time*.

153. Craig Schumacher and Rodger King, "Cosimo Matassa," Portland, OR, *Tape Op*, vol. 40, March/April 2004.

154. Monroe Berger, "Letters from New Orleans," *Annual Review of Jazz Studies 7, 1994–1995*, ed. Edward Berger, David Cayer, Henry Martin, Dan Morgenstern, and Lewis Porter. Institute for Jazz Studies, Rutgers, the State University of New Jersey (Lanham, MD: Scarecrow Press, 1996), 51.

155. Malvern Hall Tillitt, "Army-Navy Pay Tops Most Civilians," *Barron's National Business and Financial Weekly*, April 24, 1944.

156. Berger, "Letters from New Orleans," 51.

157. Mary Morrison interview.

158. "Life Goes to the Mardi Gras," *Life*, March 25, 1946, 136–138, 141.

159. Harvey, *The Life and Selected Letters of Lyle Saxon*, 213.

160. "Last Rites Today for Mrs. Werlein," *Times-Picayune*.

161. "Vieux Carré Trimming," *Times-Picayune*, March 20, 1940.

162. Ordinance 16,430 of March 25, 1946.

163. Leonard V. Huber, *Jackson Square Through the Years* (New Orleans: Friends of The Cabildo, 1982), 92–93.

164. Raymond J. Martinez, *The Story of the River Front at New Orleans* (New Orleans: Pelican Press, 1948), 186–187. This work lists fifty-one "steamship companies and steamship agencies operating at New Orleans" in 1948.

165. "Vieux Carré Trimming," *Times-Picayune*.

166. Teresa Anne Wilkinson, "Sense of Place and Preservation Planning: An Analysis of the New Orleans Vieux Carré From 1718 to 1985" (M.A. thesis, University of New Orleans, 1985), 80.

167. James J. Morrison, "Hits Vieux Carré Shrinkage," *Times-Picayune*, March 26, 1946.

168. *Vieux Carré Property Owners and Associates, Inc. et al. v. City of New Orleans, et al.*, 167 So. 2d 367, 26 La. 788, Supreme Court of Louisiana, 1964.

## Chapter 4

1. John Hypolite Coquille, "Martin Behrman Album." New Orleans Public Library, published at http://www.nutrias.org/~nopl/photos/behrphot.htm (accessed March 21, 2008).

2. Edward F. Haas, "New Orleans on the Half-Shell," *Journal of the Louisiana Historical Association* 13, no. 3 (1972): 296.

3. Edward F. Haas, *DeLesseps S. Morrison and the Image of Reform: New Orleans Politics, 1946–1961* (Baton Rouge: Louisiana State University Press, 1974), 56.

4. "Maestri Rides Again," *Time*, January 19, 1942, http://time-proxy.yaga.com/time/archive/preview/0,10987,766290,00.html (accessed July 6, 2005).

5. "Old Girl's New Boy," *Time*, November 24, 1947.

6. *Time's* later laudatory articles about Morrison include: September 12, 1955: "A New Face"; May 20, 1957: "Uplift for the Grande Dame"; and February 17, 1958: "King of the Crescent City."

7. Allan P. Sindler, *Huey Long's Louisiana: State Politics, 1920–1952* (Baltimore: The Johns Hopkins Press, 1956), 2nd printing, 1971, 139.

8. Haas, *DeLesseps S. Morrison*, 121. The impressions of Earl Long are derived from the reminiscences of several people who lived in Louisiana during the late 1940s–late 1950s.

9. Michael L. Kurtz and Morgan D. Peoples, *Earl K. Long: The Saga of Uncle Earl and Louisiana Politics* (Baton Rouge: Louisiana State University Press, 1990), 139–144.

10. Lorin Peterson, *The Day of the Mugwumps* (New York: Random House, 1961), 212.

11. Earl Long was thrice governor of Louisiana; he served out the remainder of Richard Leche's term, from 1939 to 1940, and was elected in his own right to two terms, 1948–1952 and 1956–1960. Louisiana Secretary of State, "Earl Kemp Long" entry, http://www.sos. louisiana.gov/tabid/402/Default.aspx (accessed February 28, 2008).

12. "The Tried and True Technique," *Time*, January 24, 1964, published online at http:// time-proxy.yaga.com/time/magazine/article/qpass/0,10987,875642,00.html?ticket=T%3Av1% 3A9d54355ced34cc247d28fdfd49ff5de7%3A1120745706%3A%252Ftime%252Fmagazine%252F article%252Fqpass%252F0%252C10987%252C875642%252C00.html (accessed July 7, 2005).

13. Haas, *DeLesseps S. Morrison*, 38.

14. Ibid., 202.

15. "Vice, Gaming Squad Goes Into Action," *New Orleans States*, May 7, 1946; "Scores Jailed for Loitering," *New Orleans States*, May 8, 1946; "All Slots in City to Be Destroyed Is Cripps Order," *New Orleans States*, May 9, 1946; "Nab 26 in Drive on Books," *New Orleans States*, May 30, 1946.

16. James Aswell, "New Orleans Takes the Cure," *The Saturday Evening Post*, January 25, 1947, 30.

17. Charles Winick and Paul M. Kinsie, *The Lively Commerce: Prostitution in the United States* (Chicago: Quadrangle Books, 1971), 242.

18. Aswell, "New Orleans Takes the Cure," 108.

19. Ibid., 107.

20. Winick and Kinsie, *The Lively Commerce*, 242.

21. "Police Back Liquor Demand with Threat, Saloonist Says," *Times-Picayune*, January 7, 1949, sect. 1, p. 1.

22. "Continues Fight to Suppress Vice," *Times-Picayune*, January 12, 1949, sect 1, 3.

23. Haas, *DeLesseps S. Morrison*, 111.

24. "Mayor Takes Up Long on Cleanup of Bookies," *Times-Picayune*, December 11, 1950, 1.

25. Haas, *DeLesseps S. Morrison*, 37.

26. Wayne Everard and Irene Wainwright, "Crescent City Choo Choo: A Short History of Railroads in New Orleans," New Orleans Public Library, 2002. Published online at http:// nutrias.org/~nopl/exhibits/choochoo/choochoo.htm (accessed July 30, 2007).

27. "Uplift for the Grande Dame," *Time*, May 20, 1957, http://time-proxy.yaga.com/time/ archive/preview/0,10987,809491,00.html (accessed July 6, 2005).

28. Walter W. Gallas, "Neighborhood Preservation and Politics in New Orleans: Vieux Carré Property Owners, Residents and Associates, Inc. and City Government, 1938–1983" (M.A. thesis, University of New Orleans, 1996), 32.

29. Aswell, "New Orleans Takes the Cure," 54. © 1947, The Saturday Evening Post Society. Used with permission.

30. Haas, *DeLesseps S. Morrison*, 37.

31. Teresa Anne Wilkinson, "Sense of Place and Preservation Planning: An Analysis of the New Orleans Vieux Carré from 1718 to 1985" (M.A. thesis, University of New Orleans, 1985), 78–79.

32. Ibid., 80.

33. John Foley, "Neighborhood Movements, Identity and Change in New Orleans' French Quarter" (Ph.D. diss., University of New Orleans, 1999), 66.

34. 1949 New Orleans City Directory, R. L. Polk Co., volume LXVII.

35. "Tennessean Dies of Heart Attack," *Times-Picayune*, January 1, 1950; Haas, *DeLesseps S. Morrison*, 182.

36. Peterson, *The Day of the Mugwumps*, 214.

37. Haas, *DeLesseps S. Morrison*, 181.

38. Peterson, *The Day of the Mugwumps*, 215.

39. U.S. Congress, Senate Special Committee to Investigate Organized Crime in Interstate Commerce 1951, *Third Interim Report*, 82nd Cong., 1st sess., S. Rep 307, 77–87.

40. "Grevemberg, Aids [*sic*] Raid N.O. Club, Arrest Four," *Times-Picayune*, September 11, 1952, 1.

41. Haas, *DeLesseps S. Morrison*, 202–203.

42. Ibid., 210.

43. *Roy Maggio Et Als Vs. City of New Orleans, de Lesseps S. Morrison, Mayor, Provosty A. Dayries, Superintendent of Police*, No. 364, 219. Civil District Court for The Parish of Orleans, August 6, 1958, 57.

44. Kurtz and Peoples, *Earl K. Long*, 183.

45. Peterson, *The Day of the Mugwumps*, 215.

46. Mary Foster, "Stella Maris Center Made Over into Condos," *Times-Picayune*, December 9, 1995.

47. B. I. Krebs and William E. Keith, "Eisenhower Sees Re-Enactment of Louisiana Transfer to U.S," *Times-Picayune*, October 18, 1953.

48. Jacob Morrison, *Historic Preservation Law* (New Orleans: Pelican Publishing Company, 1957); subsequent editions 1965, 1974.

49. Mrs. Jacob (Mary) Morrison, interview by John Geyser, New Orleans, Friends of the Cabildo Oral History Project, 1977.

50. "Saved From Slums, and at a Profit," *Times-Picayune Dixie Roto Magazine*, April 8, 1956, 10–12.

51. Jacob Morrison to Tony Wrenn, May 6, 1963. Mary Meeks Morrison and Jacob Morrison Papers, MSS 553, Box 117, The Historic New Orleans Collection.

52. Leon A. Pradel to Vieux Carré Restorations, Inc. Stockholders, April 25, 1961. Mary Meeks Morrison and Jacob Morrison Papers, MSS 553, Box 117, The Historic New Orleans Collection.

53. Jacob Morrison to Tony Wrenn.

54. Al Rose, *Storyville, New Orleans* (Tuscaloosa: University of Alabama Press, 1974), 15.

55. Ibid., 129.

56. Ibid., 208.

57. Pat O'Rourke, interview by Scott S. Ellis, New Orleans, March 20, 2005.

58. Ibid.

59. John Loughery, *The Other Side of Silence* (New York: Henry Holt and Company, 1998), 241–248.

60. William Manchester, *Goodbye, Darkness* (New York: Dell Publishing, 1982), 122.

61. Doug MacCash, "The Night They Raided the Quorum," *Times-Picayune*, June 27, 2004.

62. Haas, *DeLesseps S. Morrison*, illustration following 114.

63. Edward Haas to Scott S. Ellis, October 20, 2003, by e-mail.

64. *Roy Maggio Et Als Vs. City of New Orleans*, "Supplemental Memorandum of Authorities;" the ordinance was Section 5-66, CCS 18, 537. This section was repealed in its entirety March 18, 1993, by enactment of ordinance 15,767. Irene Wainwright, "Notes on Ordinance 18,537 Repeal," New Orleans Public Library, Louisiana Division, City Archives/ Special Collections, April 14, 2007. The same council session repealed ordinance 14,240, enacted March 13, 1935, that prohibited cross-dressing in public except on Mardi Gras. Dawn Ruth, "City Ban on Gay Bar Employees Repealed," *Times-Picayune*, May 17, 1993.

65. Some passages of *Roy Maggio Et Als Vs. City of New Orleans* call this the Starlit lounge; it was also referred to as the Starlight, which I think is the most probable name.

66. *Roy Maggio Et Als Vs. City of New Orleans*, 78.

67. John J. Bennett, Jr., *French Quarter Interviews* (New Orleans: Vagabond Press, 1969), 36. This work relates a long-standing impression of 738 Toulouse, which later became the Dungeon, a membership-only straight club, as a "gay address."

68. Bureau of Identification, New Orleans Police Department, Record No. 71487 of John MacFarlain and Record No. 69090 of Louis Robicheaux as included in *Roy Maggio Et Als Vs. City of New Orleans*.

69. Peterson, *The Day of the Mugwumps*, 215.

70. Mayor's Special Citizens Committee; Jacob Morrison et al., "Report of Committee on the Problem of Sex Deviates in New Orleans," New Orleans, Mayor's Special Citizens Committee, 1959.

71. Civil District Court for the Parish of Orleans, Division F, No. 364-219, Order of August 6, 1958, as included in *Roy Maggio Et Als Vs. City of New Orleans*.

72. Mayor's Special Citizens Committee, "Report of Committee on the Problem of Sex Deviates in New Orleans," 12.

73. Ibid., 7.

74. Provosty A. Dayries, Letter, "Dear Chief," July 24, 1958, N.O. superintendent of police to twenty-four police departments, New Orleans Police Department, 1958.

75. Mayor's Special Citizens Committee, "Report of Committee on the Problem of Sex Deviates in New Orleans," 6.

76. Section 5-66 of the New Orleans code of ordinances was made more homophobic by council action on January 29, 1959. Mayor Council Series (MCS) No. 1567 prohibited certain classes of persons from working in or patronizing bars. Section 42 of the New Orleans code was amended by MCS 1568; ordinances prohibiting houses of prostitution to include prohibitions against maintaining gathering places for homosexuals and lesbians. Section 5-66 was repealed in its entirety MCS 15, 767 of March 18, 1993. Wainwright, "Notes on Ordinance 18,537 Repeal."

77. Mayor's Special Citizens Committee, "Report of Committee on the Problem of Sex Deviates in New Orleans," 13.

78. *Where New Orleans Shopped*, Greater New Orleans Educational Television Foundation, DVD, New Orleans, 2002.

79. Pat O'Rourke, interview by Scott S. Ellis, New Orleans, March 20, 2005.

80. Martha Ann Samuel, "One-Man Restoration Society," *Times-Picayune Dixie Roto Magazine*, May 24, 1964.

81. Monroe Berger, "Letters from New Orleans," *Annual Review of Jazz Studies 7, 1994–1995*, ed. Edward Berger, David Cayer, Henry Martin, Dan Morgenstern, and Lewis Porter. Institute for Jazz Studies, Rutgers, the State University of New Jersey (Lanham, MD: Scarecrow Press, 1996), 68.

82. Jeff Hannusch, "The South's Swankiest Night Spot: The Legend of the Dew Drop Inn," www.ikoiko.com (accessed February 7, 2006).

83. Jason Berry, Jonathan Foose, and Tad Jones, *Up from the Cradle of Jazz: New Orleans Music Since World War II* (New York: Da Capo Press, 1992), 60.

84. Ibid., 18.

85. Buddy Dilberto, "Protest by Negro Gridders Cancels N.O. All-Star Game," *Times-Picayune*, January 11, 1965.

86. William Carter, *Preservation Hall: Music from the Heart* (New York: W.W. Norton, 1991), 116, 121–122.

87. Michael Hurtt, "Cosimo Matassa: The King of New Orleans Recording Engineers," *Offbeat*, June 2004, 64–65.

88. Ibid.

89. Rick Coleman, *Cosimo 101: 101 Reasons Why Cosimo Matassa, Who Engineered the Sound of Rhythm & Blues and Rock N Roll, Should Be in the Rock N Roll Hall of Fame*, Metairie, Louisiana, Music Commission, 3330 N. Causeway Blvd., Suite 438, http://www .louisianamusic.org/cosimo_101.htm (accessed July 2, 2003).

90. Craig Schumacher and Rodger King, "Cosimo Matassa," *Tape Op*, vol. 40, March/ April 2004.

91. Richard L. Forstall, compiler, *Louisiana Population of Counties [sic] by Decennial Census: 1900 to 1990*, Washington, D.C., U.S. Bureau of the Census, published March 27, 1995, online at www.census.gov/population/cencounts/la190090.txt.

92. "Mayor Queried on Landmarks," *Times-Picayune*, November 29, 1959, 25.

93. Gallas, "Neighborhood Preservation and Politics in New Orleans," 32–33.

94. Liva Baker, *The Second Battle of New Orleans* (New York: Harper Collins, 1996), 408–411.

95. Ibid., 398–399.

96. "D-Day in New Orleans," *Time*, November 28, 1960, http://www.time.com/time/ archive/preview/0,10987,871816,00.html (accessed July 6, 2005); "Fire Hoses Turned on Hundreds Protesting School Integration," *States-Item*, November 16, 1960, 1; "15 Treated for School Mix Violence Injuries," *States-Item*, November 17, 1960, 1; "Louisiana Nightmare," *Newsweek*, November 28, 1960, 19–20.

97. Haas, *DeLesseps S. Morrison*, 285

98. Ibid., 286, 287. Chep again ran unsuccessfully for governor in 1964. Chep Morrison, his seven-year-old son, Randy, and five others were killed in the crash of a chartered plane near Ciudad Victoria, Mexico, on May 23, 1964. "Morrison, 6 Others on Plane Dead," *Times-Picayune*, May 24, 1964.

## Chapter 5

1. Bernard Lemann, *The Vieux Carré: A General Statement* (New Orleans: Tulane University School of Architecture, 1966), 5.

2. New Orleans Ordinance CCS 16,430, enacted March 25, 1946.

3. Jonathan Mark Souther, "City in Amber: Race, Culture and the Tourist Transformation of New Orleans, 1945–1995" (Ph.D. diss., Tulane University, 2003), 38–40.

4. Bureau of Governmental Research, *Vieux Carré Historic District Demonstration Study:* Technical Report on the Environmental Study (Washington: Marcou, O'Leary and Associates, 1968), 56–57.

5. Ibid., 57.

6. Ibid.

7. Souther, "City in Amber," 41–47.

8. "Mrs. Robinson Blasts Motel," *Times-Picayune*, January 17, 1963.

9. Souther, "City in Amber," 46.

10. "Groups Battle Demolitions OK," *Times-Picayune*, December 17, 1962.

11. Teresa Anne Wilkinson, "Sense of Place and Preservation Planning: An Analysis of the New Orleans Vieux Carré from 1718 to 1985" (M.A. thesis, University of New Orleans, 1985), 82.

12. Souther, "City in Amber," 37, 40.

13. Lemann, *The Vieux Carré: A General Statement*, 76–77.

14. Souther, "City in Amber," 40–41.

15. Rick Raber, "Laws Can't Stop Hotel Expansion in French Quarter," *Times-Picayune*, July 31, 1983.

16. Kevin Fox Gotham, "Tourism Gentrification: The Case of New Orleans' Vieux Carré (French Quarter)," *Urban Studies* 42, no.7 (June 2005): 1111. The moratorium was revised in 1982 to permit new hotels in existing Quarter buildings, but retained zoning requirements.

17. Walter Lowery, *912 Orleans Street: The Story of a Rescue* (New Orleans: Hauser Printing, 1965), 23.

18. Edith Elliot Long, *Along the Banquette* (New Orleans: Vieux Carré Property Owners, Residents and Associates, 2004), 25. The stables were built by Paul Préval, and, as does Long, should properly be called Préval's Stables.

19. Martha Ann Samuel, "One-Man Restoration Society," *Times-Picayune Dixie Roto Magazine*, May 24, 1964.

20. William U. Madden, "Bourbon's Entertainment Raucous, But Improving," *New Orleans States-Item*, April 20, 1966, 25.

21. Edward F. Haas, *DeLesseps S. Morrison and the Image of Reform: New Orleans Politics, 1946–1961* (Baton Rouge: Louisiana State University Press 1974), photograph between 210 and 211.

22. Milton E. Brenner, *The Garrison Case: A Study in the Abuse of Power* (New York: Clarkson N. Potter, Inc. 1969), 15.

23. "Quarter Crime Emergency Declared by Police, DA," *New Orleans States-Item*, August 6, 1962; "Resume Quarter Raids, Arrest 14," *New Orleans States-Item*, August 14, 1962; "12 More Nabbed in Quarter Raid," *New Orleans States-Item*, September 1, 1962.

24. "Schiro Orders Bourbon St. Police Rotated; Ask Law Against Barkers," *New Orleans States-Item*, September 4, 1962.

25. "Police Apathetic in Crackdown on Vice, Says DA," *New Orleans States-Item*, August 27, 1962.

26. Howard Jacobs, "Bourbon Street Held 'Eden of Epidermis,'" *Times-Picayune*, August 21, 1973.

27. Iris Kelso, "French Quarter Cleanup Dispute Reaches Peak," *New Orleans States-Item*, September 8, 1962.

28. Brenner, *The Garrison Case*, 15.

29. "15 Nightclubs to Reopen," *New Orleans States-Item*, October 2, 1962.

30. Brenner, *The Garrison Case*, 5.

31. Ibid., 21.

32. "No Place for Seditious Libel," *Time*, December 4,1964, http://time-proxy.yaga.com/time/archive/preview/0,10987,830885,00.html (accessed July 6, 2005).

33. Shaw's indictment was compared to a hypothetical indictment of New York's Robert Moses. James Phelan, *Scandals, Scamps and Scoundrels* (New York: Random House, 1982), 143. Shaw received an outpouring of sympathy from people in all walks of life in New Orleans, including a cabdriver who refused to charge Shaw for his services. James Kirkwood, *American Grotesque* (New York: Harper Perennial, 1992), 31. Shaw was highly regarded by the public, and this regard continued after the indictment. Kirkwood, *American Grotesque*, 25.

34. Kirkwood, *American Grotesque*, 24–31.

35. Phelan, *Scandals, Scamps and Scoundrels*, 150.

36. Madden, "Bourbon's Entertainment Raucous, But Improving."

37. Hotel-Motel Greeters International, Louisiana Charter, *Greeters' Tourist Guide*, vol. 36, no. 16, August 15, 1966, 22.

38. Ibid., 23.

39. Madden, "Bourbon's Entertainment Raucous, But Improving."

40. *Greeters' Tourist Guide*, 7.

41. Catherine M. Vesey, "Tourism as Community Development: A Comparative Analysis of the Vieux Carré and the Lower Garden District from 1950 to 1990," University of New Orleans, College of Urban & Public Affairs, 1999, http://louisdl.louislibraries.org/CUPA/image/9927192072004_VESEY.pdf (accessed August 17, 2005).

42. William Carter, *Preservation Hall: Music from the Heart* (New York: W.W. Norton, 1991).

43. Judy Kolb, "Carnival Costumer Contest," *Vieux Carré Courier*, February 6, 1970, 3. The information about the origins of the Bourbon Street Awards is from the Kolb article; the remainder is from the author's experience.

44. Ordinance 16,430 of March 25, 1946.

45. "Lash Backers of Demolition in Vieux Carré," *New Orleans States-Item*, January 12, 1963.

46. "Louisiana Sugar Exchange Building, North Front & Bienville Streets, New Orleans, Orleans Parish La.," Library of Congress, Prints and Photographs Division, Historic American Buildings Survey, HABS LA-1110, 1963.

47. *Vieux Carré Property Owners and Associates, Inc. et al v. City of New Orleans, et al*, 167 So. 2d 367, 26 La. 788, Supreme Court of Louisiana, 1964.

48. "Quarter Units Hail Decision" *Times-Picayune*, July 3, 1964.

49. Bureau of Governmental Research, *Vieux Carré Historic District Demonstration Study* (Washington: Marcou, O'Leary and Associates, 1968). The volumes of the study were as follows:

> Environmental Survey
> Legal and Administrative Report
> Vieux Carré of New Orleans—Its Plan, Its Growth, Its Architecture
> New Orleans Central Business District Traffic Study
> Evaluation of the Effects of the Proposed Riverfront Expressway
> Technical Report on the Effects of the Proposed Riverfront Expressway
> Economic and Social Study
> Technical Report on the Environmental Study
> Plan and Program for the Preservation of the Vieux Carré

50. Ibid., Economic and Social Study, 36–37.

51. Ibid., 102.

52. Ibid., Technical Report on the Environmental Study, 48.

53. Ibid., Economic and Social Study, 103–104.

54. Ibid., 117–119.

55. James Nolan, "Remembering Kamas: The Square Round Is Also Round," *The New Laurel Review* 16, Annual 1988, 72. Used by permission.

56. Karen Trahan Leathem, "Luring Young Girls to Their Ruin: Liquor, Women and the 1908 Gay-Shattuck Law." Presented at the Louisiana Historical Association Annual Meeting, Lafayette, LA, March 14, 1997.

57. James Nolan, interview by Scott S. Ellis, New Orleans, October 13, 2007.

58. Darlene Fife, *Portraits from Memory: New Orleans in the Sixties* (New Orleans: Surregional Press, 2000), 1.

59. Nolan interview.

60. *The Quorum*, DVD, Door Knob Films, LLC, and Such-A-Much Productions, LLC, 2004.

61. Nolan interview.

62. Doug MacCash, "The Night They Raided the Quorum," *Times-Picayune*, June 27, 2004.

63. Nolan interview.

64. MacCash, "The Night They Raided the Quorum."

65. Nolan, "Remembering Kamas: The Square Round Is Also Round," 73.

66. Nolan interview. Used by permission.

67. *The Vieux Carré Courier*, "Collegiates," May 26–June 1, 1962, 4.

68. "Hippie" was a pejorative term that may have originated with the Beats, as a diminutive of "little hipster." Among themselves, they used the term "freak"; other appellations, like "the travelers," were also used. Darlene Fife, interview by Scott S. Ellis, September 27, 2006, by e-mail. The nonhippie mainstream culture was called "straight" before that came to mean "heterosexual."

69. Nolan interview.

70. Gene Bourg, interview by Scott S. Ellis, New Orleans, October 12, 2003.

71. Dennis McNally, *A Long Strange Trip* (London: Corgi Books, 2003), 501–502.

72. Bill Rushton, "Listless Discontent Litters Jackson Square," *Vieux Carré Courier*, April 14, 1967, 1, 4.

73. Walter Lowery, "What's It Like to Live in the Quarter?," *New Orleans Magazine*, September 1968, 22.

74. "Police Warn Loiterers After 88 Youths Booked," *New Orleans States-Item*, February 9, 1970.

75. Bill Bryan, "Carnival Crisis," *Vieux Carré Courier*, February 13, 1970, 1–2.

76. "Al Hirt's Famous Lip Cut by Brick Hurled at Float," *New Orleans States-Item*, February 9, 1970.

77. Bryan, "Carnival Crisis."

78. Thomas Griffin, "Youth Invasion for Carnival Indicated by Local Children," *New Orleans States-Item*, January 28, 1971, 31.

79. Fife interview.

80. Nolan interview.

81. Bryan, "Carnival Crisis," 2.

82. Thomas Griffin, "Youth Invasion for Carnival"; Fife, *Portraits from Memory*, 44.

83. *Vieux Carré Courier*, "OK . . . But," March 13, 1970, 4.

84. Fife interview.

85. Southern Louisiana Media Corporation, *NOLA Express*, May 9–22, 1969 .

86. Fife, *Portraits from Memory*, 41.

87. Ibid., 39.

88. Sara Jacobelli, "When Buster's Was Around," *The Dagger*, July 1995. http://www .thedagger.com/thedagger/dag_zine/busters.html (accessed August 26, 2006).

89. George Tresch, interview by Scott S. Ellis, July 29, 2006.

90. Fife, *Portraits from Memory*, 45.

91. Tresch interview.

92. Fife interview.

93. Fife, *Portraits from Memory*, 39.

94. Judy Kolb, "HEAD Clinic Helps Kids," *Vieux Carré Courier*, December 12, 1969, 1.

95. *Vieux Carré Courier*, "HEAD," January 2, 1970, 4.

96. Fife, *Portraits from Memory*, 41–44.

97. Roger Nelson, letter to the editor, *Ambush* magazine, October 16–29, 1998.

98. "Carnival, Cops and Confusion," *Vieux Carré Courier*, February 12, 1971, 1, 3; Fife, *Portraits from Memory*, 44.

99. David Cuthbert, "Quarter's Flea Market Does First Day of Trade," *Times-Picayune*, January 10, 1971.

100. Sara Jacobelli, interview by Scott S. Ellis, March 18, 2007, by e-mail.

101. Nolan interview.

102. Joyce Davis and Sandi Donnelly, "Panhandlers, Solicitors Growing Nuisance on Downtown Streets," *Times-Picayune*, February 11, 1973.

103. Fife interview.

104. McNally, *A Long Strange Trip*, 477–479.

105. Jacobelli interview.

106. Bruce Eggler, "No-Left-Turn Won't Send Tourists to Jail," *Times-Picayune*, April 9, 1994, A-1, A-8.

107. *Greta Cazenave, et al, vs. Sheriff Charles C. Foti, Jr., et al*, Civil Action 00-1246, U.S. District Court, Eastern District of Louisiana, December 21, 2006, http://www .nolastripsearch.com/casedoc/Class%20Action%20Settlement%20Agreement.pdf (accessed March 15, 2007).

108. Maureen Olle, *French Quarter Population, "Re: Request for Specific Census Data,"* e-mail to Scott S. Ellis, Louisiana State University Library, August 7, 2003.

## Chapter 6

1. Luis C. Hennick and E. Harper Charlton, *The Streetcars of New Orleans* (Gretna: Firebird Press, 2000), 5.

2. Ibid., 23.

3. Robert S. Sargent, Jr., *The New Orleans Streetcars*. Enter Stage Right, http://www .enterstageright.com/archive/articles/1004/1004neworleanssc-p1-thedemise.htm (accessed April 1, 2005).

4. Hennick and Charlton, *The Streetcars of New Orleans*, 70.

5. Ibid., 73–104.

6. Sargent, *The New Orleans Streetcars*, 2–3.

7. Hennick and Charlton, *The Streetcars of New Orleans*, 80.

8. Ibid., 75.

9. "Council Kills Monorail Plan," *Times-Picayune*, March 8, 1958, 1.

10. Bill Rushton, "Cityscape/Monorails and the UPT," *Vieux Carré Courier*, March 27, 1970, 7.

11. Matt Scallan, "Airport, CBD Railway Explored," *Times-Picayune*, June 12, 2000.

12. Robert A. Caro, *The Power Broker* (New York: Random House Vintage Books, 1975), 926–927.

13. Richard O. Baumbach, Jr., and William E. Borah, *The Second Battle of New Orleans* (Tuscaloosa: University of Alabama Press, 1981), 30. (This is not to be confused with Liva Baker's *The Second Battle of New Orleans* [New York: Harper Collins, 1996], which deals with school desegregation.)

14. Ibid.

15. Ibid., 32, 34; Edward F. Haas, *DeLesseps S. Morrison and the Image of Reform: New Orleans Politics, 1946–1961* (Baton Rouge: Louisiana State University Press, 1974), 42–43.

16. Baumbach and Borah, *The Second Battle of New Orleans*, 34–35.

17. Ibid., 36.

18. Ibid., 31.

19. Ibid., 118–119.

20. Ibid., 43.

21. Tom Bethell, "Road Foes Borah & Baumbach: A Tale of Two Citizens," *Vieux Carré Courier*, March 23–29, 1973, 4.

22. William Borah, interview by Scott S. Ellis, New Orleans, July 29, 2006.

23. Peter Graffagnino, "New Orleans in the Thirties," *Muscogee County (Georgia) Medical Bulletin* 20, no. 1 (1979).

24. Borah interview.

25. Baumbach and Borah, *The Second Battle of New Orleans*, 83.

26. Richard O. Baumbach and William Borah, "STOP! The Riverfront Expressway," *Times-Picayune*, sect. 1, 17, March 14, 1966.

27. Borah interview.

28. Baumbach and Borah, "STOP! The Riverfront Expressway."

29. Borah interview. Used by permission.

30. Elizabeth A. Masters, "Martha Robinson and French Quarter Preservation" (honors thesis, Tulane University, 1985), 24.

31. Borah interview; Bethell, "Road Foes Borah & Baumbach," 2.

32. Baumbach and Borah, *The Second Battle of New Orleans*, 43, 68–70.

33. Ibid.,44.

34. Rob Walker, *Under the Freeway*. Brooklyn: Flâneur, April 2002, http://www.flaneur.org/04_02/0402_walker.html (accessed April 1, 2005).

35. Hoke May, "New Orleans Traffic—Black Days Ahead," *New Orleans Magazine*, January 1969, 30.

36. Baumbach and Borah, *The Second Battle of New Orleans*, 28.

37. Bureau of Governmental Research, *Vieux Carré Historic District Demonstration Study:* Evaluation of the Effects of the Proposed Riverfront Expressway (Washington: Marcou, O'Leary and Associates, 1968), 9.

38. Ibid., 24–29.

39. Ibid., photo, 115.

40. Caro, *The Power Broker*, 930–939.

41. Borah interview.

42. Sargent, *The New Orleans Streetcars*; New Orleans Regional Transit Authority, "Canal Streetcar Fact Sheet," http://www.norta.com/news/canal/fact.php (accessed April 1, 2005).

43. Ronald H. Deiter, *The Story of Metro* (Glendale, CA: Interurban Press, 1990), 32.

44. Borah interview; Baumbach and Borah, *The Second Battle of New Orleans*, 140.

45. Ibid., 144.

46. Masters, "Martha Robinson," 26–27.

47. Baumbach and Borah, *The Second Battle of New Orleans*, 44, 49.

48. Caro, *The Power Broker*, 914–918.

49. Baumbach and Borah, *The Second Battle of New Orleans*, 74.

50. Ibid., 75.

51. Haas, *DeLesseps S. Morrison*, 287.

52. Baumbach and Borah, *The Second Battle of New Orleans*, 57, 75–77.

53. May, "New Orleans Traffic—Black Days Ahead," 39.

54. Baumbach and Borah, *The Second Battle of New Orleans*, 204.

55. The news broke on July 1, 1969. Baumbach and Borah, *The Second Battle of New Orleans*, 193.

56. Bethell, "Road Foes Borah & Baumbach," 4.

57. Ibid.

58. New Orleans Regional Transit Authority, "Canal Streetcar Fact Sheet."

59. Ibid.

60. Thomas Head, "Dining Out on U Street and Shaw," *Washingtonian Magazine*, December 1, 2005.

61. "Facelifting the Square," *Times-Picayune*, December 16, 1975; Frank L. Schneider, "Jackson Square: Anxiety Behind the Scenes," *Times-Picayune*, April 6, 1975.

62. University of New Orleans, College of Urban and Public Affairs, *Changing Land Use in the Vieux Carré: Managing Growth to Preserve a National Landmark District*, New Orleans, 1992, 4–17.

63. "Traffic Rules Are Announced," *Times-Picayune*, December 28, 1973.

64. Frank Donze, "Quarter Bus Ban Takes Hold; Hotel Operators Shift Operations Gradually," *Times-Picayune*, April 11, 1997.

65. Charles Green, "Council Okays Mini-Buses for French Quarter Routes," *Times-Picayune*, March 16, 1973.

66. Borah interview.

67. Frank Donze, "Morial Drops Support for Pedicabs," *Times Picayune*, August 25, 2000.

68. Gordon Russell, "Pedicab Service to Seek New Federal Trial," *Times-Picayune*, October 25, 2002.

69. Donze, "Morial Drops Support for Pedicabs."

70. Frank Donze, "Pedicab Proposal Back in Motion," *Times-Picayune*, April 30, 2001.

71. Ibid.

72. Borah interview.

73. Bernard Lemann, *The Vieux Carré: A General Statement* (New Orleans: Tulane University School of Architecture, 1966), 73.

74. Louisiana Department of Transportation, "Crescent City Connection Bridges," Baton Rouge, http://www.dotd.state.la.us/operations/cccd/bridges.asp (accessed April 6, 2005).

## Chapter 7

1. Louisiana Mid-Continent Oil and Gas Association, "Historical Highlights for the LA Oil and Gas Industry," www.lmoga.com/history.html (accessed May 5, 2005).

2. "One Down," *Time*, September 25, 1939, http://time-proxy.yaga.com/time/archive/preview/0,10987,761953,00.html (accessed July 6, 2005). Leche was eventually convicted of mail fraud unrelated to the oil issue, served nearly five years in federal prison, and was pardoned by President Truman in 1952. Louisiana Secretary of State, "Richard Webster Leche," http://www.sec.state.la.us/64.htm (accessed March 6, 2007).

3. Pam Radtke Russell, "Going with the Flow," *Times-Picayune*, September 10, 2006.

4. Ibid.

5. Ibid.

6. "The Outsider Makes It Big," *Time*, November 5, 1979, http://time-proxy.yaga.com/time/archive/preview/0,10987,912529,00.html (accessed July 6, 2005).

7. Maureen Olle, *French Quarter Population, "Re: Request for Specific Census Data,"* e-mail to Scott S. Ellis, Louisiana State University Library, August 7, 2003.

8. Jonathan Mark Souther, "City in Amber: Race, Culture and the Tourist Transformation of New Orleans, 1945–1995" (Ph.D. diss., Tulane University, 2003) 240–242.

9. Ibid., 222, note 71.

10. James R. Bobo, *The New Orleans Economy: Pro Bono Publico?* (New Orleans: University of New Orleans, College of Business Administration, 1975), 16.

11. John Maginnis, "Legislature's Bad Image Proves Useful," *Times-Picayune*, February 28, 2007.

12. Bobo, *The New Orleans Economy: Pro Bono Publico?*, 114.

13. Ibid., 128.

14. The NASA reservation is currently named the John C. Stennis Space Center.

15. Sandy Smith, "Brazen Empire of Crime, Part II," *Life*, September 8, 1967, 94–97.

16. Charles Y. W. Chai, "Who Rules New Orleans? A Study of Community Power Structure," *Louisiana Business Survey* 2 (October 1971): 11.

17. James Gill, *Lords of Misrule: Mardi Gras and the Politics of Race in New Orleans* (Jackson: University Press of Mississippi, 1997), 219–220; Lawrence M. Knopp, Jr., "Gentrification and Gay Community Development in a New Orleans Neighborhood" (Ph.D. diss., University of Iowa, August 1989), 66.

18. Walter Lowery, *912 Orleans Street: The Story of a Rescue* (New Orleans: Hauser Printing, 1965), 52. Used by permission.

19. Ibid., 23.

20. Nicholas Lemann, "Hard Times in the Big Easy; New Orleans," *Atlantic Monthly*, August 1, 1987, 1 of downloaded edition; Knopp, "Gentrification and Gay Community Development," 100–101.

21. Bobo, *The New Orleans Economy: Pro Bono Publico?*, 41.

22. Ibid., 129.

23. Vieux Carré Commission, Vieux Carré Survey, Square 82, Lot 23050-01, addendum, from the Historic American Buildings Survey 1939–1940.

24. "Gay Liberation Group Marches," *Times-Picayune*, January 24, 1971, sect. 1, 16.

25. William H. Adler, "'Liberation' Goal of Gay March," *States-Item*, January 23, 1971, 1; "Gay Lib Demonstrates," *Vieux Carré Courier*, February 5, 1971, 1, 7, 12.

26. George Tresch, interview by Scott S. Ellis, New Orleans, July 29, 2006.

27. Lili LeGardeur, "Has Cabrini Park Gone to the Dogs?," *Times-Picayune*, May 23, 2002.

28. Associated Press, "'73 Parades Will Bypass Quarter," *Times-Picayune*, August 25, 1972.

29. Mike Early, interview by Scott S. Ellis, New Orleans, July 29, 2006.

30. "Allen" (pseud.), interview by Scott S. Ellis, New Orleans, October 14, 2007.

31. Jon Newlin, interview by Scott S. Ellis, New Orleans, March 19, 2005.

32. Ibid.

33. James T. Sears, *Rebels, Rubyfruit and Rhinestones: Queering Space in the Stonewall South* (Piscataway, New Jersey: Rutgers University Press, 2001), 102.

34. Newlin interview.

35. Rev. William P. Richardson, Jr., interview by Dorothy Mahan, New Orleans, *Friends of the Cabildo: Oral History Series*, February 18, 1990.

36. Sears, *Rebels, Rubyfruit and Rhinestones*, 104.

37. Bruce Nolan and Chris Segura, "Memorial for Fire Dead Has Forgiveness Theme," *Times-Picayune*, June 26, 1973.

38. Sears, *Rebels, Rubyfruit and Rhinestones*, 100.

39. Rich Magill, *Exposing Hatred—A Report on the Victimization of Lesbian and Gay People in New Orleans, Louisiana* (New Orleans: Louisiana Lesbian and Gay Political Action Caucus, 1991), 51.

40. Richardson interview.

41. Troy D. Perry, with Thomas L. P. Swicegood, *Don't Be Afraid Anymore: The Story of Reverend Troy Perry and the Metropolitan Community Churches* (New York: St. Martin's Press, 1990), 90; Tresch interview.

42. Perry, *Don't Be Afraid Anymore*, 91. Used by permission.

43. Magill, *Exposing Hatred*, 51.

44. Perry, *Don't Be Afraid Anymore*, 101.

45. Joan Treadway, "Gay Community Surfaces in Tragedy of N.O. Fire," part 1, *Times-Picayune*, September 11,1973, sect. 1, 13; Joan Treadway, "Independent Route Taken for Personal Objectives," part 2, *Times-Picayune*, September 12, 1973, sect. 2, 8; Joan Treadway, "Homosexuals Disagree on Behavior's 'Sickness,'" part 3, *Times-Picayune*, September 13, 1973, sect. 4, 2; Joan Treadway, "Psychiatric and Clerical Views Wide Spectrum," part 4, *Times-Picayune*, September 14,1973, sect. 1, 18; Joan Treadway, "It's Not Illegal to BE Gay—Certain Acts Are Criminal," part 5, *Times-Picayune*, September 15, 1973, sect. 1, 14; Joan Treadway, "'50s 'Climate of Hostility' to Gays Gone, What Now?," part 6, *Times-Picayune*, September 16,1973, sect. 1, 21.

46. Treadway, "It's Not Illegal to BE Gay—Certain Acts Are Criminal."

47. Treadway, "'50s 'Climate of Hostility' to Gays Gone, What Now?"

48. Treadway, "Independent Route Taken for Personal Objectives."

49. Tresch interview.

50. Treadway, "It's Not Illegal to BE Gay—Certain Acts Are Criminal."

51. Ibid.

52. "946 Violations Noted in Vieux Carré Checks," *Times-Picayune*, July 20, 1973.

53. Ken Weiss, "VCC Director Criticizes Disaster Area Rhetoric," *Times-Picayune*, July 18, 1973.

54. Carol Flake, "The Lavender Hill Mob Takes on Anita Bryant," *Figaro*, New Orleans, June 29, 1977.

55. "City Quarter Plan Opposed," *Times-Picayune*, May 31, 1973.

56. "Judge Stops Sound-Light Until Plan Satisfies Laws," *Times-Picayune*, October 25, 1973.

57. Leonard V. Huber, *Jackson Square Through the Years* (New Orleans: Friends of the Cabildo, 1982), 115–116.

58. Early interview; Ann Veigle, "Changed Street Has Business Rolling on the River," *Times-Picayune*, August 31, 1986.

59. "Allen" (pseud.) interview. Used by permission.

60. New Orleans City Directory for 1985, R. L. Polk Company.

61. Veigle, "Changed Street Has Business Rolling on the River." The businessman quoted was Sidney Pampo, owner of Sidney's Newsstand.

62. Ibid.

63. Newlin interview.

64. Tresch interview .

65. James Nolan, interview by Scott S. Ellis, New Orleans, October 13, 2007.

66. Robyn Halvorsen, interview by Scott S. Ellis, New Orleans, September 29, 2006. Used by permission.

67. Ibid.

68. Nolan interview. Used by permission.

69. Paul Atkinson, "Dupuy Will Try to Keep Tujague's in Vieux Carré," *Times-Picayune*, March 22, 1974.

70. Frank L. Schneider, "Jackson Square: Anxiety Behind the Scenes," *Times-Picayune*, April 6, 1975.

71. Halvorsen interview.

72. David Cuthbert, "Quarter's Flea Market Does First Day of Trade," *Times-Picayune*, January 10, 1971.

73. Halvorsen interview.

74. Andrei Codrescu, *New Orleans, Mon Amour* (Chapel Hill: Algonquin Books, 2006), 207–209.

75. Halvorsen interview.

76. Ibid.

77. William Borah, interview by Scott S. Ellis, New Orleans, July 29, 2006.

78. Betty Carter, interview by Anne Ritchie, Women in Journalism Oral History Project of the Washington Press Club Foundation, April 10, 1990, in the Oral History Collection of Columbia University and other repositories, http://press.org/wpforal/cart.htm (accessed June 24, 2006).

79. Mary Foster, "Stella Maris Center Made Over into Condos," *Times-Picayune*, December 9, 1995.

80. Martine Geronimi, *The French Market New Orleans Style: Preservation of the Past, Patrimonal Alibi and Glorification of Commerce*, Society for the Study of Architecture in Canada (SSAC), 2001, autumn issue, http://membres.lycos.fr/mappamundi/market.html (accessed November 15, 2001).

81. J. E. Burgoyne, "Winds of Change Shift French Market Smells," *Times-Picayune*, December 17, 1972, sect. 3, 8.

82. Ibid.

83. Liz Scott, "Trials and Errors: The Saga of Clay Shaw," *New Orleans Magazine*, November 1999, 14–15.

84. "Project Reason Slated by Shaw," *Times-Picayune*, February 28, 1973.

85. Atkinson, "Dupuy Will Try to Keep Tujague's in Vieux Carré."

86. Jack Davis, "French Market Dedicated; Mayor Blasts Project's Critics," *States-Item*, April 1, 1975.

87. Millie Ball, "Last Retail Fish Stall to Leave French Market," *Times-Picayune*, February 11, 1974.

88. Chris Segura, "Last Call Morning Call; Coffee Shop Shuts Its Doors," *Times-Picayune*, March 1,1974.

89. Stella Pitts, "French Market Renovation Closes Battistella's for Good," *Times-Picayune*, October 6, 1974.

90. New Orleans Public Library, "Dedication of the Renovated French Market, April 1, 1975," photograph 7, 12 of Mayor Moon Landrieu Photograph Collection, City Archives, http://nutrias.org/~nopl/photos/landrieu/m1195.htm (accessed February 9, 2006).

91. James Kirkwood, *American Grotesque* (New York: Harper Perennial, 1992), 658.

92. New Orleans Public Library, "Dutch Alley," Mayor Ernest N. Morial Photographs Collection, City Archives, http://nutrias.org/photos/enm/enm29_417.htm (accessed February 9, 2006).

## Chapter 8

1. Rick Delaup, "Gallery of Eccentrics," http://www.eccentricneworleans.com/gallery_of_eccentrics.htm (accessed November 2, 2006).

2. Don Lee Keith, "The Bead Lady & Others," *New Orleans Magazine*, February 1991, 137. Used by permission of Renaissance Publishing.

3. The information about Ruthie's early years is from *Ruthie the Duck Girl*, DVD, Rick Delaup, New Orleans, 1999. The remainder is from the author's experience.

4. Chris Rose, "Accidental Tourist Attraction, Closed," *Times-Picayune*, December 4, 1999.

5. Chris Rose, "Rest in Peace, Ruthie," *Times-Picayune*, September 21, 2008.

6. Herbert Asbury, *The French Quarter: An Informal History of the New Orleans Underworld* (New York: Garden City Publishing, 1938), 99.

7. Robert Herndon, *Eight Days with Bob Harrington* (Nashville: Benson Printing Company, 1974), 66.

8. Ibid., 38.

9. Associated Press, "Bourbon Street Wants Protesters to Stay Away," September 3, 2004; Bruce Eggler, "City Council Restricts Bullhorns in Quarter," *Times-Picayune*, November 5, 2004.

10. Delaup, "Gallery of Eccentrics."

11. Chris Sheraouse, "New Orleans Mecca Sought by Runaways," *States-Item*, January 28, 1971, 31.

12. Christina Vella, *Intimate Enemies* (Baton Rouge: Louisiana State University Press, 1997), 273.

13. Mike Early, interview by Scott S. Ellis, New Orleans, July 29, 2006.

14. *City of New Orleans and the Vieux Carre Commission v. Board of Directors of the Louisiana State Museum, James Sefcik; Tammany Contracting Company; and the Department of Culture, Recreation and Tourism*, No. 98-C-1170. Supreme Court of Louisiana, 1998.

15. Stewart Yerton, "Mean Streets; Merchants Want Police to Curb Street People to Keep the French Quarter Out of the Gutter," *Times-Picayune*, October 15, 1995.

16. Mike Guy, "Gutterpunks," *Rolling Stone*, May 15, 2003, 59–66.

17. Yerton, "Mean Streets."

18. Elizabeth Mullener, "Clarkson's Crusade," *Times-Picayune*, June 22, 2003.

19. New Orleans Ordinance 54-412.

20. "Homeless Problem in Quarter," *Times-Picayune*, August 23, 1995, B4.

21. Susan Finch and Coleman Warner, "Destitute Pose Dilemma in Tourist Town," *Times-Picayune*, January 24, 1996.

22. Ibid.

23. Roger Nelson, letter to the editor, *Ambush* magazine, October 16–29, 1998.

24. Guy, "Gutterpunks."

25. Nikki Usher, "Gutterpunk Paradise," *Times-Picayune*, August 25, 2003.

26. Yerton, "Mean Streets."

27. Keith Spera, "El Matador Exits," *Times-Picayune*, January 9, 2004.

28. Chris Rose, "The Hustler," *Times-Picayune*, July 3, 2005.

29. John Schwartz, "For Harry Anderson, the New Orleans Magic Is Gone," *New York Times*, August 30, 2006.

## Chapter 9

1. Illinois Central Railroad, *New Orleans for the Tourist*, Chicago, 1907, unpaginated.

2. John Galsworthy, "That Old-Time Place" in *The Inn of Tranquility*, 1912. Published online by the University of Adelaide at http://etext.library.adelaide.edu.au/g/galsworthy/john/inn/ (accessed March 10, 2008).

3. Chance Harvey, *The Life and Selected Letters of Lyle Saxon* (Gretna: Pelican Publishing, 2003), 62–63.

4. John J. Bennett, Jr., *French Quarter Interviews* (New Orleans: Vagabond Press, 1969), 41.

5. Russell Levy, "Of Bards and Bawds: New Orleans Sporting Life Before and During the Storyville Era, 1897-1917" (M.A. thesis, Tulane University, 1967), 60–63.

6. Cosimo Matassa, interview by Scott S. Ellis, New Orleans, April 24, 2004. The origin of "vidalia" as a synonym for "prospective john" is uncertain. Christine Wiltz's *The*

*Last Madam* maintains that the term was adopted from the name of Norma Wallace's dog (Christine Wiltz, *The Last Madam: A Life in the New Orleans Underworld* [Cambridge, MA: Da Capo Press, 2000], 29). Cosimo Matassa told me he thought since many prostitutes were country girls lured into the life, and vidalia onions come from rural areas, that association may have been made. Another theory is that these prospective johns could, through liquor and temptation, be "peeled" of their money.

7. Anthony Stanonis, *An Old House in the Quarter: Vice in the Vieux Carré of the 1930s*, Loyola University Student Historical Journals, 1997, vol. 28, http://www.loyno.edu/~history/journal/1996-7/Stanonis.html, 6 of downloaded edition (accessed October 18, 2003).

8. Harvey, *The Life and Selected Letters of Lyle Saxon*, 177–178.

9. Federal Writers' Project, Works Progress Administration, *New Orleans City Guide*, 1st ed. (Cambridge, MA: Riverside Press, 1938). The *New Orleans City Guide*, edited by Robert Tallant, a protégé of Lyle Saxon, was revised and reissued in 1952.

10. Work Projects Administration, *A Tour Of the French Quarter for Servicemen* (New Orleans: Work Projects Administration Recreational Council for New Orleans, 1941).

11. Monroe Berger, "Letters from New Orleans," *Annual Review of Jazz Studies 7: 1994–1995*, ed. Edward Berger, David Cayer, Henry Martin, Dan Morgenstern, and Lewis Porter. Institute for Jazz Studies, Rutgers, the State University of New Jersey (Lanham, MD: Scarecrow Press, 1996), 51.

12. Fannie B. Campbell Welsh, *Mercedes, a New Orleans Hurricane!* (Houston: The Anson Jones Press, 1948), 114–116.

13. "Collegiates," *Vieux Carré Courier*, May 26–June 1, 1962, 4.

14. Al Rose, *Storyville, New Orleans* (Tuscaloosa: University of Alabama Press, 1974), 174.

15. Bennett, *French Quarter Interviews*, 41.

16. Tao Woolfe, "Cities Seek Ways to Take Party Out of Spring Break," *Times-Picayune*, April 4, 1993.

17. The Associated Press, "Spring Breakers Relocate; Panama City Is Party Central," *Times-Picayune*, March 21, 1994.

18. Columbia Broadcasting System, "Bedlam on Bourbon Street," *48 Hours*, broadcast March 10, 1993, no. 232. BurrellesLuce Transcripts, 22.

19. Nina J.Sines and John Ekman. "The Minimum Drinking Age and Alcohol Policy: An Historical Overview and Response to the Renewed Debate In Wisconsin," University of Wisconsin Law School, Resource Center on Impaired Driving, Resource Center Report 96-1, April 1996, www.law.wisc.edu/rcid/reports/report0496.htm (accessed March 10, 2008). The federal statute is 23 USC § 158.

20. Rick Bragg, "Louisiana Stands Alone on Drinking at 18," *New York Times*, March 23, 1996.

21. Stewart Yerton, "Passing the Other Bar Exam," *Times-Picayune*, December 19, 1999.

22. Michael Perlstein, "MADD Descends on Big Easy for Convention," *Times-Picayune*, September 13, 2003.

23. Mardi Gras Unmasked.com, "The Crackdown That Wasn't," 2000, www.mardigrasunmasked.com/mardigras/carnivalcourier/crackdown.htm (accessed March 10, 2008).

24. New Orleans Code of Ordinances, Sec. 54-413.

25. Mardi Gras Unmasked.com. "The Crackdown That Wasn't."

26. Ibid.

27. Earl Bernhardt, interview by Scott S. Ellis, New Orleans, December 1, 2006.

28. Elisabeth Butler, "Tourism Still Rebounding from Shock of 9-11," *New Orleans City Business*, September 9, 2002.

29. Stanonis, *An Old House in the Quarter*, 5 of downloaded edition.

30. Robert Kinney, *The Bachelor in New Orleans* (New Orleans: Bob Riley Studios, 1942).

31. Wiltz, *The Last Madam:A Life in the New Orleans Underworld*, 181.

32. Rose, *Storyville, New Orleans*, 154.

33. Matassa interview.

34. Bessiane Parker, interview by Scott S. Ellis, New Orleans, April 20, 2007.

35. This phrase, used in conjunction with Las Vegas tourism, is a registered trademark of the Las Vegas Convention and Visitors Authority. U.S. Patent and Trademark Office, http://tess2.uspto.gov/bin/showfield?f=doc&state=jnbl01.2.4 (accessed February 26, 2008).

36. Reminiscence of the author.

37. James T. Sears, *Rebels, Rubyfruit and Rhinestones: Queering Space in the Stonewall South* (Piscataway, New Jersey: Rutgers University Press, 2001), 96–97. The information about the origins of Southern Decadence is from *Rebels, Rubyfruit and Rhinestones*; the remainder is from the author's experience.

38. Keith Darce, "Southern Decadence Means Big Business; Gay Tourists Give Summer a Boost," *Times-Picayune*, September 4, 1998.

39. Jon Kemp, "Southern Decadence Just Around Corner," *Times-Picayune*, September 2, 2004.

40. James Van Dorin to Scott S. Ellis, November 5, 2007.

41. Allen G. Breed, "French Quarter Holdouts Create Tribes," The Associated Press, September 4, 2005, http://www.wwltv.com/sharedcontent/nationworld/katrina/stories/0904 05cckatrinajrfrenchquarter.26851646.html (accessed August 31, 2006).

42. John Foley, "Neighborhood Movements, Identity and Change in New Orleans' French Quarter" (Ph.D. diss., University of New Orleans, 1999), 113.

43. "Quarter Business Loss Laid to Anti-Mix Laws," *New Orleans States-Item*, September 7, 1962.

44. Marty Mulé, "Standing on Principle," *Times-Picayune*, January 24, 1995.

45. Buddy Dilberto, "Protest by Negro Gridders Cancels N.O. All-Star Game," *Times-Picayune*, January 11, 1965.

46. Jonathan Mark Souther, "City in Amber: Race, Culture and the Tourist Transformation of New Orleans, 1945–1995" (Ph.D. diss., Tulane University, 2003), 227.

47. Mulé, "Standing on Principle."

48. Souther, "City in Amber," 225–236.

49. From time to time, there have been black gay bars in the Quarter. Wolfendale's on North Rampart was one.

50. State Farm Bayou Classic, "The History of the Bayou Classic," www.statefarmbayouclassic.com/ (accessed December 2005); "Bayou Classic and Big Easy," *Times-Picayune*, November 30, 1996.

51. Lynne Jensen, "N.O. Set for Classic Party; Bayou Bash Demands Traffic Crowd Plan; 100,000 Expected to Converge for Classic," *Times-Picayune*, November 19, 2000; Pamela Coyle, "Name of Game Is See and Be Seen; 'Classic Is Cars and Chillin,'" *Times-Picayune*, November 29, 1997.

52. Allen Powell III, "Man Dies After Fight with Nightclub Bouncers," *Times-Picayune*, January 1, 2005.

53. "Restrictions on use of force by persons employed by bars, lounges, and nightclubs located within the Vieux Carré." New Orleans City Code of Ordinances, Sect. 10-187, Municode.com.

54. James Varney, "Testers Find Racial Bias by Nightclubs," *Times-Picayune*, March 30, 2005.

55. James Varney, "Old Law Among New Tools to Stop Bar Bias," *Times-Picayune*. May 22, 2005.

56. Ibid.

57. New Orleans District Attorney, "Razzoo Case," press release, October 1, 2008.

58. Arnold Genthe, *Impressions of Old New Orleans* (New York: George H. Doran Company, 1926), 13.

59. Bruce Eggler, "City Council Puts Limits on Walking Tours," *Times-Picayune*, July 18, 2003.

60. Bruce Eggler, "Walking Tours Limits Inspire Heated Debate," *Times-Picayune*, May 20, 2003.

61. Eggler, "City Council Puts Limits on Walking Tours."

62. National Park Service, "Jean Lafitte National Historical Park and Preserve," www.nps.gov/jela (accessed March 10, 2008); Mary S. Jones, "Vieux Carré National Park; Park Services Takes Turn Through the Quarter," *Times-Picayune*, January 15, 1999.

63. National Park Service, "About the Park: Our Mission." New Orleans Jazz National Historical Park Web site, www.nps.gov/jazz/mission.htm (accessed November 7, 2005).

64. Souther, "City in Amber," 307.

65. Ibid., 311.

66. Ibid., 312.

67. Bernard Lemann, *The Vieux Carré: A General Statement* (New Orleans: Tulane University School of Architecture, 1966), 29.

68. Kevin Fox Gotham, "Tourism Gentrification: The Case of New Orleans' Vieux Carré (French Quarter)," *Urban Studies* 42, no.7 (June 2005): 1111.

69. Tom Bissell, interview by Scott S. Ellis, New Orleans, March 19, 2005.

70. Ibid.

71. Bruce Eggler, "Planners Divided on Quarter Hotel," *Times-Picayune*, June 14, 2006.

72. Bruce Eggler, "Quarter Hotel Plan Is Withdrawn," *Times-Picayune*, August 3, 2006.

73. Elizabeth Mullener, "The Locals: Drawn By Charm, Driven Out by Crowds," *Times-Picayune*, May 16, 1994.

74. Souther, "City in Amber," 88–94.

## Chapter 10

1. Pierce F. Lewis, *New Orleans: The Making of an Urban Landscape*, 2nd ed. (Charlottesville: University Press of Virginia, 2003), 177, figure 65.

2. Arnold R. Hirsch and Joseph Logsdon, eds., *Creole New Orleans: Race and Americanization* (Baton Rouge: Louisiana State University Press, 1992).

3. Lyle Kenneth Perkins, "Failing the Race: A Historical Assessment of New Orleans Mayor Sidney Barthelemy, 1986–1994," Baton Rouge, Louisiana State University, 2005, 47.

4. Ibid., 40.

5. Christopher Cooper, "What Friends Are For," *Times-Picayune*, October 13, 1996.

6. Edward F. Haas, *DeLesseps S. Morrison and the Image of Reform: New Orleans Politics, 1946–1961* (Baton Rouge: Louisiana State University Press, 1974), 83.

7. Perkins, "Failing the Race," 23.

8. WTRG Economics, "World Events and Crude Oil Prices, 1981–1998," London, AR, http://www.wtrg.com/oil_graphs/crudeoilprice8198.gif (accessed May 5, 2005).

9. Louisiana Department of Labor, Office of Occupational Information Services Research and Statistics Division, "Mining in New Orleans," Excel™ spreadsheet. The New Orleans MSA, for this purpose, included Orleans, Jefferson, St. Tammany, Plaquemines, St. Bernard, St. John, and St. Charles parishes. The figures from 1982 to 1989 also include

St. James Parish. White- and blue-collar jobs were not separately recorded. Figures reflect numbers as of January of each year and are rounded in the source material to the nearest 100. Data for 1980 is absent but has been interpolated between 1979 and 1981.

10. Perkins, "Failing the Race," 28.

11. Pam Radtke Russell, "Going with the Flow," *Times-Picayune*, September 10, 2006.

12. Liva Baker, *The Second Battle of New Orleans* (New York: Harper Collins, 1996), 472–473.

13. Nicholas Lemann, "Hard Times in the Big Easy; New Orleans," *The Atlantic Monthly*, August 1, 1987.

14. Victor Gold, "Let's Get Togedder: New Orleans Mayor For-As-Long-As-He Wants Marc Morial Is Giving New Meaning to His City's Long Reform-Resistant History. Selling Out to Casino Interests Is Allowing Seediness to Displace the City's Irreplaceable Charm," *The American Spectator*, May 1, 1998.

15. Frank Bovenkerk, "The Year Without Mardi Gras: The New Orleans Police Strike of 1979," *Crime, Law and Social Change* (Kluwer Academic Publishers, Dordrecht, NL) 20 (1993): 54.

16. James Kellogg to Scott S. Ellis, April 11, 2008; Bovenkerk, "The Year Without Mardi Gras," 55.

17. Ibid., 58.

18. Ibid., 62–63.

19. Gold, "Let's Get Togedder."

20. Perkins, "Failing the Race," 7.

21. Ron Faucheux, interview by Scott S. Ellis, April 23, 2006, by e-mail.

22. Lemann, "Hard Times in the Big Easy."

23. Rick Raber, "Paradise Lost?," *Times-Picayune*, September 19, 1983.

24. Fay S. Joyce, "Garish Intruders Muffling Spirit of French Quarter," *New York Times*, June 10, 1983.

25. Reni Haley, "Pete's Place Building Is Up for Sale," *Times-Picayune*, January 24, 1987.

26. Raber, "Paradise Lost?"

27. Joan Treadway and Wes Jackson, "Quarter's Condition Defended, Attacked," *Times-Picayune*, sect. 1, 17–18, May 28, 1983.

28. Ibid; John Pope, "Al's Final Note Hurt, Quarter Feels," *Times-Picayune*, sect. 1, 9, July 5, 1983.

29. John Pope, "Block Bad, Not Quarter, Hirt Says," *Times-Picayune*, sect. 1, 1, July 12, 1983.

30. The Associated Press, "Al Hirt; The 'King of the Trumpet' Is Gone," April 26, 1999.

31. Federal Housing Finance Board, "National Average Contract Mortgage Rate: Historical Data," graphic by Mortgage-X.com, http://mortgage-x.com/general/indexes/contract_rate_history.asp (accessed March 10, 2008).

32. George Tresch, interview by Scott S. Ellis, New Orleans, July 29, 2006.

33. Combined Federal Regulations, "Historic Preservation Certifications Pursuant To Sec. 48 (g) and Sec. 170 (h) of the Internal Revenue Tax Code of 1986," 36CFR67, Change 1, Edition of July 1, 2003, 344–362, Washington, D.C., Department of the Interior, National Park Service. http://www.cr.nps.gov/hps/tps/tax/taxregs.htm#67_4 (accessed March 10, 2008).

34. Gordon Russell, "Dubious Value," *Times-Picayune*, April 4 and 5, 2004. The Louisiana legislature forced Orleans Parish to use one property assessor, effective in 2008.

35. Pat O'Rourke, interview by Scott S. Ellis, New Orleans, March 20, 2005.

36. Mary Foster, "Stella Maris Center Made Over into Condos," *Times-Picayune*, December 9, 1995.

37. University of New Orleans, College of Urban and Public Affairs, *Changing Land Use in the Vieux Carré: Managing Growth to Preserve a National Landmark District*, New Orleans, 1992. This work lists Quarter vacancy rates by decade: 1980 was 21.9 percent; 1990 was 38.4 percent. Interpolating in a linear manner, 1985 would have had a vacancy rate of 30.1 percent, which is not far from my landlord's assertion.

38. Jonathan Mark Souther, "City in Amber: Race, Culture and the Tourist Transformation of New Orleans, 1945–1995" (Ph.D. diss., Tulane University, 2003), 280–281.

39. Michael Wilkinson, interview by Scott S. Ellis, New Orleans, January 28, 2006.

40. The Sauvignet-Thomas House. J. Wesley Cooper, *Louisiana: A Treasure of Plantation Homes* (Natchez: Southern Historical Publications, Inc., 1961), 28–29.

41. "Map of Bars, Lounges and Restaurants," *Impact*, January 1, 1980.

42. "Allen" (pseud.), interview by Scott S. Ellis, New Orleans, October 14, 2007.

43. Robyn Halvorsen, interview by Scott S. Ellis, New Orleans, September 29, 2006.

44. Wood Enterprises, "What Began as One Man's Dream Has Become the Career of Many," www.woodenterprises.com (accessed June 24, 2008).

45. "Allen" interview.

46. James Kellogg, "Re: Jewel's Question," e-mail to Scott S. Ellis, October 29, 2006.

47. Alan Robinson, "Letter to the Editor," *Impact*, October 1, 1981, 2.

48. "N.O. Gay Ordinance Fails to Pass," *Impact*, April 1, 1984, 1.

49. Tresch interview.

50. Nan Perales, "Where It Faltered: A Multitude of Problems," *Times-Picayune*, November 11, 1984, 1.

51. Tom Bissell, interview by Scott S. Ellis, New Orleans March 19, 2005.

52. Rick Raber, "Laws Can't Stop Hotel Expansion in French Quarter," *Times-Picayune*, July 31, 1983.

53. "Two Decades for a Quarter," *New Orleans Magazine*, April 2003.

54. R. James Kellogg, "French Quarter Recollections," e-mail to Scott S. Ellis, November 29, 2003.

55. Perales, "Where It Faltered," 25.

56. "The World's Fair and Exposition Information and Reference Guide, 1984 Louisiana World's Fair," Earth Station 9, http://www.earthstation9.com/index.html?1984_lou.htm (accessed March 10, 2008).

57. "The New Orleans Fair Hangover," *Time*, November 25, 1984, published at http://www.time.com/time/archive/preview/0,10987,927007,00.html (accessed April 4, 2005).

58. Columbia Broadcasting System, "Come to the Fair," *60 Minutes*, broadcast December 30, 1984, vol. 17, no. 16, BurrellesLuce Transcripts.

59. The final official figure was 7,335,279 visitors. "The World's Fair and Exposition Information and Reference Guide, 1984 Louisiana World's Fair."

60. "Foul Times for a Fair," *Time*, October 1, 1984, http://www.time.com/time/archive/preview/0,10987,954394,00.html?internalid=related (accessed April 6, 2005).

61. Rebecca Mowbray and Greg Thomas, "Time Release Renewal," *Times-Picayune*, May 9, 2004.

62. Columbia Broadcasting System, "Come to the Fair."

63. Greg Thomas, "20 Years Later, Silver Lining Apparent," *Times-Picayune*, May 9, 2004

64. Mowbray, "Time Release Renewal."

65. "The New Orleans Fair Hangover, "*Time*.

66. Columbia Broadcasting System, "Come to the Fair."

67. Kathy Finn, "What's Up Dock?, Or, A Peripatetic Guide to the Riverfront," *New Orleans Magazine*, June 1, 1994.

68. Thomas, "20 Years Later, Silver Lining Apparent."

69. Russell Levy, "Of Bards and Bawds: New Orleans Sporting Life Before and During the Storyville Era, 1897-1917" (M.A. thesis, Tulane University, 1967), 76–77.

70. Roy Letson, "Gay Homicides Cause Panic in French Quarter," *Impact*, July 13, 1984, 1.

71. Richard T. Devlin et al., "An Open Letter About AIDS," *Impact*, June 17, 1983, 2.

72. O'Rourke interview.

73. F. Barre-Sinoussi, J. C. Chermann, F. Rey et al., "Isolation of a T-lymphotropic Retrovirus from a Patient at Risk for Acquired Immune Deficiency Syndrome (AIDS)," *Science*, May 20, 1983 (4599), 868-871.

74. Brobson Lutz, M.D., interview by Scott S. Ellis, New Orleans, February 25, 2006.

75. Ibid.

76. Randy Shilts, *And the Band Played On* (New York: St. Martin's Press, 1987), 303–305 et al.

77. Lutz interview.

78. Ibid.

79. Ibid.

80. O'Rourke interview.

81. University of New Orleans, *Changing Land Use in the Vieux Carré*, table 1, 2–3.

82. Mrs. Jacob (Mary) Morrison, interview by John Geyser, New Orleans, Friends of the Cabildo Oral History Project, 1977.

83. Vieux Carré Commission, "Design Guidelines, Typical Materials," https://secure.cityofno.com/portal.aspx?portal=59&tabid=36 (accessed May 2, 2007).

84. Scott S. Ellis, "Decatur Street, New Orleans 1975 and 1985," compiled 2006. Unpublished monograph on file at the Historic New Orleans Collection.

85. Ann Veigle, "Changed Street Has Business Rolling on the River," *Times-Picayune*, August 31, 1986.

86. Perkins, "Failing the Race," 8.

87. Ibid., 3.

88. Ibid., 19.

89. University of New Orleans, *Changing Land Use in the Vieux Carré*, 1–3.

90. "Protecting the Quarter," *Times-Picayune*, April 13, 1993.

91. Bruce Alpert, "Area Police Rank High in U.S. Brutality Report," *Times-Picayune*, May 20, 1992, B-1.

92. Harvey, Chance. *The Life and Selected Letters of Lyle Saxon* (Gretna: Pelican Publishing, 2003), 123. Used by permission.

93. Kathy Finn, "Vieux Carré: Charm Under Pressure," *New Orleans Magazine*, March 1, 1993.

94. Catherine M. Vesey, "Tourism as Community Development: A Comparative Analysis of the Vieux Carré and the Lower Garden District from 1950 to 1990," University of New Orleans, College of Urban and Public Affairs, 1999, 11–12. Retrieved August 17, 2005, and published online at http://louisdl.louislibraries.org/CUPA/image/9927192072004_VESEY.pdf.

95. Finn, "Vieux Carré: Charm Under Pressure."

96. Mike Early, interview by Scott S. Ellis, New Orleans, July 29, 2006.

97. New Orleans Comprehensive Zoning Ordinance, Section 8.4.3, as enacted by ordinance 20, 271 adopted August 2, 2001. Published by Lexis-Nexis at http://ordlink.com/codes/neworleans/index.htm (accessed March 10, 2008).

98. New Orleans Comprehensive Zoning Ordinance, Sect. 13.2.1.

99. Louisiana Revised Statute 9:5625, (G) 1.

100. Anthony Marino, e-mail to Scott S. Ellis, October 8, 2006.

101. Bruce Eggler, "Parking Meters Delayed to Hear Quarter Complaints," *Times-Picayune*, November 21, 1993.

102. Elizabeth Mullener, "The Locals: Drawn by Charm, Driven Out by Crowds," *Times-Picayune*, May 16, 1994.

103. Maureen Olle, French Quarter Population, "Re: Request for Specific Census Data," e-mail to Scott S. Ellis, Louisiana State University Library, August 7, 2003.

104. Elizabeth Mullener, "Exodus Leaves City with Empty Feeling," *Times-Picayune*, January 16, 1994

105. No concise terminology for residents of the Vieux Carré has ever been accepted. "French Quarter or Vieux Carré resident' is about the most well-received; "Quarterite," or, heaven forbid, "Vieux Carrean" have mercifully never caught on.

106. Lawrence M. Knopp, Jr., "Gentrification and Gay Community Development in a New Orleans Neighborhood," (Ph.D. diss., University of Iowa, August 1989), 78.

107. Federal Housing Finance Board, "National Average Contract Mortgage Rate: Historical Data."

108. Knopp, "Gentrification and Gay Community Development," 61, figures 11 and 13. Knopp's home price charts end at 1984; my extrapolation of approximately seventy thousand dollars for an average Marigny house in 1985 is based upon the 1984 mean price of eighty thousand dollars for the Marigny "Triangle" between Esplanade and Elysian Fields, and the 1984 mean price of sixty thousand dollars for the Marigny "Rectangle" between Elysian Fields and Franklin.

109. Some data sets define the Marigny's downriver boundary as Franklin Avenue; however, the community defines the railroad tracks at Press Street as the boundary shared with the Bywater neighborhood.

110. Brian J. McBride, "Press Street: A Concept for Preserving, Reintroducing, and Fostering Local History" (M.A. thesis, Louisiana State University, 2005) 11.

111. Knopp, "Gentrification and Gay Community Development," 64–65.

112. Ibid., 71–72.

113. Ibid., 142.

114. Ibid., 80–102. The story of the Marigny's gay gentrification is well set out in Knopp's thesis and could easily make a fascinating historical novel.

115. O'Rourke interview and the author's experience.

116. "Allen" (pseud.) interview.

117. Amy Spillman, "Stopping the Swarm," *Agricultural Research*, July 2003. Agricultural Research Service, U.S. Department of Agriculture.

118. Duncan Murrell, "The Swarm," *Harper's*, August 2005, 56.

119. John McQuaid, "Shredding the Soul of a City," *Times-Picayune*, June 28, 1998.

120. Mark Schleifstein, "In N.O., Bugs Go to School, and the Schools Are Failing," *Times-Picayune*, June 28, 1998.

121. Clayton Boyer, interview by Scott S. Ellis, New Orleans, September 29, 2006.

122. Murrell, "The Swarm," 56.

123. Boyer interview.

124. Lynne Jensen, "Infestation Eats Up Time and Money," *Times-Picayune*, July 1, 1998.

125. Murrell, "The Swarm," 55–56.

126. Vieux Carré Commission, "Design Guidelines, Typical Materials."

127. John McQuaid and Lynne Jensen, "History Under Fire," *Times-Picayune*, July 1, 1998.

128. Mark Schleifstein, "Federal Program Unleashes Millions to Stop Termites," *Times-Picayune*, July 1, 1998; Spillman, "Stopping the Swarm."

129. Schleifstein, "Federal Program Unleashes Millions to Stop Termites."

130. Louisiana State University Agricultural Center, "French Quarter Termite Program Expands," press release, June 8, 2006.

131. Alan Morgan, Dennis Ring, Alan R. Max, and Frank S. Guillot, "Status of the French Quarter Formosan Subterranean Termite Management Program after Hurricane Katrina." Presented at the International Union for the Study of Social Insects Congress, August 1, 2006, Washington, D.C.

132. Finn, "What's Up Dock?"

133. S. Frederick Starr, ed., *Inventing New Orleans: Writings of Lafcadio Hearn* (Jackson: University Press of Mississippi, 2001), 110.

134. Elizabeth Mullener, "Insectarium: Thrill or Threat," *Times-Picayune*, May 17, 1994.

135. Bruce Eggler, "Coming Soon to a Museum Near You: Bugs," *Times-Picayune*, August 21, 2005.

## Chapter 11

1. Robert Tallant, *Mardi Gras . . . As It Was* (Gretna: Pelican Publishing Company, 2000), 14.

2. Wayne Everard and Irene Wainwright, "Crescent City Choo Choo: A Short History of Railroads in New Orleans," New Orleans Public Library, 2002, http://nutrias.org/~nopl/exhibits/choochoo/choochoo.htm (accessed July 30, 2007).

3. Yvonne Ragas Estrade, "The Accidental Place: Louis Armstrong Park Out of Place on the North Side," University of New Orleans, 2003, 31.

4. Ibid., 38.

5. Ibid., 40.

6. Dwight Ott, "Tremé Group Demands Half Culture Center Jobs," *Times-Picayune*, March 5, 1972.

7. Estrade, "The Accidental Place," 48.

8. Ibid., 50.

9. Ibid., 51.

10. Ann Veigle, "Bright Hopes Elude N. Rampart St.," *Times-Picayune*, August 31, 1986.

11. Ibid.

12. Estrade, "The Accidental Place," 52.

13. Dan Bennet and Walt Philbin, "Tourist Killed in Armstrong Park," *Times-Picayune*, sect. 1, 1, January 8, 1987.

14. Veigle, "Bright Hopes Elude N. Rampart St."

15. Thomas Griffin, "More Praise for Art Deco Palace Called Jonathan," *States-Item*, August 13, 1977; Patrick M. Burke, "Restaurant Buildings Snubbed," *Times-Picayune*, October 3, 1987.

16. "Some Attention on N. Rampart," *Times-Picayune*, October 31, 1976.

17. "Pleasure Palace a Pleasing Sight,"*Times-Picayune Real Estate*, February 5, 1983.

18. Veigle, "Bright Hopes Elude N. Rampart St."

19. Burke, "Restaurant Buildings Snubbed"; Lettice Stuart, "Jonathan's Building Is Bought for $165,000," *Times-Picayune*, December 5, 1987.

20. Janet Plume, "Rampart Market Cooking," *Times-Picayune*, December 17, 1988.

21. Stephanie Grace, "Hotel Is Coming to Rampart Street," *Times-Picayune*, November 13, 1994.

22. Veigle, "Bright Hopes Elude N. Rampart St."

23. Ibid.

24. National Park Service, "About the Park: Our Mission," New Orleans Jazz National Historical Park Web site, www.nps.gov/jazz/mission.htm (accessed November 2005).

25. Bruce Eggler, "Park Service Given Go-Ahead for Jazz Visitor Center in Park," *Times-Picayune*, August 4, 1999.

26. Leslie Williams, "WWOZ Trumpets Spacious Park Plan; Green Space Would Be Lost, Critics Say," *Times-Picayune*, September 17, 2003; Leslie Williams, "WWOZ's Revised Park Plan Still Faces Static; Planned Expansion Too Big, Critics Say," *Times-Picayune*, July 1, 2004.

27. Mississippi Gambling Laws, Sections 87-7-1 through -5, and 97-33-1 through -51, December 2005, www.gambling-law-us.com/state-laws/mississippi (accessed December 2005).

28. Estrade, "The Accidental Place," 54.

29. Keith Spera, "Cradle of Rock: Recording Studio Named Landmark," *Times-Picayune*, December 11, 1999.

30. Renee Peck, "Vieux Redo," *Times-Picayune*, September 25, 2004.

31. U.S. Department of Transportation, Federal Transit Administration, "Desire Steetcar Line, New Orleans, LA, November 2003," http://www.fta.dot.gov/documents/NO2AA.doc (accessed March 15, 2008).

32. Spera Keith, "Farewell to the Funky Butt?," *Times-Picayune*, August 19, 2005.

33. Keith Spera, "Plan to Reopen Jazz Club in N.O. Falls on Deaf Ears; Councilwoman Says She Opposes Proposal," *Times-Picayune*, October 25, 2005.

34. Gwen Filosa, "HANO Says It Has No Plans to Demolish Iberville Complex, But Local Residents Remain Unconvinced," *Times-Picayune*, July 1, 2005.

35. Wyatt Buchanan, "S.F.'s Castro Faces Identity Crisis," *San Francisco Chronicle*, February 25, 2007, http://www.sfgate.com/cgi-bin/article.cgi?f=/c/a/2007/02/25/MNG2DOATDK1.DTL (accessed April 8, 2008).

36. "Noise Complaints Could Silence Jazz at King Bolden's," *New Orleans City Business*, March 21, 2007.

37. Allison Fenterstock, "Out of the Zone," *Gambit*, April 17, 2007.

38. New Orleans Comprehensive Zoning Ordinance Sections 8.7 and 8.8. http://ordlink.com/codes/neworleans/index.htm (accessed March 15, 2008).

39. "Noise Complaints Could Silence Jazz at King Bolden's," *New Orleans City Business*.

## Chapter 12

1. Federal Writers' Project, Works Progress Administration, *New Orleans City Guide*, 1st ed. (Cambridge MA: Riverside Press, 1938), 231.

2. Hilary Irvin to Scott S. Ellis, February 5, 2007.

3. Hilary Irvin to Scott S. Ellis, August 8, 2007.

4. John Pope and Connie Jackson, "Trash Rises to New Height," *Times-Picayune*, March 3, 1995.

5. Gordon Russell, "Nagin Scraps Tradition of Trashing Carnival," *Times-Picayune*, March 6, 2003.

6. The history of New Orleans's struggle with drainage from the 1890s to the mid-1900s is summarized in the following: Martin Behrman, "A History of Three Great Public Utilities, Sewerage, Water and Drainage and Their Influence Upon the Health and Progress of a Big City." Presented at the convention of the League of American Municipalities, Milwaukee, WI, September 29, 1914. New Orleans, Brandao Print, n.d., ca. 1914. Transcribed by Bill Thayer, http://penelope.uchicago.edu/Thayer/E/Gazetteer/Places/America/United_States/Louisiana/New_Orleans/_Texts/Behrman*.html (accessed February 1, 2007). Infrastructure

in the opening year (1936–1937) of the Maestri administration is covered in: Uncredited, *New Orleans To-Day A City Meets Its Problems* (New Orleans: Wetzel Printing, 1937).

7. John Churchill Chase, *Frenchman, Desire and Good Children and Other Streets of New Orleans,* 3rd ed. (New York: Touchstone Books, 1997), 98.

8. Richard Campanella, *Time and Place in New Orleans* (Gretna: Pelican Publishing, 2002), 60.

9. Earl Bernhardt, "Water Backs Up on Bourbon," *Times-Picayune,* March 24, 2002.

10. Leslie Williams, "Catch Basin Screens Will Help Lake; Quarter Businesses Install Them," *Times-Picayune,* June 4, 2003.

11. Earl Bernhardt to Scott S. Ellis, October 3, 2007.

12. Elizabeth Mullener, "Clarkson's Crusade," *Times-Picayune,* June 22, 2003.

13. Stacia Wilson, "French Quarter Looking Clean," WWL-TV, February 3, 2007, as hosted at http://www.sdtwasteanddebris.com/video/VTS_01.wmv (accessed July 4, 2007).

14. "New Cleaner to Make French Quarter 'Super Fresh,'" *New Orleans City Business,* April 18, 2007.

## Chapter 13

1. Mississippi Gambling Laws, Sections 87-7-1 through -5, and 97-33-1 through -51, December 2005, published by Gambling-Law-US.com at www.gambling-law-us.com/state-laws/mississippi (accessed March 15, 2008).

2. Yvonne Abraham, "Casino Workers Wary of Future," *Boston Globe,* September 10, 2005. The thirteenth Mississippi coast casino, Hard Rock, was scheduled to open in the fall of 2005 but was destroyed by Hurricane Katrina. It finally opened in 2007.

3. Lyle Kenneth Perkins, "Failing the Race: A Historical Assessment of New Orleans Mayor Sidney Barthelemy, 1986–1994," Louisiana State University, 2005, 44.

4. Victor Gold, "Let's Get Togedder: New Orleans Mayor For-As-Long-As-He Wants Marc Morial Is Giving New Meaning to His City's Long Reform-Resistant History. Selling Out to Casino Interests Is Allowing Seediness to Displace the City's Irreplaceable Charm," *American Spectator,* May 1,1998.

5. Bruce Eggler, "Tremé Group Demands Changes in Casino Plans," *Times-Picayune,* November 27, 1993.

6. Mike Hughlett, "Dame Fortune Scowled at New Orleans; Miss. Gulf Coast Won Every Hand," *Times-Picayune,* April 28, 1996.

7. Bill Toland, "Harrah's Woes in New Orleans Become Fodder for Casino Battle Here," *Pittsburgh Post-Gazette,* February 27, 2006.

8. "Vice, Gaming Squad Goes into Action," *New Orleans States,* May 7, 1946; "Scores Jailed for Loitering," *New Orleans States,* May 8, 1946; "All Slots in City to Be Destroyed Is Cripps Order," *New Orleans States,* May 9, 1946.

9. James Aswell, "New Orleans Takes the Cure," *Saturday Evening Post,* January 25, 1947, 30.

10. Hughlett, "Dame Fortune."

11. Frank Donze, "City Council Cuts a Deal with Harrah's," *Times-Picayune,* March 16, 2001.

12. Toland, "Harrah's Woes."

13. Bruce Eggler, "No-Left-Turn Won't Send Tourists to Jail," *Times-Picayune,* April 9, 1994

14. *Greta Cazenave, et al, vs. Sheriff Charles C. Foti, Jr., et al,* Civil Action 00-1246, U.S. District Court, Eastern District of Louisiana, December 21, 2006, http://www

.nolastripsearch.com/casedoc/Class%20Action%20Settlement%20Agreement.pdf (accessed March 15, 2007).

15. Jonathan Mark Souther, "City in Amber: Race, Culture and the Tourist Transformation of New Orleans, 1945–1995" (Ph.D. diss., Tulane University, 2003), 294.

16. Michael Perlstein, "Miles to Go," *Times-Picayune*. December 18, 1994.

17. Elizabeth Mullener, "Farewell to the Chief," *Times-Picayune*, May 24, 2002.

18. Federal Bureau of Investigation: Uniform Crime Reports, 1995–2002; Crime Index, Offenses Reported; Index of Crime, Metropolitan Statistical Areas. Pennington ran for mayor of New Orleans in 2002 and was defeated by Ray Nagin. Pennington subsequently became Atlanta chief of police.

19. Frank Donze, "Quarter Residents Hire Cops; Levee Officers Patrol Streets," *Times-Picayune*, May 9, 1995.

20. Frank Donze, "Quarter Loses Levee Cops; Pennington Halts Patrols," *Times-Picayune*, May 18, 1995.

21. Combined Federal Regulations. "Historic Preservation Certifications Pursuant To Sec. 48 (g) and Sec. 170 (h) of the Internal Revenue Tax Code of 1986," 36CFR67, Change 1, Edition of July 1, 2003, 344–362, Washington, D.C., Department of the Interior, National Park Service, http://www.cr.nps.gov/hps/tps/tax/taxregs.htm#67_4 (accessed March 10, 2008).

22. Kevin Fox Gotham, "Tourism Gentrification: The Case of New Orleans' Vieux Carré (French Quarter)," *Urban Studies* 42, no. 7 (June 2005): 1109.

23. Ibid., 1112.

24. Ibid.

25. Pat O'Rourke, interview by Scott S. Ellis, New Orleans, March 20, 2005.

26. Gotham, "Tourism Gentrification," 1108.

27. Elizabeth Mullener, "The Locals: Drawn by Charm, Driven Outby Crowds," *Times-Picayune*, May 16, 1994.

28. Gotham, "Tourism Gentrification," 1111. The moratorium was revised in 1982 to permit new hotels in existing Quarter buildings, but retained zoning requirements.

29. Coleman Warner, "Decatur Street Hotel Sued Over Expansion," *Times-Picayune*, March 31, 1998.

30. Anthony Marino, e-mail to Scott S. Ellis, October 8, 2006.

31. Gotham, "Tourism Gentrification," 1111.

32. Bruce Eggler, "Quarter Hotel Plan Is Withdrawn," *Times-Picayune*, August 3, 2006.

33. Skye Moody, "Illegal Guesthouses Start Row in Quarter," *Times-Picayune*, July 18, 1997.

34. David A. Fahrenthold,  "Wakeup Call Placed for Illegal N.O. Inns; City Targets Growth of Bed-and-Breakfasts," *Times-Picayune*, July 19, 1999.

35. Tom Bissell, interview by Scott S. Ellis, New Orleans, March 19, 2005.

36. Department of the Interior, National Park Service, New Orleans Jazz National Historical Park, *New Orleans Jazz History Walking Tours: Central Vieux Carré Brochure*, http://www.nps.gov/jazz/historyculture/upload/central-vc.pdf (accessed November 7, 2005).

37. Rebecca Mowbray, "The New Bourbon Royalty," *Times-Picayune*, February 10, 2002.

38. Robert Simmons, "New Orleans, America's Most Exotic City," *Coronet*, March 1956, 84–85.

39. Mowbray, "The New Bourbon Royalty."

40. New Orleans Planning Commission Master Plan, Sections 8.8.1, 8.8.3.

41. Richard Campanella, *Time and Place in New Orleans* (Gretna, LA: Pelican Publishing, 2002), 138–139.

42. Gregory Roberts, "Burgers, Baubles, Baseball Caps," *Times-Picayune*, July 13, 1996.

43. Ibid.

44. Ibid.

45. Catherine M.Vesey, "Tourism as Community Development: A Comparative Analysis of the Vieux Carré and the Lower Garden District from 1950 to 1990," University of New Orleans, College of Urban and Public Affairs, 1999, 5, http://louisdl.louislibraries.org/CUPA/image/9927192072004_VESEY.pdf (accessed August 17, 2005).

46. Charles Y. W. Chai, "Who Rules New Orleans? A Study of Community Power Structure,"*Louisiana Business Survey* 2 (October 1971): 10.

47. Mowbray, "The New Bourbon Royalty."

48. "11 Most Endangered Places," National Trust for Historic Preservation, www.nationaltrust.org/11most/list.asp (accessed January 2003).

49. Louisiana Revised Statutes, Section 25-737, "Powers of Historic District Commissions."

50. *Vieux Carré Property Owners, Residents & Associates v. Brown*, No. 87-3700, U.S. District Court, Eastern District of Louisiana, September 21, 1987, summarized as Case 133, Advisory Council on Historic Preservation, www.achp.gov/book/case133.html (accessed August 31, 2006).

51. Clarence Doucet, "Bourbon House Declared Dead," *Times-Picayune*, October 1, 1964.

52. Nathan Chapman, interview by Scott S. Ellis, New Orleans, September 29, 2006.

53. Elliot Parker, *Newsrooms Under Siege: Crime Coverage and the Louisiana Pizza Kitchen Murders* (Mt. Pleasant, MI: Central Michigan University, 1997).

54. Michael Wilkinson, interview by Scott S. Ellis, New Orleans, January 28, 2006.

55. Ibid. Used by permission.

56. George Tresch, interview by Scott S. Ellis, New Orleans, July 29, 2006.

57. Lili LeGardeur, "Has Cabrini Park Gone to the Dogs?," *Times-Picayune*, May 23, 2002.

58. J. William Thompson, "Almost Another Country," *Landscape Architecture*, American Society of Landscape Architects, July 2003, http://www.asla.org/lamag/lam03/july/feature1.html (accessed March 15, 2008).

59. Mike Early, interview by Scott S. Ellis, New Orleans, July 29, 2006.

60. John Foley and Mickey Lauria, "Plans, Planning and Tragic Choices," University of New Orleans, College of Urban and Public Affairs, 1999, 13, http://louisdl.louislibraries.org/CUPA/image/50123202072004_ACSP299.pdf (accessed August 17, 2005).

61. Ibid., 14.

62. Ibid., 19.

63. Ibid., 19. Quote used by permission.

64. John Foley and Mickey Lauria, "Historic Preservation, Urban Revitalization, and Value Controversies in New Orleans' French Quarter," University of New Orleans, College of Urban and Public Affairs, 2000, 26, http://louisdl.louislibraries.org/CUPA/image/38743202072004_UUA.pap.pdf (accessed August 17, 2005).

65. Anthony Marino, "Part V, Acquiring Community Support and Managing the 'Politics.'" Presented at Fundamentals of Real Estate Development, August 9, 2006, New Orleans.

66. Greg Thomas, "If You Build It, Will They Come?," *Times-Picayune*, July 23, 1997.

67. Bruce Eggler, "Bienville Will Get Digs in the Quarter," *Times-Picayune*, December 9, 1993.

68. Blake Pontchatrain (pseud.), "New Orleans Know It All," *Gambit*, August 2, 2005.

69. Lyle Saxon, *Fabulous New Orleans* (New York: The Century Company, 1928), 189–192; Herbert Asbury, *The French Quarter: An Informal History of the New Orleans Underworld* (New York: Garden City Publishing, 1938), 153.

70. *City of New Orleans and the Vieux Carré Commission v. Board of Directors of the Louisiana State Museum, James Sefcik; Tammany Contracting Company; and the Department of Culture, Recreation and Tourism*, No. 98-C-1170, Supreme Court of Louisiana 1998, 2.

71. Ibid., 4.

72. Ibid.

73. Ibid., 8, note 14.

74. Ibid., 5, note 10.

75. Ibid., 5–6.

76. Ibid., 6, note 11.

77. Ibid., 5, note 9.

78. Ibid., 6.

79. Ibid., 7, note 13.

80. Walter Gallas and Anthony Marino, "Cabildo Case Not Just About the Fence," *Preservation in Print*, Preservation Resource Center of New Orleans, May 1998, 32.

81. Bruce Eggler, "High Court," *Times-Picayune*, May 9, 2004.

82. *City of New Orleans and the Vieux Carré Commission v. Board of Directors of the Louisiana State Museum*, 8.

83. Ibid., 15.

84. Liz Scott, "Chris Rose by a Landslide," *New Orleans Magazine*, December 2006, 52–53.

85. James Gill, "Re: Bio Information Request," e-mail to Scott S. Ellis, January 27, 2007.

86. James Gill, *Lords of Misrule: Mardi Gras and the Politics of Race in New Orleans* (Jackson, MS: University Press of Mississippi, 1997).

87. Rick Delaup, *Ruthie The Duck Girl*, DVD, New Orleans, 1999.

88. Paul Willis, e-mail to Scott S. Ellis, July 18, 2007.

89. James Nolan, interview by Scott S. Ellis, October 13, 2007.

90. Coleman Warner, "Getting the Squeeze," *Times-Picayune*, August 4, 1999.

91. New Orleans Ordinance 18,857 of September 3, 1998.

92. *Lionhart v. Foster*, 100 Fsupp.2d 383 U.S. District Court, Eastern District of Louisiana, 1999.

93. Pamela Coyle, "Quiet Zone Law Struck Down," *Times-Picayune*, October 30, 1999.

94. Brett Martel, "Non-Stop Merrymaking Doesn't Amuse Residents of French Quarter," *Milwaukee Journal Sentinel*, December 5, 1999.

95. Rhonda Bell, "Police Sweep Square Hours Before Wedding," *Times-Picayune*, September 12, 1999.

96. Frank Donze, "Quarter Bus Ban Takes Hold; Hotel Operators Shift Operations Gradually," *Times-Picayune*, April 11, 1997.

97. "Crackdown in the Quarter," *Times-Picayune*, June 5, 2000.

98. "Protecting the Quarter," *Times-Picayune*, April 13, 1993.

99. Lili LeGardeur, "Police Hear Quarter Gripes; Complaints Include Tour Buses, Lewdness," *Times-Picayune*, October 3, 2000.

100. "Crackdown in the Quarter," *Times-Picayune*.

## Chapter 14

1. Tom Bissell, interview by Scott S. Ellis, New Orleans, March 19, 2005.

2. "Treasures Taken Away from Closed Church," *Times-Picayune*, July 12, 1997; Maria Montoya, "A Glimpse of Heaven," *Times-Picayune*, March 31, 2002.

3. John C. Hill, "Clarkson Riles Peers, Pleases Conservatives," *Times-Picayune*, April 23, 1994; James Gill, *Lords of Misrule: Mardi Gras and the Politics of Race in New Orleans* (Jackson, MS: University Press of Mississippi, 1997), 23–25, 250. The applicable ordinances

are found in the New Orleans Code of Ordinances, chapter 86, and, more specifically for Carnival organizations, section 86–39.

4. Lili LeGardeur, "Bench Warfare," *Times-Picayune*, September 17, 2002.

5. "Passing the Smell Test," *Times-Picayune*, July 18, 2002.

6. Ibid.

7. Gordon Russell, "At Rally, They're Just Wild About Jackie," *Times-Picayune*, October 21, 2002.

8. Elizabeth Mullener, "Clarkson's Crusade," *Times-Picayune*, June 22, 2003.

9. Ibid.

10. Tara Young, "Some Fear Cleanup of French Quarter Will Erase Its Charm," *Times-Picayune*, July 19, 2002.

11. Mullener, "Clarkson's Crusade."

12. Gwen Filosa, "Judge Convicts Mother of Tap Dancers," *Times-Picayune*, May 20, 2004.

13. Tara Young, "NOPD Initiative Has Colorful New Leader," *Times-Picayune*, November 15, 2004.

14. New Orleans Code of Ordinances, Sect. 54-491.1, "Prohibited Offers to Rent Property," M.C.S. 21606, July 1, 2004.

15. Philip Rucker, "Nagin Caught in Cop-Swap Crossfire; Some Say Changes Politically Motivated," *Times-Picayune*, June 26, 2004.

16. Bruce Eggler, "Incumbents Lose Seats in 3 Districts," *Times-Picayune*, May 21, 2006.

17. Frank Donze, "Clarkson Wins At-Large Council Seat," *Times-Picayune*, November 17, 2007.

18. Elizabeth Mullener, "The Locals: Drawn by Charm, Driven Out by Crowds," *Times-Picayune*, May 16, 1994.

19. Nathan Chapman, interview by Scott S. Ellis, New Orleans, September 29, 2006.

20. Michael Wilkinson, interview by Scott S. Ellis, New Orleans, January 28, 2006.

21. Elisabeth Butler, "Tourism Still Rebounding from Shock of 9-11," *New Orleans City Business*, September 9, 2002.

22. Bruce Eggler, "Event Overshadowed, But Not Overlooked; Despite Bush Absence, Celebration a Success," *Times-Picayune*, December 21, 2003.

23. Ed Anderson, "Chirac May Have Hard Time Getting La. Visa; Foster Calls French Leader 'a Snake,'" *Times-Picayune*, September 26, 2003.

24. Eggler, "Event Overshadowed."

25. James Van Dorin to Scott S. Ellis.

26. The Brookings Institution, "Hurricane Katrina Timeline," http://www.brook.edu/fp/projects/homeland/katrinatimeline.pdf (accessed July 26, 2007).

27. James Van Dorin, "Katrina Stories," unpublished manuscript, December 2005; James Van Dorin, interview by Scott S. Ellis, New Orleans, June 14, 2007.

28. Van Dorin, "Katrina Stories."

29. Angus Lind, "Doctor-Do-It-All; Brobson Lutz Did a Little of Everything for French Quarter Residents After Katrina," *Times-Picayune*, October 14, 2005; Brobson Lutz, "My Katrina Experience," *New Orleans Magazine*, December 2005.

30. Allen G. Breed, "French Quarter Holdouts Create Tribes," Associated Press, September 4, 2005, http://www.wwltv.com/sharedcontent/nationworld/katrina/stories/090405cckatrinajrfrenchquarter.26851646.html (accessed August 31, 2006).

31. Van Dorin, "Katrina Stories."

32. Van Dorin interview.

33. Ibid.

34. James Van Dorin to Scott S. Ellis.

35. Breed, "French Quarter Holdouts Create Tribes."

36. Gwen Filosa and Gordon Russell, "Faltering Safety Net," *Times-Picayune*, October 9, 2005.

37. Tara Young, "Unlikely Haven," *Times-Picayune*, December 5, 2005.

38. "The Outsider Makes It Big," *Time*, November 5, 1979, http://time-proxy.yaga.com/time/archive/preview/0,10987,912529,00.html (accessed July 6, 2005).

39. Michael Perlstein, "1st District: 'Fort Apache' Officers Draw Line at the French Quarter," *Times-Picayune*, December 18, 2005.

40. Brian Thevenot, "Canizaro Takes the Heat in Plan for City's Future," *Times-Picayune*, March 19, 2006.

41. "Storied French Quarter Nursing Home to Close," *New Orleans City Business*, September 18, 2006.

42. "New Orleans Post Katrina Funk," Associated Press, January 18, 2007, http://www.cbsnews.com/stories/2007/01/18/katrina/main2371452.shtml (accessed August 17, 2007).

43. Greg Thomas, "Glut of Houses Sends Prices Plummeting," *Times-Picayune*, June 23, 2007.

44. Virginia R. Burkett, David B. Zilkoski, and David A. Hart, "Sea-Level Rise and Subsidence: Implications for Flooding in New Orleans, Louisiana," U.S. Geological Survey, October 12, 2005, http://www.nwrc.usgs.gov/hurricane/Sea-Level-Rise.pdf (accessed July 31, 2007).

# BIBLIOGRAPHY

The bibliography includes all sources. It is formatted, in general, in accordance with the *Chicago Manual of Style*, with the following tailoring:
Second and subsequent entries by the same author are in chronological, not alphabetical, order (as preferred by CMS). Chronological order assists the reader by maintaining continuity with the narrative flow and evolving stories covered by the same reporters.
In second and subsequent entries by the same author, the 3-em dash is used. However, if the second or subsequent entry is a coauthorship, the entire name is repeated. If the first entry is a coauthorship and the second is a single authorship, the sole author is repeated.
Newspapers and institutions (as authors where no author was credited) are listed alphabetically, and articles chronologically. The article "the" is ignored in alphabetization.
URLs are listed if the source is only available online. If a source is merely a printed document reproduced online, the URL is not given.

Abraham, Yvonne. "Casino Workers Wary of Future." *Boston Globe*, September 10, 2005.
Adler, William H. "'Liberation' Goal of Gay March." *States-Item*, January 23, 1971.
"Allen" (pseud.). Interview by Scott S. Ellis. New Orleans, October 14, 2007.
Alpert, Bruce. "Area Police Rank High in U.S. Brutality Report." *Times-Picayune*, May 20, 1992.
Anderson, Ed. "Chirac May Have Hard Time Getting La. Visa; Foster Calls French Leader 'a Snake.'" *Times-Picayune*, September 26, 2003.
Asbury, Herbert. *The French Quarter: An Informal History of the New Orleans Underworld.* New York: Garden City Publishing, 1938.
Associated Press. "'73 Parades Will Bypass Quarter." *Times-Picayune*, August 25, 1972.
———. "Spring Breakers Relocate; Panama City Is Party Central." *Times-Picayune*, March 21, 1994.
———. "Al Hirt; The 'King of the Trumpet' Is Gone." April 26, 1999.
———. "Bourbon Street Wants Protesters to Stay Away." September 3, 2004.
———. "New Orleans Post Katrina Funk." January 18, 2007. Published online at http://www.cbsnews.com/stories/2007/01/18/katrina/main2371452.shtml (retrieved August 17, 2007).
Aswell, James. "New Orleans Takes the Cure." *Saturday Evening Post*, January 25, 1947.
Atkinson, Paul. "Dupuy Will Try to Keep Tujague's in Vieux Carre." *Times-Picayune* March 22, 1974.
Babin, Madelene. Interview by Christine Durbas. New Orleans, *Friends of the Cabildo: Oral History Project*, May 10, 1982.

Baker, Liva. *The Second Battle of New Orleans*. New York: HarperCollins, 1996.

Ball, Millie. "Last Retail Fish Stall to Leave French Market." *Times-Picayune*, February 11, 1974.

Barker, Danny. Interview by John Healy. New Orleans Public Library, Jambalaya Project, October 24, 1979.

Barre-Sinoussi, F., J. C. Chermann, F. Rey et al. "Isolation of a T-lymphotropic Retrovirus from a Patient at Risk for Acquired Immune Deficiency Syndrome (AIDS)." *Science*, May 20, 1983.

Barry, John M. *Rising Tide*. New York: Touchstone, 1998.

Baumbach, Richard, Jr., and William Borah. "STOP! The Riverfront Expressway." *Times-Picayune*, March 14, 1966.

———. *The Second Battle of New Orleans*. Tuscaloosa: University of Alabama Press, 1981.

Behrman, Martin. "A History of Three Great Public Utilities, Sewerage, Water and Drainage and Their Influence Upon the Health and Progress of a Big City." Presented at convention of the League of American Municipalities, Milwaukee, WI, September 29, 1914. New Orleans: Brandao Print, n.d., ca. 1914.

———. *Martin Behrman of New Orleans*. Edited by John R. Kemp. Baton Rouge: Louisiana State University Press, 1977.

Bell, Rhonda. "Police Sweep Square Hours Before Wedding." *Times-Picayune*, September 12, 1999

Bennet, Dan, and Walt Philbin. "Tourist Killed in Armstrong Park." *Times-Picayune*, January 8, 1987.

Berger, Monroe. "Letters from New Orleans." *Annual Review of Jazz Studies 7: 1994–1995*. Edited by Edward Berger, David Cayer, Henry Martin, Dan Morgenstern, and Lewis Porter. Institute for Jazz Studies, Rutgers, the State University of New Jersey. Lanham, MD: Scarecrow Press, 1996.

Bernhardt, Earl. "Water Backs Up on Bourbon." *Times-Picayune*, March 24, 2002.

———. Interview by Scott S. Ellis. New Orleans, December 1, 2006.

———. E-mail to Scott S. Ellis. October 3, 2007.

Berry, Jason, Jonathan Foose, and Tad Jones. *Up from the Cradle of Jazz: New Orleans Music Since World War II*. New York: De Capo Press, 1992.

Bethell, Tom. "Road Foes Borah & Baumbach: A Tale of Two Citizens." *Vieux Carré Courier*, March 23–29, 1973.

Bissell, Tom. Interview by Scott S. Ellis. New Orleans, March 19, 2005.

Blenk, James. *An Appeal to the Citizens of New Orleans and Louisiana to Restore St. Louis Cathedral*. New Orleans: St. Louis Cathedral, 1917.

Bobo, James R. *The New Orleans Economy: Pro Bono Publico?* The University of New Orleans, College of Business Administration. New Orleans, 1975.

Boehm, Rudolph H. "Mary Grace Quackenbos and the Federal Campaign Against Peonage : The Case of Sunnyside Plantation." *Arkansas Historical Quarterly* 50, no. 1 (Spring 1991).

Bonner, Judith H. *The New Orleans Arts & Crafts Club: An Artistic Legacy*. The New Orleans Museum of Art and the Historic New Orleans Collection. New Orleans, 2007.

Borah, William. Interview by Scott S. Ellis. New Orleans, July 29, 2006.

Boulard, Gary. *Huey Long Invades New Orleans; The Siege of a City, 1934–36*. Gretna, LA: Pelican Publishing Company,1998.

Bourg, Gene. Interview by Scott S. Ellis. New Orleans, October 12, 2003.

Bourgeois, Marsha. *The Preservation of the Vieux Carré and Its Grassroots Beginnings*. New Orleans: Loyola University Student Historical Journals, vol. 20, 1988.

Bovenkerk, Frank. "The Year Without Mardi Gras: The New Orleans Police Strike of 1979." Dordrecht, NL: *Crime, Law and Social Change*. Kluwer Academic Publishers, 20, 1993.

Boyer, Clayton. Interview by Scott S. Ellis. New Orleans, September 29, 2006.

Bragg, Rick. "Louisiana Stands Alone on Drinking at 18." *New York Times*, March 23, 1996.

Breed, Allen G. "French Quarter Holdouts Create Tribes." Associated Press, September 4, 2005.

Brenner, Milton E. *The Garrison Case: A Study in the Abuse of Power*. New York: Clarkson N. Potter, Inc. 1969.

The Brookings Institution. "Hurricane Katrina Timeline." Published online at http://www.brook.edu/fp/projects/homeland/katrinatimeline.pdf (retrieved July 26, 2007).

Bryan, Bill. "VCC Criticizes Study." *Vieux Carré Courier*, December 19, 1969.

———. "Carnival Crisis." *Vieux Carré Courier*, February 13, 1970.

Buchanan, Wyatt. "S.F.'s Castro Faces Identity Crisis." *San Francisco Chronicle*, February 25, 2007.

Bureau of the Census, Richard L. Forstall, compiler. *Louisiana Population of Counties [sic] by Decennial Census: 1900 to 1990*. Washington, D.C., March 27, 1995.

Bureau of Governmental Research. *Vieux Carré Historic District Demonstration Study: The Vieux Carré, New Orleans, Its Plan, Its Growth, Its Architecture*. Washington: Marcou, O'Leary and Associates, 1968.

———. *Vieux Carré Historic District Demonstration Study: Technical Report on the Environmental Survey*. Washington: Marcou, O'Leary and Associates, 1968.

———. *Vieux Carré Historic District Demonstration Study: Technical Report on the Effects of the Proposed Riverfront Expressway*. Washington: Marcou, O'Leary and Associates, 1968.

———. *Vieux Carré Historic District Demonstration Study: Economic and Social Study*. Washington: Marcou, O'Leary and Associates, 1968.

———.*Vieux Carré Historic District Demonstration Study: Plan and Program for the Preservation of the Vieux Carré*. Washington: Marcou, O'Leary and Associates, 1968.

———. *Vieux Carré Historic District Demonstration Study: Evaluation of the Effects of the Proposed Riverfront Expressway*. Washington: Marcou, O'Leary and Associates, 1968.

Burgoyne, J. E. "Winds of Change Shift French Market Smells." *Times-Picayune*, December 17, 1972.

Burke, Patrick M. "Restaurant Buildings Snubbed." *Times-Picayune*, October 3, 1987.

Burkett, Virginia R., David B. Zilkoski, and David A. Hart. "Sea-Level Rise and Subsidence: Implications for Flooding in New Orleans, Louisiana." Lafayette, Louisiana: U.S. Geological Survey, October 12, 2005.

Butler, Elisabeth. "Tourism Still Rebounding from Shock of 9-11." *New Orleans City Business*, September 9, 2002.

Campanella, Richard. *Time and Place in New Orleans* Gretna, LA: Pelican Publishing, 2002.

Caro, Robert A. *The Power Broker*. New York: Random House Vintage Books, 1975.

Carter, Betty. Interview by Anne Ritchie. Women in Journalism Oral History Project of the Washington Press Club Foundation, April 10, 1990, in the Oral History Collection of Columbia University and other repositories.

Carter, William. *Preservation Hall: Music from the Heart*. New York: W. W. Norton, 1991.

Casso, Evans J. *Staying in Step: A Continuing Italian Renaissance*. New Orleans: Quadriga Press, 1984.

Chai, Charles Y. W. "Who Rules New Orleans? A Study Of Community Power Structure." *Louisiana Business Survey* 2 (October 1971).

Chapman, Nathan. Interview by Scott S. Ellis. New Orleans, September 29, 2006.

Chase, John Churchill. *Frenchman, Desire and Good Children and Other Streets of New Orleans*. 3rd ed. New York: Touchstone Books, 1997.

Codrescu, Andrei. *New Orleans, Mon Amour*. Chapel Hill, NC: Algonquin Books, 2006.

Coleman, Rick. *Cosimo 101: 101 Reasons Why Cosimo Matassa, Who Engineered the Sound of Rhythm & Blues and Rock N Roll, Should Be in the Rock N Roll Hall of Fame*. Metairie: Louisiana Music Commission: http://www.louisianamusic.org/cosimo_101.htm (retrieved July 2, 2003).

Columbia Broadcasting System. "Come to the Fair." *60 Minutes*. Broadcast December 30, 1984, vol. 42, no. 16. BurrellesLuce Transcripts.

———. "Bedlam on Bourbon Street." *48 Hours*. Broadcast March 10, 1993, no. 232. BurrellesLuce Transcripts.

Combined Federal Regulations. "Historic Preservation Certifications Pursuant To Sec. 48 (g) and Sec. 170 (h) of the Internal Revenue Tax Code of 1986" 36CFR67, Change 1, Edition of July 1, 2003. Washington, D.C.: Department of the Interior, National Park Service.

Cooper, Christopher. "Renaissance Hits Decatur Street; Dreary Strip Gets New Life." *Times-Picayune*, February 23, 1997.

———. "What Friends Are For." *Times-Picayune*, October 13, 1996.

Cooper, Courtney Ryley. *Designs in Scarlett*. Boston: Little, Brown and Company, 1939.

Cooper, J. Wesley. *Louisiana: A Treasure of Plantation Homes*. Natchez: Southern Historical Publications, Inc., 1961.

Coquille, John Hypolite. "Martin Behrman Album." New Orleans Public Library, published at http://www.nutrias.org/~nopl/photos/behrphot.htm.

Coyle, Pamela. "Name of Game Is See and Be Seen; 'Classic Is Cars and Chillin.'" *Times-Picayune*, November 29, 1997.

———. "Quiet Zone Law Struck Down." *Times-Picayune*, October 30, 1999.

Cuthbert, David. "Quarter's Flea Market Does First Day of Trade." *Times-Picayune*, January 10, 1971.

Daniel, Pete. *Deep'n As It Come: The 1927 Mississippi River Flood*. Fayetteville: University of Arkansas Press, 1996.

Darce, Keith. "Southern Decadence Means Big Business; Gay Tourists Give Summer a Boost." *Times-Picayune*, September 4, 1998.

Davis, Jack. "French Market Dedicated; Mayor Blasts Project's Critics." *States-Item*, April 1, 1975.

Davis, John H. *Mafia Kingfish*. New York: Signet, 1989.

Davis, Joyce, and Sandi Donnelly. "Panhandlers, Solicitors Growing Nuisance on Downtown Streets." *Times-Picayune*, February 11, 1973.

Dayries, Provosty A. Letter, "Dear Chief," July 24, 1958. Superintendent of Police to 24 Police Departments. New Orleans Police Department, 1958.

Deiter, Ronald H. *The Story of Metro*. Glendale, CA: Interurban Press, 1990.

Delaup, Rick. *Ruthie The Duck Girl*. DVD, New Orleans, 1999.

———. "Gallery of Eccentrics." http://www.eccentricneworleans.com/gallery_of_eccentrics.htm (retrieved November 2, 2006).

Delery, Linda C., ed. "Preview to the World's Fair and Vacation Planner." New Orleans: Picayune Publishing, 1983.

Devlin, Richard T. et al. "An Open Letter About AIDS." *Impact*, June 17, 1983.

Dilberto, Buddy. "Protest by Negro Gridders Cancels N.O. All-Star Game." *Times-Picayune*, January 11, 1965.

Donze, Frank. "Quarter Residents Hire Cops; Levee Officers Patrol Streets." *Times-Picayune*, May 9, 1995.

———. "Quarter Loses Levee Cops; Pennington Halts Patrols." *Times-Picayune*, May 18, 1995.

———. "Quarter Bus Ban Takes Hold; Hotel Operators Shift Operations Gradually." *Times-Picayune*, April 11, 1997.

———. "Morial Drops Support for Pedicabs." *Times-Picayune*, August 25, 2000.

———. "City Council Cuts a Deal with Harrah's." *Times-Picayune*, March 16, 2001.

———. "Pedicab Proposal Back in Motion." *Times-Picayune*, April 30, 2001.

———. "Clarkson Wins At-Large Council Seat." *Times-Picayune*, November 17, 2007.

Door Knob Films, LLC, and Such-A-Much Productions, LLC. *The Quorum*, DVD, 2004.

Doucet, Clarence. "Bourbon House Declared Dead." *Times-Picayune*, October 1, 1964.

Dreyer, Edward. *Some Friends of Lyle Saxon*. New York: Hastings House, 1948. Published under same cover as Lyle Saxon's *The Friends of Joe Gilmore*.

Early, Mike. Interview by Scott S. Ellis. New Orleans, July 29, 2006.

Edwards, Louise. "Yellow Fever and the Sicilian Community in New Orleans." Minneapolis: University of Minnesota, May 30, 1989.

Eggler, Bruce. "Proposal Tightens Quarter Growth." *Times-Picayune*, May 10, 1993.

———. "Parking Meters Delayed to Hear Quarter Complaints." *Times-Picayune*, November 21, 1993.

———. "Tremé Group Demands Changes in Casino Plans." *Times-Picayune*, November 27, 1993.

———. "Bienville Will Get Digs in the Quarter." *Times-Picayune*, December 9, 1993.

———. "No-Left-Turn Won't Send Tourists to Jail." *Times-Picayune*, April 9, 1994.

———. "Park Service Given Go-Ahead for Jazz Visitor Center in Park." *Times-Picayune*, August 4, 1999.

———. "Walking Tours Limits Inspire Heated Debate." *Times-Picayune*, May 20, 2003.

———. "City Council Puts Limits on Walking Tours." *Times-Picayune*, July 18, 2003.

———. "Event Overshadowed, But Not Overlooked; Despite Bush Absence, Celebration a Success." *Times-Picayune*, December 21, 2003.

———. "High Court." *Times-Picayune*, May 9, 2004.

———. "The Final Link, Last Vestige of Chinatown May Fall; Old Site Slated to Be Garage for New Hotel." *Times-Picayune*, October 15, 2004.

———. "City Council Restricts Bullhorns in Quarter." *Times-Picayune*, November 5, 2004.

———. "Coming Soon to a Museum Near You: Bugs." *Times-Picayune*, August 21, 2005.

———. "Historic Doll House for Sale." *Times-Picayune*, August 14, 2005.

———. "Incumbents Lose Seats in 3 Districts." *Times-Picayune*, May 21, 2006.

———. "Planners Divided on Quarter Hotel." *Times-Picayune*, June 14, 2006.

———. "Quarter Hotel Plan Is Withdrawn." *Times-Picayune*, August 3, 2006.

Ellis, Scott S. "Decatur Street, New Orleans 1975 and 1985." Compiled 2006. On deposit with the Historic New Orleans Collection.

Estrade, Yvonne Ragas. "The Accidental Place: Louis Armstrong Park Out of Place on the North Side." New Orleans: University of New Orleans, 2003.

Everard, Wayne, and Irene Wainwright. "The Evil Wind: Hurricanes in South Louisiana." New Orleans Public Library, 1995. Published online at http://www.nutrias.org/~nopl/exhibits/hurricane1.htm (retrieved December 15, 2008).

———. "Crescent City Choo Choo: A Short History of Railroads in New Orleans." New Orleans Public Library, 2002. Published online at http://nutrias.org/~nopl/exhibits/choochoo/choochoo.htm (retrieved July 30, 2007).

Fahrenthold, David A. "Wakeup Call Placed for Illegal N.O. Inns; City Targets Growth of Bed-and-Breakfasts." *Times-Picayune*, July 19, 1999.

Faucheux, Ron. Interview by Scott S. Ellis. E-mail, April 23, 2006.

Federal Bureau of Investigation: Uniform Crime Reports, 1995–2002; Crime Index, Offenses Reported; Index of Crime, Metropolitan Statistical Areas.

Federal Housing Finance Board. "National Average Contract Mortgage Rate: Historical Data." Graphic by Mortgage-X.com, http://mortgage-x.com/general/indexes/contract_rate_history.asp.

Fenterstock, Allison. "Out of the Zone." *Gambit*, April 17, 2007.

Fife, Darlene. *Portraits from Memory: New Orleans in the Sixties*. New Orleans: Surregional Press, 2000.

———. Interview by Scott S. Ellis. E-mail, September 27, 2006.

Filosa, Gwen. "Judge Convicts Mother of Tap Dancers." *Times-Picayune*, May 20, 2004.

———. "HANO Says It Has No Plans to Demolish Iberville Complex, But Local Residents Remain Unconvinced." *Times-Picayune*, July 1, 2005.

Filosa, Gwen, and Gordon Russell. "Faltering Safety Net." *Times-Picayune*, October 9, 2005.

Finch, Susan, and Coleman Warner. "Destitute Pose Dilemma in Tourist Town." *Times-Picayune*, January 24, 1996.

Finn, Kathy. "Vieux Carré: Charm Under Pressure." *New Orleans Magazine*, March 1, 1993.

———. "What's Up Dock?, Or, a Peripatetic Guide to the Riverfront." *New Orleans Magazine*, June 1, 1994.

Flake, Carol. "The Lavender Hill Mob Takes on Anita Bryant." *Figaro*, New Orleans, |June 29, 1977.

Foley, John. "New Orleans' French Quarter: Framing Diverse Visions of Urban Living." University of New Orleans, College of Urban and Public Affairs. Presented at Association of Collegiate Schools of Planning (ACSP) Annual Conference, November 5–8, 1998, Pasadena, CA.

———. "Neighborhood Movements, Identity and Change in New Orleans' French Quarter." Ph.D. diss., University of New Orleans, 1999.

Foley, John, and Mickey Lauria. "Plans, Planning and Tragic Choices." University of New Orleans, College of Urban and Public Affairs, 1999.

———. "Historic Preservation, Urban Revitalization,and Value Controversies in New Orleans' French Quarter." University of New Orleans, College of Urban and Public Affairs, 2000.

Formento, Dennis. "The Golden Triangle: An Interview with James Nolan." *Exquisite Corpse*, May 19, 1999, www.corpse.org/issue_5/broken_news/formento.htm.

Foster, Mary. "Stella Maris Center Made Over Into Condos." *Times-Picayune*, December 9, 1995.

*Frank Leslie's Illustrated Weekly.* "The First Night at the French Opera . . . ," December 11, 1902.

Gallas, Walter. "French Quarter Group Pushes Preservation of Buildings and Neighborhood Since 1920s." *Preservation in Print*, August 1995.

———. "Neighborhood Preservation and Politics in New Orleans: Vieux Carré Property Owners, Residents and Associates, Inc. and City Government, 1938–1983." M.A. thesis, University of New Orleans, 1996.

Gallas, Walter, and Anthony Marino. "Cabildo Case Not Just About the Fence." *Preservation in Print*, New Orleans, May 1998.

Galsworthy, John. "That Old-Time Place" in *The Inn of Tranquility*. New York: Charles Scribner's Sons, 1912.

Gambino, Richard. *Vendetta*. Toronto: Guernica, 1998.

Gatewood, Willard B., Jr. "Sunnyside: The Evolution of An Arkansas Plantation." *Arkansas Historical Quarterly* 50, no. 1 (Spring 1991).

Gayarré, Charles. *History of Louisiana*. Vol. 3, ch. 4 (1788 fire); vol. 3, ch. 6 (1794 fire). New York: William J. Widleton, 1867.

Gelman, Ari. *A River and Its City: The Nature of Landscape in New Orleans*. Berkeley: University of California Press, 2003.

Genthe, Arnold. *Impressions of Old New Orleans*. New York: George H. Doran Company, 1926.

Geronimi, Martine. *The French Market New Orleans Style: Preservation of the Past Patrimonal Alibi and Glorification of Commerce*. Ottawa: Society for the Study of Architecture in Canada (SSAC), 2001 autumn issue.

Gill, James. *Lords of Misrule: Mardi Gras and the Politics of Race in New Orleans*. Jackson: University Press of Mississippi, 1997.

———. "Re: Bio Information Request." E-mail to Scott S. Ellis, January 27, 2007.

Gold, Victor. "Let's Get Togedder: New Orleans Mayor For-As-Long-As-He Wants Marc Morial Is Giving New Meaning to His City's Long Reform-Resistant History. Selling Out to Casino Interests Is Allowing Seediness to Displace the City's Irreplaceable Charm." *The American Spectator*, May 1,1998.

Gordon, John Steele. "We Banked On Them." *American Heritage Magazine*, July/August 1995.

Gotham, Kevin Fox. "Tourism Gentrification: The Case of New Orleans' Vieux Carré (French Quarter)." *Urban Studies* 42, no.7 (June 2005).

Grace, Stephanie. "Hotel Is Coming to Rampart Street." *Times-Picayune*, November 13, 1994.

Graffagnino, Peter. "New Orleans in the Thirties." *Muscogee County Medical Bulletin* 20, no. 1 (1979).

Greater New Orleans Community Data Center. "French Quarter Neighborhood: Housing & Housing Costs." 2004.

———. "French Quarter Neighborhood: Transportation." 2004.

———. "French Quarter Neighborhood: People & Household Characteristics." 2004.

———. "French Quarter Neighborhood: Income & Poverty." 2004.

Greater New Orleans Educational Television Foundation. *Where New Orleans Shopped*. DVD, 2002.

Green, Charles. "Council Okays Mini-Buses for French Quarter Routes." *Times-Picayune*, March 16, 1973.

*Greta Cazenave, et al, vs. Sheriff Charles C. Foti, Jr., et al*. Civil Action 00-1246, U.S. District Court, Eastern District of Louisiana, December 21, 2006.

Griffin, Thomas. "Youth Invasion for Carnival Indicated by Local Children." *States-Item*, January 28, 1971.

———. "More Praise for Art Deco Palace Called Jonathan." *States-Item*, August 13, 1977.

Guy, Mike. "Gutterpunks." *Rolling Stone*, May 15, 2003.

Haas, Edward F. "New Orleans on the Half-Shell." *Louisiana History, Journal of the Louisiana Historical Association* 13, no.3 (1972).

———. *DeLesseps S. Morrison and the Image of Reform: New Orleans Politics, 1946–1961*. Baton Rouge: Louisiana State University Press, 1974 .

———. "Re: The Image of Reform." E-mail to Scott S. Ellis, October 20, 2003.

Hair, William Ivy. *Carnival of Fury*. Baton Rouge: Louisiana State University Press,1976.

Hale, Allean. "Two on a Streetcar." *The Tennessee Williams Literary Journal* 1, no. 1 (1989).

Haley, Reni. "Pete's Place Building Is Up for Sale." *Times-Picayune*, January 24, 1987.

Halvorsen, Robyn. Interview by Scott S. Ellis. New Orleans, September 29, 2006.

Hannusch, Jeff. "The South's Swankiest Night Spot: The Legend of the Dew Drop Inn." www.ikoiko.com (retrieved February 7, 2006).

Hardy, Arthur. "Re: Parades Ending In Vieux Carre?" E-mail to Scott S. Ellis, December 19, 2004.

Harvey, Chance. *The Life and Selected Letters of Lyle Saxon*. Gretna, LA: Pelican Publishing, 2003.

Head, Thomas. "Dining Out on U Street and Shaw." *Washingtonian Magazine*, December 1, 2005.

Heard, Malcolm. *French Quarter Manual: An Architectural Guide to New Orleans' Vieux Carré*. New Orleans: Tulane School of Architecture, 1997.

Heleniak, Roman. "Local Reaction to the Great Depression in New Orleans." *Louisiana History, Journal of the Louisiana Historical Association* 10, no. 4 (1969).

Hennick, Luis C., and E. Harper Charlton. *The Streetcars of New Orleans*. Gretna, LA: Firebird Press, 2000.

Herndon, Joseph L., and Mary L. Oehrlein. "Historic Structures Report: 1850 House Museum, Lower Pontalba Building, Jackson Square, New Orleans, Louisiana." Washington, D.C.: Building Conservation Technology, August 1, 1977.

Herndon, Robert. *Eight Days with Bob Harrington*. Nashville: Benson Printing Company, 1974.

Hill, John C. "Clarkson Riles Peers, Pleases Conservatives." *Times-Picayune*, April 23, 1994.

Hirsch, Arnold R., and Joseph Logsdon, eds. *Creole New Orleans: Race and Americanization*. Baton Rouge: Louisiana State University Press, 1992.

Historic American Buildings Survey/Historic American Engineering Record. "Louisiana Sugar Exchange, North Front & Bienville Streets, New Orleans, Orleans Parish, LA." Library of Congress, Prints & Photographs Division, HABS LA,36-NEWOR,58-; HABS Number LA-1110. http://hdl.loc.gov/loc.pnp/hhh.la0055 (retrieved July 14, 2007).

The Historic New Orleans Collection. "The Long Weekend: The Arts and the Vieux Carré Between the World Wars 1918–1941." Part 1, The 1920s: From Armistice to the Crash. Exhibit of January 16–May 1, 1993.

Hoffmann, Marie Louise. "The St. Vincent's Hotel." M.A. thesis, Tulane University, 1933.

Hotel-Motel Greeters International. *Greeters' Tourist Guide*, Louisiana Chapter. Vol. 36, No. 16. New Orleans: August 15, 1966.

Huber, Leonard V., and Samuel Wilson, Jr. *Baroness Pontalba's Buildings and the Remarkable Woman Who Built Them*. 2nd ed. New Orleans: New Orleans Chapter of the Louisiana Landmarks Society and the Friends of the Cabildo, 1966.

———. *The Basilica on Jackson Square*. New Orleans: St. Louis Cathedral, 1972.

Huber, Leonard V. *Jackson Square Through the Years*. New Orleans: The Friends of the Cabildo, 1982.

Hughlett, Mike. "Dame Fortune Scowled at New Orleans; Miss. Gulf Coast Won Every Hand." *Times-Picayune*, April 28, 1996.

Hungerford, James. *The Personality of American Cities*. New York: McBride, Nast & Company, 1913.

Hurtt, Michael. "Cosimo Matassa: The King of New Orleans Recording Engineers." *Offbeat*, June 2004.

Illinois Central Railroad. *New Orleans for the Tourist*. Chicago, 1907.

*Impact*. "Map of Bars, Lounges and Restaurants." New Orleans, January 1, 1980.

Irby, William Ratcliffe. Excerpt from will regarding bequest of Lower Pontalba Building to the Louisiana State Museum, May 11, 1926. Pontalba File, Louisiana State Museum.

Irvin, Hillary S. "Vieux Carré Commission History." New Orleans: Vieux Carré Commission, 1986.

———. "Socially Tolerant and Sensually Pleasing Vieux Carré Still Charms." New Orleans: *Preservation In Print*, December 1993.

———. E-mail to Scott S. Ellis, February 5, 2007.

Jackson, Joy. "Prohibition in New Orleans: The Unlikeliest Crusade." *Louisiana History, Journal of the Louisiana Historical Association* 19 (1978).

Jacobelli, Sara. "When Busters Was Around." *The Dagger*, July 1995. http://www.thedagger .com/thedagger/dag_zine/busters.html.

———. Interview by Scott S. Ellis. E-mail, 2006–2007.

Jacobs, Howard. "Bourbon Street Held 'Eden of Epidermis.'" *Times-Picayune*, August 21, 1973.

Jarrell, Sanford. *New Orleans—The Civilized and Lively City*. Little Blue Book No. 1410. Girard, KS: Haldeman-Julius Publications, 1929.

Jensen, Lynne. "Infestation Eats Up Time and Money." *Times-Picayune*, July 1, 1998.

———. "N.O. Set for Classic Party; Bayou Bash Demands Traffic Crowd Plan; 100,000 Expected to Converge for Classic." *Times-Picayune*, November 19, 2000.

Jones, Mary S. "Vieux Carré National Park; Park Services Takes Turn Through the Quarter." *Times-Picayune,* January 15, 1999.

Joor, Harriet. "New Orleans, the City of Iron Lace." *Craftsman*, November 1905.

Joyce, Fay S. "Garish Intruders Muffling Spirit of French Quarter." *New York Times*, June 10, 1983.

Kane, Harnett T. "Guns, Barflys, Petticoats Feature Vieux Carré Bar War." *New Orleans Item*, May 22, 1941.

———. *Queen New Orleans: City by the River*. New York: William Morrow & Company, 1949.

Katz, Leonard. *Uncle Frank: The Biography of Frank Costello*. New York: Pocket Books, 1975.

Keith, Don Lee. "The Bead Lady & Others." *New Orleans Magazine*, February 1991.

Kellogg, R. James. "French Quarter Recollections." E-mail to Scott S. Ellis, November 29, 2003.

———. "Re: Jewel's Question." E-mail to Scott S. Ellis, October 29, 2006.

———. E-mail to Scott S. Ellis, April 11, 2008.

Kelso, Iris. "French Quarter Cleanup Dispute Reaches Peak." *New Orleans States-Item*, September 8, 1962.

Kemp, Jon. "Southern Decadence Just Around Corner." *Times-Picayune*, September 2, 2004.

Kendall, John S. *History of New Orleans*. Chicago: Lewis Publishing,1922.

———. "The Pontalba Buildings." *Louisiana Historical Quarterly* 19, no.1 (January 1936).

———. "The French Quarter Sixty Years Ago." *Louisiana Historical Quarterly* 34, no. 2 (April 1951).

Kennedy, Richard S., ed. *Literary New Orleans in the Modern World*. Baton Rouge: Louisiana State University, 1998.

Kinney, Robert. *The Bachelor in New Orleans*. New Orleans: Bob Riley Studios, 1942.

Kirkwood, James. *American Grotesque*. New York: Harper Perennial, 1992.

Knopp, Lawrence M., Jr. "Gentrification and Gay Community Development in a New Orleans Neighborhood." Ph.D. diss., University of Iowa, August 1989.

Kolb, Judy. "HEAD Clinic Helps Kids." *Vieux Carré Courier*, December 12, 1969.

———. "Carnival Costumer Contest." *Vieux Carré Courier*, February 6, 1970.

Krebs, B. I., and William E. Keith. "Eisenhower Sees Re-Enactment of Louisiana Transfer to U.S." *Times-Picayune*, October 18, 1953.

Kurtz, Michael L., and Morgan D. Peoples. *Earl K. Long: The Saga of Uncle Earl and Louisiana Politics*. Baton Rouge: Louisiana State University Press, 1990.

La Maison Hospitaliere Web site, http://www.maisonhospitaliere.org/ (retrieved June 14, 2005).

Larson, Susan. *The Booklover's Guide to New Orleans*. Baton Rouge: Louisiana State University Press, 1999.

Le Petit Théâtre du Vieux Carré. *Le Petit Théâtre du Vieux Carré*. New Orleans, 1940.

Leathem, Karen Trahan. "Luring Young Girls to Their Ruin: Liquor, Women and the 1908 Gay-Shattuck Law." Presented at the Louisiana Historical Association Annual Meeting, Lafayette, LA, March 14, 1997.

LeGardeur, Lilli. "Police Hear Quarter Gripes; Complaints Include Tour Buses, Lewdness." *Times-Picayune*, October 3, 2000.

———. "Bench Warfare." *Times-Picayune*, September 17, 2002.

———. "Has Cabrini Park Gone to the Dogs?" *Times-Picayune*, May 23, 2002.

Lemann, Nicholas. "Hard Times in the Big Easy; New Orleans." *The Atlantic Monthly*, August 1, 1987.

Lemann, Bernard. *The Vieux Carré: A General Statement*. New Orleans: Tulane University School of Architecture, 1966.

Letson, Roy. "Bath House Raided on 'Obscenity' Charges." *Impact*, June 1984.

———. "Gay Homicides Cause Panic in French Quarter." *Impact*, July 13, 1984.

Levy, Russell. "Of Bards and Bawds: New Orleans Sporting Life Before and During the Storyville Era, 1897–1917." M.A. thesis, Tulane University, July 28, 1967.

Lewis, Peirce F. *New Orleans: The Making of an Urban Landscape*. 2nd ed. Charlottesville: University of Virginia Press, 2003.

*Life*. "Life Goes to the Mardi Gras." March 25, 1946.

Lind, Angus. "Doctor-Do-It-All; Brobson Lutz Did a Little of Everything for French Quarter Residents After Katrina." *Times-Picayune*, October 14, 2005.

Liuzza, Ted. "Spring Fiesta Opens with Crowning of Queen Sunday." *New Orleans Item*, March 6, 1942.

Long, Edith Elliot. *Along the Banquette*. New Orleans: Vieux Carré Property Owners, Residents and Associates, 2004.

Long, William. "Listless Discontent Litters Jackson Square." *Vieux Carré Courier*, April 14, 1967.

Loughery, John. *The Other Side of Silence*. New York: Henry Holt and Company, 1998.

*Louisiana et al v. United States*. 380 US 145 (1965).

Louisiana Department of Labor, Office of Occupational Information, Services Research and Statistics Division. "Mining in New Orleans." Excel spreadsheet.

Louisiana Department of Transportation. "Crescent City Connection Bridges." Published at http://www.dotd.state.la.us/operations/cccd/bridges.asp.

Louisiana Historical Society. "Programme of the Celebration in Honor of the Hundredth Anniversary of the Transfer of Louisiana from France to the United States." December 18–20, 1903. The Historic New Orleans Collection, 57-10-L.5.

Louisiana Mid-Continent Oil and Gas Association. "Historical Highlights for the LA Oil and Gas Industry." www.lmoga.com/history.html (retrieved May 5, 2005).

Louisiana Revised Statutes, Section 25-737. "Powers of Historic District Commissions."

Louisiana Secretary of State. "Richard Webster Leche." http://www.sec.state.la.us/64.htm (retrieved March 6, 2007).

Louisiana State University Agricultural Center. "French Quarter Termite Program Expands." Press release, June 8, 2006.

Louisiana World Exposition. *1984 World's Fair New Orleans Official Guidebook*. New
    Orleans: Picayune Publishing, 1984.
Lowery, Walter. *912 Orleans Street: The Story of a Rescue*. New Orleans: Hauser Printing,
    1965.
——. "What's It Like to Live in the Quarter?" *New Orleans Magazine*, September 1968.
Lutz, Brobson, M.D. "My Katrina Experience." *New Orleans Magazine*, December, 2005.
——. Interview by Scott S. Ellis. New Orleans, February 25, 2006.
MacCash, Doug. "The Night They Raided the Quorum." *Times-Picayune*, June 27, 2004.
Madden, William U. "Bourbon's Entertainment Raucous, But Improving." *States-Item*, April
    20, 1966.
Magill, Rich. *Exposing Hatred—A Report on the Victimization of Lesbian and Gay People
    in New Orleans, Louisiana*. New Orleans: Louisiana Lesbian and Gay Political Action
    Caucus, 1991.
Maginnis, John. "Legislature's Bad Image Proves Useful." *Times-Picayune*, February 28, 2007.
Manchester, William. *Goodbye, Darkness*. New York: Dell Publishing, 1982.
Mardi Gras Unmasked.com. "The Crackdown That Wasn't." www.mardigrasunmasked.com/
    mardigras/carnivalcourier/crackdown.htm, 2000.
Marino, Anthony. "Part V, Acquiring Community Support and Managing the 'Politics.'"
    Presented at Fundamentals of Real Estate Development, New Orleans, August 9, 2006.
——. E-mail to Scott S. Ellis, October 8, 2006.
Martel, Brett. "Non-Stop Merrymaking Doesn't Amuse Residents of French Quarter."
    *Milwaukee Journal Sentinel*, December 5, 1999.
Martin, Joan M. "*Plaçage* and the Louisiana *Gens de Couler Libre*." In *Creole: The History
    and Legacy of Louisiana's Free People of Color*, edited by Sybil Kein. Baton Rouge:
    Louisiana State University Press, 2000.
Martinez, Raymond J. *The Story of the River Front at New Orleans*. New Orleans: Pelican
    Press, 1948.
Maselli, Joseph, and Dominic Candelero. *Italians in New Orleans*. Charleston: Arcadia
    Publishing, 2004.
Masters, Elizabeth A. "Martha Robinson and French Quarter Preservation." Honors thesis,
    Tulane University, 1985.
Matassa, Cosimo. Interviews by Scott S. Ellis. New Orleans, April 24, 2004, and March 19,
    2005.
May, Hoke. "New Orleans Traffic—Black Days Ahead." *New Orleans Magazine*, January
    1969.
McBride, Brian J. "Press Street: A Concept for Preserving, Reintroducing, and Fostering
    Local History." M.A. thesis, Louisiana State University, May 2005.
McMain, Eleanor. "Behind the Yellow Fever in Little Palermo." *Charities* 15 (November 4,
    1905).
McNally, Dennis. *A Long Strange Trip*. London: Corgi Books, 2003.
McQuaid, John. "Shredding the Soul of a City." *Times-Picayune*, June 28, 1998.
McQuaid, John, and Lynne Jensen. "History Under Fire." *Times-Picayune*, July 1, 1998.
Meis, Jerry. E-mail to Scott S. Ellis, April 7, 2006.
Milani, Ernesto R. "Peonage at Sunnyside and the Reaction of the Italian Government."
    *Arkansas Historical Quarterly* 50, no. 1 (Spring 1991).
Mississippi Code, Sections 87-7-1 through -5; and 97-33-1 through -51 et seq. December
    2005.
Montoya, Maria. "A Glimpse of Heaven." *Times-Picayune*, March 31, 2002.
Moody, Skye. "Illegal Guesthouses Start Row in Quarter." *Times-Picayune*, July 18, 1997.

Morgan, Alan, Dennis Ring, Alan R. Max, and Frank S. Guillot. "Status of the French
     Quarter Formosan Subterranean Termite Management Program after Hurricane
     Katrina." Presented at the International Union for the Study of Social Insects Congress,
     Washington, D.C., August 1, 2006.
Morrison, Jacob H. "Hits Vieux Carré Shrinkage." *Times-Picayune*, March 26, 1940.
     Although this letter has a printed signature of James J. Morrison, this must be a misprint;
     it cannot be James H. Morrison, then congressman from Louisiana and not related to the
     half-brothers deLesseps S. or Jacob H. Morrison.
———. Letter to Tony Wrenn, May 6, 1963. Mary Meeks Morrison and Jacob Morrison
     Papers, MSS 553, Box 117, The Historic New Orleans Collection.
Morrison, Mary Meeks, and Jacob Morrison Papers, MSS 553, The Historic New Orleans
     Collection.
Morrison, Mary (Mrs. Jacob H.). Interview by John Geyser. New Orleans, Friends of the
     Cabildo Oral History Project, 1977.
Mowbray, Rebecca. "The New Bourbon Royalty." *Times-Picayune*, February 10, 2002.
Mowbray, Rebecca, and Greg Thomas. "Time Release Renewal." *Times-Picayune*, May 9,
     2004.
Mulé, Marty. "Standing On Principle." *Times-Picayune*, January 24, 1995.
Mullener, Elizabeth. "Exodus Leaves City with Empty Feeling." *Times-Picayune*, January 16,
     1994.
———. "The Locals: Drawn by Charm, Driven Out by Crowds." *Times-Picayune*, May 16,
     1994.
———. "Insectarium: Thrill or Threat." *Times-Picayune*, May 17, 1994.
———. "Farewell to the Chief." *Times-Picayune*, May 24, 2002.
———. "Clarkson's Crusade." *Times-Picayune*, June 22, 2003.
Murrell, Duncan. "The Swarm." *Harper's*, August 2005.
National Commission on Law Observance and Enforcement. "Report on the Enforcement
     of the Prohibition Laws of the United States" (The Wickersham Commission Report on
     Alcohol Prohibition). Washington, D.C., January 7, 1931.
National Park Service. "About the Park: Our Mission." New Orleans Jazz National Historical
     Park Web site, www.nps.gov/jazz/mission.htm (retrieved November 2005).
———. "Jean Lafitte National Historical Park and Preserve." www.nps.gov/jela.
———. "New Orleans Jazz Neighborhood History Map." New Orleans Jazz National
     Historical Park, http://www.nps.gov/archive/jazz/Maps_neighborhoods.htm (retrieved
     July 7, 2007).
Nelson, Roger. Letter to the editor. *Ambush*, October 16–29, 1998.
New Orleans. Mayor's Special Citizens Committee; Jacob Morrison et al. "Report of
     Committee on the Problem of Sex Deviates in New Orleans." 1959.
*New Orleans City Business*. "New Cleaner to Make French Quarter 'Super Fresh.'" April 18,
     2007.
———. "Storied French Quarter Nursing Home to Close." September 18, 2006.
———. "Noise Complaints Could Silence Jazz at King Bolden's." March 21, 2007.
New Orleans Code of Ordinances: "Vieux Carré Pontalba Buildings. Accepting from the
     Pontalba Building Museum Association, Inc., that certain portion of ground and the
     improvements there on known as the Upper Pontalba Building, and fixing the terms and
     conditions controlling said donation." CCS 11,949. 1930.
———. "Exempting Ordinance." CCS 16,430. March 25, 1946.
———. MCS 1567, January 30, 1959. Amended Section 5-66. Prohibited certain classes of
     people from employment in, or patronizing of, bars.

———. MCS 1568, January 30, 1959. Prohibited the rental of property to certain classes of
people for certain acts.
———. CCS 18,537. Repealed in its entirety March 18, 1993, by enactment of ordinance MCS
15,767, which also repealed Section 5-66.
———. "Vieux Carré Malls." Section 154-608. August 17, 1995.
———. "Noise." 18,857, September 3, 1998.
———. "Prohibited Offers to Rent Property." Section 54-491.1, MCS 21,606, July 1, 2004.
———. "Restrictions on use of force by persons employed by bars, lounges, and nightclubs
located within the Vieux Carré." MCS 22,027, August 4, 2005.
New Orleans Comprehensive Zoning Ordinance.
New Orleans District Attorney. "Razzoo Case." Press release, October 1, 2008.
*New Orleans Item.* "Vieux Carré Folk Meet Thursday to Advance Plans for Improvement."
February 5, 1920.
———. "Vieux Carré Group Raps Commission." January 12, 1939.
———. "Vieux Carré Charges to Be Studied." May 16, 1940.
———. "5464 French Quarter Arrests Shown in Report by Reyer." August 13, 1940.
———. "Push Drive to Mop Up Quarter." August 13, 1940.
*New Orleans Item-Tribune.* "Push Drive for Cleanup in Quarter." May 19, 1940.
*New Orleans Magazine.* "Around the Belt." August 1967.
———. "Two Decades for a Quarter." April 2003.
*New Orleans Morning Tribune.* "Mrs. Werlein to Lead State Wet Forces." May 3, 1932.
New Orleans Planning Commission Master Plan. Sections 8.8.1, 8.8.3.
New Orleans Public Library. "Dedication of the Renovated French Market, April 1, 1975."
Photograph 7 of Landrieu Photograph Collection, City Archives. http://nutrias
.org/~nopl/photos/landrieu/m1195.htm.
———. "Yellow Fever Deaths in New Orleans." http://nutrias.org/~nopl/facts/feverdeaths
.htm.
———. "Dutch Alley." City Archives, Mayor Ernest N. Morial Photographs Collection.
http://nutrias.org/photos/enm/enm29_417.htm.
———. "The Louisiana Purchase Sesquicentennial in New Orleans." http://www.nutrias
.org/~nopl/monthly/february2003/february2003.htm.
New Orleans Regional Transit Authority. "Canal Streetcar Fact Sheet." Published at http://
www.norta.com/news/canal/fact.php.
*New Orleans States.* "Father Antoine Favors Cleanup." May 4, 1920.
———. "Open Letter Asks Law in Vieux Carré." May 15, 1940.
———. "Vice, Gaming Squad Goes into Action." May 7, 1946.
———. "Scores Jailed for Loitering." May 8, 1946.
———. "All Slots in City to Be Destroyed Is Cripps Order." May 9, 1946.
———. "Nab 26 in Drive on Books." May 30, 1946.
*New Orleans States-Item.* "Fire Hoses Turned on Hundreds Protesting School Integration."
November 16, 1960.
———. "15 Treated for School Mix Violence Injuries." November 17, 1960.
———. "Quarter Crime Emergency Declared by Police, DA." August 6, 1962.
———. "Resume Quarter Raids, Arrest 14." August 14, 1962.
———. "Police Apathetic in Crackdown on Vice, Says DA." August 27, 1962.
———. "12 More Nabbed in Quarter Raid." September 1, 1962.
———. "Schiro Orders Bourbon St. Police Rotated; Ask Law Against Barkers." September 4,
1962.
———. "Quarter Business Loss Laid to Anti-Mix Laws." September 7, 1962.

————. "15 Nightclubs to Reopen." October 2, 1962.

————. "Lash Backers of Demolition in Vieux Carré." January 12, 1963.

————. "Al Hirt's Famous Lip Cut by Brick Hurled at Float." February 9, 1970.

————. "Police Warn Loiterers After 88 Youths Booked." February 9, 1970.

Newlin, Jon. Interview by Scott S. Ellis. New Orleans, March 19, 2005.

*Newsweek.* "Vieux Carré." August 12, 1940.

————. "Louisiana Nightmare." November 28, 1960.

*New York Times.* "Chief Hennessey Avenged." March 15, 1891.

The Nobel Foundation. *Nobel Lectures, Physiology or Medicine, 1901–1920: Paul Ehrlich 1908.* Amsterdam: Elsevier Publishing Company, 1967.

Nolan, Bruce, and Chris Segura. "Memorial for Fire Dead Has Forgiveness Theme." *Times-Picayune,* June 26, 1973.

Nolan, James. "Remembering Kamas: The Square Round Is Also Round." *The New Laurel Review* 16, Annual 1988.

————. Interview by Scott S. Ellis. New Orleans, October 13, 2007.

Olle, Maureen. French Quarter Population, "Re: Request for Specific Census Data." E-mail to Scott S. Ellis. Louisiana State University Library, August 7, 2003.

O'Rourke, Pat. Interview by Scott S. Ellis. New Orleans, March 20, 2005.

Ott, Dwight. "Tremé Group Demands Half Culture Center Jobs" *Times-Picayune,* March 5, 1972.

Padgett, John B. "William Faulkner." The Mississippi Writers Page, published online at http://www.olemiss.edu/mwp/dir/faulkner_william/index.html.

Parker, Bessiane. Interview by Scott S. Ellis. New Orleans, April 20, 2007.

Parker, Elliot. *Newsrooms Under Siege: Crime Coverage and the Louisiana Pizza Kitchen Murders.* Mt. Pleasant, MI: Central Michigan University, 1997.

Peck, Renee. "Vieux Redo." *Times-Picayune,* September 25, 2004.

Perales, Nan. "Where It Faltered: A Multitude of Problems." *Times-Picayune,* November 11, 1984.

Perkins, Lyle Kenneth. "Failing the Race: A Historical Assessment of New Orleans Mayor Sidney Barthelemy,1986–1994." Baton Rouge: Louisiana State University, 2005.

Perlstein, Michael. "Miles to Go." *Times-Picayune,* December 18, 1994.

————. "MADD Descends on Big Easy for Convention." *Times-Picayune,* September 13, 2003.

————."1st District: 'Fort Apache' Officers Draw Line at the French Quarter." *Times-Picayune,* December 18, 2005.

Perry, Rev. Troy D., with Thomas L. P. Swicegood. *Don't Be Afraid Anymore: The Story of Reverend Troy Perry and the Metropolitan Community Churches.* New York: St. Martin's Press, 1990.

Peterson, Lorin. *The Day of the Mugwumps.* New York: Random House, 1961.

Phelan, James. *Scandals, Scamps and Scoundrels: The Casebook of an Investigative Reporter.* New York: Random House, 1982.

Pitts, Stella. "French Market Renovation Closes Battisella's for Good." *Times-Picayune,* October 6, 1974.

Plume, Janet. "Rampart Market Cooking." *Times-Picayune,* December 17, 1988.

Plyer, Allison. Greater New Orleans Community Data Center. "Your Data Request." E-mail to Scott S. Ellis, July 15, 2003.

R. L. Polk Company. 1949 New Orleans City Directory.

————. 1975 New Orleans City Directory.

————. 1985 New Orleans City Directory.

Pontchatrain, Blake (pseud.) "New Orleans Know It All." *Gambit*, August 2, 2005.

Pope, John. "Al's Final Note Hurt, Quarter Feels." *Times-Picayune*, July 5, 1983.

———. "Block Bad, Not Quarter, Hirt Says." *Times-Picayune*, July 12, 1983.

Pope, John, and Connie Jackson. "Trash Rises to New Height." *Times-Picayune*, March 3, 1995.

Pope, John. "A Hundred Years Ago, New Orleans Declared War on the Mosquito." *Times-Picayune*, July 17, 2005.

Powell, Allen III. "Man Dies After Fight with Nightclub Bouncers." *Times-Picayune*, January 1, 2005.

Pradel, Leon A. to Vieux Carré Restorations, Inc. Stockholders, April 25, 1961. Mary Meeks Morrison and Jacob Morrison Papers, MSS 553, Box 117, The Historic New Orleans Collection.

Raber, Rick. "Laws Can't Stop Hotel Expansion in French Quarter." *Times-Picayune*, July 31, 1983.

———. "Paradise Lost?" *Times-Picayune*, September 19, 1983.

Raffray, Jeannette S. "Origins of the Vieux Carré Commission 1920–1941: A Reappraisal." M.A. thesis, University of New Orleans, 1993.

Ramsey, Jan. "North Rampart Needs a Savior." *Offbeat*, May 27, 2007.

Rececher, Edward M., and the editors of *Consumer Reports* magazine. *The Consumers Union Report on Licit and Illicit Drugs*. Yonkers: Consumers Union, 1972.

Reeves, Sally. "Re: 1903 Colonial Museum History Inquiry." E-mail to Scott S. Ellis, March 12, 2008.

Reynolds, George M. *Machine Politics in New Orleans 1897–1926*. 2nd ed. New York: AMS Press, 1968.

Richardson, Rev. William P., Jr. Interview by Dorothy Mahan. *Friends of the Cabildo: Oral History Series*. New Orleans, February 18, 1990.

Roberts, Gregory. "Burgers, Baubles, Baseball Caps." *Times-Picayune*, July 13, 1996.

Robinson, Alan. "Letter to the Editor." *Impact*, October 1, 1981.

Rose, Al. *Storyville, New Orleans*. Tuscaloosa: University of Alabama Press, 1974.

Rose, Chris. "Accidental Tourist Attraction, Closed." *Times-Picayune*, December 4, 1999.

———. "The Hustler." *Times-Picayune*, July 3, 2005.

———. "Rest in Peace, Ruthie." *Times-Picayune*, September 21, 2008.

Rosenberg, Daniel. *New Orleans Dockworkers: Race, Labor, and Unionism, 1892–1923*. Albany: State University of New York Press, 1988.

Rosenman, Samuel I., ed. *The Public Papers and Addresses of Franklin D. Roosevelt*, 1943 volume, "The Tide Turns." New York: Harper Brothers, 1950.

*Roy Maggio Et Al Vs. City of New Orleans, de Lesseps S. Morrison, Mayor, Provosty A. Dayries, Superintendent of Police*, No. 364,219, Civil District Court for The Parish of Orleans, August 6, 1958.

Rucker, Philip. "Nagin Caught in Cop-Swap Crossfire; Some Say Changes Politically Motivated." *Times-Picayune*, June 26, 2004.

Rushton, Bill. "Cityscape/Monorails and the UPT." *Vieux Carré Courier*, March 27, 1970.

Russell, Gordon. "At Rally, They're Just Wild About Jackie." *Times-Picayune*, October 21, 2002.

———. "Pedicab Service to Seek New Federal Trial." *Times-Picayune*, October 25, 2002.

———. "Nagin Scraps Tradition of Trashing Carnival." *Times- Picayune*, March 6, 2003.

———. "Dubious Value." *Times-Picayune*, April 4 and 5, 2004.

Russell, Pam Radtke. "Going with the Flow." *Times-Picayune*, September 10, 2006.

Ruth, Dawn. "City Ban on Gay Bar Employees Repealed." *Times-Picayune*, May 17, 1993.

Samuel, Martha Ann. "One-Man Restoration Society." *Times-Picayune Dixie Roto Magazine*,
      May 24, 1964.

Sanchez, Tanya Marie. "The Feminine Side of Bootlegging: Women, Drink and Prohibition
      in New Orleans." M.A. thesis, University of New Orleans, 1998.

Sargent, Robert S., Jr. *The New Orleans Streetcars.* Sudbury ON: Enter Stage Right, published
      at http://www.enterstageright.com/archive/articles/1004/1004neworleanssc-p1-thedemise
      .htm (retrieved October 11, 2004).

Saxon, Lyle. "French Opera House to Rise Again From Ruins." *Times-Picayune*, December
      5, 1919.

———. "Baroness Pontalba Portrait Goes Home." *Times-Picayune*, October 10, 1926.

———. *Fabulous New Orleans.* New York: The Century Company, 1928.

———. *A Walk Through the Vieux Carré.* 4th ed. New Orleans: Dinkler Hotels, 1940.

———. *Fabulous New Orleans.* 2nd ed. New Orleans: Robert Crager & Company, 1950.

Scallan, Matt. "Airport, CBD Railway Explored." *Times-Picayune*, June 12, 2000.

Schleifstein, Mark. "In N.O., Bugs Go to School, and the Schools Are Failing." *Times-
      Picayune*, June 28, 1998.

———. "Federal Program Unleashes Millions to Stop Termites." *Times-Picayune*, July 1, 1998.

Schneider, Frank L. "Jackson Square: Anxiety Behind the Scenes" *Times-Picayune*, April 6,
      1975.

Schumacher, Craig, and Rodger King. "Cosimo Matassa." *Tape Op*, vol. 40, March/April
      2004.

Schwartz, John. "For Harry Anderson, the New Orleans Magic Is Gone." *New York Times*,
      August 30, 2006.

Scott, John Wyeth II. "William Spratling and the New Orleans Renaissance." *Louisiana
      History, Journal of the Louisiana Historical Association* 45, no. 3 (Summer 2004).

———. "Natalie Vivian Scott: The Origins, People and Times of the French Quarter
      Renaissance (1920–1930), Volume I." Ph.D. diss., Louisiana State University,1999.

Scott, Liz. "Trials and Errors: The Saga of Clay Shaw." *New Orleans Magazine*, November
      1999.

———."Chris Rose by a Landslide." *New Orleans Magazine*, December 2006.

Sears, James T. *Rebels, Rubyfruit and Rhinestones: Queering Space in the Stonewall South.*
      Piscataway, New Jersey: Rutgers University Press, 2001.

Segura, Chris. "Last Call-Morning Call; Coffee Shop Shuts Its Doors." *Times-Picayune*,
      March 1, 1974.

Sheraouse, Chris. "New Orleans Mecca Sought by Runaways." *States-Item*, January 28, 1971.

Shilts, Randy. *And the Band Played On.* New York: St. Martin's Press, 1987.

Simmons, Robert. "New Orleans, America's Most Exotic City." *Coronet*, March 1956.

Sindler, Allan P. *Huey Long's Louisiana: State Politics, 1920–1952.* Baltimore: The Johns
      Hopkins Press, 1956; 2nd printing, 1971.

Sines, Nina J., and John Ekman. "The Minimum Drinking Age and Alcohol Policy: An
      Historical Overview and Response to the Renewed Debate in Wisconsin." University of
      Wisconsin Law School, Resource Center on Impaired Driving, Resource Center Report
      96-1, April 1996.

Smith, Sandy. "Brazen Empire of Crime, Part II." *Life*, September 8, 1967.

Souther, Jonathan Mark. "City in Amber: Race, Culture and the Tourist Transformation of
      New Orleans, 1945–1995." Ph.D. diss., Tulane University, 2003.

Southern Louisiana Media Corporation. *NOLA Express*, May 9–22, 1969.

Spera, Keith. "Cradle of Rock: Recording Studio Named Landmark." *Times-Picayune*,
      December 11, 1999.

———. "El Matador Exits." *Times-Picayune*, January 9, 2004.

———. "Farewell to the Funky Butt?" *Times-Picayune*, August 19, 2005.

———. "Plan to Reopen Jazz Club in N.O. Falls on Deaf Ears; Councilwoman Says She Opposes Proposal." *Times-Picayune*, October 25, 2005.

Spillman, Amy. "Stopping the Swarm." *Agricultural Research*, July 2003, Agricultural Research Service, U.S. Department of Agriculture.

Stanonis, Anthony. *An Old House in the Quarter: Vice in the Vieux Carré of the 1930s*. New Orleans: Loyola University Student Historical Journals, vol. 28, 1997.

———."'A Woman of Boundless Energy': Elizabeth Werlein and Her Times." *Louisiana History, Journal of the Louisiana Historical Association* 46, no.1 (Winter 2005).

Starr, S. Frederick, ed. *Inventing New Orleans: Writings of Lafcadio Hearn*. Jackson: University Press of Mississippi, 2001.

State Farm Bayou Classic. "The History of the Bayou Classic." www.statefarmbayouclassic .com (retrieved December 2005).

*State of Louisiana vs. Phillip Anthony*, No. 98-KA-0406, Supreme Court of Louisiana, 1998.

Stier, Emile V., and James B. Keeling. *Glorified French Market*. New Orleans: The French Market Corporation, 1938.

Stuart, Lettice. "Jonathan's Building Is Bought for $165,000." *Times-Picayune*, December 5, 1987.

Tallant, Robert. *Mr. Preen's Salon*. Garden City: Doubleday, 1949.

———. *The Romantic New Orleanians*. New York: E. P. Dutton, 1950.

———. *Mardi Gras . . . As It Was*. Gretna, LA: Pelican Publishing Company, 2000.

*Time*. "A Matter of Record." December 31, 1923.

———. "For Tarpon." May 10, 1937.

———. "One Down." September 25, 1939.

———. "Maestri Rides Again." January 19, 1942.

———. "Old Girl's New Boy." November 24, 1947.

———. "Uplift for the Grande Dame." May 20, 1957.

———. "D-Day in New Orleans." November 28, 1960.

———. "The Tried and True Technique." January 24, 1964.

———. "No Place for Seditious Libel." December 4, 1964.

———. "The New American Samaritans." December 27, 1971.

———. "The Outsider Makes It Big." November 5, 1979.

———. "Foul Times for a Fair." October 1, 1984.

———. "The New Orleans Fair Hangover." November 25,1984.

*Times-Democrat*. "Opening of the Louisiana Transfer Celebration." December 19, 1903.

———. "Tributes by Representatives of the People of Three Nations." December 20, 1903.

———. "The Colonial Museum Is Formally Opened." December 21, 1903.

*Times-Picayune*. "Cathedral Dynamited." April 26, 1909.

———."Noted Gin Mills May Turn Tamely to Coffee Houses." January 17, 1919.

———. "Dry Agents Find Orleans Largest Whiskey Factory." October 14, 1921.

———. "'Imported Rum' Factory Found by Dry Raiders." January 6, 1922.

———. "Dry Agents Seize Alcohol Still." June 22, 1923.

———. "Perfumery Rivals Coconut as Shield in Liquor Circles." January 9, 1925.

———. "French Quarter Guardians Named." November 25, 1925.

———. "W. R. Irby Calls at Undertakers and Shoots Self." November 21, 1926.

———. "Offer of Work Causes Rioting Among Jobless." March 11, 1930.

———. "City Breweries Sell Out; Joyous Throngs Toast New and Old." April 14, 1933.

———. "Vieux Carré Trimming." March 20, 1940.

——. "Last Rites Today for Mrs. Werlein." April 25, 1946.

——. "Police Back Liquor Demand with Threat, Saloonist Says." January 7, 1949.

——. "Continues Fight to Suppress Vice." January 12, 1949.

——. "Dope Raid Ends in Nine Arrests." June 9, 1949.

——. "Tennessean Dies of Heart Attack." January 1, 1950.

——. "Mayor Takes Up Long on Cleanup of Bookies." December 11, 1950.

——. "Grevemberg, Aids [sic] Raid N.O. Club, Arrest Four." September 11, 1952.

——. Dixie Roto Magazine, "Saved from Slums, and at a Profit." April 8, 1956.

——. "Council Kills Monorail Plan." March 8, 1958.

——. "Mayor Queried on Landmarks." November 29, 1959.

——. "Groups Battle Demolitions OK." December 17, 1962.

——. "Mrs. Robinson Blasts Motel." January 17, 1963.

——. "Morrison, 6 Others on Plane Dead." May 24, 1964.

——. "Quarter Units Hail Decision." July 3, 1964.

——. "Gay Liberation Group Marches." January 24, 1971.

——. "Project Reason Slated by Shaw." February 28, 1973.

——. "946 Violations Noted in Vieux Carré Checks." July 20, 1973.

——. "City Quarter Plan Opposed." May 31, 1973.

——. "Judge Stops Sound-Light Until Plan Satisfies Laws." October 25, 1973.

——. "Traffic Rules Are Announced." December 28, 1973.

——. "Facelifting the Square." December 16, 1975.

——."Some Attention on N. Rampart." October 31, 1976.

——. Real Estate. "Pleasure Palace a Pleasing Sight." February 5, 1983.

——. "Protecting the Quarter." April 13, 1993.

——. "Homeless Problem in Quarter." August 23, 1995.

——. "Bayou Classic and Big Easy." November 30, 1996.

——. "Treasures Taken Away from Closed Church." July 12, 1997.

——. "Crackdown in the Quarter." June 5, 2000.

——. "Passing the Smell Test." July 18, 2002.

Thevenot, Brian. "Canizaro Takes the Heat in Plan for City's Future." Times-Picayune, March 19, 2006.

Thomas, James W. Lyle Saxon: A Critical Biography. Birmingham, AL: Summa Publishing Inc., 1991.

Thomas, Greg. "If You Build It, Will They Come?" Times-Picayune, July 23, 1997.

——. "20 Years Later, Silver Lining Apparent." Times-Picayune, May 9, 2004.

——. "Glut of Houses Sends Prices Plummeting." Times-Picayune, June 23, 2007.

Thompson, J. William. "Almost Another Country." Washington, D.C., American Society of Landscape Architects. Landscape Architecture, July 2003.

Tillitt, Malvern Hall. "Army-Navy Pay Tops Most Civilians." Barron's National Business and Financial Weekly, April 24, 1944.

Toland, Bill. "Harrah's Woes in New Orleans Become Fodder for Casino Battle Here." Pittsburgh Post-Gazette, February 27, 2006.

Trask, Benjamin H. Fearful Ravages: Yellow Fever in New Orleans 1796–1905. Center for Louisiana Studies, University of Louisiana at Lafayette, 2005.

Treadway, Joan. "Gay Community Surfaces in Tragedy of N.O. Fire," Part 1. Times-Picayune, September 11,1973.

——."Independent Route Taken for Personal Objectives," Part 2. Times-Picayune, September 12, 1973.

——. "Homosexuals Disagree on Behavior's 'Sickness,'" Part 3. *Times-Picayune*, September 13, 1973.

——. "Psychiatric and Clerical Views Wide Spectrum," Part 4. *Times-Picayune*, September 14,1973.

——. "It's Not Illegal to BE Gay—Certain Acts Are Criminal," Part 5. *Times-Picayune*, September 15,1973.

——. "50s 'Climate of Hostility' to Gays Gone, What Now?," Part 6. *Times-Picayune*, September 16,1973.

Treadway, Joan, and Wes Jackson. "Quarter's Condition Defended, Attacked." *Times-Picayune*, May 28, 1983.

Tresch, George. Interview by Scott S. Ellis. New Orleans, July 29, 2006.

Uncredited. *New Orleans To-Day a City Meets Its Problems.* New Orleans: Wetzel Printing, 1937.

U.S. Congress. Senate Special Committee to Investigate Organized Crime in Interstate Commerce 1951. *Third Interim Report.* 82nd Cong. 1st sess. S. Rep 307.

U.S. Department of the Interior, National Park Service, New Orleans Jazz National Historical Park. New Orleans Jazz History Walking Tours: Central Vieux Carré Brochure. http://www.nps.gov/jazz/historyculture/upload/central-vc.pdf (retrieved March 15, 2007).

U.S. Department of Transportation, Federal Transit Administration. "Desire Streetcar Line, New Orleans, LA, November 2003." http://www.fta.dot.gov/documents/NO2AA.doc (retrieved March 15, 2008).

University of New Orleans, College of Urban and Public Affairs. *Changing Land Use in the Vieux Carré: Managing Growth to Preserve a National Landmark District.* New Orleans, 1992.

——. School of Hotel, Restaurant and Tourism. "Facing Change in the French Quarter of New Orleans: Trends and Developments." New Orleans, 1984.

Ursuline Guest House. "Ursuline's French Quarter Guide." New Orleans, 1980.

Usher, Nikki. "Gutterpunk Paradise." *Times-Picayune*, August 25, 2003.

Van Dorin, James. "Katrina Stories." Unpublished manuscript, December 2005.

——. Interview by Scott S. Ellis. New Orleans, June 14, 2007.

Varney, James. "Testers Find Racial Bias by Nightclubs." *Times-Picayune*, March 30, 2005.

——. "Old Law Among New Tools to Stop Bar Bias." *Times-Picayune*, May 22, 2005.

Veigle, Ann. "Bright Hopes Elude N. Rampart St." *Times-Picayune*, August 31, 1986.

——. "Changed Street Has Business Rolling on the River." *Times-Picayune*, August 31, 1986.

Vella, Christina. *Intimate Enemies.* Baton Rouge: Louisiana State University Press, 1997.

Vesey, Catherine M. "Tourism as Community Development: A Comparative Analysis of the Vieux Carré and the Lower Garden District from 1950 to 1990." University of New Orleans, College of Urban and Public Affairs, 1999.

——."Tourism Impacts in the Vieux Carré: An Analysis of Cultural Issues, Residential Perspectives and Sustainable Tourism Planning." Ph.D. diss., University of New Orleans, 1999.

Vieux Carré Commission. "Design Guidelines, Typical Materials."

——. Property records for Square 82, Lot 23050-01. Addendum. From Historic American Buildings Survey 1939–1940.

*The Vieux Carré Courier.* "Collegiates." May 26–June 1, 1962.

——. "HEAD." January 2, 1970.

——. "OK . . . But." March 13, 1970.

——. "Gay Lib Demonstrates." February 5, 1971.

———. "Carnival, Cops and Confusion." February 12, 1971.

*Vieux Carré Property Owners and Associates, Inc. et al v. City of New Orleans, et al*, 167 So. 2d 367, 26 La. 788, Supreme Court of Louisiana, 1964.

*Vieux Carré Property Owners, Residents and Associates v. Brown*, No. 87-3700, U.S. District Court, Eastern District of Louisiana, September 21, 1987. Summarized as Case 133, Advisory Council on Historic Preservation, www.achp.gov/book/case133.html.

*The Voice of the People*. "State Machine Ticket Hand Picked Product." Baton Rouge, January, 1936.

Vyhnanek, Louis. *Unorganized Crime: New Orleans in the 1920s*. Lafayette, LA: The Center for Louisiana Studies, 1998.

Wainwright, Irene. "Notes on Ordinance 18,537 Repeal." New Orleans Public Library, Louisiana Division, City Archives/Special Collections, April 14, 2007.

Walker, Rob. *Under the Freeway*. Brooklyn: Flâneur, April 2002, published at http://www .flaneur.org/04_02/0402_walker.html.

———. "Decatur Street Hotel Sued Over Expansion." *Times-Picayune*, March 31, 1998.

———. "Getting the Squeeze." *Times-Picayune*, August 4, 1999.

Weiss, Ken. "VCC Director Criticizes Disaster Area Rhetoric." *Times-Picayune*, July 18, 1973.

Wells-Barnett, Ida B. *Mob Rule in New Orleans: Robert Charles and His Fight to the Death, the Story of His Life, Burning Human Beings Alive, Other Lynching Statistics*. Chicago: Unknown publisher, 1900.

Welsh, Fannie B. Campbell. *Mercedes, a New Orleans Hurricane!* Houston: The Anson Jones Press, 1948.

Werlein, Elizabeth (Mrs. Phillip). *The Wrought Iron Railings of the Vieux Carré, New Orleans*. Publisher unknown, n.d., ca. 1912–1921.

Wilkinson, Michael. Interview by Scott S. Ellis. New Orleans, January 28, 2006.

Wilkinson, Teresa Anne. "Sense of Place and Preservation Planning: An Analysis of the New Orleans Vieux Carré from 1718 to 1985." M.A. thesis, University of New Orleans, 1985.

Williams, Leslie. "Catch Basin Screens Will Help Lake; Quarter Businesses Install Them." *Times-Picayune*, June 4, 2003.

———. "WWOZ Trumpets Spacious Park Plan; Green Space Would Be Lost, Critics Say." *Times-Picayune*, September 17, 2003.

———. "WWOZ's Revised Park Plan Still Faces Static; Planned Expansion Too Big, Critics Say." *Times-Picayune*, July 1, 2004.

Williams, T. Harry. *Huey Long*. New York: Alfred A. Knopf, 1969.

Williams, Thomas (Tennessee). *Vieux Carré*. New York: New Directions Publishing, 2000.

Willis, Paul. E-mail to Scott S. Ellis, July 18, 2007.

Wilson, Stacia. "French Quarter Looking Clean." WWL-TV, broadcast February 3, 2007, as hosted at http://www.sdtwasteanddebris.com/video/vts_01.wmv (retrieved July 4, 2007).

Wiltz, Christine. *The Last Madam: A Life in the New Orleans Underworld*. Cambridge, MA: Da Capo Press, 2000.

Winick, Charles, and Paul M. Kinsie. *The Lively Commerce: Prostitution in the United States*. Chicago: Quadrangle Books, 1971.

Wood Enterprises. "What Began as One Man's Dream Has Become the Career of Many." www.woodenterprises.com (retrieved June 24, 2008).

Woolfe, Tao. "Cities Seek Ways to Take Party Out of Spring Break." *Times-Picayune*, April 4, 1993.

Work Projects Administration. Photograph Collection, New Orleans Public Library, Series 11.54 through 11.56, Upper Pontalba, 1935–1937. http://www.nutrias.org/~nopl/photos/wpa/wpaphotos.htm (retrieved July 14, 2007).

———. Federal Writers' Project. *New Orleans City Guide*. 1st ed. Cambridge, MA: Riverside Press, 1938.

———. Federal Writers' Project. *A Tour of the French Quarter for Servicemen*. New Orleans Work Projects Administration Recreational Council for New Orleans, 1941.

———. Federal Writers' Workers Project. *The New Orleans City Park, Its First Fifty Years*. Edited by Robert Tallant. New Orleans: Gulf Printing Company, 1941.

———. Photograph Collection Series Number 36.109; "Recreation; Recreation Project for Whites. Regular recreational activities are conducted by WPA recreation leaders at the Iberville Housing Project. Shown here is a track meeting which boy residents of the project participated. Exterior." June 15, 1942, http://nutrias.org/~nopl/photos/wpa/wpa36.htm (retrieved August 2, 2007).

———. *New Orleans City Guide*. 2nd ed. New York: Houghton Mifflin, 1952.

The World's Fair and Exposition Information and Reference Guide, 1984 Louisiana World's Fair. Earth Station 9, published at http://www.earthstation9.com/index.html?1984_lou.htm.

WTRG Economics. "World Events and Crude Oil Prices, 1981–1998." http://www.wtrg.com/oil_graphs/crudeoilprice8198.gif (retrieved May 5, 2005).

Wyatt-Brown, Bertram. "Leroy Percy and Sunnyside: Planter Mentality and Italian Peonage in the Mississippi Delta." *Arkansas Historical Quarterly* 50, no. 1 (Spring 1991).

Yerton, Stewart. "Mean Streets; Merchants Want Police to Curb Street People to Keep the French Quarter Out of the Gutter." *Times-Picayune*, October 15, 1995.

———. "Passing the Other Bar Exam." *Times-Picayune*, December 19, 1999.

Young, Tara. "Some Fear Cleanup of French Quarter Will Erase Its Charm." *Times-Picayune*, July 19, 2002.

———. "NOPD Initiative Has Colorful New Leader." *Times-Picayune*, November 15, 2004.

———. "Unlikely Haven." *Times-Picayune*, December 5, 2005.

Zeringer, Lillian Fortier. *Accent on Dedication: The Story of La Maison Hospitaliere*. New Orleans: La Societé des Dames Hospitalieres, 1985.

# INDEX

Page numbers in *italics* refer to illustrations.